WOMEN'S PRESS ORGANIZATIONS, 1881–1999

WOMEN'S PRESS ORGANIZATIONS, 1881–1999

Edited by
Elizabeth V. Burt

GREENWOOD PRESS
Westport, Connecticut • London

Library of Congress Cataloging-in-Publication Data

Women's press organizations, 1881–1999 / edited by Elizabeth V. Burt.
    p. cm.
   Includes bibliographical references and index.
   ISBN 0–313–30661–3 (alk. paper)
    1. Women in journalism—United States—Societies, etc.—History—20th century. 2.
Women in journalism—United States—Societies, etc.—History—19th century. 3. Women
journalists—United States—Societies, etc.—History. I. Burt, Elizabeth V., 1943–
PN4872.H57   2000
070.4'06'073—dc21   99–049045

British Library Cataloguing in Publication Data is available.

Library of Congress Catalog Card Number: 99–049045
ISBN: 0–313–30661–3

First published in 2000

Greenwood Press, 88 Post Road West, Westport, CT 06881
An imprint of Greenwood Publishing Group, Inc.
www.greenwood.com

Printed in the United States of America

The paper used in this book complies with the
Permanent Paper Standard issued by the National
Information Standards Organization (Z39.48–1984).

10 9 8 7 6 5 4 3 2 1

This book is dedicated to the memory of Donna Allen (1920–1999), who fought for women's voice in the media and served as a role model to all of us who care to protect and preserve freedom of speech and the press.

Contents

Elizabeth V. Burt

Preface

When I first began my research on women's press organizations in 1995, only two academic articles had been published on the topic, and journalism histories—even those on women journalists—made only a few brief references to these groups. When I talked about my research, the general response in the journalism and academic communities was one of surprise that such organizations, with the exception, of course, of one or two fairly prominent twentieth-century groups, had existed. Yet, at least one hundred such organizations have been established in the United States in the past 120 years. Some survived only a few years, others decades, and a few more than a century. Some have left permanent records of their existence, others have disappeared, leaving behind only a few scattered references. It is my hope that this volume will correct this void in the historical record.

This book does not attempt to chronicle all the women's press organizations established since the first, the Ladies' Press Club, was established in Washington, D.C., in 1881. Indeed, this would be impossible given the scarcity of documentary records as well as the practical limits of space and time. Starting with a "wish list" of seventy-five organizations identified in preliminary research, I contacted potential contributors and called for volunteers to participate in the project. The list was narrowed down when willing researchers were unable to locate adequate material on organizations that seem to have disappeared with barely a trace. New organizations were added, however, as contributors, some of them members of present-day press organizations, came forward with their own suggestions.

The final selection presented here offers an eclectic and wide-ranging group of women's press organizations established in all parts of the country since 1885. It attempts to include organizations that represent geographical as well as chronological diversity, that were significant in their contributions to press women, and whose history and development could be adequately documented so that significant conclusions might be reached.

Ironically, some of the organizations that were probably key to what can be called the women's press club movement of the nineteenth century, that are frequently mentioned in individual chapters, could not be profiled in this volume. Although they are often referred to in journals and publications of the period, little is actually known about their organization, goals, and activities, and no substantive records have been located. Thus this book does not contain chapters on the Ladies' Press Club, founded in Washington, D.C., in 1881 and renamed the Woman's National Press Association in 1883; the National Woman's Press Association, established in New Orleans in 1885 and renamed the International Woman's Press Association in 1887; or the National Federation of Women's Press Clubs, established in 1891.

The thirty-seven organizations described in this volume, however, are a representative sample. They include some of the earliest organizations established in the mid-1880s, such as the still-flourishing Illinois Woman's Press Association, as well as more recent groups established in the last fifteen years, such as the Association for Women in Sports Media. They represent national, regional, state, and local organizations, from the National Federation of Press Women to the New England Woman's Press Association to the Denver Woman's Press Club. Some are no longer in existence, but more than half continue today. Of these, several are struggling with increasing challenges at the turn of the twenty-first century while a few are thriving and have bright hopes for the future.

Beyond the elemental function of establishing a basic record of the existence of these women's press organizations, it is the goal of this volume to identify some of the social, economic, professional, and even political forces that led to their establishment; identify and describe the women responsible for their creation and continuation; describe the ways in which these organizations responded to and interacted with significant events and issues of the times; place them in the context of developments in the journalism community and the communications industry of the period and assess their contributions to those institutions; and, above all, identify how they contributed to the definition of the "woman journalist" and her professionalization.

Throughout this project, the location of documentary records has been a major challenge. As most women's historians know only too well, records of women and women's groups are rarely thought to be of enough importance to be kept, preserved, and archived. Records of most women's press organizations, therefore, are frequently no longer in existence; those few that are, are generally incomplete and scattered. Records of more recent groups are often moved around informally from the home of one officer or meeting place to another with the result that they are often misplaced, lost, or inadvertently destroyed. In a few exceptional cases, records of organizations have been donated to libraries or historical societies, and even here, they tend to be incomplete. Although several women's press organizations published some form of newsletter or bulletin, for example, few of these have been preserved and few of those collections are complete.

Anecdotes abound. In the case of the New England Woman's Press Association (NEWPA), founded in 1885, the first twenty-three years of the association's records went up in flames with the home of the association secretary in the 1908 Chelsea (Massachusetts) fire. The bulk of the next twenty-four years of records went missing after NEWPA member Myra Lord collected them to publish a history on the organization in which she laments the loss of the earlier records! Some of the association's records from 1920 to 1959 are miraculously preserved in a collection at the Massachusetts Historical Society, but the last twenty-three years of NEWPA's records, from 1959 to 1982, are available only in bits and pieces kept by a few of the association's surviving officers. In the case of the National Federation of Press Women (NFPW), records of the federation's early years are misfiled in the voluminous records of the Illinois Woman's Press Association (which was instrumental in organizing the federation) at the Chicago Historical Society Research Center. Their "disappearance" is, ironically, noted in correspondence between an NFPW officer and former officer (preserved in the NFPW Collection at the Chicago Historical Society) in which the current officer asks her predecessor where the early records might be. Her predecessor replies that although she has been ill and her memory is no longer what it used to be, she seems to remember giving the files to the Chicago Historical Society! In the case of the Michigan Woman's Press Association newsletter, the *Interchange*, published 1892 to 1902, a collection was once housed at the Michigan State Library in Lansing, but to the dismay of the researcher, the complete collection disappeared in 1998.

Yet even these incomplete collections are a blessing to the historian and offer a base line for research in this topic. Libraries and historical societies to be lauded in their efforts to preserve such material and encouraged to continue these efforts include the Kansas State Historical Society, the Ohio Historical Society in Columbus, the Chicago Historical Society Research Center, the Massachusetts Historical Society, the Western Reserve Historical Society in Cleveland, the Cincinnati Historical Society, the Indiana Historical Society in Indianapolis, the Michigan Historical Center in Lansing, the Mississippi Department of Archives and History in Jackson, the University of Illinois at Chicago Library, the Western Historical Manuscript Collection at the University of Missouri at Columbia, the Broadcast Pioneers Library of American Broadcasting at the University of Maryland, the Washington Press Club Foundation, and the public libraries in Boston, Denver, and Detroit.

Notwithstanding the existence of these collections, most of the material contained in this volume came from a wide variety of sources and the contributors performed a Herculean task in tracking down the information necessary to put together a thorough, well-documented, and insightful history of each organization. A lucky few located the pertinent archival collections and organization newsletters in existence; beyond this, they located material about the organizations, their members, and activities in trade journals, contemporary newspapers, obituaries, city and state histories and directories, city and state records, biographical dictionaries, and oral histories collected in the last twenty years. In the case of more recent organizations that were still in existence during the 1950s and 1960s, a few diligent contributors tracked down former members, some of whom are now in their eighties or nineties, to interview them about their recollections or to clarify a particular point. Contributors researching organizations in existence today encountered a different problem. Some, such as the National Federation of Press Women, the Association for Women in Communications, and National Federation of Press Women/Missouri Affiliate, are in a state of flux as they reorganize or refocus their goals in an attempt to meet challenges of rising costs, declining membership, and wavering participation. Some of these issues were being addressed at annual conventions even as this book was nearing completion. In one case, the co-presidents of the Missouri group explained by e-mail the logistics and rationale behind their recent reorganization. In the case of the National Federation of Press Women, the researcher called in an update of her manuscript virtually from the convention floor.

The individuals and institutions to be thanked for their contributions to this volume, therefore, are many. First, the contributors should be thanked for all their work in the preparation of their manuscripts through various revisions in which they constantly fine-tuned their material, always looking for the telling detail and interpretation. I thank them, especially, for their good-natured and generous responses to numerous e-mail messages and late-night phone calls. The librarians from the many institutions who helped the researchers should also be thanked. The Schlesinger Library at Radcliffe College, the Massachusetts Historical Society, the Butler Library at Columbia University, the Ohio Historical Society, and the Ellis Library at the University of Missouri at Columbia are just some of those that come to mind. In addition, I would particularly like to thank Maurine Beasley and Marion Marzolf, two outstanding journalism historians, and Harvey Jassem, the director of the School of Communication at the University of Hartford, for their constant support and encouragement. I also thank the University of Hartford for its partial support of the research for this book provided by a 1995–96 Vincent B. Coffin Grant and a 1998–99 Faculty Fellowship in the Humanities, and the National Endowment for the Humanities for a 1997 Summer Research Stipend that supported travel expenses to various archives to complete my own research on this project.

A few technical details should be explained here. The reader will note that several chapters bear the title of an organization followed by "(Formerly the . . .)." Since some of these organizations changed their name up to three times, it was decided that the *most recent* name would be used, but that previous names would be included in chronological order in parentheses, and that name changes would be described in the text and outlined in the Institutional Profile at the end of the chapter.

In a few cases, where a chapter describes several attempts at organizing press women in a particular city or state, the chapter title is "Women's Press Organizations in . . . ," rather than the name of a particular organization. In the cases of Missouri and Mississippi, for example, press women first organized in those states during the 1890s, though little is known about those organizations. They did, however, create a tradition that was instrumental in the establishment of women's press organizations some fifty years later. Therefore, it was decided they should be granted as full an account as possible.

The reader will note that several chapters are unable to give the exact year in which an organization was disbanded or discontinued and the final year is placed in parentheses. Given the incomplete state of most records concerning these organizations, proof of their evidence can be found only in scattered references in newspaper stories, city directories, and announcements of programs, and it is often impossible to discover when they finally ceased activity. Thus, several authors speculate that a particular organization ceased "sometime after" a particular year in which the last evidence of activity can be found. In fact, in several cases, the organization never officially disbanded: in the words of former members, they simply "faded away" or "ran out of steam." In these cases, the author attempts to identify the last evidence of the organization's existence.

Since the names of some of these organizations are sometimes quite lengthy, the authors have adopted the acronyms they used immediately following the first reference as a way of simplifying the text. However, wherever possible, authors have attempted to avoided creating an "alphabet soup" by using other words and phrases such as "the group" or the "women" to denote the organization and revert to the full name where confusion would otherwise occur.

Asterisks that appear after the name of an organization throughout the various chapters denote press organizations that are profiled elsewhere in this volume.

The chapters are arranged alphabetically by the names of the organizations. Each chapter offers a historical essay that provides information about the organization's founding, its members and the character of the membership, its activities, some of the issues in which it became involved, and its contributions. An Informational Sources section at the end of each chapter offers a selected bibliography of sources pertinent to that particular press organization. An Institutional Profile provides significant dates in the organization's history, any name changes, the name or names of any newsletters, the location of papers or manuscript collections, and, if the organization is still in existence, contact information. The chapters are followed by a chronological listing of women's press organizations, a bibliography of all pertinent works cited in this book, and a list of the contributors.

I hope this volume will prove useful to students of journalism and women's history and that it will encourage them to develop further research suggested by this material in areas yet unexplored.

Elizabeth V. Burt

Introduction

Women's press organizations in the United States have played an active role in the preparation, professionalization, recognition, and assimilation of women in journalism. Since the first organizations were founded during the early 1880s, the number of women in the journalistic work force has increased from less than 3 percent to more than 48 percent.[1] The roles they routinely occupy in the news industry have expanded from correspondent, society writer, and woman's page editor to include positions as print and broadcast reporter, managing editor, and publisher. In the expanding communications industry of the twentieth century, women writers found their place in related fields as well, including public relations and advertising. And with the growth of journalism schools and programs in the last century, women have slowly but gradually come to represent nearly a third of the faculty.[2]

As women's place in the profession has changed in the last century, so too have the interests, goals, and strengths of women's press organizations. These changes have contributed to an evolving vision of the role of the woman journalist. For just as surely as these organizations assisted women in defining themselves as journalists, they contributed to women's acceptance as journalists by the profession as well as the public. In addition, women's press organizations, often closely related to major women's movements of the nineteenth and twentieth centuries, have often put women's issues on the public agenda.

EARLY YEARS: 1881–1919

Although women started organizing reform groups as early as the 1840s and social clubs in the late 1860s, they were slow to organize professional clubs, simply lacking the critical mass to make such clubs feasible.[3] Press clubs existed in many cities and states, but these were organized by men and typically closed to female membership on the grounds that a place where men smoked, drank, and gambled was no place for a lady.[4] A few exceptions, such as the Missouri Press Association, founded in 1867, permitted a few women members in the early years, but these women often attended meetings as the wife of an editor; because they had married an editor, they found themselves, almost inadvertently, it would seem, to be newspaperwomen.[5]

For the most part, however, the few women journalists employed full time on newspaper staffs occupied positions as society writers or editors. A larger number, uncounted by the census, were correspondents or contributors who wrote for several publications at the same time and were paid space rates (by the column inch for published material). Thus, women journalists, who were already at a disadvantage because of their numerical inferiority and the secondary positions they occupied, were further disadvantaged by being cut off from the professional networking and collegiality available to their male colleagues through city and state press clubs.

It was not until the 1880s, when up to a half-dozen women in a given city might find full-time positions on the staff of daily papers or women working there as correspondents might number twice that, that women journalists banded together to create their own press clubs and associations. The first of these was a group of "lady correspondents" in Washington, D.C., who, out of "Necessity and Ambition" formed the Ladies' Press Club in 1881 with Emily Edson Briggs ("Olivia" of the *Philadelphia Press*) as their first president. (By 1883, the club had renamed itself the Woman's National Press Association.)[6] These women, some of whom had been selling their work to newspapers for more than twenty years, identified the purpose of the organization as providing a source of "mutual help and encouragement" for the female correspondents working in the nation's capital, especially for the "coming generation" of women journalists.[7]

Next to organize were a group of women attending the North, South, and Central American Exposition in New Orleans in 1885. The group, which included journalists from Boston, St. Louis, and Indianapolis, formed the National Woman's Press Association (later renamed the International Woman's Press Association to avoid confusion with the Washington association). Their hope was that it would serve as an umbrella organization that would spark the establishment of city and state organizations throughout the country.[8] Their goal of providing women journalists with an opportunity for networking, enhancing their skills, and finding work is clear in their founding document:

The object of this organization is to provide a medium of communication between journalists of the country and to secure all the benefits that will result from organized effort. Such information as is continually needed by writers will always be rendered available, and new avenues will be opened to individuals for journalistic work. Innumerable benefits will arise from mutual help and encouragement. One aim of the association is to forward the interests of working women in every possible way by combined action of newspaper women.[9]

By the early 1900s, some two dozen women's press organizations had been established, many of them through the efforts of the National Woman's Press Association. There were organizations in more than seventeen states as well as regional organizations serving New England, the South, and the West Coast. Several national and international groups had also been established, including the National Federation of Women's Press Clubs in 1891 and the Woman's International Press Union in 1898.[10]

Women's press organizations became so popular, in fact, that by the early 1900s, some states claimed organizations in several cities. Thus, women journalists in Ohio could choose among the Cleveland Woman's Press Club,* founded in 1886, the Woman's Press Club of Cincinnati,* founded in 1888, and the Ohio Newspaper Women's Association,* founded in 1902. Pennsylvania had women's press organizations located in both Philadelphia and Pittsburgh, and Michigan had three.[11]

The principal goal of the women's press organizations during these years was to provide a venue where women journalists could talk about their work, provide advice to beginners, and mingle with their professional sisters—a luxury often denied them in the workplace where hiring practices were all too often dictated by the "one woman is enough" policy. Their meetings and conventions featured speeches and papers on the practical side of the profession with such titles as "Women in Journalism," "The Ethics of Our Profession," "In What Line of Newspaper Work Are Women Most Fitted to Constitutionally Excel," and "How Many Departments Can a Woman Successfully Edit Each Week?"[12] Discussion often centered on professional issues of the period, such as copyright law, the poor pay for space writers, and sensationalism. Some organizations, such as the New England Woman's Press Association,* the Pacific Coast Women's Press Association,* and the Illinois Woman's Press Association,* made resolutions, signed petitions, and sent them to newspapers and Congress.[13]

But the existence of these organizations also served another purpose: that of promoting the legitimacy of women journalists. As other women's organizations had done before them, they sought publicity through the press. First they sought exposure by seeking space in the society columns of the general circulation press, the columns of women's publications such as the *Woman's Journal*, and the "club notes" of the trade journals such as *The Journalist* and *The Fourth Estate*. Next, they began seeking news coverage of organizational activities in the mainstream press. Thus by 1900, the society columns in local papers regularly ran reports of the doings of the individual clubs, including their weekly meetings, their fund raisers, and their annual balls.[14] Other events, such as annual conventions and even weekly meetings, attracted news coverage when prominent social or political figures were invited as speakers.

The women's press organizations also gained recognition in the trade journals, although not all of it was positive. For whereas some like *Journalist* publisher Allan Forman and *Journalist* columnist Margherita Arlina Hamm praised them as essential to the advancement of the journalism profession in general and women journalists in particular,[15] others spoofed them as unprofessional gatherings of "gossips" and "dabblers" who had little to do with the journalism trade.[16]

Unlike these critics, many of these early organizations did not distinguish among journalists, published authors, and occasional writers or contributors. Truly democratic and nurturing, and quite practical in accepting the fact that few women were actually employed full time at newspapers, many accepted any woman who wielded the pen. The Illinois Woman's Press Association,* for example, included "authors, editors, poets, contributors, correspondents, reporters, and publishers."[17] The Cleveland Woman's Press Club* always welcomed nonjournalists, and in fact, eventually evolved into the Cleveland Writers' Club.* The League of American Pen Women* was founded in 1897 by journalists and writers alike, whose goal was to bring together "women journalists, authors, and illustrators for mutual benefit and strength that comes with union."[18]

Others, however, attempted to define the level of professionalism of members through different categories of membership; active membership might be open only to women earning money with their writing while associate membership might be offered to women who only occasionally published their work. In fact, exactly who might qualify as a member became a point of bitter debate and division in some cases. When newspaperwomen disagreed with a decision by the Michigan Woman's Press Association* in 1892 to expand membership to include "any woman resident of Michigan who is regularly connected in a literary way with any reputable newspaper or magazine, or *who is engaged in literary work for publication* [italics added]," they walked out and established an organization of their own, the Michigan Woman's Press Club,* which was restricted to women "connected with newspapers."[19] These debates continued over the years and well into the next century, often surfacing as pressures rose to increase membership or as developments in the industry opened new opportunities to women.

Many of the founders of women's press organizations were active in the woman's club movement, which linked these press organizations to the broader movement. Sallie Joy White, the first president of the New England Woman's Press Association,* was an active suffragist and a former officer of the Middlesex County Suffrage Association in Massachusetts.[20] Jane Cunningham Croly, "Jennie June," who established the Woman's Press Club of New York City* in 1889, is credited with launching the woman's club movement in 1868 when she founded Sorosis and was instrumental in establishing the General Federation of Women's Clubs in 1890.[21] Julia Ames and Frances E. Willard, founding members of the Illinois Woman's Press Association,* were both officers of the Women's Christian Temperance Union.[22]

It is no surprise, therefore, that the early women's press organizations were closely allied to the woman's club movement of the period. Many shared its benevolent and reformist characteristics and interests and, in fact, planned to use their position with the press to forward those interests. The New England

Woman's Press Association,* for example, explicitly stated that one of its goals was to forward "by concerted action through the Press such good objects in social, philanthropic and reformatory lines as may from time to time present themselves."[23] It formed a benefit society called Samaritana in 1893 that distributed funds among a number of local charitable institutions and established a journalists' fund that it maintained for the next eighty years to aid "distressed newspaper people in need of assistance."[24] One of the early projects of the Illinois Woman's Press Association* was to provide a cheap lodging house for working women and in 1886 the association announced a campaign to raise $1,500 to fund the project.[25] The Pacific Coast Women's Press Association* lobbied for a slew of municipal reforms, including the public improvement of roads, streets, parks, libraries, kindergartens, "and anything and everything that tends to the building up of the country."[26]

Many of the women involved in press associations were also active in the suffrage movement. Suffrage was frequently a topic of debate at meetings and conventions, and several press clubs eventually took a formal position on the reform. In 1911, the Kansas Woman's Press Association "declare[d] unanimously for equal suffrage" and the Southern California Women's Press Club* endorsed suffrage by a straw vote of 34 to 4.[27] In 1914, the New England Woman's Press Association sent a delegation to march in the May 2 suffrage parade in Boston, and in October 1915 and October 1917, the Woman's Press Club of New York City* marched "in a body" in the suffrage parades in New York.[28] This is not to say that all press women were suffragists, however, and not all press clubs endorsed the reform. The Woman's Press Club of Cincinnati,* in fact, studiously avoided the explosive topic so as to avoid a split in the ranks that might have proved fatal to the group's cohesiveness.[29]

The close ties between the press clubs and reform movements were frequently strengthened by the fact that the official newsletters of the press clubs were often reform publications or publications supportive of women's reforms, especially women's rights and suffrage. Thus the pro-suffrage *Woman's Exponent* became the official organ of the Utah Woman's Press Club,* Caroline Huling's short-lived *Justitia* (1887–88) became the organ of the Illinois Woman's Press Association,* and Charlotte Perkins Stetson's (later Gillman) socialist and progressive *Impress* (1894–95) served as the official organ of the Pacific Coast Woman's Press Association.*[30] All women's press organizations, as well as their members, received ample coverage in the suffrage *Woman's Journal*, edited by NEWPA charter member Alice Stone Blackwell. From the late 1880s until 1914, the weekly *Journal* often ran articles on women's press organizations and, in 1891, started publishing a regular column, "Women of the Press," written by Florence M. Adkinson, a founding member of the National Woman's Press Association and a member of NEWPA.[31]

Given their stature in these movements, it was not unusual for officers of the women's press organizations to appear on the podium at national and even international conventions promoting women's rights, economic development, peace, and education. At the 1893 World's Fair in Chicago, many press club officers participated in the Press Club Fair and the International Congress of Literary Women, including Sallie Joy White of the New England Woman's Press Association and Cynthia Westover Alden of the Woman's Press Club of New York City.* After 1890, press club officers often became the press chairs of the biennial conventions of the General Federation of Women's Clubs (GFWC) and in this capacity were, to a certain degree, able to orchestrate newspaper coverage of the GFWC activities.

By 1900 the U.S. Census reported 2,193 women journalists—7 percent of the journalistic workforce—and their press associations, which claimed more than seven hundred members across the nation, were established in at least seventeen states.[32] In 1909, as a result of universities opening their doors to women and their enrollment in the first journalism programs, a women's fraternal organization, Theta Sigma Phi (TSP; later renamed Association for Women in Communications*), was established at the University of Washington. This journalism sorority eventually became a national organization, with chapters in most states and universities with journalism programs.[33] Women journalists were not quite so uncommon as they had been in the 1880s, and it might be said that their exposure to the public through their activity in women's press clubs legitimized them to a certain degree.

Some press organizations, such as the National Editorial Association (NEA), founded in 1885, had begun to enroll both men and women as members, and in 1890, several woman's press associations sent delegates to NEA's annual convention held in Boston.[34] By the end of the century, woman's press groups were also affiliated with a dozen state, regional, and city male press organizations such as the Pennsylvania State Editorial Association, the Oregon Press Club, the Northwest Missouri Press Association, the East Texas Press Association, the St. Paul Press Club, and the Kansas City (Missouri) Press Club.[35] Some of these typically male-dominated organizations also began to admit female members, as in the case of the Pennsylvania State Editorial Association, and the St. Paul Press Club.[36] In yet other cases, limited though they might be, press associations were formed by men and women working together. In 1891, the International League of Press Clubs was organized, and within two years a woman (NEWPA's Sallie Joy White) was elected a first vice president.[37] And in 1895, the newspaper men and women of Nevada met to organize a press club.[38]

THE SECOND GENERATION: 1920–1937

Because the activities and interests of many of the women's press organizations founded during the last decades of the nineteenth century were so closely linked to the general woman's movement, which in turn was linked with the suffrage movement, it was perhaps inevitable that like many other women's organizations of the period, they lost much of their vitality with the passage of the federal woman suffrage amendment in 1919. The energetic women journalists who had established a beachhead in the 1880s were aging, retiring, and dying; in some cases, their organizations died with them. Thus the Woman's National Press Association had lost most of its members to old age, infirmity, and the grim reaper by 1920 and became inactive during the mid-1920s. The Michigan Woman's Press Club* and the Missouri Woman's Press Association* suspended meetings during the early years of World War I, and other organizations, such as the Woman's Press Association of the South,* the Woman's Press Club of Kentucky (founded in 1890), and the Mississippi Women's Press Club (founded in 1894), vanished quietly without leaving more than the faintest trace for future historians.

As so often happens in woman's history, the next generation of women journalists not involved in the surviving organizations seem to have been oblivious to the women who had preceded them. When Washington women journalists organized the Women's National Press Club (WNPC)* in 1919, they ignored the still active Woman's National Press Association.[39] But like the women who came before them, the women who established the WNPC had two basic motivations: their exclusion from the dominant male press organization, and the need to network with other (female) journalists in a similar position. The WNPC offered visibility to Washington women journalists and allowed them to seek the same access to news sources as male journalists enjoyed through the prominent male-only National Press Club. Like the National Press Club, the WNPC invited prominent speakers to its luncheons; unlike the National Press Club, those speakers were often *women*.

Another women's press organization established during this period was the New York Newspaper Women's Club,* established in 1922. Many of its founders, like those of the WNPC, had been active in and reported on the suffrage movement. Also like the founders of the WNPC, they apparently ignored the existence of the previously established Woman's Press Club of New York City* in order to create a new organization for a new generation. The New York Newspaper Women's Club, unlike its predecessor, was to be devoted entirely to women working for newspapers.[40]

Those organizations that survived the turn of the century, the stresses of World War I, and the triumph of the suffrage movement focused on securing women's positions in the press. Some that had originally limited membership to newspaperwomen, such as the New England Woman's Press Association,* revised requirements to embrace women professionals in the emerging communication fields, such as public relations and radio, as well as in the broader field of literature and magazine writing.[41] Some devoted special attention to the next generation, sponsoring activities such as scholarships and youth auxiliaries in the hope of attracting women to the profession and securing their allegiance to the organization. The Woman's Press Club of New York City* in 1921 was the first to establish a scholarship fund; by the 1960s, this became a common practice.

Notwithstanding the increase in the number of women employed in the communications industry in these decades—by 1930 women made up 22.9 percent of the journalistic workforce—participation in some of the older press organizations began to falter toward the end of the 1920s.[42] In some cases, it would appear that women's very success in finding full-time employment in the press siphoned off the energy they might otherwise have been able to devote to leadership and participation in press organizations. In other cases, such as the Utah Woman's Press Club,* Pacific Coast Women's Press Association,* and Southern California Women's Press Club,* the fiery reformist spirit that had characterized their early years died out with the end of the Progressive Era, the passage of woman suffrage, and the death of founding members. Finally, the economic crisis of the Depression made it difficult for many women to maintain their membership and participation in press organizations. By the end of the 1930s, the Utah Woman's Press Club,* the Michigan Woman's Press Association,* the Pacific Coast Women's Press Association,* and the Southern California Women's Press Club* had all disbanded or ceased activity.

FEDERATION AND RESURGENCE: 1937–1970

A resurgence of energy was infused into women's press organizations in the second half of the 1930s. No doubt a combination of factors—the growing unrest in Europe, the relocation of male reporters to cover the escalating European crisis, the increasing number of female journalism graduates dissatisfied with the job market, and the constant awareness of the disparity between their abilities and the jobs available to them—encouraged women journalists once again to look for the support and networking that would come with strong women's press organizations.

Interest in reestablishing a national network began in the Illinois Woman's Press Association* in the late 1920s and eventually coalesced into the idea of establishing a national federation of clubs that would adhere to rigid membership requirements. By 1936, four state organizations—Illinois Women's Press Association,* Ohio Newspaper Women's Association,* Presswomen of Portland (Oregon), and the Woman's Press Club of Indiana*—had federated to form the National Federation of Press Women (NFPW).*[43] Like the National Woman's Press Association founded in 1885, the NFPW was to serve as an umbrella organization with state affiliates. An early requirement that affiliated clubs restrict their membership to women working for newspapers discouraged some existent press organizations from joining, but this was eventually changed so that the NFPW and its affiliates came to embrace a wide variety of women in communications, including those in advertising, public relations, and broadcast.

The coming of World War II also created new opportunities for women journalists who suddenly found themselves filling positions formerly reserved for men only. Undoubtedly these new opportunities—and perhaps the realization that they could easily be snatched away—created a greater awareness of the need for the camaraderie and support to be provided by women's press organizations. During the 1940s, responding to these developments as well as the recruiting efforts of the NFPW, several new organizations were created, some in areas where none had ever existed, others where older organizations had died out. In Kansas, where a women's press association had flourished in Topeka for some years during the 1890s, a second organization, Kansas Press Women,* was established in 1941. Following the same pattern, Minnesota Press Women* was established in 1940, Colorado Press Women* in 1941, Idaho Press Women in 1944, and Mississippi Press Women* in 1947.

At the same time, women were finding their way into the once restrictive radio industry and the newly emerging television industry. Though some radio script writers had joined the traditional women's press clubs, no organization was devoted specifically to their needs until 1942, when the National Association of Broadcasters (NAB) established a department specifically for women, the Association of Women Directors (AWD), which was renamed the Association of Women Broadcasters (AWB)* in 1946. Although tightly controlled by the parent organization, AWB did provide a venue for women in broadcasting to network and bring up issues specific to women in the industry. NAB dissolved AWB when personality and political issues interfered with its control over the group, but it immediately sponsored the creation of a second organization, American Women in Radio and Television (AWRT),* which continues to exist today.

Organizations founded during this period became especially active in encouraging education for women in journalism through writing workshops, scholarships, and awards. Through these activities, the women's press organizations were able to create a living chain from one generation to the next in which working journalists became both role models and mentors to students entering the field and women just starting out. By naming awards and scholarships after particular women journalists, they were also assuring that these women, unlike their predecessors of the nineteenth century, would not be forgotten by future generations.

As we have seen, many of the women who founded and joined women's press associations did so largely because they were excluded from male press organizations and isolated within the journalism profession, which for most of its existence has been (and continues to be) male dominated. They soon learned, however, that rather than serving as a *substitute* for something believed to be, by definition, *better*, the women's press organizations provided a sense of power, solidarity, and *identity* women could rarely have experienced in mixed-sex organizations. Nevertheless, as women gained legitimacy in journalism, the barriers excluding women from male-only press clubs began to come down slowly, starting in the 1890s in a handful of city clubs and state associations. By the early 1960s women in some localities had the option of choosing whether to belong to a women's organization, a mixed-sex organization, or both.

The process was accelerated by the women's movement of the 1960s when the concerted action of women activists and organizations brought continual attention to the inequities of "male-only" policies within the journalism profession and the news industry. Once again many women's press organizations became involved in debate over a social movement—the movement for the ratification of the Equal Rights Amendment (ERA). As in the period of the suffrage movement, many women journalists were feminists who supported the amendment. But there were also conservatives, and debate was often long and fiery. Several organizations, including NFPW,* Women in Communications, Inc.,* Delaware Press Women,* and Idaho Press Women,* eventually endorsed the ERA. Others entertained debate but did not take a position; still others, like Missouri Press Women,* made the conscious decision *not* even to discuss the issue, perhaps in an effort to avoid conflict within the organization.

As the women's movement brought pressure through public opinion and legal action, the most recalcitrant of male press organizations—the National Press Club and Sigma Delta Chi—removed their exclusionary policies and admitted their first women members in 1971 and 1972, respectively. The Women's National Press Club* had anticipated the National Press Club's move a month earlier by changing its name to the Washington Press Club and voting to admit men.[44] Following these developments, many women's press organizations abandoned their membership designations that defined members in term of gender, although they usually retained the word *women* or *woman's* in their name and continued to adhere to their purpose of supporting "the efforts of women within the profession to realize their full rights and privileges," in the words of Kansas Press Women.*[45] Other women's press organizations, in addition to admitting male members, dropped the word *women* from their title. In 1995, Texas Press Women* (founded in 1893 as Texas Woman's Press Association) changed its name to Texas Professional Communicators in an effort to attract new members. In 1997, Delaware Press Women* changed its name to Delaware Press Association after men came to represent 20 percent of the membership.[46] Other NFPW affiliates have made similar decisions, and twelve of the federation's forty-four affiliates now use a name without the designation *women*.[47]

DECLINE AND NEW DIRECTIONS

Even as women's and men's press organizations merged and once male-only or female-only groups accepted members of the opposite sex after 1970, participation in established press organizations declined across the board. Changing lifestyles, a decrease of available time for voluntary and professional activities, and increasing demands for organizational effort seem to have doomed some of these organizations. The Woman's Press Club of New York City* dissolved in 1980; Minnesota Press Women* disbanded in 1982; the Woman's Press Club of Cincinnati* disbanded after its centennial anniversary in 1988. Others simply became inactive without taking formal action: the New England Woman's Press Association* ceased activity after 1982; and during the 1990s, at least four NFPW affiliates became inactive. Others have succeeded in hanging on by capping costs, reducing the frequency of meetings, redefining their mission, and stepping up recruiting efforts. The urgency of these attempts is illustrated by NFPW's ambitious "Blueprint for 2000," which aims to refocus the federation in the twenty-first century.[48]

At the same time, following the patterns established early in the twentieth century, new women's press organizations are rising in response to emerging issues and needs; they are fueled by the passion of strong leaders with the feminist goal of erasing continuing gender inequities. In 1985, a group of women journalists and journalism educators established JAWS: Journalism and Women Symposium* to support "the personal growth and empowerment of women in the newsroom." Members meet at an annual "camp" to mingle, discuss issues, and participate in training activities; by 1999, there were about four hundred.[49] In 1987, women sports journalists created the Association for Women in Sports Media (AWSM)* to address the difficulties they faced in covering male athletes, the poor coverage of women's sports, the lack of legitimacy accorded women athletes and women sports reporters, and inequities of pay. Today AWSM has more than six hundred members and is active in responding to individual cases regarding discrimination against and harassment of women sports journalists.[50]

This introduction highlights some of the common themes running through the stories of the many women's press organizations profiled in this book. Most groups were established at a time when women were excluded from positions of power and authority within the communications industry, whether as women correspondents of the 1880s, radio announcers of the 1940s, or sports reporters of the 1980s and 1990s. These press organizations provided the support they needed to function, to survive gracefully during times of little progress, and to eventually overcome some of the barriers that prevented them from gaining full access to their profession. Many today would argue that full access has not yet been attained and that women's press organizations are still needed.

Another theme running through the stories of these organizations is the debate over who should be allowed to join. The debate might have changed in relation to professional opportunities, technological developments, and the social status of women in a particular place or time, but it often determined whether an organization would be inclusive or exclusive. Should members be all writers or just newspaper writers? Should they be anyone who wrote, only those who wrote for publication, only those who received pay for their work, or only those who supported themselves with their work? Should they be limited to newspaper-women or include magazine writers, publicity writers, radio scriptwriters, television reporters, women in advertising, college professors? Should they be restricted to women or allow men to join?

Most also grappled with the question of whether they should restrict their activities to purely professional concerns or larger social issues. Should they restrict their discussions to copyright law and "pure press," how to write a lead and get a story published, and recent changes in the libel law—or should they become embroiled in debates over municipal reform, woman suffrage, child labor laws, pay equity, and the ERA?

Another theme running through these stories is the sense that these organizations needed to keep a constant vigil in order to remain vital to their constituents. All the organizations profiled here, with perhaps the exception of those established in the last fifteen years, at some point dealt with waning energy, declining membership, and faltering participation. Some succeeded in re-creating themselves in response to changing conditions, whereas others failed. Some ignored already existing organizations, setting up instead a competing group to follow a particular agenda or serve as a platform for a particular organizer. This highlights yet another common theme—the constant tension between cooperation and competition, sisterhood and professionalization, which became increasingly noticeable within these organizations as the twentieth century progressed.

This volume provides many starting points for those interested in the story of women journalists, their networks and publications, their development as professionals, and the relationship between their craft and their social position. It is this editor's hope that this volume will serve both as a resource and as a source of inquiry for future research on these subjects.

NOTES

1. Maurine H. Beasley and Sheila J. Gibbons, eds., *Taking Their Place: A Documentary History of Women and Journalism* (Washington, D.C.: American University Press, 1993), p. 10; "Table Number 637, Employed Civilians by Occupation, Sex, Race, and Hispanic Origin, 1983 and 1993," *Statistical Abstract of the United States* (Washington, D.C.: United States Department of Commerce, Economic and Statistics Administration, 1994), p. 637.

2. Pamela J. Creedon, ed., *Women in Mass Communication*, 2d ed. (Newbury Park, Calif.: Sage, 1993), p. 17. Creedon cites a 1992 survey of faculty members of the Association for Education in Journalism and Mass Communication.

3. For discussion of women's reform groups and women's clubs of the nineteenth century, see Karen J. Blair, *The Clubwoman as Feminist: True Womanhood Redefined, 1868–1914* (New York: Holmes and Meier, 1980), and Eleanor Flexner, *Century of Struggle: The Woman's Rights Movement in the United States*, rev. ed. (Cambridge, Mass.: Belknap Press of Harvard University, 1975), pp. 182–96.

4. In 1891, California journalist Maude S. Peaselee quoted a Boston Press Club decision that "women might do as good work as men in newspaper offices, but *were out of place in an ordinary men's club* [italics added by Peaselee]." Maude S. Peaselee, "Here's Hopin'," *The Journalist*, 31 January 1891, p. 12.

5. Jewell Ross Mehus and Maude Freeland, eds., "Forward," *Missouri Press Women, History and Directory, 1965*, Missouri Press Women Papers, folder 15, Western Historical Manuscript Collection, Ellis Library, University of Missouri, Columbia, Missouri.

6. S. D. Fry, "Newspaper Women," *The Journalist*, 19 December 1892, p. 11, reprinted from the Philadelphia *Herald*, n.d.; "Woman's National Press Association," *Woman's Journal*, 26 January 1901, p. 28. Other founders were Mary Clemmer (Ames), correspondent for the *Independent*, Martha D. Lincoln, and Rose P. Breandle, who wrote under the pen name "Pips."

7. Marion McBride, "Report to the 1890 Convention of the National Editorial Association," *The Journalist*, 5 July 1890, p. 12.

8. The name was changed in 1888. McBride, "Report," p. 12.

9. Ibid.

10. Elizabeth V. Burt, "A Bid for Legitimacy: The Woman's Press Club Movement, 1881–1900," *Journalism History* 23, no. 2 (summer 1997): 72–84.

11. Ibid.

12. E. Cora DePuy, "Southern Michigan," *The Journalist*, 5 July 1890, p. 5; "Annual Meeting of the Illinois Woman's Press Association," *The Journalist*, 4 February 1891, p. 10; "Topeka," *The Journalist*, 26 March 1898, p. 225; E. Cora DePuy, "Southern Michigan," *The Journalist*, 13 May 1899, p. 264; "Woman's Press Club of Illinois," *The Journalist*, 18 December 1886, p. 14.

13. Myra B. Lord, *History of the New England Woman's Press Association* (Newton, Mass.: Graphic Press, 1932), pp. 27–28, 314; Pacific Coast Woman's Press Association, Annual Program, September 1892, pp. 21–23.

14. The *Boston Post*, for example, regularly ran notices of NEWPA events.

15. Margherita Arlina Hamm, "Among the Newspaper Women," *The Journalist*, 3 September 1892, p. 10; Allan Forman, "Hardly Gallant," *The Journalist*, 23 January 1892, p. 8.

16. See, for example, "Boston Beanlets," *The Journalist*, 24 July 1897, p. 110; "Boston Beanlets," *The Journalist*, 1 January 1898, p. 130.

17. "The Illinois Woman's Press Association," *The Fourth Estate*, 23 May 1895, p. 3.

18. Claracy Lee M. Waldrop, "We Make History," *The Pen Woman* (June/July/August 1997), p. 11. The league changed its name in 1921 to the National League of American Pen Women.

19. Will Chaddock, "Michigan," *The Journalist*, 27 August 1892, p. 5.

20. "Results of Election," Middlesex County Suffrage Association, Sallie Joy White Papers, Collection A126 (hereafter SJW Papers), box 2, vol. 2, Schlesinger Library, Radcliffe College, Cambridge, Massachusetts.

21. Flexner, pp. 183, 190.

22. *Prominent Women of Illinois* (Chicago: Illinois Woman's Press Association, 1932), pp. 10, 15.

23. Jean Kincaid (Estelle M. Hatch), "New England Woman's Press Association," *The Journalist*, 26 January 1889, p. 7.

24. "Boston," *The Journalist*, 17 June 1893, p. 14; "The Club Women," *The Fourth Estate*, 10 December 1898, p. 5.

25. "Boston," *The Journalist*, 18 December 1886, 14.

26. Emilie Tracy Y. Parkhurst, "Pacific Coast Women's Press Association," *Californian*, September 1893, pp. 528–29.

27. "Press Women of Kansas Declare Unanimously for Equal Suffrage," *Woman's Journal*, 3 June 1911, p. 169; Rose L. Ellerbe, *History of the Southern California Women's Press Club* (Los Angeles: Rose Ellerby, 1930), p. 36.

28. Lord, *History*, p. 305; Minutes of Business Meeting of Woman's Press Club of

New York City, 9 October 1915 and 13 October 1917, Archives of the Woman's Press Club of New York City, box 4, Butler Library, Columbia University, New York.

29. Martin Hogan, Jr., "Press Club: That's All She Wrote: Woman's Group Brings to an End 100-Year Entity," *Cincinnati Enquirer*, 14 August 1988, p. B4 Metro.

30. The *Impress* ("A Journal for Men and Women") was initially published by the PCWPA but was sold to Stetson in 1894. She devoted one or more pages in each issue to the PCWPA, but she also devoted considerable space to political and economic issues.

31. The *Woman's Journal* dropped its column on women in journalism (as well as columns on women in teaching, medicine, and business) after 1914, reflecting its shift from a general women's rights publication to one devoted specifically to passage of the suffrage amendment.

32. Beasley and Gibbons, *Taking Their Place*, p. 10; Burt, "A Bid for Legitimacy," p. 79.

33. In the early 1970s, after pressure generated and supported by the women's move-ment, women were admitted to the male national fraternity Sigma Delta Chi and the women's group evolved into Women in Communication, Inc. (WICI).

34. "The Ladies' Dinner," *The Journalist*, 5 July 1890, p. 19. Associations to send delegates to the 1890 convention included the women's press associations of New Eng-land, Illinois, and the Pacific Coast. The first women's press association to become an auxiliary to the National Editorial Association was the Illinois Woman's Press Associ-ation. (McBride, "Report," p. 12.)

35. *The Journalist*, 1886–1900, passim; *The Fourth Estate*, 1894–1900, passim.

36. "Female Reporters," *The Journalist*, 25 April 1891, p. 13; "Ruth Kimball," *The Journalist*, 6 May 1893, p. 7.

37. "International League Convention," *The Journalist*, 27 May 1893, p. 4.

38. "Notes among the Clubs and Associations," *The Fourth Estate*, 17 October 1895, p. 15.

39. Maurine Beasley, "The Women's National Press Club: Case Study of Professional Aspirations," *Journalism History* 15, no. 4 (winter 1988): pp. 112–121.

40. Emma Bugbee, Minutes, 22 March 1922, Newswomen's Club of New York Pa-pers, Newswomen's Club of New York, National Arts Club Building, New York.

41. "NEWPA Constitution," *NEWPA Yearbook, 1946*, New England Woman's Press Association Papers, Massachusetts Historical Society, Boston, Massachusetts.

42. According to the 1930 census, there were 11,924 female and 39,920 male editors and reporters. "Table I: General Report on Occupations," *Fifteenth Census of the United States: Population*, vol. 5 (Washington, D.C.: Government Printing Office, 1933), p. 20.

43. *Pen Points*, May 1937, p. 2, Illinois Woman's Press Association Collection, Chi-cago Historical Society Research Center, Chicago.

44. The National Press Club's action followed, it should be noted, the decision by the Women's National Press Club to accept male members and to drop the word *women* from its name and change it to the Washington Press Club. Beasley. "The Women's National Press Club," p. 120.

45. *Kansas Press Women Handbook*, 1974; *Kansas Press WomeNewsletter*, September 1983; both in Kansas Press Women Papers, Manuscript Collection 223, boxes 9 and 11, Manuscripts Department, Kansas State Historical Society, Topeka.

46. Katherine Smigie, DPA historian, e-mail correspondence to author, 17 August 1998.

47. NFPW Membership List, NFPW Web page, <http://www.nfpw.org>, 4 June 1999.

48. NFPW, "Blueprint for 2000," 1988.

49. JAWS Web page, <http://www.jaws.org>.

50. *AWSM Newsletter*, <http://users.southeast.net/~awsm>, 20 May 1999.

1

Sonya Forte Duhé

American Women in Radio and Television, 1951–Present

BEGINNINGS

Back in 1929, we had crystal sets . . . you had to listen with earphones, and some of them had big horns. We were heard ninety miles away from where we were broadcasting one night, and it caused, oh, it caused a furor. Everybody would say, oh, just think, we heard you ninety miles away. I worked a program in the morning, and I worked a program on KWEA [Shreveport, Louisiana]. Then I'd run over to KWKH [Shreveport], and I'd run a program over there. . . . Everything was live in those days. We played records, but they were those awful 78 records . . . and we blocked them off in fifteen-minute periods. Our microphones, they were all carbon mikes, great, big old mikes, that you see both ends. If you didn't stand right in the middle of that thing, you couldn't be heard. If you turned your head to sneeze, it was just too bad.[1]

"Those were all the little interesting things that made radio in those days pioneering," broadcast pioneer Judy Bryson told delegates at the 1977 American Women in Radio and Television National Convention.[2]

"I've broadcast from the kitchen. I had a doctor from India who came and cooked curried chicken right out in the kitchen. Of course, it's radio, but you could hear that chicken boiling," Annabell Webb reminisced to the delegates.[3]

It was kitchen talk, singing, acting, and how to be a good housewife. A woman's place in early radio was also in research, off-air interviewing, and writing. Women pioneers in broadcasting, like Webb and Bryson, did not announce or read the news—at least in the early years.[4] It was the women who made radio a logical extension of the home that became the foundation for American Women in Radio and Television (AWRT)—the oldest continuing professional broadcast organization in the country.[5]

AWRT was formed in 1951, but women's path to journalism and the broadcast industry began well before the organization was conceived. During the suffrage campaign when women fought for the right to vote, new opportunities were created for women to express themselves journalistically. Metropolitan newspapers hired a few women journalists to cover the woman's movement. A few women moved into newsrooms to replace men during World War I.

Nationally, the number of women working as print reporters and editors more than doubled from 7,105 in 1920 to 14,786 in 1930. But most of those women worked in one of three areas: women's pages, magazines, and book publishing. Women rarely covered politics or other forms of hard news. Editors told women they were biologically unsuited to reporting, as did Philip Porter and Norval Luxon in their 1935 reporting textbook: "The general tempo—with the deadline-fighting element always present—is such to bar many women because of nervous temperament. . . . Most women are incapable of covering police and court news."[6]

The tempo was much the same for women in radio. With the advent of commercial radio in the 1920s, women found their opportunities severely limited. According to early broadcaster Ruth Crane, "Newscasting was reserved for men because station managers and advertisers held that men's voices alone carried authority and believability."[7] By 1943, there were more than twenty thousand men in radio and television compared to about five thousand women.[8] Management believed women weren't tough enough; that they got married and had babies, and that as soon as they were trained, they were gone.[9]

The women who did find a place behind the microphone were largely restricted to traditional women's fare.[10] At that time, a career in broadcasting meant being an actress on a popular radio soap opera or in a nighttime drama. Women sang, sold products, and were entertainers. When Mary Margaret McBride, a well-established magazine and newspaper reporter began her radio career in 1934 in New York, she was told to pretend to be something she was not. But in the middle of a broadcast, the irrepressible McBride burst out, "Oh, what's the use? I can't do it! I'm not a grandmother! I'm not a mother. I'm not even married. . . . The truth is I'm a reporter and I would like to come here every day and tell you about places I go and people I meet. Write me if you'd like that. But I can't be a grandmother anymore!"[11] Her listeners responded positively, and McBride launched one of the most successful careers in radio history. She became known as "Lady Number One of the Air" for her daily interview program that continued on network radio until her retirement in 1960.[12]

At the same time, television was becoming a popular medium. Some women were beginning to be taken seriously—if they worked hard enough. In 1946, ABC hired Pauline Frederick to cover regular news assignments for those times that male reporters were not available. Even after getting exclusive stories at the United Nations, she still wasn't allowed on-air. She continued to persevere. By 1948, she made the move to television and became TV's first successful newswoman, covering the United Nations for NBC from 1953 until her retirement in 1972. Like so many other TV newswomen of her time, Frederick made the move from radio to TV.[13]

But still, in the words of Ruth Crane, female broadcasters had "no opportunity to know or communicate with each other."[14] Women needed a forum for expression and career development.

ORGANIZATION

The Association of Women Broadcasters (AWB),* the first national organization for women professionals in broadcasting, was an adjunct of the National Association of Radio and Television Broadcasters (NARTB), the predecessor of the National Association of Broadcasters (NAB). The women's organization was financed by NARTB and its successor, and its membership was limited to women designated by member station managers to represent their stations. NARTB was a management trade association, which meant that the women's organization would be comprised only of women working for NARTB stations and designated by their station managers as their representative.

Uncomfortable with some of the personalities and politics, particularly early feminist politics, involved in the AWB, NARTB discontinued its women's division in October 1950.[15] But there remained an interest within the group to provide a forum for women in broadcasting, and NARTB executives, led by President Harold Fellows, called a group of women to Washington, D.C., to discuss the formation of an independent organization. As a result of that meeting, the NARTB board voted to underwrite the expense of forming an independent operation that would later become AWRT.[16]

The librarian of CBS News, Agnes Law, acting as chair, set up a steering committee of eleven women. Law and her committee met later that year and gave the new women's organization its name—American Women in Radio and Television. The committee set the date for its first convention to be held at the Hotel Astor in New York City, April 6–8, 1951. Edythe Meserand, of station WOR-Mutual, New York, was the convention chair and was elected AWRT's first president during the convention.[17] Members of the executive board were Doris Corwith, supervisor of talks and religious programs at NBC; Edythe Fern Melrose, WXYZ, Detroit; Marjorie Christopher, WQAM, Miami; Izetta Jewel, KCBQ, San Diego; and Dorothy Fuller, WBET, Brockton (Massachusetts). Completing the board's roster were five directors-at-large who represented a variety of industries and agencies. Chosen to represent trade associations was Harriet Sabine, Can Manufacturers' Institute; representing the commercial group was Betty Stuart Smith of J. Walter Thompson, New York. Elizabeth Marshall, who worked at WBEZ, Chicago, was chosen to represent educational radio and TV, and Natalie Flatow, radio and TV director of the Girl Scouts of America, represented service organizations. Gertrude Broderick of the Federal Security Agency, Office of Education, Washington, D.C., represented governmental agencies on the board.[18]

By the end of the first year, AWRT leadership had established a stable foundation with headquarters in the Grand Central Terminal Building in New York City and pushed enrollment up to 672. Active membership, requiring dues of $12 per year, was available to any professional woman broadcaster or woman employed in an executive or creative position by a radio or television station or network or by a client using station or network time. Members holding "active" membership status were allowed to vote, but associate members were not. Associate membership was open to any woman employed in radio or television by noncommercial organizations, including educational and religious institutions and service and government agencies. Dues for associate members were $15 per year. Women employed in radio or television by commercial organizations, including trade associations and advertising and public relations agencies, were also considered associates, but their dues cost $25 a year.[19] Membership categories continued to evolve and fees to escalate. By 1998, there were three categories: active, corporate, and individual. An active member's dues cost $125 a year. Corporate membership ranged from $2,500 to $10,000. Individual membership ranged from $62.50 to $350.

At its inception, the organization's structure was basic. Geraldine Zorbaugh was appointed as counsel. Five national committees were established: membership, eligibility, publications, projects, and public relations. State chairs were appointed, and they worked closely with the committees and board. Local, city, and state chapters were formed throughout the country.[20]

PROGRAMS AND ACTIVITIES

In April 1951, AWRT held an organizing convention in New York City. The program, which was attended by 282 women, included a visit to the new UN Building and Delegation Headquarters. Assistant Secretary of State Edward Barrett and the Honorable Madame Vijaya Lakshmi Pandit, Indian ambassador to the United States, spoke on "Women's Role in International Affairs." Other speakers included Frieda Hennock, member of the Federal Communications Commission, and Jack Gould, radio editor of the *New York Times*. The delegation adopted a constitution, bylaws, code of ethics, and its first governing body.[21] Like most conventions, this one included business as well as social meetings. *McCall's Magazine* hosted a buffet supper, and the Better Shoe Guild and the New York Dress Institute put on a fashion show. But the women's convention was taken seriously; New York's *Radio Television Daily* reported the event with an article headlined "Woman Broadcasters Elect; Set Radio-TV Code."[22]

In the next several years, membership and participation in the annual conventions grew and these meetings served as a springboard for launching campaigns and programs. At the 1952 convention in Detroit, Doris Corwith, from NBC, New York, was elected to a two-year term as president. Corwith employed the theme of "Women Are First Class Citizens" during her presidency and reinforced her vision for the organization through such campaigns as "Get Out the Vote." At the 1954 convention in Atlanta, hosted by one of the first local chapters in the South, Corwith launched the establishment of a $500 college scholarship fund.

By 1955, AWRT boasted more than one thousand members. Jane Dalton, of WSPA-TV in Spartanburg, South Carolina, oversaw that year's convention in Chicago, and the following year's enclave in Boston. An Industry Information Committee was appointed to publish a newsletter, *Digest*, to provide members with news in the broadcasting industry. Meanwhile, state chapters were expanding into metropolitan areas. The next year, AWRT opened a new, larger headquarters. The organization's president, Edythe Fern Melrose of WXYZ-TV, Detroit, invited the press to its opening. Former first lady Eleanor Roosevelt, an honorary member who had long been a staunch supporter of female journalists, attended the event.

The mid-1950s were anxious years for members, for a nationwide programming shift was occurring among radio and television stations. Hints of the women's liberation movement were beginning to take form, and more and more broadcast operations were switching from homemaking shows to more diversified programs to satisfy a broader female audience. This was a switch that could benefit women in radio, but could at the same time displace those who had made their careers on the homemaking shows. At the same time, women were slowly gaining in employment in the broadcasting industry. In 1958, an AWRT survey, "Woman Power in Radio-Television Stations and Networks," revealed that women accounted for 22 percent of all employees in the broadcasting industry.[23] At the same time, women were beginning to demand equality and struck out at the assumption that men and women should occupy separate and unequal spheres in journalism.

With the women's liberation movement now in full swing, Nena Badenoch, a radio and TV consultant working in Chicago, was elected president. During Badenoch's two-year tenure (1958–60), the organization's constitution was revised and full voting privileges were given to all members. It was also under Badenoch's presidency that AWRT established its Educational Foundation as an outgrowth of its sustained interest in providing scholarships to women broadcasting students. This marked the first time a professional broadcasting organization established such a fund.[24] Today, the foundation sponsors educational programs, charitable activities, scholarships, and special projects to benefit the community, the electronic media, and women and men employed in the communications industries. The foundation remains nonprofit and educational, and it is funded by contributions, directed by a volunteer board of trustees, and advised by a board of honorary trustees made up of industry leaders. It is chartered in the District of Columbia with a mission to "use the media to create change through charitable, educational and literary initiatives."[25]

Speakers at the AWRT conventions over the years included political as well as industry leaders. In 1959, for example, the speaker at the convention's opening banquet was presidential candidate John F. Kennedy, who was generally supportive of women's equal employment and later went on to establish the Presidential Commission on the Status of Women.

GROWTH, DECLINE, AND CHANGES IN MEMBERSHIP

By the organization's tenth anniversary in 1961, AWRT was 1,600 members strong. In the next two years, AWRT president Esther Van Wagoner Tufty, of Tufty News Service and NBC News, actively recruited new members. She traveled thousands of miles to attend regional conferences to help in the organization of new chapters across the country. As the number of women in the broadcasting industry grew, so did the AWRT. From the organization's first small headquarters in New York's Grand Central Terminal Building, AWRT repeatedly moved to larger quarters, first to a suite at 501 Madison Avenue, then to 75 East 55th Street, and then in 1969 to 1321 Connecticut Avenue, N.W., in Washington, D.C. By 1975, AWRT membership had grown to nearly three thousand members, including attorneys, station owners, station managers, vice presidents, newscasters and correspondents, producers, librarians, technicians, salespersons and sales managers, programming and music directors, broadcast standards and continuity directors, copywriters, unit managers, corporate officers, planning directors and analysts, advertising and promotion professionals, and public relations practitioners.

The continual growth would not continue, however, and after 1975, membership numbers began to decline. It is unclear exactly what brought about this decline in membership; like many other women's organizations of the time, it may have been that women simply believed they had won the battle for employment equality and opportunity and no longer needed a united front to fight for their interests. Twenty years later, the membership stands at 1,800.

Although AWRT was originally created as an organization for women, during the 1960s the question of opening membership to all qualified professionals—male and female alike—became a topic of discussion. At the 1974 convention, a committee on male membership recommended against including men at that time, but to continue to review the matter on a regular basis. During the next two years the organization's National Public Relations Committee took on this responsibility and though making no specific recommendation, concluded that the organization was delaying the inevitable and that it eventually would become a broadcast organization open to "all qualified persons without regard to sex."[26] Shortly after, following the lead of other women's press organizations such as the Women's National Press Club* and Women in Communication, Inc.,* AWRT voted to open membership to men.

Men did join, and eventually some even served as officers, a step Tom Markely, an account executive for KMTV-Omaha, explained as a positive career move:

Some may think it unusual that a man would aspire to a board position in AWRT, but I have found my participation in AWRT to be rewarding, fulfilling and consistent with my belief that electronic media must be fully representative of all people who compose the industry. As one of the first male members of the national Board of Directors, I can attest to the fact that AWRT is indeed an organization for everyone who believes that success knows no gender.[27]

Markley is testimony to AWRT's commitment to women *and men* in the 1990s and is reflected in the organization's homepage welcome message, which states "American Women in Radio and Television is a national, non-profit, professional organization of women *and men* who work in the electronic media and closely allied fields. . . . AWRT is for everyone, including men, women and corporations, who believe in competitive opportunity and want to speak together in an articulate, unified voice on AWRT issues."[28]

MISSION

During its first years, the mission of AWRT was to provide a medium for the exchange of ideas that would help women to become "greater assets to their station, networks and employers." It also aimed at encouraging "greater cooperation among women in radio and television and those in closely allied fields and to increase women's opportunities to be of service to the broadcasting industry as a whole."[29] Nearly fifty years later, that mission has remained, although the exact wording has been changed and men have been included as members.[30]

One of the most important functions of AWRT during the 1980s and 1990s has been representing women's rights and issues in Washington, D.C. In the late 1990s, for example, AWRT representatives testified at a Federal Communications Commission hearing on spectrum policy and urged the commission to adopt policies that would ensure that women might become owners. AWRT also urged the commission to enforce equal employment opportunity rules to ensure that women would be ensured nondiscriminatory access to senior-level management positions. During the same period, in conjunction with Capital Cities/ABC, it developed an award-winning radio and television public service announcement campaign, "Stop Sexual Harassment."[31]

To keep members up-to-date and address issues concerning the broadcasting industry, particularly those that affect women, AWRT organization produces four publications. Its newsletter *News and Views*, which replaced the AWB's *The Beam* in August 1951, is published every two weeks.[32] The AWRT *Resource Directory*, which is published in the fall of each year, includes a comprehensive list of contacts in the industry, including AWRT members and officers, as well as bylaws, policies, and procedures. A third publication, *Tech Talk*, is a quarterly newsletter available via facsimile that addresses converging technology issues. *Careerline* provides a list of available positions in the broadcasting industry.

Another AWRT mission has been to track studies monitoring progress in women's employment in broadcasting and the coverage of women in the news through the 1980s and 1990s. These studies have shown gains in employment, compensation, and promotion as well as a reduction in the number of obstacles faced by women as journalists and as objects of news and feature coverage. At the same time, they have shown, women in journalism have still not reached parity with their male colleagues.

By 1994, women held about one-third (36 percent) of the jobs in both TV and radio news, up from just 13 percent in 1972. By 1997, although broadcast newsrooms were still male dominated, some women in TV newsrooms had broken through the glass ceiling by taking over as news directors at about one-fourth of all U.S. commercial TV station newsrooms. Whereas only two or three of the nation's 630 news directors in 1972 were women, they had increased to an estimated 205 out of a total of 850 news directors in 1996. Furthermore, trends in 1990 indicate women will hold one-third of all TV news director positions by 2001.[33]

As AWRT nears its fiftieth anniversary in 2001, the reminiscing at its national convention will probably be somewhat different from what it was back in 1977, when Bryson and Webb addressed the gathering. Instead of discussing crystal sets and huge microphones, war stories may be about radios with microphones that can barely be seen. Instead of reminiscing about broadcasts heard ninety miles away, the buzz may be about live television broadcasts from across the globe. Instead of laughing about the idiosyncrasies of cooking shows, the chatter may center on the popularity of talk shows and, of course, broadcasting before the advent of digital technology, notebook computers, cellular phones, pagers, e-mail, the Internet, and the World Wide Web.

Furthermore, there is sure to be continued discussion on a woman's place in the radio and television industry—certainly where they've been and, no doubt, where they're headed.

NOTES

1. Judy Bryson, "Do you remember when . . . ?" AWRT Convention, Minneapolis, Minnesota, 29 April 1977, American Women in Radio and Television Collection (hereafter AWRT Collection), Broadcast Pioneers Library of America, Hornbake Library, University of Maryland, College Park, Maryland.

2. Ibid.

3. Annabell Webb, "Do you remember when . . . ?" AWRT Convention, Minneapolis, Minnesota, 29 April 1977.

4. Judith A. Cramer, "Radio: A Woman's Place Is on the Air," in *Women in Mass Communication*, 2d ed., ed. Pamela J. Creedon (Newbury Park, Calif.: Sage, 1993), pp. 154–66.

5. "The AWRT Story," American Women in Radio and Television, 6 January 1975, AWRT Collection.

6. Philip W. Porter and Norval N. Luxon, *The Reporter and the News* (New York: D. Appleton-Century, 1935), p. 8.

7. Maurine H. Beasley and Sheila J. Gibbons, eds., *Taking Their Place: A Documentary History of Women and Journalism* (Washington, D.C.: American University Press, 1993), p. 165.

8. U.S. Department of Commerce, *Statistical Abstract of the United States*, vol. 64 (Washington, D.C.: Government Printing Office, 1943).

9. Edward Bliss, Jr., *Now the News: The Story of Broadcast Journalism* (New York: Columbia University Press, 1991).

10. Beasley and Gibbons, *Taking Their Place*, p. 165.

11. Morleen G. Rouse, "Daytime Radio Programming for the Homemaker, 1926–1956," *Journal of Popular Culture* 12 (fall 1978): 315–19; quoted in Beasley and Gibbons, *Taking Their Place*, p. 165.

12. David H. Hosley and Gayle K. Yamada, *Hard News: Women in Broadcast Journalism* (Westport, Conn.: Greenwood Press, 1987), pp. 3–4; Beasley and Gibbons, *Taking Their Place*, p. 165.

13. Beasley and Gibbons, *Taking Their Place*, p. 166.

14. Typed transcript of "Mower Interview" with Ruth Crane Schaefer, 1975, from the oral history project of AWRT, AWRT Collection, p. 1.

15. According to Ruth Crane, "The winds that later blew in Women's Lib were growing stronger and the AWB Executive Committee, together with representatives of the National Association of Broadcasters, mutually agreed that a separation would be best for all concerned." "Mower Interview," p. 12.

16. "The AWRT Story," 6 January 1975, AWRT Collection.

17. "Back to Our Beginnings," *Impact: Magazine of American Women in Radio and Television*, 1977, p. 5.

18. "Women Broadcasters Elect; Set Radio-TV Code," *Radio Television Daily*, 10 April 1951.

19. *The Beam*, January 1951.

20. "Women Broadcasters Elect; Set Radio-TV Code."

21. Official Program, American Women in Radio and Television, Hotel Astor, New York City, April 1951, AWRT Collection.

22. "Women Broadcasters Elect; Set Radio-TV Code," *Radio Television Daily*, 10 April 1951.

23. "Back to Our Beginnings," p 11.

24. Upon completing her term as president, Badenoch was made chair of the foundation.

25. American Women in Radio and Television homepage, <http://www.awrt.org> (May 1998).

26. Letter from Audrey Hunt, national AWRT president, 10 April 1978, AWRT Collection.

27. Tom Markley, "A Few Good Men," AWRT homepage, <http://www.awrt.org> (May 1998).

28. AWRT homepage, <http://www.awrt.org> (May 1998).

29. "Women Broadcasters Elect; Set Radio-TV Code."

30. AWRT homepage, <http://www.awrt.org> (May 1998).

31. AWRT homepage, <http://www.awrt.org/advocacy> (2 February 1999); "Banner

Year for Women's Organization: AWRT Membership Up; Harassment Effort Honored,"
Billboard, 24 April 1993.

    32. "Twenty Years of Progress: 1951–1971," AWRT publication, Washington, D.C.,
AWRT Collection.

    33. Vernon Stone, "MU Researcher Tracks Women's Gains as TV News Directors,"
University of Missouri homepage, <http://www.missouri.edu~jourvs> (26 February
1997).

INFORMATIONAL SOURCES

American Women in Radio and Television Collection. The Broadcast Pioneers Library
        of American Broadcasting, The University of Maryland, College Park, Maryland.
American Women in Radio and Television homepage, <http://www.awrt.org>.
Bliss, Edward, Jr. *Now the News: The Story of Broadcast Journalism.* New York: Co-
        lumbia University Press, 1991.
Cramer, Judith A. "Radio: A Woman's Place Is on the Air." In *Women in Mass Com-
        munication*, ed. Pamela Creedon. Newbury Park, Calif.: Sage, 1993.
Hosley, David H., and Gayle K. Yamada. *Hard News: Women in Broadcast Journalism.*
        Westport, Conn.: Greenwood Press, 1987.
Rouse, Morleen G. "Daytime Radio Programming for the Homemaker, 1926–1956."
        Journal of Popular Culture 12 (fall 1978): 315–19.

INSTITUTIONAL PROFILE

American Women in Radio and Television

Dates: Organized April 1951, New York City, New York.

Publications: *News and Views*, published every two weeks (1951–present); *Resource
    Directory*, published annually in the fall; *Tech Talk*, a quarterly newsletter available
    via facsimile; *Careerline*, lists available broadcasting positions.

Archive: AWRT Collection, Broadcast Pioneers Library of American Broadcasting,
    Hornbake Library, University of Maryland, College Park, Maryland.

Contact: AWRT, 1650 Tyson Boulevard, Suite 200, McLean, VA 22102, tel. (703) 506–
    3290, Web site: <http://www.awrt.org>.

2

Victoria Goff

Association for Women in Communications, 1909–Present
(Formerly Theta Sigma Phi and Women in Communications, Inc.)

ORGANIZATION

In 1909, seven young women enrolled in the University of Washington's new journalism department.[1] In April 1909, Professor Merle Thorpe encouraged them to produce the first women's edition of the college newspaper, the *Pacific Daily Wave*. Helen Ross, an associate editor on the general staff, was editor. Georgina "Jean" MacDougall and Helen Graves were assistant editors. The day after the edition came out, the *Wave* reported, "The women even read proof and the mistakes are few, and the paper is a credit to the women."[2]

The experience gave MacDougall (later Davis) an idea. She wanted to tell her best friend Ross about her project and waited impatiently outside Ross's philosophy class. "It was the longest hour of my life," MacDougall recalled.[3] As Helen Ross (later Lantz) remembered, MacDougall "was fairly bursting with a plan. It was nothing less than to start an honorary [women's] journalism fraternity to which none but the best might hope for admittance and from which would come all the great women writers of the future."[4]

The next day MacDougall and Ross recruited the other women students— Graves, Blanche Brace, Rachel Marshall, Olive Mauermann, and Irene Somerville.[5] They created the Alpha chapter of Theta Sigma Phi (TSP) on April 8, 1909.[6] Ross wrote that "Greek dictionaries, fraternity dictionaries, books on heraldry ... were held in front of the Thorpe fireplace where I firmly believe the name was conjured out of the dancing flames."[7] The organization also adopted an official insignia. "All the obvious symbols of the writer's craft had been taken long ago," Ross wrote. "We found ourselves always coming back to a little gold pin of odd shape which Mr. Thorpe habitually wore in his coat lapel and which he told us formed the letters in the linotype. One night we took a secret ballot and each of the seven had drawn a matrix on her slip of paper."[8] The symbol was also chosen for the word's broader meaning as a place where something takes form or develops.

MacDougall was chosen president of the new organization. Ross, the group's secretary, was the only member with a typewriter.[9] She wrote the constitution and bylaws and corresponded with universities that were establishing journalism departments. MacDougall was the telegraph editor for the university paper, which had a pony service through United Press linking it with other colleges. Word about the new fraternity, therefore, spread quickly. The University of Wisconsin was the first school that asked to join. In October 1910, the Alpha chapter granted a charter to the University of Wisconsin's Beta chapter, and the fledgling fraternity became a national organization. A third chapter was founded at the University of Missouri, and by 1915, there were chapters at the universities of Indiana, Kansas, Oklahoma, and Oregon and Ohio State University. Once there were eight chapters, alumnae decided to elect national officers separate from Alpha chapter officers, who had been acting as national officers. Ross was the first national grand president.[10]

ACTIVITIES AND GROWTH

In 1915, the Alpha chapter started publishing *The Matrix, a Magazine for Women Journalists*. Published over the years as a monthly, bimonthly, and quarterly, the newsletter provided information on the national organization, the various chapters, their activities, and some of the issues involving women journalists and professionals.[11] Articles were often written by prominent women journalists, such as Ida Tarbell, who wrote the lead story in the first issue, and prominent women leaders, such as Eleanor Roosevelt, who became an honorary member in 1934.[12]

Interest in TSP continued as the United States entered World War I. With the advent of the war, in fact, many members moved into newspaper jobs that had previously been held by men, and several became war correspondents. For instance, Peggy Hill, a *Cleveland Plain Dealer* reporter, was the first woman accredited to the War Department.[13] By the end of the war in 1918, TSP had grown to fourteen chapters and approximately five hundred members. In that year, it held its first convention at the University of Kansas in Lawrence, with William Allen White as one of the convention speakers. President Helen Ross Lantz told delegates to go back to their chapters and tell their members that "they are part of a big national writers' club composed of women who are doing things, a working organization seeking definite achievement in the field of letters calculated to raise the standard of journalism, to improve working conditions for the women of the profession and to insure the individual to greater effort."[14]

In addition to electing national officers, delegates revised the constitution, made plans to expand *The Matrix*, and devised ways to improve communication between chapters and alumnae. They also passed measures to establish a fraternity employment bureau and to support the appointment of women journalism professors.[15] Merze Marvin of the advertising staff at the *Des Moines Register-Tribune* stressed how important it was for women to contribute to journalism education:

[O]ne-third of the students enrolled in schools and departments of journalism today are women. The percentage is steadily increasing, just as the number of women employed on our newspapers is increasing. . . . The schools boast of their progress, their up-to-datedness. . . . Are they now to fall behind, to fail to keep up with the newspapers in giving women their opportunity? I think not. Before another Theta Sigma Phi convention the woman instructor in journalism will have come into her own.[16]

That year also saw the establishment of the first alumnae chapter, from Kansas City, which organized a tour of the *Kansas City Star* for the delegates.[17] Alumnae chapters (later known as professional chapters) were founded in Des Moines, Indianapolis, and Chicago shortly after.[18] As for the employment bureau planned during the convention, this was opened in Chicago as the Woman's National Journalistic Register, Inc. on September 1, 1920. Professors at ten colleges, and universities, including the universities of Missouri, Wisconsin, Washington, Michigan, Vassar, Cornell, and Northwestern, endorsed the bureau. Its advisory council included women authors and journalists and presidents of the New York Federation of Business and Professional Woman's Clubs, the League of Advertising Women, and the Woman's Press Club of New York City. The employment bureau increased job placement for members by 200 percent during the 1920s.[19]

To raise money for the employment bureau, the University of Illinois Pi chapter held the first Matrix Table, a formal banquet and lecture, on April 6, 1921. The banquet honored Sinclair Lewis, who was the featured speaker. Students, faculty women, and prominent women from Champaign and Urbana attended. The lecture-banquet combination was so successful that it was held each spring, and soon other chapters organized banquets to honor the achievements of their campus and community women.[20] Another event that became a tradition still practiced today was TSP's College Weekend, first held in Chicago during spring break in 1922. This first weekend attracted ten women from the universities of Illinois, Iowa, and Indiana. Prominent men and women in the field of journalism spoke to students about opportunities in Chicago and in other parts of the country.[21]

The 1920s were years of growth and opportunity for TSP members, but the Great Depression created special challenges for this cohort. By 1931, many journalism graduates were jobless or underemployed and many chapters' dues were delinquent. According to the editor of *The Matrix*, it was impossible for women journalists to find reporting jobs unless they took lower pay than men. *The Matrix* suggested some alternatives for the Depression graduate: She could work for experience, not pay; develop her own business; or break into reporting by starting in a clerical position.[22] Women journalists who were working in

Washington were given a boost during this period by First Lady Eleanor Roosevelt, who held weekly press conferences open only to women reporters. Roosevelt became friends with Ruby Black, who covered the first lady for the United Press Association and was the editor of *The Matrix*, TSP's first employment bureau manager, and a national president. Roosevelt contributed articles to *The Matrix* and became an honorary member in 1934.[23] The same year, TSP hired a professional director and founded a central office in New York.

Despite the Depression, opportunities for women in fields other than print—especially advertising and radio—began to increase. Member Kathryn Cravens of St. Louis was the first female radio news commentator, and members Mary Margaret McBride and Dorothy Thompson had network interview and analysis programs. *The Matrix* ran features on successful TSP members, including *Detroit Times* reporter Vera Brown, who learned to fly her own plane to write a series on aviation; Alice Keith, who opened the National Academy of Broadcasting in Washington; and Marguerite Harrison, who was a foreign correspondent for the *Baltimore Sun*. To celebrate the success of members such as these, TSP inaugurated the Headliner Awards in 1939.

By 1940, TSP had thirty-nine campus chapters and twenty-three alumnae chapters. As World War II expanded opportunities for women in print and broadcast journalism, several TSP members served as overseas correspondents— Inez Robb, Inez and Ruth Cowen, Esther Van Waggoner Tufty, Leah Burdette, Bonnie Wiley, Dickey Chapelle, and Marguerite Higgins. Member Margaret Bourke-White, *Life* magazine photojournalist, became the first female correspondent accredited to the Army Air Force.

Although TSP members experienced increased professional opportunities during World War II, some of the organization's activities were curtailed by wartime conditions. Thus, conventions were cancelled from 1942 to 1945 because of travel restrictions. Local chapters, nonetheless, kept busy with patriotic activities. Some were organized into emergency units under the director of civilian defense; others created news bureaus at United Service Organizations (USO) clubs and sent stories about servicemen and women to their hometown newspapers. In 1946, the Chicago chapter initiated the Hospitalized Veterans Writing Project (HVWP), which helped veterans express their feelings in writing.

By 1950, TSP had grown to forty-seven campus chapters and twenty-nine alumnae groups as more women entered the workplace. In 1951, National adopted the HVWP, encouraged members to work one-on-one with hospitalized veterans, and awarded cash prizes for the patients' writing. Members continued to work as foreign correspondents in the 1950s. Higgins covered the Nuremberg war trials and the Berlin blockade for the *New York Herald Tribune*. Later she was made Tokyo bureau chief and was the only woman reporting the North Korean invasion. Her account of the battle earned her TSP's 1951 Headliner Award as well as the Pulitzer Prize.

United States involvement in the Korean conflict also encouraged TSP leadership to call for a global view, and the organization sponsored membership tours to Europe, South America, Hawaii, Japan, Bermuda, and Taiwan. With eighty-eight members living abroad, the fraternity formed Theta Sigma Phi Internationale in 1954, and *The Matrix* began to regularly feature articles on members living and working in foreign countries as well as articles about customs and etiquette abroad. During this decade, *The Matrix* also recorded the growing tension between the demands of raising children and work. It printed articles on how to cope as a career woman and how to write at home while being a housewife. It also kept members informed of expanding opportunities in television, medical journalism, and scientific and technical writing. During the next decade, *The Matrix* published informative articles about new job opportunities, how-to articles about writing techniques, and pieces about the history of women journalists by scholars such as Kathleen Endres. Chapter involvement in social and public policy issues were also reflected in articles such as one by member Ponchitta Pierce, an editor at *Ebony*: "Negro News—Why Isn't More on Women's Pages."

WOMEN IN COMMUNICATIONS, INC.

The 1960s and 1970s brought some fundamental changes to TSP's structure and self-image. In 1964, the organization moved its national headquarters from New York City to Austin, Texas, and Jo Caldwell Meyer retired after serving as executive secretary for twenty-four years. At the 1972 national convention, the sixty-three-year-old organization was renamed Women in Communications, Inc. (WICI). The reason given for the change was that the Greek name and letters were too easily confused with sororities and did not reflect the organization's professional purpose and function.[24] At the same time, delegates voted to allow men to become active rather than honorary members. This came shortly after Sigma Delta Chi, the national male professional journalism society, added "Society of Professional Journalists" to its name and began admitting women.[25] Some of the first men to join WICI included Edward L Bernays, pioneer public relations practitioner; Walter A. Schwartz, president of ABC Television; John Mack Carter, editor of *Ladies' Home Journal*; Allen H. Neuharth, president of the Gannett newspaper chain; and Sey Chasler, editor of *Redbook*. Delegates also called for more women journalism professors and an end to discriminatory practices that prevented their academic advancement.

During the next years, WICI continued and expanded its previous programs and became actively involved in social and political issues. In 1973, it created the National Awards Program (later named the Clarion Awards) to recognize excellence in all types of communication. A new monthly, *National Newsletter*, joined *Matrix* and ran articles about pollution and environmental issues, violence on college campuses, and racial barriers. Chapters became more aggressive in minority recruitment. The Chicago chapter, for instance, launched a Minority

Recruitment program, which set up a scholarship fund and provided high school students from twenty-one schools with information about careers in communication.[26]

The biggest challenge of the 1970s was women's rights. After much discussion, WICI put its strength behind passage of the Equal Rights Amendment (ERA). It joined ERAmerica, the national ERA coalition, to fight mounting opposition to the amendment and raised money for its ERA effort at regional meetings. In 1980, WICI was one of 250 organizations that participated in a national ERA march in Chicago on May 10 and that summer gathered other women's groups for a media event outside the Republican National Convention. The organization was also involved in the 1975 International Women's Year meeting in Mexico City and the Houston Women's Conference in 1977.[27]

WICI became increasingly organized in its approach to the issues that interested its membership. During the 1980s, it opened a public affairs office in Washington to monitor legislation and represent WICI's views. Besides fighting for equal rights and opportunity for women, the organization became active in the fight for freedom of information legislation in the aftermath of Watergate. In 1979, WICI and eleven other communication organizations founded the First Amendment Congress, which works to preserve First Amendment rights. In 1983, the organization protested the news blackout during the Grenada invasion. Leaders testified before Congress against possible changes to the Freedom of Information Act that would restrict the public's access to federal documents and deliberations, and more than one hundred chapters organized congressional letter-writing campaigns. Other issues to win WICI's support were pay equity, medical and maternity leave, and civil rights. The organization joined the National Committee on Pay Equity and supported the Family & Medical Leave Act (FMLA) and the Civil Rights Act.[28]

DECLINE

Ironically, the successes of the second women's movement have been blamed for a decline in membership in many women's organizations, including WICI. However, WICI's dwindling membership base, which became apparent in the 1970s, was the result of other factors as well. Early in that decade, there was trouble at the student chapter level. MaryAnn Yodelis Smith, longtime adviser of the University of Wisconsin at Madison chapter, wrote in her annual Faculty Adviser's Report that she found it difficult to " 'sell' students on the benefit of national affiliation; they find it hard to see what national does for them." She also noted that WICI, at least at Madison, had competition from other student organizations, including the ad club, the Society of Professional Journalists (SPJ), Public Relations Students' Society of America (PRSSA), and the photography club. "It is difficult to compete with SPJ. Most young women now see more advantage in a joint organization; few can afford the dues for both," she wrote.[29]

By the 1990s, national's relationship with its professional chapters was also problematic as chapters became particularly disenchanted with the national leadership. For example, the Madison (Wisconsin) Professional Chapter in 1996 seriously discussed dissolving and forming a new local women's communication organization. According to *Signature*, the chapter newsletter, this decision to consider seceding from WICI national was the result of frustration with national. The Madison WICI Board had expressed its concern as early as February 1995, when it had voted to give the national one year to "improve its membership and overall responsiveness to chapter boards." In April of that year, the Madison board wrote to WICI's national director, identifying issues that needed immediate attention. These were the financial management of the national organization; its reduction of important membership services; the lack of communication to members concerning the national Clarion competition; the decrease in publications; and "the National Board's lack of communication with local boards."[30]

Probably in response to growing unrest among WICI student and professional chapters, Ellsworth and national president Carol Fernstermacher made presentations at the annual meeting in October 1995. They promised a restructured national and a better, stronger organization. The Madison newsletter referred to their proposals as "a mixed bag of 'bandaid' approaches to the organization that appeared to be skirting National's difficulty in retaining members and meeting monthly bills."[31]

The Fundamentals for the Future Task Force was formed that fall as part of the restructuring effort and was commissioned by the National Board to restore WICI's financial stability. At a February 1996 Task Force meeting in Phoenix, a decision was made to meet with local chapters across the country to tell them about national's plan and to obtain input. When Christine Bulkeley, the task force chair, met with the Madison WICI board in March 1996, the board concluded that the plan Bulkeley presented did not address member needs, basic services, escalating dues, leadership development opportunities, and publications. Several members suggested that the chapter take another year to look at how national was progressing with its changes and revisit the issue in 1997.[32]

Before that happened, delegates at the annual conference in fall 1996 voted to dissolve Women in Communications, Inc., and replace it with the Association for Women in Communications. The new structure has an eleven-member board with broad geographic and chapter-size coverage. Management is handled under contract by Bay Media, Inc., of Arnold, Maryland. It is too soon to know the fate of the recently restructured organization. It would be unfortunate if an organization that has provided women with networking, leadership and professional development opportunities since 1909 were not to survive into the twenty-first century.

NOTES

1. It was the second journalism program in the nation.

2. "College Girls Get Out Daily Wave," as quoted in Anne Hecker, "The Beginning," *Matrix*, summer 1976. p. 5. The article added that a "large part of the paper is devoted to women's sports, something new in a college paper."

3. Ibid., p. 4.

4. Helen Ross Lantz, "The Founding of Theta Sigma Phi," *The Matrix*, April 1926.

5. Brace became a reporter on the *New York Herald Tribune*, a publicist, and a short story writer; Marshall wrote short stories and movie scripts in Hollywood; Mauermann was a writer in Hawaii and New York; Somerville became a captain of the women's department of the Seattle Police Department.

6. In the same year, male students at DePauw University formed Sigma Delta Chi, an honorary journalism fraternity that excluded women.

7. Lantz, "The Founding of Theta Sigma Phi."

8. Ibid.

9. MacDougall married and moved to Oregon, where she founded the Portland chapter in 1938. She wrote children's books and during the 1950s taught a children's poetry workshop on Mercer Island. Ross became a staff writer for the *Seattle Times* and a Seattle correspondent for the *Christian Science Monitor*. She also wrote for national magazines, including *Colliers* and the *Saturday Evening Post*.

10. "History of Women in Communications, Inc.," *1993 Directory*, p. 27; Hecker, p. 5.

11. In 1967 the publication's name was shortened to *Matrix*; it was later converted back to *The Matrix*.

12. *1993 Directory*, p. 27.

13. Larissa C. Kulczycky et al., *The First 85 Years: The History of Women in Communications, Inc.* (Arlington, Va.: Women in Communications, Inc., 1994), p. 3.

14. Helen Ross Lantz, "The Mythical Notebook," *The Matrix*, July 1918.

15. Mary Smith, "Convention Report," *The Matrix*, March 1918.

16. "Why Not Women Instructors in Journalism?" *The Matrix*, May 1918.

17. Some accounts say that the first alumnae chapter was not founded until May 1919.

18. Letter from Susan Shaffer, co-founder Pi (Chicago) chapter, to Theta Sigma Phi national office, Seattle, Washington, 1920.

19. Kulczycky, p. 4. The other three Universities whose professors endorsed the bureau were Kansas, New York, and Ohio State Universities.

20. Norma Green, *Leading Change for 75 Years: WICI-Chicago, 1919–1994* (Chicago: Women in Communications, Inc., Chicago Professional Chapter, 1994), p. 3. The Chicago chapter was the only group to set up a house to provide living space for young women journalists. For thirty years, rents were kept low, and the house was a self-governing unit, with a housekeeper and cook.

21. Ibid.

22. *1993 Directory*, p. 27.

23. Ibid.

24. "AWC History," Association for Women in Communications Web page, <www.womcom.org>.

25. Maurine H. Beasley and Sheila J. Gibbons, eds., *Taking Their Place: A Docu-*

mentary History of Women and Journalism (Washington, D.C.: American University Press, 1993). p. 28.

26. "AWC History."

27. *1993 Directory.*

28. Ibid.

29. MaryAnn Yodelis Smith, WICI Faculty Adviser's Report Form, University of Wisconsin at Madison Chapter, 1978. MaryAnn Yodelis Smith Papers, State Historical Society of Wisconsin, Madison, Wisconsin.

30. *Signature, Madison's Professional Chapter of Women in Communications, Inc.,* August 1996, p. 1.

31. Ibid.

32. Ibid.

INFORMATIONAL SOURCES

Association for Women in Communications, Madison (Wisconsin) Chapter Records. State Historical Society of Wisconsin, Madison, Wisconsin.

"AWC History," Association for Women in Communications Web site, <http://www.womcom.org>.

Georgina MacDougall Davis Papers. Manuscripts and University Archives, University of Washington, Seattle, Washington.

Green, Norma. *Leading Change for 75 Years: WICI-Chicago 1919–1994.* Chicago: Women in Communications, Inc., Chicago Professional Chapter, 1994.

"History of Women in Communications, Inc." *1993 Directory.* Arlington, Va.: Women in Communications, Inc., 1993.

Kulczycky, Larissa C., *The First 85 Years: The History of Women in Communications, Inc.* Arlington, Va.: Women in Communications, Inc., 1994.

MaryAnn Yodelis Smith Papers. State Manuscripts and Archives, Historical Society of Wisconsin, Madison, Wisconsin.

The Matrix, July 1918–present, passim.

Signature, August 1996.

INSTITUTIONAL PROFILE

The Association for Women in Communications

Dates: Founded as **Theta Sigma Phi** in 1909 at University of Washington, Seattle, Washington; became a national organization in 1910; first convention 1918 at Lawrence, Kansas; opened national office in New York City, 1934; headquarters moved to Austin, Texas, in 1964. Name changed to **Women in Communication, Inc.,** in 1972 and membership was opened to men. Dissolved in 1996 and replaced by the **Association for Women in Communications**.

Newsletter: *The Matrix,* 1916–present.

Papers: Records and correspondence regarding the founding of the organization are in the Georgina MacDougall Davis Papers, Manuscripts and University Archives, University of Washington, Seattle, Washington. Papers of various chapters are held by local universities and historical societies.

Contact: Association for Women in Communications, 1244 Ritchie Highway, Suite 6, Arnold, MD 21012–61887. Patricia Troy, Executive Director, tel. (410) 544–7442, Web site: <http://www.womcom.org>.

3

Tina V. Hall

Association for Women in Sports Media, 1987–Present

The Association for Women in Sports Media (AWSM) was established in 1987 to address issues confronting women sports journalists.[1] Many scholars have documented the problems that women faced as they made their way from the women's pages to the front page.[2] Women seeking a career in sports reporting were no exception to these struggles; they faced obstacles unique to their discipline, including denial of access to locker rooms, sexual harassment, and condescension.[3] The formation of AWSM provided a unified front to address these problems.

AN "AWESOME" BEGINNING

When Michele Himmelberg became a full-time sports reporter in 1979, only a handful of women were working major sports beats or were employed at major dailies. "We were isolated from each other and fighting all the battles of the pioneers on our own," she said nearly two decades later. "Slowly we got to know each other better, and there was less animosity and more of a willingness to help each other."[4]

While covering the July 1985 Olympic Festival in Baton Rouge, Louisiana, for the *Orange County* (California) *Register*, Himmelberg met with Julie Cart of the *Los Angeles Times*, Melanie Hauser of the *Houston Post*, Sally Jenkins of the *Washington Post*, and Denise Tom of *USA Today* to discuss the plausibility of an organization for women sports writers. A month later Himmelberg did a mass mailing to newspaper sports departments proposing an association that would help women pull together to fight difficulties with locker room access, discrimination, and acceptance.

After a year of developing a mailing list, Himmelberg had lunch with three colleagues, Kristin Huckshorn, Nancy Cooney, and Susan Fornoff, in San Francisco to develop a plan. They launched AWSM (pronounced "awesome") with a few preliminary newsletters and scheduled a convention to be held May 1988 in Oakland.

"It was remarkable, really, that the convention came off at all. Publicity mostly was word of mouth," said Christine Brennan, a sports writer at the *Washington Post* who was elected president at the inaugural convention.[5] Forty women attended the three-day convention, with quite a few paying their own way. Their primary objective was "to assist in supporting, retaining, and recruiting women in the sports journalism ranks."[6]

Membership in AWSM was open to women and men of any profession—journalists and nonjournalists alike—who supported women sports journalists.[7] Any member was eligible for office, and the organizational structure eventually consisted of a president, secretary-treasurer, and several vice presidents assigned to specific activities such as finances, conventions, the job bank, and the newsletter. Regional coordinators were selected as the association grew. By 1999, a regional coordinator chairperson supervised a total of eleven regions located throughout the country.[8]

MAJOR ISSUES

The first issue for AWSM to tackle was locker room access, which was a longstanding issue for women sports journalists. Women in the profession suffered a definite disadvantage to their male counterparts, who generally had free access to male athletes before and after a game or competition. Team management and coaches often determined whether women sports writers were granted access to locker rooms.[9] A few breakthroughs had been made during the 1970s. On one occasion, coaches allowed two Canadian women journalists in the locker room after the 1975 National Hockey League All-Star game. Another breakthrough occurred when Coach Bud Grant of the Minnesota Vikings granted entry to *Washington Post* sports writer Betty Cuniberti in 1977.

But complete access for women journalists was granted only after legal action was taken on their behalf. In 1977, for example, Time, Inc., filed suit against the commissioner of Major League Baseball and the New York Yankees when *Sports Illustrated* writer Melissa Ludtke was not allowed in the locker room during the World Series. New York federal district court judge Constance Baker Motley concluded "that all reporters, regardless of sex, should have equal access to the athletes, including the locker room if necessary."

After two decades of similar incidents, not all of which ended in victory, AWSM took organized action. Members of the newly formed group placed numerous phone calls to sports teams and leagues after women sports writers were denied access to locker rooms. "If we heard of someone being denied access, we called the offending parties (team, league, etc.) and got them on the phone and complained," said Brennan. AWSM gained the support of the

Associated Press sports editors and was eventually able to get all the major professional sports leagues to establish equal access policies for postgame interviews.[10]

Gaining locker room access resulted in a different set of problems for women sports journalists. The September 1990 locker room incident involving *Boston Herald* sports reporter Lisa Olson and three New England Patriots brought the issue of sexual harassment to public attention. Olson had specifically requested—twice—that her interview of one of the players be conducted in the media room at the Patriots' stadium, but the player asked her to come to the locker room, since that would be more convenient for him. While she was conducting the interview, "a naked Patriots player taunted Olson with lewd comments and suggestive body language. Encouraged by several other players, he accused her of 'looking, not writing.' "[11] When Olson complained, Patriots owner Victor Kiam appeared to side with the players. The three players were eventually fined, and the team and Kiam apologized to Olson in a letter and full-page newspaper ads.[12] AWSM responded to the highly publicized incident by conducting interviews and writing articles about it—thus raising public awareness about sexual harassment encountered by women sports journalists.

Though incidents continued to occur through the 1990s, they now often received widespread media coverage and brought action from team managers, who either fined their players or demanded that they make public apologies for their behavior. In 1996, for example, after baseball player Albert Belle screamed obscenities at NBC sportscaster Hannah Storm, Major League Baseball fined Belle $50,000. In 1997, Storm was verbally assaulted again, this time by basketball player Charles Barkley, who told her that women should not be allowed to cover men's sports. Barkley later consented to an on-air interview with Storm at which time he made a public apology for his comments.[13]

But one of the greatest challenges of women sports journalists entering the profession has been fighting discrimination, that is, convincing editors and colleagues they are capable of understanding and writing about sports.[14] A 1995 survey of AWSM members found that "although females are appearing in sports newsrooms across the nation in increasing numbers, women feel they are, in many ways, invisible to their colleagues, expected to know less and accept more menial assignments, while being the target of sexist language."[15] Other AWSM members complained of unequal opportunities for job assignments and salaries. "Women get chances, but only in the less coveted jobs," wrote one respondent. "It's unthinkable that a woman would get a major beat over a man, partly due to the opinion that you can't know a sport unless you've played it."[16]

The survey found that not only were women given less coveted assignments and passed over for promotions, but they also made less money than their male counterparts. One woman reported that men who had been hired five to six years after her, and in lower positions, made more money. Several others reported that some of their male colleagues, with the same education and job description, made as much as $10,000 a year more.[17] This, of course, was not a condition particular to women in sports journalism, or to women journalists, for that matter. Despite some improvement in women's salaries in the last two decades, women still earned just 76 percent of a man's income in 1998. This was an increase from 63 percent in 1979, the first year that compared earnings were made available.[18] By documenting these inequities and publicizing them, AWSM has, if nothing else, provided a forum in which women sports journalists can raise and discuss these issues.

ACTIVITIES

To carry out its objective of supporting, retaining, and recruiting women in sports journalism, AWSM established a yearly scholarship and internship program in 1990 for women planing to pursue a career in sports writing, sports copyediting, sports broadcasting, or sports public relations.[19] Since then, program participants have worked for *Sports Illustrated*, Gannett newspapers, the *Washington Post*, ESPN, the National Football League, and the *St. Petersburg Times*. AWSM also created a job bank, available on the organization's Web site, and sponsors a job fair at its annual convention to inform sports journalists of employment opportunities. It keeps members and non-members abreast of its activities through the *AWSM Newsletter*, which is published quarterly and is available on the association's Web site.

By 1998, AWSM membership included more than six hundred women and men employed in sports writing, editing, broadcast, and production. Since its founding in 1987, it "has addressed many of the individual concerns of female sports journalists with a unified voice, making sports journalism a better place to work for women (and, we like to think, for men, too)," according to founder Himmelberg.[20] As the century neared its end, the organization continued to grow and reach out to the next generation of women sports journalists. In 1999, AWSM launched a mentoring program to nurture young women sports journalists. Jill Agostino, president, urged members to become involved in the program with a salute to the founders and a challenge to the membership:

AWSM was started in 1987 by a handful of women who sought to help women in sports media overcome roadblocks. We need to continue their mission and reach out to help the women who are coming behind us. . . . New members, young members, are the future of AWSM. They are the future of our professions. We need to give them the guidance and wisdom we've gained from our years in the field—years filled with trying to prove that we can do our jobs and do them very well, thank you, and help them believe that they can do it, too.[21]

NOTES

1. AWSM Web page, http://users.southeast.net/~awsm>.
2. See Maurine H. Beasley and Sheila J. Gibbons, eds., *Taking Their Place: A Doc-*

umentary History of Women and Journalism (Washington, D.C.: American University Press, 1993); Kay Mills, *A Place in the News: From the Women's Pages to the Front Page* (New York: Columbia University Press, 1990); Nan Robertson, *The Girls in the Balcony* (New York: Random House, 1992); Marion Marzolf, *Up from the Footnote* (New York: Hastings House, 1977).

3. Wallace B. Eberhard and Margaret Lee Myers, "Beyond the Locker Room: Women in Sports on Major Daily Newspapers," *Journalism Quarterly* 65 (fall 1988): 595–99.

4. Michele Himmelberg, e-mail to author, 21 July 1998.

5. Christine Brennan, e-mail to author, 27 June 1998.

6. Pamela J. Creedon, ed., *Women, Media, and Sport* (Thousand Oaks, Calif.: Sage, 1994), p. 100.

7. Brennan, e-mail to author.

8. Ibid.; AWSM Web page. Presidents have included Christine Brennan of the *Washington Post* (1988–90), Michele Himmelberg of the *Orange County Register* (1990–91), Tracy Dodds of the *Los Angeles Times* (1991–92), Cathy Henkel of the *Seattle Times* (1992–93), Mary Schmitt of the *Milwaukee Journal* (1993–94), Lynn Zinser of the *Philadelphia Daily News* (1994–95), Linda Robertson of the *Miami Herald* (1995–96), Kim Pendery of the *St. Petersburg Times* (1996–97), Anita Cechowski of Pinnacle Brands (1997–98), and Jill Agostino of the *New York Times* (1998–99).

9. Creedon, *Women, Media, and Sport.*

10. Himmelberg, e-mail to author.

11. Beasley and Gibbons, *Taking Their Place*, p. 275.

12. Ibid.

13. Barkley escaped receiving a fine from the National Basketball Association. Terry Pluto, "He Knows Men Should Never Intimidate Women," *Beacon Journal*, 1 March 1996; Associated Press, "Rodman: Fine Not Justified," 13 June 1997; Associated Press, "Baseball Rings up Belle for $50,000 Fine," 29 February 1996.

14. Marzolf, *Up from the Footnote.*

15. Phyllis and Randy Miller, "The Invisible Woman: Female Sports Journalists in the Workplace," *Journalism and Mass Communication Quarterly* 72 (winter 1995): 883.

16. Ibid., pp. 886–87.

17. Ibid.

18. "Highlights of Women's Earnings in 1998," U.S. Department of Labor, Bureau of Labor Statistics Web page, <http://stats.bls.gov/blshone.html> (April 1999).

19. AWSM Web page.

20. Himmelberg, e-mail to author.

21. Jill Agostino, "AWSM Tackles Mentoring," *AWSM Newsletter*, fall 1998, p. 1.

INFORMATIONAL SOURCES

Agostino, Jill. "AWSM Tackles Mentoring." *AWSM Newsletter*, fall 1998, p. 1.
Association for Women in Sports Media. Web page. <http://users.southeast.net/ ~awsm>.
Creedon, Pamela J., ed. *Women, Media, and Sport: Challenging Gender Values.* Thousand Oaks, Calif.: Sage, 1994.
Eberhard, Wallace B., and Margaret Lee Myers. "Beyond the Locker Room: Women in

Sports on Major Daily Newspapers." *Journalism Quarterly* 65 (fall 1988): 595–99.

Miller, Phyllis, and Randy Miller. "The Invisible Woman: Female Sports Journalists in the Workplace." *Journalism and Mass Communication Quarterly* 72 (winter 1995): 883–89.

INSTITUTIONAL PROFILE

Association for Women in Sports Media (AWSM)

Dates: Organized 1987; first convention, May 1988 in Oakland, California; other convention sites have included Baltimore, Colorado Springs, Dallas, New York, and San Francisco.

Publication: *AWSM Newsletter*, published quarterly; available to members and on-line at <http://users.southeast.net/~awsm>.

Contact: P.O. Box 17536, Fort Worth, Texas 76102; most recent phone numbers and e-mail addresses available on Web site: <http://users.southeast.net/~awsm>.

4

Michael P. McCauley

Association of Women Broadcasters, 1942–1950

(Formerly Association of Women Directors)

In the 1920s, when radio was in its infancy, the medium offered new opportunities for women. Some like Bertha Brainard, a manager at New York's WJZ, argued that sex discrimination was less than in other industries, that radio gave men and women "equal opportunities and equal pay for equal work."[1] But contemporary scholars would have difficulty accepting that statement. Early radio newscasting was mainly the province of men; (male) station managers thought authority and credibility could only be conveyed through the masculine voice. Indeed, women who succeeded in radio during its first four decades typically did so as homemakers of the air—companions to the legions of lonely wives who spent most of their waking hours in the home.[2]

Women in broadcasting took their first steps toward claiming recognition with the founding of the Association of Women Broadcasters (AWB) in the 1940s.[3] The AWB was not a grassroots activist organization like many of the women's press organizations founded during the late nineteenth and the twentieth centuries; in fact, it sometimes seemed a puppet to its parent organization, the National Association of Broadcasters. The tastes and interests of its members also varied widely, ranging from a drive for better children's programming to the communication of the latest fashion trends to the development of commercial advertising support. In spite of these myriad pressures and commitments, the AWB ultimately helped foster the gradual development of feminist consciousness among women broadcasters.

EARLY RADIO WOMEN

"A woman's place in early radio was in singing . . . giving household hints . . . off-air interviewing, and writing."[4] This statement is a largely accurate description of women broadcasters in the 1930s and 1940s. Articles and books written in 1932 do mention twenty-two women who held "important executive positions" at radio stations and networks; yet other statistics paint a picture that is more sober. Only one-quarter of all people who worked in radio in 1936 were women. The three big networks of the day—NBC, CBS, and Mutual—employed about six hundred women, but only one-fifth of them held professional jobs.[5]

For those women who did work behind the microphone, the menu of daily topics seems, by today's standards, unfocused and largely trivial. Here's how Judith Cary Waller, a former station manager and public service director with NBC, described the variety of topics dished up for women listeners by women broadcasters through the mid-1940s:

Food, handicrafts, household hints, party plans, quilts, home sewing, style, beauty, health, problems of child care, human-interest stories, book reviews, interviews with interesting people, social principles, stunts and special features, poetry, featured musical numbers, news, interior decoration, pets, the romance of common things around the house, plans for a postwar world, home canning, ways of meeting contemporary shortages and curtailment, juvenile delinquency—anything that's pertinent to the home and community life of an American woman or which can help her to be a more interesting dinner-table companion for her family.[6]

Some women broadcasters, like Ruth Crane of Detroit's WJR and Mary Margaret McBride of WOR–New York, gained a solid measure of fame by hosting local women's programs. Others like Helen Sioussat, director of talks at CBS, and Alice Weel Bigart, a news writer with the same network, enjoyed success in off-air roles. During the late 1930s and early 1940s, a few women had the good fortune to be in Europe at precisely the right time to feed news reports to America prior to its entry into World War II. Sigrid Schultz, Mary Marvin Breckenridge, Helen Hiett, and Betty Wason all made their mark in this fashion. Their development into radio personalities was, however, atypical; most had college degrees and other specialized experience, and some enjoyed independent financial security. Even with these advantages, it took skill, determination, and luck for these women to make it. And some faced behavior from male colleagues that would, today, be called discriminatory.[7]

In spite of these pioneering efforts, radio stations and networks treated female broadcasters as something other than equal partners with men. Take, for example, the soap opera called *Wendy Warren and the News*. This broadcast, which chronicled the adventures of a "big city girl reporter," debuted in 1947. It was preceded by a two- or three-minute regular newscast after which a male anchor would ask "Wendy," played by an actress, to give the "ladies' news."[8] It is difficult to imagine the opposite circumstance—a female news anchor first reading the top stories of the day, and then turning the show over to Edward

R. Murrow for "men's news" and a dramatized chronicle of his escapades in wartime London.

GETTING ORGANIZED: THE ASSOCIATION OF WOMEN DIRECTORS

Though this condescension toward women in the industry would persist into the 1970s, the years of World War II saw the birth of an organization that began working for the advancement of women broadcasters. In 1942, the male-dominated National Association of Broadcasters (NAB) created the Association of Women Directors (AWD). It bears emphasis that the AWD was tightly controlled by its parent organization; this stands in contrast to other women's organizations of the day, whose officers were more freely elected by their membership.

The AWD's first executive director was Dorothy Lewis, a former chair of the National Society of New England Women."[9] Lewis had joined the NAB staff as coordinator of Listener Activities in 1941, a position she used to promote the concept of local radio advisory councils. She and other women present at the AWD's organizational meeting decided the group would parcel its membership into seventeen districts that mirrored exactly the structure of the NAB, ostensibly to ensure that it would "be possible to get together occasionally" through both district and national meetings. There would be no dues, since NAB would bear all operating expenses and supervise the new group through its Public Relations Department. Only women who worked for NAB stations and were designated by their station managers could become active members.[10] Initially, Dorothy Lewis appointed temporary officers and district chairmen herself. Ruth Chilton, who hosted a women's program on WSYR in Syracuse, was appointed national president. This arrangement would hold through the time of AWD's first elections in 1943, when the initial slate of officers and district chairpersons were elected to complete full two-year terms.[11]

Three classes of membership were adopted: active, inactive, and associate. For women whose stations belonged to NAB, those who were actually involved in the broadcast of radio programs for women or children would be classified as active members, whereas those who held positions in administration, sales, or engineering were granted inactive membership. Other women who were interested in radio but not connected with any station could join as associate members.[12]

Only about thirty women—either on-air broadcasters or executives—attended the 1942 NAB convention in Cleveland at which the AWD was founded; but within two years 650 had joined the organization. This was the first time American women in radio had an organized venue for sharing their concerns, which included the fostering of good programs and listening habits, improvement in the quality of children's programming, and discussion of various issues confronting homemakers during wartime. Certainly, the founding of the AWD was well timed. Employment of women in radio soared during World War II as many of that industry's male employees went into military service. In fact, women made up about one-third of the staff at NBC during the wartime years.[13]

The AWD's early mission was hazily defined. At first it was apparently intended to provide a venue where women broadcasters could occasionally get together, share information and ideas, and maintain contact with advertisers and nonprofit agencies alike. Members also joined in the effort to sell War Bonds, recruit young people to military service, and broadcast information supplied by various government agencies involved in the war effort.[14] One of the group's proponents, Congresswoman Frances Bolton of Ohio, noted simply that most members of the association conducted daily radio programs of interest to women. Another observer described the AWD as a "clearing house for the exchange of ideas and techniques" that would help women attract audiences to their wartime informational programs. Thus, in early 1945, the AWD held a conference to kick off its "Women of the United Nations" campaign. The purpose of the campaign was fourfold: to develop understanding among women of the world; to meet returned veterans' enlarged horizons; to share mutual experience and encourage a respect for differences; and to build a foundation for lasting peace. Sessions at the conference included "Women of the Americas," "Babies, Bullets, Ballots" and "I Knew Your Soldier."[15] One senses the overall goal of this campaign was for women broadcasters to promote peace and tranquility on the home front or, more crassly, to "put a happy face on the war."

By 1946, about one thousand women belonged to AWD. This increase in membership reflects the growing presence of women in the radio industry. In 1946, women made up 28 percent of the total employees in radio, although only one-third of these held positions in the so-called glamour job category that included "artists, writers, announcers, and technical experts."[16]

REORGANIZATION: THE ASSOCIATION OF WOMEN BROADCASTERS

The AWD's annual meeting in 1946 brought with it some organizational change. First, the categories of membership were collapsed from three to two; all women from NAB member stations—whether broadcasters, managers, or engineers—would become active members. In recognition of this move, the organization's name was changed to The Association of Women *Broadcasters* (AWB).[17]

The organization stated its objectives in its constitution. These were to promote the interests of women broadcasters and executives, encourage closer cooperation, and increase their opportunities for service; act as a central agency through which to clear information relating to the work of women broadcasters; formulate standards and principles for the work of women broadcasters throughout the United States in all fields of activity; and further the principles and objectives of the National Association of Broadcasters.[18] Further insight into the

AWB's goals can be found in the trade publication *Radio Daily*, which stated that women broadcasters were "valuable in building good public relations for radio stations and networks . . . because women are socially minded. At heart, they are—for the most part—'do gooders.' Give them a 'cause' and they will run with it."[19]

AWB activities were promoted in the association's quarterly newsletter, *The Beam*, which featured "news, articles, and gossip." Many of these activities were service oriented. On 1947, for example, the group sponsored a letter-writing contest on the topic "What I Think about Radio," formed a committee on the March of Dimes Infantile Paralysis Drive, and conducted local "Adopt-a-Family" and "Juvenile Delinquency Clean-Up" programs.[20] But other activities seemed purely social, such as the AWB convention in Washington, in April 1948, which was described in *The Beam* in terms usually reserved for the society columns.

Perhaps the biggest surprise of the convention was the presence of the President at the White House Tea. . . .

Among the "regulars" who can always be counted on to show us a swell time was Steve Shannon and the Greeting Card Association. His Valentine party saw twelve AWB members presented with huge Valentines for wearing the best looking hats. . . .

Huge gardenias vied with juicy ham to tempt early risers at Swift and Company's breakfast Saturday.[21]

IDENTITY CRISIS

Although the AWB was organized and sponsored by the NAB, the relationship between the two was never smooth. Information about NAB's motivation for founding the women's group is scarce, but it appears that the parent organization wanted women to serve *it*—and not the other way around. Ruth Crane, who hosted a women's radio program and helped found the association, recalled that most station managers who belonged to the NAB were tolerant of the women's group, with some even supporting it. But she and others note that some stations took a dim view of the AWB, partly because of the sometimes controversial leadership of Dorothy Lewis.[22]

Indeed, Lewis's tenure at the association helped focus a rift between members who wished to use radio as a vehicle for community service and those who, like the NAB, were more concerned about public relations and the pursuit of profit. Prior to her work with AWB, Lewis chaired the Radio Council on Children's Programs, also sponsored by NAB. Following that experience, she became a leading figure in the movement to form radio councils in major medium- and large-sized cities across the nation. The radio council movement started in the 1930s and by 1942, Lewis reported that progress had been made toward starting 120 local groups. Simply put, these councils tried to mediate the interests of broadcasting stations and their audiences. A typical example was the Portland

(Oregon) Radio Council, organized in 1940, whose goals were to stress the importance of more discriminate radio listening; publicize radio programs of merit; publish information on what was new in radio, and establish a speaker's bureau. The council surveyed children and parents in the Portland area and found "disapproval of programs built around crime, horror, gun-play and those of 'cliff-hanger' variety." Respondents favored "more programs built on humor, music, Bible stories, children's activities, story telling, and dramatization of good children's books, history, and lives of famous men and women."[23]

These values were consistent with those held by many middle-class women— the sort of genteel, family-oriented values that persist to this day. But men and women working in radio during World War II were often leery of such talk. For one thing, these values simply did not mesh with those of the hard-boiled businessmen who ran the radio networks and virtually all the local stations. If crime and horror programs helped pay the bills, it would do no good for civic groups to try to replace them.

It is important to note that men were not the only ones to blame for this state of affairs. In the 1940s, many women working in radio also subscribed to the "business first" ethos of their male superiors, despite their own confinement to the world of women's programs. Ruth Crane spoke for a critical mass of women broadcasters who did not embrace the concept of radio councils, or the fact that Dorothy Lewis of AWB had become one of their leading proponents:

We were not opposed to the formation of listener groups, if handled in a constructive manner—would have welcomed them—but we could not approve forming what might be construed as militant pressure groups . . . the last thing we needed was a lot of women's clubs demanding they-knew-not-what.[24]

Dissatisfaction with Lewis's leadership, and even the perception that she posed a danger to the radio industry's business practices, may have prompted NAB leaders to force her from power and, eventually, to disband AWB altogether. Early in 1948, NAB president Harold Fellowes urged a hand-picked group of women broadcasters to form their own organization. Lewis was not included in the group. After this meeting, and a concurrent decision to move the AWB offices from Lewis's home state of New York, Lewis promptly resigned her positions in both the AWB and the NAB.[25]

The AWB would soon yield to a new women's broadcasting group. It was announced in 1949 that AWB, heretofore "an informal type of organization," would become a full-fledged NAB department with an executive director reporting directly to top management.[26] Next, delegates to the 1950 AWB convention voted to establish an independent group for women in radio and the newly emerging television industry. The new organization—American Women in Radio and Television (AWRT)*—held its first convention in New York the following year. Nearly three hundred members of the old AWB attended and became charter members.[27]

WHY THE CHANGE?

The nature of AWB was hotly debated from 1948 on. According to Pat Griffith, a former broadcaster and public relations specialist who succeeded Dorothy Lewis as executive director after her resignation, some women felt the group was unduly dominated by NAB; others had friends who wanted to join AWB but could not because their station did not belong to the parent organization.[28]

Comments by Edythe Meserand, a former news writer and forty-two-year veteran of the radio industry, suggest that NAB leaders were uncomfortable with the prospect that a self-sponsored women's group might veer out of control. Dorothy Lewis also noted that some members of the NAB board feared that through her work with radio councils, she would "build a Frankenstein" that might demand changes in the broadcasting formulas designed to appeal to mass audiences.[29]

The membership of many radio councils was skewed heavily toward middle-class civic organizations such as Parent-Teacher Associations, church groups, and women's groups. But these councils did not effectively represent the low- and medium-income housewives who made up the typical daytime radio audience in the mid-1940s. The networks served these women a heavy diet of soap operas that provided companionship on one level . . . and promoted consumer goods on another. Radio councils, like those organized by AWB's Dorothy Lewis, instead favored milder, more family-oriented programs. Through their efforts to encourage more discriminate radio listening, they sought to minimize some of the entertainment programs that were the networks' economic bread and butter.[30]

If the NAB considered radio councils a threat to the economic well-being of member stations, and equated these councils with Dorothy Lewis and the AWB, one can see why it began to withdraw its support from both Lewis and the AWB in the late 1940s.

CONCLUSION

At first blush, it is difficult to assess AWB's role in the development of women's place in radio. The organization clearly had value at an elemental level, as it provided a forum where women broadcasters could learn the tricks of the trade and experience support and camaraderie among their female colleagues. This observation is less than satisfying, though, when one considers the apparent lack of political consciousness among AWB members. Though individual women of the World War II era like Dorothy Lewis and NBC commentator Dorothy Thompson did take to activism, there is no indication that such issues were ever on the AWB agenda. More often than not, the trade press described members of the association in terms that now seem patronizing. In 1948, for example, the *Radio Daily* described the members as women who "put on their

Sunday best" and acted a bit "giddy" in anticipation of the "three days' social whirl" promised by organizers of their national convention.[31]

Men held all the cards in broadcasting, and most of them viewed women with ambivalence. In the early 1940s, with thousands of potential male employees preparing for war, broadcasting managers welcomed women who wanted to try their hand at radio. But they also followed the lead of 1920s broadcasters who thought women's voices were not of suitable quality for "serious" announcing, despite the success of a few women like Dorothy Thompson, who was once declared by a poll to be the country's "most popular commentator."[32] More than eight hundred women held jobs as radio commentators in 1956; yet their roles were largely limited to the hosting of homemakers' programs.[33]

Though documentary evidence from the early years of AWD/AWB is hard to come by, we can make some reasonable inferences about the relationship of this organization to the NAB. It seems clear that the organization's first executive director, Dorothy Lewis, spoke for a group of early radio critics who agitated for better educational and children's programming and the monitoring of stations and networks by organized listener groups. With the onset of World War II and the exodus of men from the broadcasting industry, NAB member stations were forced to approach women as potential employees and as pillars of support in their communities. When the NAB brought Dorothy Lewis on board, its male executives doubtless knew that she would agitate for "better broadcasts" and closer monitoring by listeners. This it was willing to endure, in the spirit of wartime public service. But when the war ended, the need to embrace this particular kind of service went by the wayside. With men returning home after 1945, the focus in broadcasting shifted back to the bottom line.[34] Women like Dorothy Lewis, who continued the fight for better broadcasting, became expendable. The NAB first tried to draw its women's association closer into the corporate fold by closing its New York office and effectively forcing Lewis to resign. Later, the two organizations parted ways completely.

The history of the AWB can be seen, then, as an attempt by the male-dominated broadcasting industry to control and co-opt the energy of American women during wartime. At the same time, it must also be studied as part of the broader development of feminist consciousness during and after World War II. Some women who "filled in" for men at war returned to their place at home when peace ensued. Others, including many AWB members, did not. They came to love the radio industry and wanted to succeed in their own right. In the decades before the uncovering of what Betty Friedan later called the "feminine mystique," many women broadcasters knew that while they worked hard and well, they failed to garner pay and promotions equal to those awarded their male counterparts. Women who earned a place in broadcasting in the 1940s and 1950s did so knowing that they would continually have to prove their worth to their station or network.

These women clearly did prove themselves as equals to male broadcasters. Few, however, had much consciousness of the movement that would later be known as women's liberation. Women broadcasters of the 1940s and 1950s worked extraordinarily hard, often sacrificing their personal lives in the process. Like their sisters in other professions, many of them had little patience for those women who chose to keep saner hours or to complain about their status as second-class citizens of the airwaves. Many also had little patience with female bosses who acted like bosses. In a classic example of the double standards applied to women professionals, even by women themselves, Helen Sioussat, who succeeded Edward R. Murrow as director of talks at CBS, gave the following advice to would-be women broadcasters:

You've got to "show 'em," girls. Not by affecting low-heeled shoes and masculine garb, by acting self-important or bossy. If you have the stuff of which executives are made, don't be tactless or step on other's toes or over the boy ahead. Swaggering females are even more intolerable than swaggering males. . . . Too often it is the fault of the woman when a man remarks: "Female executives, ugh! Deliver me!" I have more than once had this same feeling, myself. Women can do much toward changing this sort of thinking. Not by fighting the men but by proving to them that all the aggravating little habits and traits attributed to the fair sex are missing in their particular make-up. . . . It isn't easy, I know, as there'll always be "sisters-under-the-skin" who'll do exasperating things that will make it hard for the rest of us.[35]

What, then, is the historical significance of the Association of Women Broadcasters? It could hardly be classified as part of the twentieth century's women's movement; indeed, its members met largely to share information about the specialty programs they produced for women and children. To stop with this realization, though, is to miss the true importance of AWB in the long run. By examining the discord within the organization over its very mission, and by analyzing the NAB's reactions, one can sense the presence of an important intellectual moment—a debate over women's rightful place in the broadcast spectrum. We might best call this moment one of proto-feminism, the kind that would keep the prospect of better pay and treatment on the table until later circumstances could make direct action possible.

NOTES

1. Marion Marzolf, *Up from the Footnote* (New York: Hastings House, 1977), pp. 123–24.

2. Anne McKay, "Speaking Up: Voice Amplification and Women's Struggle for Public Expression," in *Technology and Women's Voices: Keeping in Touch*, ed. Cheris Kramarae (New York: Routledge & Kegan Paul, 1988), pp. 198–202. See also Ruth Crane Schaefer, "Early Days in Broadcasting," in *Taking Their Place: A Documentary History of Women and Journalism*, ed. Maurine H. Beasley and Sheila J. Gibbons (Washington, D.C.: American University Press, 1993), pp. 165, 170.

3. This organization was founded in 1942 as the Association of Women *Directors*.

The name was changed to AWB in 1946. In this chapter, the two organizational names are used interchangeably.

4. Judith A. Cramer, "Radio: A Woman's Place Is on the Air," in *Women in Mass Communication*, 2d ed., ed. Pamela J. Creedon (Newbury Park, Calif.: Sage, 1993), p. 154.

5. Marzolf, *Up from the Footnote*, p. 32.

6. Judith C. Waller, *Radio: The Fifth Estate* (Boston: Houghton Mifflin, 1946), pp. 149–50.

7. David H. Hosley and Gayle K. Yamada, *Hard News: Women in Broadcast Journalism* (Westport, Conn.: Greenwood Press, 1987), pp. 2–21, 42–49.

8. Ibid., p. 62.

9. Eventually, the NAB reserved the right to appoint the AWD's executive vice president, a new title for the position Dorothy Lewis first occupied. See Constitution and By-Laws for the Association of Women Broadcasters of the National Association of Broadcasters, p. 2, American Women in Radio and Television Collection (hereafter AWRT Collection), box 5, Broadcast Pioneers Library of American Broadcasting (hereafter BPLAB), College Park, Maryland.

10. Dorothy Lewis to District Directors (NAB), American Women in Radio and Television Papers (hereafter AWRT Papers), American Women in Radio and Television, McLean, Virginia; Ruth Crane Schaefer and Pat Griffith Mower, "Historical Record of the Association of Women Broadcasters," Transcript of tape recording, 7 January 1976, BPLAB, p. 2.

11. Schaefer and Mower, "Historical Record," pp. 3–4.

12. Ibid., pp. 3–5.

13. Ibid., p. 1; Marzolf, *Up from the Footnote*, p. 41.

14. Schaefer and Mower, "Historical Record," pp. 4–5.

15. "Congresswoman Bolton Salutes AWB in House," *The Beam*, April 1948, p. 2; Marzolf, *Up from the Footnote*, p. 143; "Women of the United Nations" (Conference Program), AWRT Papers–McLean, pp. 2, 6.

16. Marzolf, *Up from the Footnote*, p. 143; Sue A. Lafky, "The Progress of Women and People of Color in the U.S. Journalistic Workforce," in Creedon, *Women in Mass Communication*, p. 90.

17. Schaefer and Mower, "Historical Record," pp. 6–7.

18. "Constitution and By-Laws," p. 1.

19. "Radio Women Invaluable, Kitchell Tells NAB Meet," *Radio Daily*, 24 October 1946, pp. 1, 3.

20. "Report on Letter Contest," "AWB Committee on March of Dimes Infantile Paralysis Drive," and "Alma Kitchell Reports," *The Beam* 5, no. 1 (January 1947): pp. 2–3, 6.

21. "President Reports on Washington Convention," *The Beam*, April 1948, p. 3.

22. Schaefer and Mower, "Historical Record," p. 6; Edythe Meserand, interview by Fern Ingersoll (no. 1), transcript of tape recording, Esperance, New York, 31 August 1990, "Women in Journalism," Washington Press Club Foundation Oral History Project, p. 39; Jane Barton, telephone conversation with author, 10 December 1998.

23. Donald L. Guimary, *Citizens Groups and Broadcasting* (New York: Praeger, 1975), pp. 24–26; Schaefer and Mower, "Historical Record," pp. 6–7.

24. Schaefer and Mower, "Historical Record," pp. 6–7.

25. Meserand interview, p. 41; Guimary, *Citizens Groups*, p. 32; "Dorothy Lewis

Resigns as NAB Coordinator," *The Beam*, April 1948, p. 1; Schaefer and Mower, "Historical Record," p. 8.

26. Though the NAB exists to this day, its full-fledged "women's department" lasted less than two years. In fall 1950 the NAB board approved a plan to separate the AWB from its parent organization. The move took effect on January 1, 1951. See "AWB Separates from NAB," *The Beam*, January 1951, p. 1.

27. "AWB Proposed Plan" and "Proposed Re-organization of AWB Structure," two loose documents contained in the Pat Griffith Mower folder, AWRT Collection, BPLAB; Schaefer and Mower, "Historical Record," pp. 11–13.

28. Schaefer and Mower, "Historical Record," pp. 9, 12.

29. Meserand interview, p. 41; Dorothy Lewis to Donald Guimary, 27 January 1971, cited in Guimary, *Citizens Groups*, p. 32.

30. "Money and Martha," *Newsweek*, 26 June 1950, p. 44; Guimary, *Citizens Groups*, 144–45; Waller, *Radio: The Fifth Estate*, pp. 126–127, 143.

31. "AWB Convention Opening Today," *Radio Daily*, 29 January 1948, p. 1.

32. That same year, however, Thompson's contract with General Electric, one of her sponsors, was not renewed because of the "belligerent tone" of her broadcasts on wartime topics. Apparently, her announcing was too serious. See Hosley and Yamada, *Hard News*, pp. 28–31.

33. "Money and Martha," p. 44; Marzolf, *Up from the Footnote*, p. 157.

34. We can even find evidence of this shift in *The Beam*, AWB's newsletter. Starting in October 1948, *The Beam* ran a series of front page articles featured under the headline "What Did You Sell—How Did You Sell It?" These articles contained case studies of successful sales and advertising campaigns related to womens' programs—content that was vastly different from the community service focus championed by Dorothy Lewis.

35. Helen Sioussat, *Mikes Don't Bite* (New York: L. B. Fischer, 1943), pp. 249–50.

INFORMATIONAL SOURCES

Primary Sources

AWRT Collection, Broadcast Pioneers Library of American Broadcasting, College Park, Maryland.
AWRT Papers, American Women in Radio and Television, McLean, Virginia.
The Beam (AWB newsletter), 1947–51, passim.
Radio Daily, 1943–51, passim.

Published Materials

Beasley, Maurine H., and Sheila J. Gibbons, eds. *Taking Their Place: A Documentary History of Women and Journalism*. Washington, D.C.: American University Press, 1993.
Cramer, Judith A. "Radio: A Woman's Place is on the Air." In *Women in Mass Communication*, 2d ed., ed. Pamela J. Creedon, pp. 154–66. Newbury Park, Calif.: Sage, 1993.
Hosley, David H., and Gayle K. Yamada. *Hard News: Women in Broadcast Journalism*. Westport, Conn.: Greenwood Press, 1987.

McKay, Anne. "Speaking Up: Voice Amplification and Women's Struggle for Public Expression." In *Technology and Women's Voices: Keeping in Touch*, ed. Cheris Kramarae, pp. 187–206. New York: Routledge & Keegan Paul, 1988.

Pecora, Norma. "Ruth Franklin Crane (1902–1989)." In *Women in Communication: A Biographical Sourcebook*, ed. Nancy Signorielli, pp. 79–91. Westport, Conn.: Greenwood Press, 1996.

Schaefer, Ruth Crane, and Pat Griffith Mower. "Historical Record of the Association of Women Broadcasters," transcript of tape recording, 3 January 1976, Broadcast Pioneers Library, College Park, MD.

Sioussat, Helen. *Mikes Don't Bite*. New York: L. B. Fischer, 1943.

Waller, Judith C. *Radio: The Fifth Estate*. Boston: Houghton Mifflin, 1946.

INSTITUTIONAL PROFILE

The Association of Women Broadcasters

Dates: Founded 1942 as the **Association of Women Directors**; name changed in 1946 to the **Association of Women Broadcasters**; dissolved in spring 1950 when members voted to reorganize as American Women in Radio and Television.*

Headquarters: New York City (1942–48); Washington, D.C. (1948–51).

Newsletter: *The Beam* (1943–51). Editors: Jane Weaver (WTAM-Cleveland); Eleanor Hanson (WHK-Cleveland), Marie Houlahan (WEEI-Boston). Available on microfiche at the Billy Rose Theatre Collection of the New York Public Library for the Performing Arts.

Archives: Records, correspondence, and interviews available in AWRT Collection, Broadcast Pioneers Library of American Broadcasting, College Park, Maryland, and AWRT Papers, American Women in Radio and Television, McLean, Virginia.

5

Jan Whitt

Colorado Press Women, 1941–Present

ORGANIZATION

A line drawing of a woman sowing seeds as she walks across an open field adorns the cover of the June 1976 *Press Woman*, a publication of the National Federation of Press Women (NFPW).* The illustration symbolically captures both the purpose and the energy behind Colorado Press Women (CPW) and similar state organizations that are part of the federation.

The fifty-nine women who formed the Colorado chapter of the NFPW on August 16, 1941, in Denver were committed to several goals. Early pamphlets state that the founding members wanted to secure the benefits of organized effort, to foster mutual improvement, and to provide the highest ideals of journalism. According to Lucille Hastings, charter member and state president from 1954 to 1955, she and the other fifty-eight charter members of the CPW were motivated by "a keen awareness of the power of writing women to influence opinion in times of national crisis" and by "a desire to advance mutual interests and professional standards."[1]

Although the official goals of the charter members are logical and remain true to the present day, female journalists in Colorado had other reasons for banding together as well. For example, the women gathering during the pre–Pearl Harbor summer of 1941 were deeply concerned about the role of the press in a time of international turmoil. At an earlier meeting on July 26, concerns about how the press could help to preserve national security were central to the discussion. The thirty women who met that day in the tearoom of the Denver Dry Goods Co. suggested that an organization such as CPW would allow them a forum to discuss important issues.

Although no one remembers who called the initial meeting, female journalists in Colorado had for some time been individually and collectively corresponding with the NFPW, which was established in 1937, about a state affiliate. Even as early as 1941, female journalists in Colorado were beginning to realize that if America were drawn into war, they would be needed to keep communication networks going. (In fact, an estimated 25 percent of NFPW's members "handled communications jobs abandoned by newsmen called to war," although most of them lost their jobs when the men returned.[2])

The NFPW also had strong constituencies fighting for social equality in the United States as well as for peace abroad, and some of the women who gathered in Denver were especially supportive of those goals. According to current members and historians of the CPW, finding ways to gather and distribute food for the needy in the United States and to publicize that effort motivated many early members.

Colorado women journalists also were committed to increasing the connection among women reporters and editors living in rural areas of the state. To that end, CPW named nine district vice presidents during their organizational meeting. These women would serve rural areas such as Salida, Alamosa, Rocky Ford, Sterling, and Brighton. Clearly, members of the organization were determined to sow their ideas outside of the state's metropolitan areas and to support isolated writers throughout the state.

More reasons for the formation of the organization were reported in the August 1941 issue of the *Colorado Editor*, published by the Colorado Press Association in Denver. Reporters who covered the formation of the CPW said the group came together "with the avowed purpose of improving professional standards of writing as well as increasing the scope of the woman's voice in matters of national and local interest." In addition, the *Colorado Editor* reported, the organization hoped to become "the organ through which women writers in newspaper and professional fields throughout the state may become acquainted, and find inspiration."[3]

Furthermore, because it was committed to equal rights for women, freedom of the press, and journalistic professionalism, the NFPW was a logical organization for Colorado women journalists to join. Conceived in the mid-1930s and organized in Illinois in 1937, the federation was committed to being the central organization for autonomous state groups. Begun by women journalists in Illinois, Indiana, Michigan, Ohio, Pennsylvania, New York, Washington, D.C., and Missouri, the national group had grown quickly. More than forty delegates attended the first national convention in New York City in 1939, and two hundred press women attended the convention banquet that year.

The growing clout of the NFPW attracted members at the state level and helped to empower the fledgling Colorado affiliate. For many women in the state, this was their first opportunity to belong to a press organization. There was a women's press club in Denver, founded in 1898,* but it was not readily accessible to many women working in other parts of the state. Although there was a statewide Colorado Press Association, which was created in 1878, this was dominated by men; women rarely met the criteria for membership—few women, for example, were either editors or publishers of Colorado newspapers, one of the requirements for Colorado Press Association membership. Some women were married to editors and publishers who were members of the Colorado Press Association, but they could attend only certain designated events and participate only as the spouses of official members. This situation improved somewhat during World War II, when more women began working steadily in full-time positions at newspapers and began to qualify for membership in the Colorado Press Association. By then, however, CPW had been established, was growing, and had gained the loyalty of its early members.

MEMBERSHIP AND ACTIVITIES

The founding members of Colorado Press Women represented women with a variety of experience in writing. They included Elisabeth Kuskulis, a Denver author, poet, and businesswoman who became the first president; Catherine Dines Prosser, a woman's section editor at the *Denver Post* who later served as NFPW president in 1947–48; Helen Black, drama editor of the *Rocky Mountain News*; Ellen Kate Dier, co-publisher and editor of the *Alamosa Courier*; Katherine Prescott Bemis, former editor of the *Littleton Independent*; and Eudochia Bell Smith, former reporter for the *Rocky Mountain News* and the *Houston Chronicle*.

CPW became the thirteenth affiliate of the NFPW in January 1942. By 1948, CPW boasted 114 members, making it second in size only to the Illinois affiliate. CPW was incorporated on March 16, 1962; and in 1965, the group joined the Colorado Coordinating Council, a formal group of state clubs interested in civic development, politics, and social issues. Membership continued to grow, and by the mid-1970s the group had 165 members; by 1982, that number increased to 200.

Although CPW was originally home to women working full time in newspapers, by the late 1950s that unspoken condition for membership had begun to loosen to reflect the expanding opportunities in the media industry. The growing membership soon embraced women in print and electronic media, public relations, advertising, graphic design, education, freelance work, public information, photojournalism, and publishing. CPW members have occasionally been media owners. Notable examples include Ruth Lehman, publisher of the *Longmont Times-Call*, the *Cañon City Daily News*, and the *Loveland Reporter-Herald*; Cosette Henritze, editor and publisher of the *Trinidad Chronicle-News*; and Anne Thompson, publisher of the *Rocky Ford Daily Gazette*. Members were required to be in the communication field at least one year before membership. Educators, as well as others who had been in communication fields less than a year, could become associate members.

During its first anniversary meeting in 1942, members recommitted themselves to two goals in particular: promoting higher journalistic standards and facilitating contact between women writers, especially in rural areas of the West. Many of those who joined the group later put a personal twist on these formal goals. Judy Taylor, who was CPW vice president in 1986 said that she had joined the group because it both helped her "fine-tune" her professional skills and provided "camaraderie" and an essential "support system."[4]

CPW has developed numerous programs and fund-raising activities over the years, many of which mirror activities sponsored by the NFPW. Beginning in 1942, CPW began to sponsor statewide writing contests in various categories and send submissions to the national organization's competitions. In 1949, it began to provide an annual scholarship for a female student in the University of Colorado School of Journalism and Mass Communication, and in 1958, the group established an annual "Woman of Achievement Award." CPW also provides its members with annual workshops, job referral, writing contests, annual conventions, scholarship programs, and contact with other media organizations. Since its formation, the organization has provided its members with the opportunity to network with other journalists working in the state by participating in the monthly activities and meetings of the Colorado Press Association. In addition, the group hosted two NFPW conventions, the first in Estes Park in 1946, the second in Denver in 1962.

Since 1965, more than half of the members of CPW have been Denver residents, and the goals of the organization have changed along with the nature of the membership and the media industry itself. Today, the organization lists the following as its challenges: to advance the practice of ethical journalism and professional communication; to promote a better understanding of and appreciation for the First Amendment; to offer a nurturing atmosphere for career enhancement through networking with other members in similar professions; to encourage improvement of skills by providing workshops and seminars on media and communication topics; and to provide communication contests to foster and recognize the high standard of work submitted by members.

DEALING WITH CONTROVERSIES

Colorado Press Women has been no stranger to controversy. During the 1940s, for example, members of both the NFPW and its state affiliates argued vehemently about whether or not to support the Equal Rights Bill. In 1946 the group voted to write to the Colorado congressional delegation to say it did not support the Equal Rights Bill, though no reason for this position is given in the organization's minutes. The same debate occurred over the Equal Rights Amendment during the 1970s. In this instance, however, the CPW was more supportive of women's rights and in 1976 joined a coalition to save the Equal Rights Amendment in Colorado. (The NFPW also voted to support the Equal Rights Amendment.)[5]

Members of the local chapter often illustrated their support of Colorado women by joining other state residents in social causes. For example, in 1950,

CPW joined others in the state in a campaign to raise consciousness about and to prevent violent crime against women. The crusade, called the "Porchlight Campaign," was begun by member Catherine Dines Prosser, women's page editor of the *Denver Post*, and was supported by women statewide. The Porchlight Campaign organizers urged homeowners to leave on their house lights at night in order to make it safe for women to walk home at night and to symbolize their concern about violent crime against women.[6]

One of the most disruptive events for the CPW, though, occurred in its own backyard. In 1960, two members resigned when the organization refused to admit an African American newspaperwoman as a member. The would-be member was Denver resident Betty Wilkins, who had worked for six years as associate editor and society editor for *The Call*, a "negro weekly" published in Kansas City and distributed throughout the West. Wilkins was described by colleagues as being "very well qualified" for membership, and one of the women who resigned, Helen Fletcher Collins, former national board member and assistant editor of the *American Horologist and Jeweler*, told the *Denver Post* that Wilkins's qualifications "outrank those of most of us."[7] Wilkins said she was as surprised by her rejection as were many of the members. "It just doesn't seem possible this would happen in Colorado," she said in a second *Denver Post* article on the issue. "I entered the journalistic field with the belief that this was one of the more liberal professions—and now to be faced with this. I would have expected such treatment in Mississippi, but Colorado supposedly has a reputation of being a liberal mecca."[8]

The CPW bylaws in 1960, however, dictated that if a candidate received more than three "no" votes, she would be rejected. Of the twenty women present on the day of the election, five voted against Wilkins in a secret ballot. Because of this case, the bylaws were changed the following year, allowing candidates for membership to be approved by a simple majority. Wilkins did not reapply, however, and was never granted membership.

EVOLVING GOALS AND PROGRAMS

As CPW historian Sandy Graham writes, "Records of CPW's first years make meetings sound very much like ladies' teas, replete with descriptions of centerpieces and corsages, and profuse thanks to hostesses. But professional education and national affairs were never neglected."[9] Graham grounds her words of praise in fact. Although centerpieces and refreshments might often have been the topics of discussion at meetings, the CPW could not avoid the fact that it was born in a time of great global upheaval. One of its first resolutions, in fact, passed five days after the bombing of Pearl Harbor, supported civilian defense efforts. "How Press Women Can Meet the War Emergency" was one of its first program topics. And in 1947, the CPW campaigned for a "secretary of peace" to be appointed to the cabinet of President Harry Truman.

Certainly, social issues and the international scene have changed dramatically since the 1940s, but in 1999, the ninety members of the CPW continued to support one another, to strive for ethics in media, to crusade for social justice, and to provide inspiration for women in journalism. As these words are written on the eve of a new century, CPW continues to sponsor programs in understanding international affairs and political issues; gaining further expertise in writing, editing, and photography; and supporting women in media.

Although membership numbers have dropped from two hundred to fewer than one hundred since the early 1980s, the early goals of CPW remain contemporary concerns. Networking, improving professional skills, and maintaining connections among women in urban and rural areas of Colorado are still central goals of the organization. With every new year and every accomplishment, members of CPW continue to reap what they have sown since 1941.

NOTES

1. Lucille Hastings, "Colorado," *Press Woman*, June 1976, p. 30.
2. Jean Wiley Huyler, "Past Is Prologue," *Press Woman*, June 1976, p. 1.
3. "Chapter of National Press Women Formed in Denver August 16," *Colorado Editor*, August 1941, p. 9.
4. Quoted in "Colorado Press Women Offers Contacts, Potential for Growth," *Rocky Mountain Business Journal*, 30 June 1986, p. 8.
5. Sandy Graham, "A Brief History," in "Colorado Press Women Inc.: 55 Years of Service to Communications" brochure (Denver, Colo.: Colorado Press Women, 1996), p. 3.
6. Graham, "A Brief History," p. 3.
7. "Press Women Resign after Negro Is Rejected," *Denver Post*, 13 September 1960, p. 3.
8. "Ban on Membership Shocking to Negro," *Denver Post*, 14 September 1960, p. 3.
9. Graham, "A Brief History," p. 2.

INFORMATIONAL SOURCES

Graham, Sandy. "A Brief History." In "Colorado Press Women Inc.: 55 Years of Service to Communications" brochure. Denver, Colo.: Colorado Press Women, 1996.
Hastings, Lucille. "Colorado." *Press Woman*, June 1976, pp. 30–31.
Huyler, Jean Wiley. "Past Is Prologue." *Press Woman*, June 1976, p. 1.

INSTITUTIONAL PROFILE

Colorado Press Women

Dates: Organized 16 August 1941 in Denver, Colorado.

Contact: Colorado Press Women, National Federation of Press Women, P.O. Box 5556, Arlington, VA 22205, tel. 1–800–780–2715.

6

Katherine Ward

Delaware Press Association, 1977–Present

(Formerly Delaware Press Women)

The Delaware Press Association (DPA), an affiliate of the National Federation of Press Women (NFPW),* was founded as Delaware Press Women (DPW) in April 1977 and operated under that name until October 1997. Originally, DPW served to provide support for female journalists and business communicators and to propel them into the leadership roles they were being denied at newspapers, in the corporate world, and even in various communications organizations, "which offered programs and networking more beneficial to the predominantly male members."[1] Over the years, DPW held meetings that focused on issues of importance to women in the workplace and sponsored workshops that centered on professional development—initially for those in print journalism and public relations, and later for an increasingly diverse membership as women in fields such as radio, television, advertising, and photojournalism were drawn to the supportive network of talented women.

As DPW grew from fifteen members to almost one hundred by 1996, the organization found itself in the position of being the only all-encompassing press association active in the state. DPW bylaws never precluded men, so when the organization's excellent programs, good reputation for working with high school journalism students, and a competitive statewide annual communications contest attracted a number of men, several joined in 1995. Their representation increased to 20 percent in less than a year, demonstrating the need for such an organization by men as well as women.

The question then arose: "Does our name reflect who we are today?" A committee debated the question before recommending that "a name change—not a values change" would serve to expand the network of professional colleagues devoted to practicing excellence in communication. The membership voted almost unanimously in 1977 to change the name of the organization from "Delaware Press Women" to "Delaware Press Association."

FOUNDING

In 1963, Bob Dylan sang, "the times are a-changin'." Many women moving into the last third of the twentieth century, whether homemakers or professional women trying to establish a career, however, would not have agreed with Bob. "The 1970's," wrote DPW charter member and first president Priscilla Tuminello, "was a time of real awakening by women in the U.S. and around the world to the many inequities in society due to gender bias. There was no family leave act; there was no diversity training; there was no pay equity; there was minimal understanding of the true meaning of sexual harassment or sexual discrimination."[2]

A copy of the quarterly feminist newspaper *New Directions for Women in Delaware* caught the eye of Shirley Wagener, a regional director of the NFPW in 1976. Wagener contacted editor Gloria Stuber to propose an idea: form a statewide group to affiliate with NFPW, a national network of communications professionals organized in 1937 to support female journalists. Fighting for First Amendment rights, tapping into education and personal growth opportunities, entering professional communications contests, working with high school journalists, attending annual communications conferences, and promoting the highest standards of journalism were all part of the NFPW package.

A member of the International Association of Business Communicators (IABC) and friends with women working at Delaware's largest newspaper, the *Wilmington News Journal*, Stuber believed that NFPW could help women in the field of communications throughout Delaware. She spoke with fellow IABC members Priscilla Tuminello, a community relations assistant at St. Francis Hospital in Wilmington, and Frances Naczi, the director of marketing for First Federal Savings and Loan and former editor and publisher of the *Atlantic City News*. They began calling friends such as Margaret Towers, a communications specialist for Blue Cross and Blue Shield of Delaware, and Suzanne Bush, supervisor of creative services and coeditor of the News Journal Company's in-house publication, *Viewpoints*.

At that time, women working at the *News Journal* were facing significant discrimination in terms of job responsibilities, promotions, and involvement in key professional activities. The women who agitated to meet and discuss the situation were told that management could levy severe reprisals if such a meeting took place. Stung by ongoing discrimination but propelled by the courage of their convictions, "they posted meeting notices in the ladies' room with little fear of being found out because *no one* in management was of the gender that would use the ladies' room."[3]

Stuber and her committee spoke with women throughout the state, and in April 1977, fifteen women—mainly journalists, but several in public relations and a few freelance writers—paid $15 each to join the newly created Delaware Press Women, with $10 of that amount going to membership in the NFPW. On April 29, NFPW president Jean Wiley Huyler presented the group with its charter as a state affiliate of the national organization.

DPW's organizational structure was simple and efficient: a president, a vice president, a secretary, a treasurer, and a newsletter editor, who planned the meetings, took care of any business, and kept the membership informed of programs and activities. The focus at the monthly meetings was to be on women's rights and equality in the workplace, professional development, and the ever-important support through networking. Anyone interested in joining the newly minted organization had to have been working as a professional communicator for at least a year and was to send three samples of recent work with her membership application.

In May, nine more women joined. President Tuminello announced that for its first official meeting the new affiliate would sponsor a behind-the-scenes press tour at the Marine Studies Complex of the University of Delaware College of Marine Studies in Lewes.

DPW quickly launched an active program of workshops, contests, and projects aimed at supporting professional development. In October, the group held a workshop on entering the highly competitive freelance arena. The workshop was successful, attracting not only women from the state but also members of the Pennsylvania and New Jersey NFPW affiliates.

Because the subject of women in the workplace was a central issue for the organization when election of officers took place in January 1978, those planning the installation dinner asked DPW member Judith Just, executive secretary of the Delaware International Women's Year Coordinating Committee, to speak. Members were buoyed by her remarks about her experience as Delaware's delegate-at-large at the 1977 National Women's Conference in Houston and by the wide-ranging implications of the conference for all American women.

By March 1978 and nearly forty strong, the group sponsored its first statewide communications contest, with Sandra Michel, co-owner of Lenape Publishing Co., as director. First place winners' entries were sent on to the NFPW competition, and all award winners were recognized at a spring program. At that same time, freelance photojournalist Marjorie Nudge directed DPW's first high school journalism contest. Student winners received cash prizes ranging from $3 to $10.

DPW next launched a *pro bono* community outreach project. Members donated their time to develop a promotional program to raise funds for the Chesapeake Bay Girl Scout Council. Working with a local ad agency, DPW originated the theme "The Cookie with a Cause" and had it printed on posters and brochures. The Scouts then developed single-serving packages of their famous cookies, whose sales support camping facilities. Local businesses bought the packages and gave them to customers to publicize their own participation. The program DPW initiated was successful in Wilmington and was copied in a number of other cities. The activity resulted in funds for the Scouts and in publicity and new members for DPW.

During that first year, DPW did not confine its activities to professional issues alone; it took a position on two important political issues. In early 1978 it opposed a move by Delaware senator Winnie Spence to rescind the General

Assembly's vote in support of the national Equal Rights Amendment (ERA). When DPW decided to fight for the ERA, member Cari De Santis, assistant editor of *Delaware Today Magazine*, testified at hearings before state legislators. According to Tuminello, De Santis's eloquent testimony contributed to the defeat of the move to rescind the state's approval of the federal amendment.[4]

Other political issues surfaced. Several months later, the *Wilmington Morning News* printed a letter by Tuminello that called for others to join DPW in pledging support of the peaceful integration in the schools. "The members of DPW who are involved in the communication of information related to desegregation have pledged that they will strive to impart that news in a strictly factual, non-inflammatory and unbiased manner," Tuminello wrote. "Such action will help protect the rights of all persons, of all races and ages, involved in the implementation of desegregation."[5]

By April 1978, the first anniversary of its founding, the forty-three active, committed women who joined DPW from cities and towns throughout the state during that seminal year had set the example and the pace for the coming years. Supported by funds from the Delaware Humanities Forum, they rounded out 1978 by offering a seminar called "Women in Communications: Are We Getting Through?"

More than a decade later, founding member Margaret Towers answered that question in a letter written in April 1992: "Corporations began opening their doors to women. A number of women in the Wilmington area who had jobs on small newspapers and in public relations moved up into working for the DuPont Company and other corporations in communications capacities."[6] When Gannett bought the News Journal Company in 1978, for example, the status of women on staff improved. Suzanne Bush, who had begun as a clerk typist in the advertising department, soon became the *News Journal*'s promotions director in Wilmington. Within a few years, she was head of promotions for the Gannett Newspaper Division, then became president and publisher of the *Lansdale* (Pennsylvania) *Reporter*.

PROGRAMS AND ACTIVITIES

As DPW matured during the 1980s, it continued to offer professional development through workshops and informative meetings. And as the group became ever more diverse—including not only women in print journalism and public relations but also those in broadcasting, corporate communications, marketing, advertising, graphic design, photojournalism, and journalism education—membership became an increasingly important way for individuals to network with a variety of communications professionals.

In 1985, DPW sponsored a public forum about how information is disseminated in a democracy. Project director Rita Katz Farrell, who had proposed the forum, enlisted the University of Delaware journalism program as co-sponsor and helped obtain a Delaware Humanities Forum grant to fund the event. On

April 12, 1986, "The Free Press in a Democracy—Messenger or Meddler?" drew an audience of 350 and was the basis for a television documentary produced by DPW member Sharon Baker and narrated by Ed Asner. University of California at Los Angeles (UCLA) journalism dean and media critic Ben Bagdikian gave the keynote address. Others speakers included Pulitzer Prize winner James B. Steele of the *Philadelphia Inquirer*, White House correspondent David Hoffman of the *Washington Post*, Philadelphia mayor Frank Rizzo, and about a dozen others who either made news, covered it, or analyzed it.

Ironically, as their place in the communications field became more secure, women had less time to devote to professional organizations and the programs and activities associated with them. By 1990, most DPW members were working full time, DPW membership was declining, and some of its activities, such as the professional and high school communications contests, were no longer being offered. Current members credit Katherine Smigie—author, editor, school administrator, and teacher—with breathing new life into the group while serving as president for two consecutive two-year terms from 1990 to 1994. Experienced at starting and running organizations, she began to publish a quarterly newsletter, *DelAware Press Woman*, that went out not only to the membership but also to hundreds of communicators throughout Delaware. She created a working board, consisting of a president, three vice presidents (responsible for membership, programs, and student activities), a secretary, and a treasurer—all elected for two-year terms. She also established the appointed positions of parliamentarian, newsletter editor, communications contest director, publicity director, and historian.[7] Smigie revived the professional communications contest and ran the high school journalism contest for the first time in years. She also represented DPW on NFPW committees and committed to co-sponsor a major regional one-day conference on technology and jobs in conjunction with the NFPW affiliates from New Jersey, Pennsylvania, and Maryland.

The October 1993 conference, "News, Information and Technology: Redefining the Media in the 21st Century," featured technology and communications experts from around the country to give perspective to the revolution in the field of communications wrought by the new technology. At a time when the term "information superhighway" was first being uttered and few people had heard of e-mail, participants suddenly found themselves ahead of the information curve as they not only learned about the developing technology but also saw a prototype of an on-demand personal news tablet created in the Knight-Ridder Information Design Labs in Boulder, Colorado.

DPW also broadened its focus by reaching out into the community, especially to high school journalists. When Curtis Smith, speech writer for President George Bush and former national affairs editor of the *Saturday Evening Post*, addressed the press women just six weeks before the 1992 national election, DPW invited the journalism students at Alexis I. du Pont High School to attend. Two years later DPW organized a one-day high school workshop, "The Power of the Student Press: A First Amendment Workshop," which was attended by one hundred high school journalism students and their advisers. The event featured award-winning journalist and former NFPW president Marj Carpenter as the keynote speaker and offered three separate discussion sessions on censorship of the student press, ethics and editorial responsibility, and the information superhighway. And in 1996, DPW raised more than $1,100 toward a scholarship for one of du Pont's journalism students to attend the rigorous four-week NFPW National Journalism Scholars Academy at the Peddie School in Hightstown, New Jersey.

THE TIMES THEY ARE A-CHANGIN'

Eventually, Bob Dylan proved to be right. In the mid-1990s, DPW continued to grow and attract new members. This was the result of the continuation of outstanding programs and workshops during the presidencies of Marion Rechsteiner (1994–96) and Susan Dods (1996–2000) as well as to increased interest in the annual communications contest, which, by 1994, was open to *all* Delaware professional communicators rather than to DPW members only. In 1995, one of those new members was Allan Loudell, the award-winning program director of WILM Newsradio and the first man to join the organization. Within a year, male membership rose to 20 percent of the nearly one hundred members.

Although DPW had been founded in 1977 largely to provide support for female journalists and business communicators, the membership began asking if its name in 1996 reflected the changes that had occurred in the workplace, in the field of communications, and in the organization itself during the previous two decades. For ten months a name evaluation committee weighed information. On the one hand, DPW was increasing in size under its original name and was a well-respected organization with good name recognition in the Delaware communications community; on the other, although DPW remained an advocate for women, changing times had brought increased opportunities and leadership roles for Delaware women in media-related jobs. The organization's main focus had shifted to professional development, and the name "Delaware Press Women" seemed likely to discourage male membership at a time when DPW found itself in the unique position of being the only professional communications association active in the state.[8]

The committee concluded that "a name change—not a values change" would serve to build a more inclusive community of women *and* men in Delaware devoted to practicing excellence in communication, respecting the craft and professional standards of journalism and defending First Amendment rights."[9] The matter was put to a vote. When ballots were counted on October 6, 1997, shortly after the organization celebrated its twentieth anniversary, "Delaware Press Association" was adopted as the new name by almost universal acclaim.

As the association grows ever stronger, DPW's first president, Priscilla Tuminello, is certain that under its new signature, "DPA will continue to help both women *and* men rise above society's inequities, realize their individual potential, support each other and the young people who follow after us, and contribute to an honorable and effective communications community."[10]

NOTES

1. Frances Naczi to Katherine Smigie, 29 March 1996, Delaware Press Association Collection (hereafter DPA Collection), Katherine Smigie, DPA Historian, 1012 Kent Road, Wilmington, Delaware.

2. Priscilla Tuminello to Katherine Smigie, 2 February 1997, DPA Collection.

3. Suzanne Bush, speech at DPW meeting, 19 April 1994.

4. Tuminello to Smigie, 2 February 1997, DPA Collection.

5. Tuminello's signature identified her as DPW's "political action chairperson." Priscilla Tuminello, "They Pledge Support," *Wilmington Morning News*, 24 August 1978, p. 13.

6. Margaret Towers to Katherine Smigie, 3 April 1992, DPA Collection.

7. In 1995, DPA began to name a Communicator of Achievement (COA) each December; the member named COA assumes a one-year board position the following April.

8. The Delaware Press Club, founded in 1967 and composed of both men and women, had been defunct for more than a decade. The Society of Professional Journalists and Women in Communications, Inc.,* were active regionally but not locally. Public relations and business communicators were served in Delaware by the Public Relations Society of America and IABC, respectively, and those in advertising by the Advertising Club of Delaware, but there was no all-encompassing communication organization other than DPW.

9. Barbara Roewe, "A Rose by Any Other Name," *DelAware Press Woman*, September 1998, p. 2, DPA Collection.

10. Tuminello to Smigie, 2 February 1997, DPA Collection.

INFORMATIONAL SOURCES

Delaware Press Association Collection, Katherine Smigie, Delaware Press Association Historian, 1012 Kent Road, Wilmington, Delaware.

DelAware Press Woman, 1990–present, passim.

INSTITUTIONAL PROFILE

Delaware Press Association

Dates: Founded April 1977, Wilmington, Delaware, as **Delaware Press Women**; name changed in 1997 to **Delaware Press Association**.

Newsletter: *DelAware Press Woman*, quarterly, 1990–present. Editors: Katherine Smigie (June 1990–November 1997), Cheryl Carson (November 1997–present).

Papers: Delaware Press Association Collection, Katherine Smigie, DPA Historian, 1012 Kent Road, Wilmington, Delaware.

7

Jan Whitt

Denver Woman's Press Club, 1898–Present

INTRODUCTION

In spring 1898, *Rocky Mountain News* reporter Minnie J. Reynolds refused to admit to officers of a national women's organization that Denver had no women's press club. Asked if such an organization existed, Reynolds replied, "Of course." She then hurriedly asked several women Denver journalists to meet her at a home in central Denver to form a club. Because telephones were scarce, reporters often tracked down news stories by riding their bicycles through the city. Thus, on March 18, the women Reynolds summoned rode their bicycles to journalist Helen Wixson's house at 1424 Clarkson Street. That day they established the Denver Woman's Press Club (DWPC), and in 1998, the group celebrated its 100th anniversary.

In the hundred years since it was founded, the DWPC has provided scholarships for female journalism students, bought and renovated its own clubhouse, sponsored fund-raising and educational activities, and provided encouragement to women in journalism. In 1998, its 150 members included reporters, columnists, photographers, artists, editors, freelance writers, essayists, poets, and public relations and advertising practitioners.

Established in order to honor professional women writers and to encourage the pursuit of literacy through educational and philanthropic activities, the DWPC has regularly hosted monthly dinner and lunch meetings that spotlight politicians, journalists, novelists, poets, and other guest speakers. Other traditional activities include an informal writers group that meets regularly, an annual "In-House Writing" contest that honors the work of members, and an "Unknown Writers" contest that in 1998 attracted more than eight hundred entrants. This contest, which started in the 1970s, is open to Colorado writers who have not been paid more than

$50 for any one work of fiction, nonfiction, poetry, or personal essay. In addition, the club sponsors a variety of workshops to discuss freelance writing, children's stories, poetry, fiction, and nonfiction. The DWPC also supports literacy programs and scholarships for groups and organizations such as the Rocky Mountain Women's Institute, Community College of Denver, the Denver School of the Arts, and the Colorado Committee for Women's History.

ORGANIZATION

The Denver Woman's Press Club is but one example of the many women's public and professional organizations formed at the turn of the twentieth century. In Denver, as in other parts of the country, men's press clubs predated women's clubs. The all-male Denver Press Club, which was founded on July 28, 1884, did not permit membership to women until 1970, when Virginia Culver of the *Denver Post* and Marjorie Barrett of the *Rocky Mountain News* were admitted.

In a circuitous way, the DWPC owes its existence to members of the General Federation of Women's Clubs (GFWC), which was founded in 1890. The national federation represented the interests of women and promoted a broad social and political agenda. It supported various reform issues, especially child welfare, sanitation, and education. When the GFWC decided to hold its biennial meeting in Denver in 1898, organizers began fielding inquiries from women writers asking if Denver had a women's press club. Since Reynolds was the convention's local publicity chair, the officers of the federation asked her about a club. Reynolds, always an activist, saw to it that an organization was formed without delay.

Reynolds and the other founders of the DWPC—Minnie Peck Hall (later Krauser), Reva Sapp (later O'Connor), Caroline Sheridan (later Baker), and Helen Wixson—wrote a constitution and bylaws for the club and presented them later in March to a group of seven women for approval. With characteristic humor, Reynolds, the newly elected president, included "Bars to Membership" in the document. A woman might be excluded from membership, she wrote, if she were a "bore," one who "holds out on news reporters," one who "does not have proper respect for the power of the press," or one who "cannot do something to drive dull care away."[1]

The group also agreed that copyreaders and proofreaders were to be "forever barred from membership in this club."[2] Membership also was denied to women who "didn't read newspapers," "had a deficiency of brains," or were literary critics.[3] The group later added an amendment stating that "literary critics cannot enter into the Kingdom of Heaven, and . . . there is no hell for authors in the next world because critics and publishers furnish it in this world."[4] When the press club was incorporated in 1908, its nineteen charter members declared the purpose of the group was "to advance and encourage women in literary work, to cultivate acquaintance and friendship among women of literary taste, to engage in educational effort, charity and philanthropy, to secure the benefits arising from organized effort, and to drive dull care away."[5]

To be eligible for active membership, a woman must have received money for her writing. But the DWPC also offered associate membership to women in Denver who had spacious homes that could serve as a place where the growing group could meet. These women, such as celebrity Molly Brown, "were graciously permitted to pay dues, offer their houses for meetings, sing or play for us and otherwise make themselves useful or ornamental but . . . were NOT to vote," wrote founding member Minnie Peck Hall Krauser some forty years later.[6] Although these membership policies excluded from policy decision making those women simply interested in journalism, they highlight the underlying seriousness with which members of the DWPC treated their identity as professional journalists.

Of all the founders, officers, and members, it is Reynolds (later Scalabrino) who best captures the spirit of the group, whose members were typically involved in a number of women's and community issues. Thus, the DWPC was only one of Reynolds's causes. For example, she battled for suffrage for three decades and at least one biographer argues that her efforts contributed to Colorado's distinction of being the first state to grant women the vote.[7]

The younger sister of suffragist Helen M. Reynolds and a friend of Carrie Lane Chapman Catt (who later became the president of the National American Woman Suffrage Association), Reynolds served not only as president of the DWPC but also as press secretary for the Colorado Equal Suffrage Association. She also ran (unsuccessfully) as the first woman candidate for the Populist Party in Colorado in 1894.

Born in 1865, Reynolds moved to Denver in 1890. Hired by the editors of the *Rocky Mountain News* on the basis of the work she had done as a reporter in New York, Reynolds was startled to learn that the editors thought they were hiring a man. Obviously, her New York byline, "M. J. Reynolds," had confused them. Like many women journalists of the time, she was relegated to the society page, where, "a bit disgruntled," she started as society editor. She eventually moved to women's page editor, and finally became a leading political writer.[8] Though Reynolds eventually returned to New York, she kept in close touch with the DWPC, to which she referred on at least one occasion as her "daughter."[9]

Largely because of its connection with nationally recognized activists such as Reynolds, the DWPC quickly became well known. By May 1898, the group had joined the Colorado Federation of Women's Clubs, and in June of that year, the GFWC. In 1899 the DWPC became a member of the International League of Press Clubs.

PROGRAMS AND ACTIVITIES

Club programs during the early years of the Denver Woman's Press Club included social events and discussions of topics such as "The Problems of Journalism" and "What Makes a Play Bearable." The group also sponsored a "gentleman's night" for members and their partners. Cost was $1 for a dinner for two. Until 1925, balls and pageants sponsored by the group were the biggest fund-raising activities. One of the reasons the gatherings were so successful, according to one historian, was that some of the members organizing the colorful pageants were society editors at local newspapers who, in those days, "had great clout. . . . They could make or break a socialite."[10]

One of the goals of the group was to secure a permanent meeting place, and abundant proceeds from the balls made it possible in 1924 to purchase a clubhouse at 1325 Logan Street, a few blocks from the state capitol. The purchase of the house itself made history, since real estate transactions by women during this time were far from commonplace. "This was quite an undertaking for women in the 1920s," remarked member Nancy Peterson in 1998. "It took a lot of courage."[11] The building was the former home of western landscape artist and engraver George Elbert Burr and, among other architectural distinctions, features a slanting skylight on the north side of the house that provides the direct morning sun and floods the central gathering room with light. Built in 1910, it was declared a historic landmark by the Denver Landmark Preservation Commission in 1969 and was listed on the state register of historic properties in 1995. It remains the gathering place for DWPC meetings and social functions to this day.

Since the founding of the DWPC in 1898, guest speakers have included politicians such as George McGovern; journalists such as Robert MacNeil, Anna Quindlen, Ann Landers, Abigail ("Dear Abby") Van Buren, William Safire, and Edwin Newman; and writers, playwrights, and poets such as Judith Viorst, Robert Frost, James Michener, Barbara Kingsolver, Gail Sheehy, Colleen McCullough, William Faulkner, Irving Stone, and H. G. Wells. In 1981, one of these guest speakers was the prolific romance novelist Barbara Cartland. She arrived in a limousine adorned with a pink floral wreath and wearing a pink sequined dress, pink shoes, and a pink rose corsage. Delighted members watched her arrival through second-floor windows and then ran down to meet her. When one member told her, "Oh, Miss Cartland. I have read fifty of your books," Cartland replied, "Oh, good, my dear. You have only one hundred to go."[12]

But these nationally known speakers were not the only notables in the club's history. Its own membership included the first female physician in Denver, Dr. Eleanor Lawney, and the first woman state senator in the United States, Helen Ring Robinson. Robinson crusaded for the minimum wage for women, a minimum salary law for Colorado teachers, and a longer compulsory school term for rural schools. Another pioneer was Mary Florence Lathrop, the first female lawyer in Denver, the first woman member of the Denver and Colorado Bar associations, and one of the first women invited to membership in the American Bar Association. Lathrop was also an influential member of the Society of Friends. Yet another was Helen Marie Black, the first woman business manager of the Denver Symphony Orchestra (now the Colorado Symphony Orchestra) and the co-founder of the famous Central City Opera. Other influential members included Colorado's first poet laureate, Alice Polk Hill, who wrote a history of pioneer life; Mary Coyle Chase, the Pulitzer Prize–winning author of the play *Harvey*; and novelist Katherine Anne Porter.

Other local celebrity members included Helen Bonfils and Mary Elitch Long (whose portrait hangs in the living room of the clubhouse). Both were members of founding Denver families and were devoted philanthropists. Antoinette Arnold Hawley, a magazine writer and national president of the Woman's Christian Temperance Union from 1899 to 1904, also joined. Hawley was nominated in 1900 to run for mayor on the Prohibition ticket and, as reporter Frances Melrose suggested in a 1988 article in the *Rocky Mountain News*, would probably be "outraged to see today's members drinking wine in the club rooms."[13]

ACCOMPLISHMENTS

By March of 1899, the DWPC had begun to publish *The Woman's Crier*, a publication "Issued Whenever Opportunity Offers and Occasion Demands." Although it was published for only a short time and few issues still exist, members of the club were able to build relationships with other women's organizations by sharing the newsletter with women in the Young Women's Christian Association, the Women's Christian Temperance Union, and the City Improvement Society.

Over the years, membership in the club helped women journalists accept and recognize their unique qualities as women journalists well into the twentieth century. Denverite Pat Benero, for example, who "wanted to grow up and be a newspaperman," gave credit to the DWPC for her becoming a "newspaperwoman." Benero, who wrote for the *Littleton Independent* during the 1960s, has also published columns for the *Denver Post* and the *Rocky Mountain News*, as well as articles for several Denver magazines since then.[14]

Contributing to this process, the club frequently offered panels and papers on issues faced by women in journalism. In May 1941, for example, the topic of a panel was "Why Do Women Go into Journalism?" On the panel were Katherine Prescott Bemis, former coeditor of the *Littleton Independent*; Rebecca Strasser, secretary of the Colorado Tourist Bureau; Georgia Marrs Barber, former society editor of the *Denver Post*; and Thora Wiseman, publicity director for the DWPC. According to the panelists, young women went into journalism "either in hopes of emulating the thrilling adventures of the 'girl reporter' in the movies or with the belief that they can be an influence for good, even in the columns of the society page." Panelists said that if political writing were open to women, they would "have the necessary courage and persistence to cope with this 'man's world.'" Panelists also criticized women for certain alleged flaws: "Believing that men consider newspaper women as their inferiors in intellect and ability, women have been their own worst enemies. . . . The things which men do hold against newspaper women are their being late, their pettiness, and sensitiveness."[15]

The club also remained active and innovative over the years, launching new programs when the need arose. During the 1990s, a major project was the renovation of the clubhouse, which, at the cost of $140,000, required a substantial commitment. Another project successfully launched during this period was a mentoring program for elementary school children.

The Denver Woman's Press Club remains active today, more than one hundred years after it was founded, with 150 members. Its membership qualifications have expanded to include women employed in the broadcast media, public relations, advertising, and journalism education. In order to be accepted as members, they must submit examples of their publications and, if they work in print and broadcast media or public relations and advertising, verification of their employment. Benefits of membership include participation in programs, seminars, and author receptions, as well as networking opportunities and the chance to enter the writing contests.

Founder and first president Minnie J. Reynolds could not have known that the Denver Woman's Press Club would survive more than one hundred years, but she might not have been surprised. In fact, Reynolds predicted the club would persist and thought its history would be of interest to future generations, writing, "Since the club has lived a third of a century, there's no reason it should not live a century. And on its hundredth anniversary, these records will possess very great interest."[16] In 1998, centennial planning chair Nancy Peterson confirmed the accuracy of Reynolds's prophecy, saying, "We want our members to treasure the memories and continue the work our founding members set for us— to continue the goals and dreams."[17]

Following its centennial, the DWPC has adopted a new theme: "Our Second Century." The group advertises itself nationally as the oldest continuing press club and the one women's press club with its own building. Members do not take their long, notable history for granted. As Peterson told the group during a meeting on June 6, 1998, "Sometimes when we step through the front door, we hear voices from the past. We listen and are humbled."

NOTES

1. Dolores Plested, "Amazing Minnie: A 19th Century Woman of Today," *Colorado Heritage* 1 (1984): 24.

2. Ibid.

3. Jane Houston, "Writers in Residence: The Home of the Denver Woman's Press Club," *Colorado Homes and Lifestyles*, January/February 1990, p. 77.

4. "Ladies of the Press," *Denver Post Empire Magazine*, 22 June 1958, p. 10.

5. Undated, untitled brochure, Denver Woman's Press Club Papers, Denver Woman's Press Club Clubhouse, Denver, Colorado.

6. Minnie Peck Hall Krauser, "Story of the Denver Woman's Press Club," *Colorado Editor*, May 1941, p. 8.

7. Plested, "Amazing Minnie," p. 19. In 1893, Colorado was the first state in the nation to award women the right to vote. Wyoming, which granted woman suffrage in 1890, is often recognized as the first, but it was actually only a territory at the time.

8. Plested, "Amazing Minnie," p. 19.

9. Ibid., p. 24. Reynolds returned to New York City to write for the *Times*, the *Post*,

and the *Tribune*. She married Salvatore Scalabrino in 1905 and was active in the campaigns to win suffrage for New York (which passed in 1917) and New Jersey (which did not pass until the ratification of the Nineteenth Amendment in 1920). She died of a stroke in 1936.

10. Quoted by Lori Tobias, "Join the Club: Denver Woman's Press Group May be the Nation's Oldest," *Denver Post*, 6 June 1996, p. 2E.

11. Nancy Peterson, interview with the author, 6 June 1988.

12. Ibid.

13. Frances Melrose, "Women's Press Club Celebrates 90th Year," *Rocky Mountain News Sunday Magazine*, 11 December 1988, p. 25M.

14. Quoted by Libby DeBlasio, "Press Women Celebrate Club's First 100 Years," *Rocky Mountain News*, 22 March 1998, p. 28A.

15. Betty Crippen, "Press Club Discusses Newspaper Woman's Place in World Today," *Colorado Editor*, May 1941, p. 13.

16. Quoted by Tobias in "Join the Club," p. 2E.

17. Peterson, interview with author.

INFORMATIONAL SOURCES

Cervi, Clé, and Nancy Peterson. *The Women Who Made Headlines: The First 100 Years.* Lakewood, Colo.: Western Guideways, 1998.

DeBlasio, Libby. "Press Women Celebrate Club's First 100 Years." *Rocky Mountain News*, 22 March 1998, p. 28A.

Denver Woman's Press Club Papers. History Department, Denver Public Library, Denver, Colorado.

Denver Woman's Press Club Papers. Denver Woman's Press Club Clubhouse, Denver, Colorado.

Houston, Jane. "Writers in Residence: The Home of the Denver Woman's Press Club." *Colorado Homes and Lifestyles*, January/February 1990, pp. 77–78.

Plested, Dolores. "Amazing Minnie: A 19th Century Woman of Today." *Colorado Heritage* 1 (1984): 18–27.

INSTITUTIONAL PROFILE

Denver Woman's Press Club

Dates: Organized March 1898; incorporated 23 April 1908.

Newsletter: *Woman's Crier*, 1899; "Denver Woman's Press Club Page," *Colorado Editor*, February 1936–July 1952; *DWPC Newsletter* published intermittently during the 1960s and nine to ten times per year since 1970.

Organizational records: DWPC Papers, History Department, Denver Public Library; DWPC Papers, DWPC Clubhouse.

Address: 1325 Logan St., Denver, CO 80203, tel. (303) 839–1519.

8

Marion Marzolf

Detroit Women Writers, 1900–Present

(Formerly Detroit Press Club, Detroit Women's Press Club, Detroit Women Writers Club)

Detroit Women Writers (DWW) will celebrate its centennial on June 5, 2000, making it the oldest existing writers club in Michigan. Founded in 1900 as the Detroit Press Club by thirteen women journalists and literary writers, the organization took on an increasingly literary focus early in the twentieth century. Journalists have always formed part of the membership, but poets, novelists, essayists, dramatists, nonfiction, short story, and children's writers have long outnumbered them.

Elsewhere in the nation, women's press clubs were formed because women were not allowed in the men's clubs. In Detroit, however, women were the first to organize. The founders of the Detroit Press Club organized during a convention of the Woman's International Press Union (WIPU), which was holding its convention in Detroit between May 30 and June 2, 1900. Not only were these women active in the WIPU, they were also active in other women's state and national press organizations, such as the Michigan Woman's Press Association (MWPA),* founded in 1890, and the Michigan Woman's Press Club (MWPC),* founded in 1892. The new Detroit club provided the women writers with a local meeting place for professional advancement, workshops, and critiques.

The time was right for such an organization. Seventy-five delegates from the United States and abroad attended that convention of the WIPU, its third annual congress. Speakers celebrated women's rising presence in the press—and some even took credit for it. A leading local publisher and editor, for example, James E. Scripps of the *Detroit News*, told the group that he had hired "the first woman in the reportorial field, Miss Clara Bates, now Mrs. Doty," and that he currently employed forty "ladies" at his paper. (Although he did not specify their jobs, the majority were probably clerical rather than reportorial or editorial.) The delegate from New York and New Jersey, Cynthia Westover Alden, told the attendees there were one thousand women working on newspapers in the United States, and one-tenth of those were Michigan women. "You have the greatest number and are the leaders if you want to be," she challenged, "but you do not appreciate yourselves." She also noted that only twenty years earlier the press had enjoyed making fun of women's activities, but that the development of the department store and the woman's club movement had led to "treating women with the respect they deserved."[1]

The WIPU convention closed with an afternoon boat trip on the Detroit River and a fish supper in the St. Clair Flats, a popular resort area of islands in the St. Clair River delta. In this heady atmosphere, the idea of the women's Detroit press club, which had been discussed earlier, was put into action. On June 5, thirteen women, whose credits ranged from regular employment as journalists on Detroit's four leading daily newspapers, the *Detroit News, Free Press, Journal*, and *Tribune*, to contributing writers of stories and poetry for local and national publications, met and organized.[2]

FOUNDING MEMBERS

When the Detroit Press Club was founded, there was already a long tradition of involvement by Detroit women in the city's political, cultural, and social life and in the woman's club movement.[3] In 1897, there were nineteen women's clubs in the city that were linked to a state federation of about one hundred women's clubs. Michigan could claim the nation's first ladies literary club (established 1872 in Kalamazoo) and its first journalism school, established in 1886 by Martha Louise Rayne.[4]

The press club's first officers wrote for a variety of publications. Lucy A. Leggett, who was elected honorary president, was a book author, teacher, and special writer for the *Detroit Sunday News-Tribune*; Alice E. Bartlett, elected president, published prose and poetry under the pen name Birch Arnold and was a department head at the *Detroit Journal* and a special writer for several other newspapers. Pruella Janet Sherman, who was elected vice president, was a special writer and woman's page editor for the *Detroit Sunday News-Tribune*, and Ida F. Wain, elected recording secretary, was a reviewer for two Detroit papers, the *Evening News* and the *Tribune*. Mabel L. Ayers, who was elected corresponding secretary, was a journalist at the *Detroit Free Press* and Josephine Voss, who became treasurer, described herself as a book author.[5]

Of the other seven founding members, four were devoted to newspaper work. Journalist Aristine Anderson wrote for two Detroit papers, the *Evening News* and the *Sunday News-Tribune*; Hattie C. Sleeper, the owner of the Michigan Press Clipping Bureau, was also a writer for several newspapers; Emma Stark Hampton was a writer for weekly magazines; and Sarah J. LaTour was a weekly columnist for a Freemason paper. The three remaining members were devoted more to literary writing. Mrs. Franc Nicols was the vice principal of the Sprague Correspondent School for Writers from 1909 to 1910; Hester J. Spinner wrote poetry for Sunday newspapers and magazines, and Hulda T. Hollands published poetry and stories in the *Detroit Free Press*.[6]

In naming Lucy Leggett, the honorary president, the group was acknowledging her significance in the women's press club movement. Leggett was a former vice president of the National Woman's Press Association (formed May 13, 1885) and an active member of the WIPU, for which she had been corresponding secretary and a delegate to the Chicago World's Fair in 1893. No doubt she was involved in bringing the WIPU to Detroit for its convention in 1900 and was one of the speakers on that occasion. Leggett also ran the Rayne journalism school from 1890 to 1900, after its founder moved to Oak Park, Illinois.

Other early members were equally involved in women's organizations and press groups. Etta Wilson, who in 1886 was the first woman journalist employed by a Grand Rapids newspaper (the *Herald*), was also secretary of the Grand Rapids Press Club, a mixed-sex club founded in 1885. Wilson founded the Michigan Woman's Press Club in 1892 for women journalists working on Michigan publications. She did this after the older Michigan Woman's Press Association, to which she also belonged, expanded membership to include any published woman writer living in the state.[7] E. Cora DePuy, another early member, covered all news about Michigan journalism and journalists for the national professional magazine, *The Journalist*, which was published in New York City. Jennie O. Starkey, an editor of several columns including the "Letter Box" and "Society" for the *Detroit Free Press* was also an early member.

ACTIVITIES

The Detroit Press Club began meeting every other Tuesday night, first at the Buhl block in downtown Detroit, where Hattie C. Sleeper had located her Michigan Press Clipping Bureau in 1898.[8] All published writers, they welcomed as potential members "all women writers and authors living in Detroit." Prospective members were required to submit a copy of a story, article, or poem they had published in an established newspaper or magazine. Associate membership was available to women who lived outside Detroit. This group, like the Michigan Woman's Press Association, made it clear that published writing, not simply employment on a Michigan publication, was the criterion for eligibility.

A dynamic bunch, the members of the club appreciated the value of support and healthy professional criticism, and from the start brought in noted editors and writers to speak and hold vigorous workshops. Meetings opened with a "critics' half hour" of readings from the Manuscript Shop, a wooden model of Shakespeare's cottage made by a member's son, which served as a place for members to deposit their manuscripts to be read.

By 1904, the club began to be referred to as the Detroit Women's Press Club, apparently because its name, the Detroit Press Club, was appropriated by the city's male journalists. In May 1904, according to an article by E. Cora DePuy in *The Journalist*, 125 male journalists in Detroit formed their own Detroit Press

Club.[9] According to DePuy, the new group was to host the International Press League, a mixed-sex organization, in summer 1905. "The Detroit Women's Press Club," the article reported, "was part of the entertainment committee" for a trip to St. Clair Flats.[10] This story does not discuss the change of name for the women's club, but a 1938 article in a local newspaper quotes an early member, explaining that the word *Women's* was added to the original name to avoid confusion with the men's club.[11] On October 13, 1908, the women officially changed their club name to Detroit Women's Press Club.[12]

Membership in the Detroit Women's Press Club had grown to twenty-nine by 1913. The next year, the group once again changed its name. Perhaps in an attempt to attract more members, it changed the word *press* to *writers* as the Detroit Women Writers Club opened membership to semi-professionals. The 1914 constitution specified that the object of the group was to foster "a spirit of unity and good will among all the women in the city writing for publication." Membership was for women "regularly connected in a literary way with any reputable newspaper or magazine or professionally engaged in writing for publication." Growth continued steadily to a peak of sixty-five active members in 1928 and remained between fifty and sixty until the 1970s, when it doubled. Inactive membership was offered to those no longer living in the Detroit area or occasionally to those who could not attend for health reasons.

Meetings in the 1920s ranged from discussions of writing techniques, manuscript preparation, and marketing to specialized writing genres. The group also held regular writing contests for poetry and fiction and recognized each member's publications. By 1959 the club published an annual list of achievements or published works, conferences, lectures, and workshops by members.

At various times members formed subgroups around specific genres in order to focus on the specifics of topics such as rhyme schemes for poetry and plot development for the novelist, for example. These groups in the 1920s met before the regular biweekly meetings, and in the 1980s met in members' homes. The club newsletter, *The Bulletin*, which began publication in January 1924, listed coming events, presidential messages, board meeting reports, information on new members, and members' accomplishments. The newsletter editor was appointed by the president.

Social affairs were a high priority on the agenda during the 1930s. The club held Mother and Daughter dinners and President's Day teas. At meetings committees reported on social legislation such as child welfare, home economics, public health, civics, Americanization, and conservation. During World War II, the women writers participated in home front activities and volunteer activities along with their professional writing.

By the late 1930s, any woman journalist working in Detroit might join one or more professional organizations. Theta Sigma Phi, (later renamed Association for Women in Communications*), which was founded in 1909 by women journalism students at the University of Washington, opened a Detroit professional chapter in 1938. The local chapter was fed by graduates of the Michigan college chapters and professionals and over the years gradually expanded its membership to include all professional jobs in communications.[13] Elsewhere in the state, women journalists were likely to join the MWPA, which affiliated with the National Federation of Press Women* in 1937. The Detroit Women Writers Club, however, was the choice for those with literary credits and aspirations.

Like most women's press and writers clubs, the Detroit group did not have a home of its own and met in various locations over the years. In 1907 the group considered finding a permanent home and conducted a fund-raising sale of two hundred autographed books by famous authors. But the effort ceased without comment in the records, presumably because the writers decided to focus on writing and not on fund-raising. Thus they met at various locations, often libraries, until 1937, when the club program first listed its official meeting place as the Woman's City Club, which had a membership of about five thousand prominent women. Located in the heart of the city, the Woman's City Club was a popular luncheon and meeting site for the writers group until 1967. It is fondly remembered by a few members for its connections, good food, and smoke-filled-room critique sessions, where newer writers fearfully read before an impressive group of successful published novelists, like Joyce Carol Oates and Judith Guest, and poets and magazine writers for national and local publications.

The Detroit group did not typically take stands on political or social issues; instead, it focused on encouraging and promoting "creative writing of the highest professional standard." But in 1966 an exception was made in a matter of social conscience over the racist exclusionary policies of the Woman's City Club, where the group had been meeting for nearly thirty years. The women writers had no such exclusionary policies for their own membership, and they set about making that absolutely clear in April 1966 with new wording of the membership requirements that stated "membership would not be restricted by race, creed, or color." At the same time, the Detroit Women Writers Club voted to drop the word "club" from its name.

These two issues indicate the more professional and less social character of the contemporary group. At the time the group specified its nonracial membership policy it had been considering the admission of a black woman poet. (Her membership application was approved in 1967.) They knew her membership in their organization would challenge the Woman's City Club's unwritten, race-restrictive policy and she would not be allowed entry to the building's second-floor meeting rooms. The writers began looking for another meeting location, even as they wrote to the City Club hoping for a change in its policy. The City Club, however, would not change. In May 1967, the writers organization—now called Detroit Women Writers—moved its meetings to Wayne State University. The issue hit the newspapers, and Lenore Romney, the wife of Michigan's governor, resigned from the Woman's City Club a few days later when she learned about its policy.[14]

In the meantime, the group continued to sponsor activities aimed at providing support for women writers. In 1962, it joined with Oakland University in Rochester, Michigan, to launch a highly successful annual writing conference that typically drew four to five hundred participants. The conference, which continues today, provides participants with contacts to New York editors and agents, though it also functions as an appropriate and distinctive community service. It also attracts new members to the writers organization, and by the 1970s, many were from outside Detroit.

By the mid-1990s, DWW also began to include male members. If the issue of race preference was a very public matter, the issue of admitting male members was quiet indeed. Rarely in its ninety-year existence had the membership committee been faced with a male applicant. But in the feminist and equal rights era of the 1970s and 1980s, this became a matter of concern and private discussion. What would happen if the club became a writers group for men and women? Very quietly the board interpreted the membership rules as not barring male members, and in 1994 a retired male English professor with solid writing credentials joined the group. A second joined in 1998.

In 1970, DWW had moved its meetings to the Detroit Public Library in downtown Detroit, but by the 1990s, the city's deterioration and high crime rate caused concern. Some members wanted to move the group to a suburban location. Others, just as determined, wished to stay with the city and work for Detroit's anticipated rebirth. During the 1990s the board tried various means to serve members' conflicting needs and calm their fears. Several meetings each year were held at suburban libraries and in private homes. Luncheon meetings held at area restaurants continued to attract a sizeable group of thirty or so, but the regular meetings ranged from three to ten, a far cry from the vigorous group of twenty or more that had attended regularly in the 1970s. Finally, when the suburban libraries hiked their fees for nonsuburban group meetings and a new Detroit mayor promised a resurgence for the city, the DWW board voted to hold all regular meetings for 1997–98 once again at the Detroit Public Library. DWW had provided a sizeable contribution to the Friends of the Detroit Public Library throughout this era, and in return the Friends supported DWW activities, including writing workshops and readings.

CHALLENGES

From the founding members to the working journalists, authors, poets, and freelance writers of the present day, DWW has served to promote women writers, encourage their aspirations, offer sound and tough criticism and useful information and advice. Since its founding in 1900, the organization has had 481 active members. It now has 142 members, nearly a third of whom have reached the "life membership" status of twenty-five or more years with DWW. Sixteen of its past presidents are living and active as mentors and in committee work.

With the nearing of its centennial anniversary, DWW faces challenges typical of organizations of the late twentieth century. The organization's structure, with its regular activities of readings and writing conferences, requires the active work of twenty officers and chairs. Although the organization's first president held office for twenty years, two-year terms are now the maximum for any one office and have been typical for most of DWW's history. But filling these posts has become more and more difficult as the membership ages and substantial numbers of members have begun to tire after years of active service.

Changing family and work routines and the growth of the businesses located in the suburbs have also made an impact on a group that has spent most of its years in the central city, where lunch meetings could be worked into a busy work schedule. It is clear that the members' needs are changing and that daytime and lunch meetings are a problem for writers with full-time jobs outside the home office.

At the same time, DWW's central focus on encouraging creativity and subjecting the experienced and novice writers to thoughtful criticism has held the group together and continues to attract four or five new members each year. DWW makes an effort to bring these newer members into the active running of the organization and to groom them for leadership.

Members' work can be found in some of DWW's publications. It has published *Echos from the Moon*, an anthology of poetry and verse (undated) and *Voices on Writing Fiction* (1987). In 1999 it published *Century of Voices: Detroit Women Writers Anthology, 1900–2000*. DWW will celebrate its 100th birthday in 2000 at several events to underscore its significant contributions to the literary world and the independence of modern women.[15]

NOTES

1. *Detroit Free Press*, 31 May 1900, p. 3.

2. "The Detroit Woman's Press Club," *The Journalist*, 27 February 1904, p 1.

3. Alice Tarbell Crathers, *In Detroit . . . Courage Was the Fashion* (Detroit: Wayne State University Press, 1953), pp. 170–75.

4. *The Journalist*, 28 February 1891, pp. 1–2; James Stanford Bradshaw, "Mrs. Rayne's School of Journalism," *Journalism Quarterly* 60 (1983): 513–17. Rayne is one of the seven women in the Michigan Journalism Hall of Fame. See Induction Ceremony Program, Michigan State University, Michigan Journalism Hall of Fame, 18 April 1998.

5. *Detroit Federation of Women's Clubs Directory, 1909–1910* (Detroit: Detroit Federation of Women's Clubs Directory, 1910), p. 37; *The Journalist*, 27 February 1904, pp. 309–14, 316.

6. Ibid.

7. *The Journalist*, 27 August 1892, p. 5; *The Journalist*, 2 August 1890, p. 11; "Michigan Woman's Press Association," *Michigan History Magazine* 24 (summer 1940): 309–312; Willah Weddon, *Michigan Press Women, Today and Yesterday*. (Stockbridge, Mich.: Weddon Press, 1996), p. 1456.

8. *The Journalist*, 6 September 1903, p. 360.

9. There were other press clubs in the city. The Detroit Printers' Club, established in 1904, was open to women compositors. The male journalism fraternal organization,

Sigma Delta Chi, was headquartered in Detroit from 1914 into the 1920s. (Sigma Delta Chi did not permit women members until the 1970s.)

10. *The Journalist,* 22 July 1905, p. 217.

11. *Detroit Saturday Night,* undated clipping, Detroit Women Writers Archives (hereafter DWW Archives), Burton Historical Collection, Detroit Public Library, Detroit, Michigan. The article reports on the May 11, 1938, meeting.

12. No doubt the women discussed this, but there are no records or reports on the subject. It was eventually assumed the women had formed their press club because they could not get into the men's press club. Their pioneering status was forgotten until recent research turned up the story.

13. During the 1960s, TSP changed its name to Women in Communication, Inc.

14. "DWW President's Report, 1965–1966," DWW Archives; *Detroit Free Press,* 3 May and 19 May 1967.

15. Material for the bulk of this history was taken from the author's personal search of DWW Archives of correspondence, yearbooks, board meeting reports, clippings, and treasurer's reports. The records are extensive but incomplete.

INFORMATIONAL SOURCES

Bradshaw, James Stanford. "Mrs. Rayne's School of Journalism." *Journalism Quarterly* 60 (1983): 513–17.

Crathers, Alice Tarbell. *In Detroit . . . Courage Was the Fashion.* Detroit: Wayne State University Press, 1953.

Detroit Women Writers Archives. Burton Historical Collection, Detroit Public Library, Detroit, Michigan.

"Michigan Woman's Press Association." *Michigan History Magazine* 24 (summer 1940): 309–12.

Weddon, Willah. *Michigan Press Women, Today and Yesterday.* Stockbridge, Mich.: Weddon Press, 1996.

INSTITUTIONAL PROFILE

Detroit Women Writers

Dates: Founded 5 June 1900, Detroit, Michigan, as the **Detroit Press Club**; renamed **Detroit Woman's Press Club** 13 October 1908; renamed **Detroit Women Writers Club**, 13 January 1914; renamed **Detroit Women Writers**, 12 April 1966.

Newsletter: *The Bulletin,* January 1924–66; renamed *DWW Newsletter.* Only a partial collection is held in the DWW Archives. The secretary and current newsletter editor retain some recent files.

Archives: Detroit Women Writer Archives. Burton Historical Collection, Detroit Public Library, Detroit, Michigan.

Contact: Kathleen Ripley Leo (president 1999), 42185 Baintree Circle, Northville, MI 48167, tel. (248) 349–4827. Mailing address: DWW, c/o Friends Office, Detroit Public Library, 5201 Woodward Ave., Detroit, MI 48202.

9

Sandra L. Haarsager

Idaho Press Women, 1944–Present

INTRODUCTION

For much of the first half of the twentieth century, female journalists in Idaho faced difficulties beyond gender-based limitations on what jobs in the newsroom they could fill. Comparatively few in number in this sparsely populated state, they were often separated by significant distances and geographical barriers. They found themselves isolated professionally in rural communities without much ability to either network or find professional development geared to their needs. These were conditions that the Idaho Press Women (IPW), founded in 1944, helped alleviate.[1]

Born of World War II activism and the "can do" spirit of a handful of organizers who traveled the state to create the professional association, IPW provided its members professional training through annual conferences, support and reinforcement at annual meetings, and most important to some, a sense of being engaged in and belonging to a profession. Indeed, professionalism was built into the group's requirements for membership. From its earliest years prospective members were required to present evidence of publication as well as the sponsorship of an existing member to qualify. The organization focused on professional development and eschewed politics in a state where regional divisions often infused politics.

At the time of IPW's founding, other predominantly female writers organizations already existed in the state, such as the still very active Idaho Writers League. These organizations tended more toward fostering creative writing endeavors in poetry and fiction, however, and did not require that members be working professionals as did Idaho Press Women. Membership rolls of these organizations sometimes overlapped, but IPW retained as its primary focus the development of its members' journalistic skills to make each "a better press woman," as one longtime member put it.[2] It also fostered outreach through a high school writing contest and college scholarship program and established an annual awards program to recognize members' best work.

It has been difficult for IPW to maintain a statewide membership and regular activities, and over the years its membership has been well under one hundred. However, the women who joined tended to stay in the organization, often for decades. They were eager to have the kind of support, networking, and recognition that IPW provided as an antidote to professional isolation and newsroom job assignment stereotyping. The organization's achievements, besides providing professional camaraderie, included annual workshop conventions, recognition of members' work through annual writing contests and awards, outreach through student writing contests and scholarships, and participation in community literacy programs.

Through its affiliation with the National Federation of Press Women (NFPW),* the Idaho organization was able to establish national connections through the activities of its members who entered NFPW contests and attended NFPW meetings. IPW strengthened these connections on the three occasions that it hosted the NFPW conventions—in 1967, 1975, and 1989. It also established a tradition of recognizing outstanding Idaho writers and leaders with its "Woman of Achievement" awards, later renamed the "Communicator of Achievement" award, for lifetime service to the profession.

ORGANIZATION AND MEMBERSHIP

What made the Idaho experience for press women unique was what is unique about Idaho itself—its geography, with great distances between population centers, its sparse population, its late development from territory to statehood in 1890, the early passage of woman suffrage in 1896, and a tradition of sometimes irascible and iconoclastic editors of dozens of mostly small newspapers, all but a handful of them male. By 1910, women had established a vigorous club movement in the state. Many women found a professional outlet in women's club work, which for many was a covert and acceptable way to work for expansion of woman's rights.[3] The movement through study clubs often fostered and trained members to become researchers, writers, and activists, requisite skills for those who later aspired to become journalists.

Gradually, small towns in Idaho grew into cities and economic development led to community development, especially as agricultural tracts made possible through irrigation and federal land policies opened up land to settlement and development. Newspapers and other publications in the state became increasingly professionalized, and as they expanded women began to fill jobs as writers that enabled them and their publishers to utilize their education. Often in rural Idaho the chance to be a published writer came in the form of working first as a correspondent filing stories from places distant from the publication. This process enabled publications to extend their staffs and gave women entry-level positions and opportunities to become published, albeit as writers of community news. It was as correspondents or freelance writers that women began to see the benefits of a professional network, spurred by what was happening nationally with the NFPW and similar organizations in the 1930s.

One of those women was Gladys Rae Swank, a freelance writer and correspondent. She first attended a NFPW meeting in Chicago at the end of the 1930s. Swank, who later became a legislator and a judge, discussed the idea of an Idaho organization with other professional women and was inspired early in the 1940s to begin work to create an NFPW affiliate to support and recognize women writers in Idaho. She enlisted the help of fellow attendee and novice writer Dorine Goertzen, who later enjoyed a long career in public relations as a writer based in the southern part of the state. Goertzen had begun writing for what became the *Twin Falls Times-News* after she graduated from high school in the mid-1930s. The two women traveled the state for months, despite limitations imposed by wartime gas rationing, and succeeded in enlisting the interest and help of Boise newspaper editor Claire Goldsmith.

Ultimately the organization they created adopted the mission of the NFPW as its own. Membership required sponsorship of a current member and approval by officers, and the application had to include samples of professional work. IPW is run by five elected officers (president, two vice presidents, a secretary, and a treasurer) and a board consisting of several directors serving two-year terms. IPW also has a number of standing committees, including public relations, parliamentarian, newsletter, communicator of achievement, communications contest, and youth contest.

The founders' timing was good. The end of the war meant the beginning of a surge of activity as women channeled their wartime energy and activism, and their career-oriented independence, into other endeavors, writing among them. Within a few years, the organization was stable and its membership had grown to over two dozen members.

IPW's membership regulations were demanding, and the general trend within the news industry toward the professionalization of journalism was reflected in the organization's structure. In a bid for legitimacy through both recognition and exclusion—a strategy typical of professional organizations—IPW set lofty goals and limited its membership to working communication professionals. Here it was similar to other women's organizations that since the beginning of the century had typically used enforcement of standards of merit, lofty professional ideals, and professional norms to counter some of the rigid standards applied to professional women. Such professional associations created for and by women walked the tightrope between representing allied women's interests and advocating gender blindness in the professions, including journalism. This made their identity and programming sometimes problematic.

In the case of IPW, the resolution to this dilemma came in the form of professional, skills-oriented development and mutual support rather than political or social advocacy. The organization was "dedicated to promoting the highest ideals in journalism; to providing exchange of journalistic ideas and experiences; to coordinating efforts on matters of national interest to women communications professionals."[4]

Thus, IPW required evidence that prospective members were working writers. Prospective members had to submit three pieces of writing published during the prior year. With the emergence of broadcast news, video production, and other communications media, the publication standard broadened. By 1950 membership requirements specified that three examples of work from an applicant "taken from files of the past two years" must accompany the application for membership. Those eligible for membership are defined as "anyone who qualifies as a professional communicator actively engaged in any aspect of communications for remuneration."[5]

Although IPW was originally established for women, the organization opened its membership to men by 1970, anticipating other women's press organizations such as the Women's National Press Club* and Women in Communications, Inc.,* which extended membership to men in the 1970s. IPW members had become wary of maintaining a single-sex organization in the context of discussions about equal rights (Idaho passed the Equal Rights Amendment in 1972), and they also wanted to expand their membership. However, male members at any one time never numbered more than two or three, although they generally participated in the meetings.

PROGRAMS AND ACTIVITIES

Because people were often prone to dismiss women's clubs as social rather than professional groups, IPW's leaders eschewed the connotation of "club" for their organization. As former president Elayne Bybee said in an interview, "We were not a club—the goal was to help make each of us become a better press woman." IPW, in fact, initially focused on developing the journalistic skills of its members, but it gradually broadened its interests to include a wider rubric of communication skills, such as those found in broadcast or public relations. By the 1970s IPW was offering a broad array of workshop topics and speakers on editing, photography, advertising, and even fiction.

Like many women's organizations, IPW saw itself as apolitical. There was little direct political activism on the part of the organization over the years, although issues such as affirmative action and the Equal Rights Amendment— which it eventually endorsed—were frequently discussed at annual meetings.[6] This sense of political neutrality helped foster the professional support, comfort, and congeniality that made the IPW prosper over the decades as the group got together each year for its annual conventions in the spring and professional workshops in the fall.

Almost from its founding, IPW sponsored annual writing contests in a variety of publication categories in line with the NFPW's annual competition and many of the state winners became national winners as well. These national award winners illustrate the wide variety of jobs and topics women came to cover in Idaho journalism: Joy Morrison, of the *Idaho State Journal* in Pocatello, for example, was awarded for her feature writing; JoJane Hammes, publisher of the *St. Maries Gazette*, was awarded for her columns on civic and community issues; former NFPW president Louise Shadduck was awarded for her features published in Spokane and North Idaho publications; Betty Penson Ward of the *Idaho Statesman*, Boise, won several awards for her travel pieces and columns, and Loris Jones Dudley, of the *Moscow Idahonian*, won awards from the mid-1970s to mid-1980s for her pieces about agriculture and education.

IPW's annual workshops typically covered professional topics and issues such as effective leads, photography, feature writing, the First Amendment, and the Freedom of Information Act. Speakers included such noted authors as crime writer Ann Rule and raptor expert and writer Morley Nelson. In the 1960s, workshops for radio and television writing and production were added to the agenda.

By the 1980s, IPW had established a number of broad ongoing activities. It supported regional literacy programs, sponsored a high school writing contest and scholarship, and offered the annual Ann Adams scholarship (named after the deceased editor of the *Idaho Free Press*, published in Grangeville), awarded to a junior or senior Idaho college student majoring in communications. In addition, IPW published a regular (usually quarterly) newsletter for members, *IPW Presswoman*, with information on upcoming events, awards, contests, new members, member activities, and other news of interest.[7]

IPW maintained its connection to the NFPW and hosted national conventions of that group on three separate occasions; in 1967 and 1975 in Sun Valley, and in 1989 in Coeur d'Alene.

CONTRIBUTIONS

One of IPW's most important contributions is the role it has played in nurturing Idaho's women communication professionals, some of whom went on to become state leaders in a variety of capacities. The organization also enhanced these members' professional identities and allowed them to act as role models who might inspire others. One such woman was Betty Penson-Ward, who worked as society editor, women's editor, lifestyle editor, and columnist for the *Idaho Statesman* in Boise for some fifty years; she joined IPW in 1958 and inspired others to join. Penson-Ward, who began her professional career in 1934 at the *Boise Capital News*, described what it was like to be female and working in journalism in the days before the IPW came into being in 1944: "In earlier years, the 'girls' who staffed a newspaper's women's department were not recognized as journalists of importance because they were allowed little identity of their own," she wrote. "Slowly we made changes in our image, from society desk to women's department to the Arts of Living."[8]

Another woman who credits some of her success to her membership in IPW is award winner Loris Jones Dudley, who like many women in journalism before the 1960s began her newspaper career not as a reporter but behind a receptionist's desk (at a small daily in Moscow). "I got such a feeling of support and camaraderie," she said of IPW, "a sense that we're all in this together and we can help one another."[9] Margaret Hawkes Lindsley, who served as IPW's secretary for many years, found the professional contacts she made through the IPW most helpful "because I was out in a rural area where there were not many people interested in writing,"[10]

Becoming IPW's "better press woman" served many members well. Founder Swank, who worked for twenty-five years as a feature writer and photographer for the *Spokane Chronicle*, wrote broadcast news, and edited a weekly for five years, served two terms in the Idaho legislature as a Democrat from 1965 to 1969 and worked in a variety of legislative positions before and after her term.[11] Swank also became the NFPW's National Youth Chairman for the high school girls' editorial writing contests and served as the third president of the Idaho Writers League in 1943. In addition to organizing Idaho Press Women, she helped organized Washington Press Women, which became a NFPW affiliate.

In 1971, IPW honored Swank as its "Woman of Achievement" and named its annual high school writing and photography contest and scholarship after her. Another IPW member to achieve recognition was co-founder Dorine Dimond Goertzen, who began working for the South Idaho daily later known as the *Twin Falls Times News* after graduating from high school in the 1930s. She later worked for a publishing company and did public relations work for various organizations, edited a magazine, *Scenic Idaho*, and won the IPW "Woman of Achievement" award in 1973.[12]

Louise Shadduck, who served as president of the NFPW from 1971 to 1973 and successfully fostered closer relations between the national organization and the White House, was the only IPW member to earn the IPW Woman of Achievement award twice.[13] Shadduck had a highly visible career working for U.S. Congressman Orval Hansen (R-Idaho). She wrote for the *Coeur d'Alene Press* and later the *Spokesman-Review* in Spokane, Washington. Shadduck became noted as an effective writer and spokesperson for the forestry industry and congressional representatives and later wrote several popular regional histories. The state named a building in her honor in 1998.

CONCLUSION

Like many women's press organizations, Idaho Press Women faces an uncertain future at the end of the twentieth century. Some fifty years after it was first established, its major concerns center around sustaining its membership, meeting expenses through the collection of dues (increased to $60 a year in 1998), and bringing together its members from the northern and southern extremes of the state (a distance of 500 miles). These have been perennial issues for women's organizations in the state since women first began meeting in goal-oriented groups at the turn of the century.[14]

Always a relatively small group with a statewide membership that hovered around fifty to seventy members statewide, the group's membership peaked at one hundred in 1989 when it hosted the NFPW in Coeur d'Alene. However, like other voluntary organizations, IPW faced a membership decline in the 1990s, dropping to just over thirty members by the end of the decade. Notwithstanding its contests and scholarships and attempts to recruit male and minority members, the organization was hard pressed to increase its numbers. New members and recruits were often daughters of earlier members or associates of existing members. Journalists, both male and female, tended to gravitate instead to the Idaho Press Club, a Boise-based group founded in the 1960s, for professional reinforcement. The long-term future of IPW, in the face of declining membership, was uncertain as the twenty-first century approached.

NOTES

1. The author is grateful to several longtime members of Idaho Press Women who shared their time to be interviewed for this chapter. Much of its content is based on their comments and recollections.

2. Elayne Bybee, former IPW president, interview by the author, Pocatello, Idaho, 8 July 1998. Bybee joined the organization in 1958.

3. See Sandra Haarsager, *Organized Womanhood: Cultural Politics in the Pacific Northwest, 1840–1920* (Norman: University of Oklahoma Press, 1997).

4. "Idaho Press Women Invite You . . . ," IPW informational brochure, no date.

5. The applications and samples are reviewed by the IPW's first vice president and secretary. "Idaho Press Women Invite You . . ."; Margaret Hawkes Lindsley, e-mail correspondence with the author, 30 July 1998.

6. Idaho initially passed the ERA in 1972 but rescinded it in 1977.

7. IPW brochure.

8. Betty Penson-Ward, *Idaho Women in History: Big and Little Biographies and Other Gender Stories*, vol. 1 (Boise: Legendary Publishing Co., 1991), p. 214.

9. Loris Jones Dudley, interview by the author, Moscow, Idaho, 24 July 1998. Dudley joined the organization in 1971, inspired to join after hearing member writers Betty Penson-Ward and former state treasurer Marjorie Ruth Moon speak at a meeting of student journalists.

10. Margaret Hawkes Lindsley, interview by the author, Idaho Falls, 27 July 1998.

11. Gladys Rae Swank, "Ladies of the House (And Senate): A History of Idaho Women in the Legislature since Statehood," unpublished manuscript, 1978, pp. 69–70, Special Collections, University of Idaho, Moscow, Idaho.

12. "Biographies of Idaho Women," unpublished manuscript, compiled by the Altrusa Club of Boise, 1979, Day Northwest Collection, Special Collections, University of Idaho, Moscow, Idaho.

13. Elayne Bybee, correspondence to the author, 16 July 1998. Bybee was president in the mid-1990s.

14. When the Idaho Federation of Women's Clubs began in Idaho in 1900, the state

organization met in three districts because of the difficulties and expense of transportation in the expansive and rugged state. See Haarsager, *Organized Womanhood*, pp. 300–302.

INFORMATIONAL SOURCES

Altrusa Club of Boise. "Biographies of Idaho Women." Unpublished manuscript, 1979. Day Northwest Collection, Special Collections, University of Idaho, Moscow, Idaho.

Haarsager, Sandra. *Organized Womanhood: Cultural Politics in the Pacific Northwest, 1840–1920*. Norman: University of Oklahoma Press, 1997.

Hogsett, Vernetta Murchison. *The Golden Years: A History of the Idaho Federation of Women's Clubs, 1905–1955*. Caldwell: Idaho Federation of Women's Clubs, Caxton Printers, 1955.

Idaho Press Women. Brochures and newsletters, 1990–98, passim.

Penson-Ward, Betty. *Idaho Women in History: Big and Little Biographies and Other Gender Stories*. Boise: Legendary Publishing Co., 1991.

Swank, Gladys Rae. "Ladies of the House (and Senate): A History of Idaho Women in the Legislature since Statehood." Unpublished manuscript, 1978. Special Collections, University of Idaho, Moscow, Idaho.

INSTITUTIONAL PROFILE

Idaho Press Women

Dates: Founded October 1944, Boise, Idaho.

Newsletter: *IPW Presswoman*, 1945–present, generally published quarterly. Current editor Meg Donahue, P.O. Box 405, Challis, ID 83266. Back issues located in archives (below) and with Elizabeth Laden, IPW Historian, P.O. Box 410, Island Park, ID 83429.

Archives: IPW Papers, Idaho State Library, Boise, Idaho.

Contact: Cathy Koon, 425 E. 4th St., St Anthony, ID 84445, e-mail:<current @idahonews.com>, Web site:<www.webpak.net/~handj/ipw/ipw.htm>.

10

Norma Fay Green

Illinois Woman's Press Association, 1885–Present

The roots of the Illinois Woman's Press Association can be traced to May 1885 when the National Woman's Press Association was organized at the World's Industrial and Cotton Centennial Exposition in New Orleans by Marion A. McBride of the *Boston Post*. McBride "envisioned the new group patterned after the Women's Christian Temperance Union which organized state societies auxiliary to the national" and encouraged NWPA founding members to start up their own state or regional associations.[1] One of the founders, Chicago newspaper writer Frances A. Conant, agreed to recruit other women writers for a local group when she returned home. After consulting with *Chicago Evening Post* writer Antoinette Van Hoesen Wakeman, author and publisher Dr. Alice Bunker Stockham, and others, Conant decided to organize an auxiliary in Chicago.

Despite Conant's initial efforts, the Illinois organization was "only partially effected in June 1885."[2] The group met at the Chicago office of lawyer Myra Bradwell, the founder and editor of *Legal News* and a publisher of law books. Bradwell was chosen president but declined because of the press of business. Further attempts at local organizing were suspended until the fall when it was decided to form an independent state association. In January 1886, "a score of earnest workers met by invitation at the home of Dr. Julia Holmes Smith [a physician, medical writer, and former drama critic for the *New Orleans Picayune* who had been at the exposition], and the formal organization was completed. The new society was named the Illinois Woman's Press Association [IWPA]. Its object, stated in its constitution, was to provide a means of communication between women writers, and to secure all the benefits resulting from organized effort."[3]

FOUNDING MEMBERS

Mary Allen West, editor of the Women's Christian Temperance Union's (WCTU's) *Union Signal*, was elected the group's first president and served for seven years until 1893. Other officers included medical writer Dr. Sarah Hackett Stevenson, vice president; newspaper and magazine writer Frances Conant, corresponding secretary; book publisher Belle Gorton, recording secretary and newspaper writer Antoinette Wakeman, treasurer. The officers reflected the diversity of member occupations and interconnecting alliances to other women's organizations. Stevenson later became president of the Chicago Woman's Club, a literary-turned-service organization begun in 1876, and Wakeman later headed the Press League, a newspaperwomen's group organized in 1892.[4]

The more than forty women who became charter members represented a variety of fields in which women could earn a living by their writing. Perhaps the best known was Frances Willard, president of the WCTU and author, publisher, writer, and editor. She was joined by Elizabeth Boynton Harbert, creator of "Woman's Kingdom" at the *Chicago Inter-Ocean* and a regular contributor to a number of publications, including the *New York Independent, Cincinnati Gazette, Chicago Post*, and *Des Moines Register*. She was also publisher of the suffrage magazine *New Era*. Other members included Ursula Gestefeld, an author of metaphysical healing books; Frances E. Owens, editor of *Journal of Industrial Education* and pioneer subscription cookbook publisher; and Mary C. Van Benschoten, editor at the *Chicago Record and Appeal*. Also among the charter members were poet and children's book author Sarah Wilder Pratt and lawyer Mary A. Ahrens, who wrote on suffrage and other reform movements. Six women physicians were among the founders: Sarah Hackett Stevenson; Julia Holmes Smith, who became a *Chicago Record Herald* reporter, playwright, and author of short stories and magazine articles; Alice Stockham, author and publisher of a best-selling book on women's health and publisher of *Kindergarten* magazine; Mary Weeks Burnett, editor and publisher of the *Journal of Heredity*; Florence Hunt, a medical writer specializing in mental illness; and Odelia Blinn, publisher, medical research correspondent, and contributor to various publications.

Caroline Huling became the oldest surviving charter member and lived until 1941 working as a newspaper writer, magazine editor, publisher, and novelist. A native of Saratoga Springs, New York, she came to Chicago in 1884 at age twenty-nine to attend a woman suffrage convention and stayed on. She responded to a newspaper notice about the fledgling IWPA and became one of its founders. Huling remained active in IWPA for five decades and edited many of its publications, including its first newsletter, *Stylus*, and *Prominent Women of Illinois*, a biographical collection published in 1932 as a fund-raiser.

INITIAL STRUCTURE

The IWPA elected a slate of officers, including a president, a single vice president, both recording and corresponding secretaries, a treasurer, and two assistants. By 1890, the slate of general officers expanded to include three vice presidents and two librarians. The executive committee consisted of the general officers along with the chairmen of standing committees, and three other women elected by the association. The general officers, elected by ballot at the annual meeting in January, were to hold office "till their successors are elected," whereas other Executive Committee members could be elected at any regular meeting. The number of years an officer could serve, consecutively or otherwise, was not mentioned in the bylaws of the early years.

The association's committees reflected many of the issues of the era in which the group was formed, including those of professionalization and social reform. Professional concerns were addressed by four committees: The task of the Literary Criticism Committee was to advise members on manuscript merit; the Revising Manuscript Committee vetted members' work, a service for which it was "at liberty to charge usual prices for such service"; the role of the Literary Information Committee was to "point out correct and reliable sources of information"; and the Work and Workers Committee served as a job clearinghouse.[5] The association denied any intention "to make [itself] in any sense a trade union for newspaper workers only, . . . [though] it did propose to advance the interest of women as writers and along kindred lines." In 1890, it reported the success of the committees, which "in doing the work assignment, have rendered efficient aid to authors in the publication of their books, to novices in preparing manuscripts, and have assisted many in securing employment."[6]

Other committees were directed more toward outreach and networking. The Publication Committee, for example, was to issue all IWPA printed material (which came to include annual manuals and the association newsletter) and advise authors on publishing. The task of the Reporting Committee went beyond publicizing IWPA functions; it was charged with arranging to have "suitable reports made of all women's meetings throughout the state" so that members could network and the state press might cover such activities. The task of the Education Committee was to bring IWPA "influence to bear in the direction of wise and practical efforts" in the education movement, and the Philanthropy Committee researched worthy causes seeking volunteer time and talent as well as money and then recommended "the wisest methods of securing the best results."[7]

The IWPA met monthly, except during the summer, for professional programs and executive sessions. A typical program included a musical or literary selection followed by a talk on a professional topic. The association never had its own headquarters and met at a variety of locations over the years. Several early meetings were held at that bastion of male journalism, the Chicago Press Club, even though women were excluded from membership and had to use the ladies' entrance.[8] Later it would meet at area hotels, and in 1890, with more than one hundred members, it had its own downtown clubroom, Monica Hall, in a downtown office space funded by Stockham and others. During the twentieth century, IWPA met at the new Chicago Press Club facilities, the Chicago Woman's Club, Chicago Literary Club, Women's City Club, and a number of hotels.

MEMBERSHIP

The IWPA accepted women from all over the state, and eventually the country, who were sympathetic with its mission and eager to connect with a sisterhood of scribes. The association's Membership Committee was both selective and inclusive in screening and recruiting applicants. It divided the membership into categories by line of work and type of professional expertise that defined members as authors, editors, correspondents, contributors, reporters, and publishers. There were three initial classifications of membership: Regular active members were those who had been previously or were currently being paid for their writing; associated members were defined as those "who write in the interest of reforms, or to gratify their taste"; and honorary members were those recognized for achievement and prominence. The latter two categories had no voting privileges. By 1892, the active category was amended to include paid illustrators as well as wordsmiths. By 1898, poets were officially added to the member groupings.

Both factual reporting and creative fiction were represented in members' work, a fact noted in 1890 by IWPA president Mary Allen West in an address before the all-male Illinois Press Association:

[T]he lines between journalistic and literary work are . . . dissolving into each other, and our leading newspapers throughout the country are publishing in supplement[s] and so-called magazine[s] not only the work of the best writers of the day, but other original literary work of merit. Not only is it true that journalism is a fitting field of labor for woman, but it is also more accessible to her than most professions.[9]

IWPA members published popular as well as scholarly work. This was illustrated by the work of its early presidents, such as Helen Elkin Starrett (January 1893–January 1894), an editorial writer and contributor to the *North American Review*; Elizabeth Armstrong Reed (January 1894–June 1896, June 1902–June 1904), who wrote several books on Hindu and Persian literature; Sallie M. Moses (June 1896–June 1898), a staff member of the *Chicago Saturday Evening Herald*; and Hannah Effa Webster (June 1898–June 1900), who came to be known as "the dean of Chicago newspaper women" and was an editorial writer for the *Chicago Mail* and *Chicago Daily News Journal*.[10]

The IWPA also expanded its membership to reach other women and expand its influence through auxiliaries and honorary memberships. In 1899, it started a young ladies auxiliary to welcome aspiring writers into its ranks. By the early twentieth century, the honorary roster included women of national prominence such as Jane Addams, Julia Ward Howe, Susan B. Anthony, Ellen Henrotin, president of the General Federation of Women's Clubs, and Anna Ballard, a *New York Sun* staff writer who had the distinction of being the "only woman ever on the roster of the New York Press Club."[11] International honorary members included Finland's Baroness Alexandra Grippenberg, an editor, newspaper publisher, and Finnish legislator; England's Lady Isabel Somerset of England, an editor of the WCTU's *Union Signal* and the suffrage publication *Woman's Herald*; and Lady Somerset's countrywoman Henrietta M. Lord, a London County Council member, book publisher, and magazine editor.

Membership rules continued to change over the years. In 1902, the association limited regular membership to those who had received payment for their work within two years of the date of application. In 1903 another category—corresponding member—was added to retain and attract those who had moved or lived out of state. In later years, as the IWPA broadened its definition of "press" to include "authors, editors, reporters, playwrights, publishers, poets, copywriters for advertising matter, song and musical composers, illustrators and continuity writers," the regular active member qualifications were tightened.[12] Thus in 1907, the active category was once again restricted to those currently doing paid work who could prove it by submitting at least three published articles and "other credentials as evidence of eligibility as may accompany them" for examination.[13] Voting was done by secret ballot of the entire membership, and three negatives were sufficient to bar an applicant from membership; those who were barred could not be proposed for membership again for one year. In 1939, as early members aged, IWPA created a new dues-exempt emerita category for those who had joined at least twenty-five years earlier. This replaced the life membership category that had listed IWPA founder and veteran newswoman Conant as its sole member from 1890 onward.

NETWORKS AND CONNECTIONS

By 1891 IWPA was connected with several other professional and women's groups. It was affiliated with the National Editorial Association (NEA) and International League of Press Clubs, both of which were mixed-sex press organizations. It remained affiliated with the NEA for about thirty years and had a representative on its executive board; Huling was the NEA's first woman officer elected in 1890 as assistant recording secretary. In 1892, the IWPA was a member of the International Federation of Women's Press Clubs and became an auxiliary to the Illinois Woman's Alliance, a group of twenty-four local community, religious and professional organizations mobilized to form a labor union to improve working conditions for women and children.[14]

Like many other women's press organizations of the period, the IWPA was firmly embedded in the woman's club movement of the turn of the twentieth century. In February 1920, with a membership of more than two hundred, its newsletter *Pen Points* boasted: "There are more professional lecturers and read-ers—some of national reputation—in IWPA than in any other woman's club in Chicago. A list of IWPA speakers is being compiled for the Speaker's Bureau of the Illinois Federation of Woman's Clubs. This bureau represents six hundred women's clubs and has many calls for paid speakers." It was affiliated with the General Federation of Women's Clubs for thirty years until 1922, when mem-bers decided that a strictly professional organization had no place in a federation of general clubs and withdrew from membership.[15]

The association's connections to other women's professional groups contin-ued, and monthly program speakers included the presidents of the local chapters of the National League of American Pen Women* and the Woman's Advertising Club. The IWPA was an early supporter of the Chicago-based Woman's Na-tional Journalistic Register initiated in 1920 by Theta Sigma Phi (later renamed Association for Women in Communications*), a women's national college jour-nalism honorary society founded in 1909. During the 1930s, IWPA president Leona Alford Malek (a syndicated columnist who wrote for the *Chicago Herald-Examiner* under the byline "Prudence Penny") also was an officer in the Chicago Women's Association of Commerce and the Women's Advertising Club of Chi-cago. Affiliations like these kept communication lines open for exchange of ideas among working women in many professional spheres.

ACTIVITIES

One way in which the IWPA sought to promote its ideas and interests was through the many publications it issued over the years. By 1888 it had begun to publish a program calendar that soon evolved into an annual yearbook that listed officers, bylaws, and meeting schedules; a directory of members with their mailing address; and advertisements for local businesses, especially those of female entrepreneurs. Only one directory, issued at the time of the World's Columbian Exposition in Chicago in 1893, detailed the professional affiliation of all members. The directories in 1894 and 1898–99 identified members by categories of work such as author, editor, and correspondent. In 1903, IWPA started publishing a newsletter known as the *Stylus: A Journal for Writers*, which was supported by advertisements and edited until 1905 by founding member Caroline Huling. According to Huling, the newsletter had three major goals: "to give association news, to establish a home for women writers and to aid young authors."[16] Even after two years of publication, she felt compelled to explain the publication's purpose:

The reason for being of the *Stylus* seems to be misunderstood, especially by some new members. . . . The membership of the IWPA is scattered over a wide territory, literally from Japan to England, as well as all over Illinois, it being a state, not a local, organi-zation. Most of these absentees joined the Association when residing here and retained their membership after moving away. To foster their interest it was desirable to keep them posted as to our work. . . . Several of the members are also becoming aged and infirm, the IWPA being nearly twenty years old, and it was suggested that a philanthropic work be taken up for the relief of such persons and other women writers. To properly keep this work before the people, some regular medium of publicity was necessary, hence the *Stylus* came into existence. . . . The *Stylus* makes no pretensions to being a Literary journal . . . aiming simply to give news matter about the Association and its members. Later, as the patronage increases and the income justifies, it is proposed to enlarge and broaden the policy still, however, keeping it true to its purpose and making it still more useful to writers, by giving more of the practical article that will be helpful alike to all who hope to earn money with their pen and to publish items to further the sale of manuscripts. Few authors disdain to receive hints in this direction, and wise ones profit thereby. The *Stylus* aims particularly to help new writers, however.[17]

In 1905, under president Ada Barton Bogg, the IWPA launched a second monthly newsletter, the *Quill*, which provided upcoming programs, member news, and service articles. No extant copies of it have been found, but it is listed as the organization's official organ in both the 1905 and 1906 annual directories. It had apparently ceased publication by 1909, for in that year in a report to the NEA, Huling notes, "A small publication on the interests of the Association was maintained several years and may be revived." By 1920 the association was issuing a newsletter again, which it named *Pen Points*; in 1930 its editor was made a member of the Executive Committee.

Beyond internal publications, the IWPA also published several books, including, in 1914, a hardbound *Memory Book* "wherein the members of the IWPA have written bits of feminine philosophy and fancy, and wherein you may write your own." During the Depression, the association planned to raise money by publishing a two-volume series entitled *Prominent Women of Illinois* and *Prominent Men of Illinois* that would be sold to the people profiled. Only the women's book was completed, but this apparently raised $1,300 "to be used as a permanent loan fund for the benefit of needy women."[18] The IWPA did not restrict itself to the printed word, but also took advantage of developing technologies to publicize its presence and the accomplishments of its members. In 1933, members contributed to a weekly fifteen-minute radio program of skits, poems, short stories, and lectures on such topics as children's literature and interior decorating broadcast on WCFL (the Chicago Federation of Labor station). Later, in 1937, IWPA members broadcast a weekly five-minute series of radio shows during *Homemaker Hour* on WLS (owned by Sears, Roebuck & Co., whose call letters stood for "World's Largest Store"). And in the 1990s, as a means to increase its visibility and credibility as a professional organization, it established a telephone hotline and a Web site on the Internet to disseminate information about meetings, membership, and current activities and to field queries about the organization and its activities.

The association was also active in social and philanthropic causes. During its early years, it regularly provided textbooks to needy youth and sent books to Appalachian schools. In the 1890s, IWPA was part of the Chicago Protective

Agency, a housing and escort service for working women established by the
Chicago Woman's Club. In memory of early member Eliza Bowman, editor of
the *Newsboy's Appeal*, IWPA furnished a room in the McKinley Home for
Working Girls in the early 1900s as part of its affiliation with the Model Lodging
House Association. By the 1920s, it was providing social services such as an
emergency loan fund, pensions, burials, and even a cemetery plot for indigent
women journalists (not just IWPA members) and poor children. Huling hoped
to establish a home for aged and infirm women writers, but this costly venture
never materialized.[19]

FEDERATION AND GROWTH

Although during its early years the IWPA was a member of the National
Woman's Press Association and the International Federation of Women's Press
Clubs, these organizations did not survive beyond the turn of the twentieth
century. The idea of a federation of women's press clubs reemerged in 1920,
the same year woman suffrage became a reality. The October 1920 edition of
Pen Points mentions that Renee B. Stern, chairman of IWPA's Special Committee of Club Affiliations, had begun to compile a list of various women's
press clubs and associations in the United States and elsewhere "with the idea
of forming a loose federation for the mutual exchange of courtesies." This federation would allow traveling IWPA members to obtain information about
women's press clubs in the cities they were visiting, and conversely, the IWPA
would be able to host press women from other parts of the country when they
were visiting Chicago.

But not until the mid-1930s did IWPA president Helen Miller Malloch successfully mobilized press women. The catalyst was the debate over IWPA's
lobbying efforts for copyright legislation that would protect women writers
whose creative work was being used without monetary compensation on radio
broadcasts. Recognizing the need for women to band together in an organized
fashion, those involved in the debate began to envision a national group that
would allow the "interchange of ideas, plans and speakers, prestige coming from
rigid membership requirements, assistance to members new in the community
both socially and in a business way."[20] Taking Malloch's suggestion, Martha
Dunlap, a new IWPA member who had been appointed chairman of the Illinois
Committee on Federating Women's Press Organizations, sent letters proposing
such a federation to one hundred newspaperwomen in many different states. Of
these women, thirty-five pledged to become members at large, and by November
1936, three women's press associations joined IWPA's Illinois Committee on
Federating Women's Press Organizations. The Ohio Newspaper Women's Association* was the first to endorse the national program, followed by Press
Women of Portland, Oregon, and the Woman's Press Club of Indiana.* The
resulting organization was named the National Federation of Press Women
(NFPW),* and Malloch was elected president at the first official meeting in

1937.[21] IWPA became 100 percent affiliated with NFPW in 1945, meaning membership in the Illinois association, which remained autonomous, automatically included national membership as well.

By World War II, the IWPA had become more geographically diverse than in its early days, when meetings and members were concentrated in the Chicago metropolitan area. It held its first regional conference in downstate Springfield in 1940 and in the next year established the Mate Palmer Awards to publicize members' media work. Named for IWPA's ninth president, a writer and long-time editor of the *Banner of Gold* who served from June 1907 to June 1908, the annual communication contest continued through the 1990s with more than ninety categories for statewide entries. Despite the global crisis, new members continued to join; and in 1944, after reporting the addition of fourteen, IWPA Membership Committee chairman Marion Carey boasted, "A club, whose members work so hard to bring in suitable new blood, will survive war, famine—in fact, the four horsemen."[22] In the early 1950s, IWPA actively recruited prominent women as honorary members, including columnist Dorothy Thompson, Senator Margaret Chase Smith, and author Cornelia Otis Skinner.

DECLINE

During the 1960s, when a dozen of IWPA's oldest members died, efforts were made to increase membership and attract younger journalists. A step-by-step guide was published to assist in recruiting friends and acquaintances, and initiatives were continued to connect with journalism students at the high school and college level. Despite these efforts, however, the IWPA, founded in the nineteenth century before journalism schools became widespread, was beginning to lose ground to college journalism honorary societies created in the first decade of the twentieth century. Theta Sigma Phi, founded in 1909, had chapters at most journalism programs as well as alumnae chapters throughout the country. The Illinois chapter eventually competed for membership among the same women who might join IWPA, and the competition increased in 1972, when the sorority changed its name to Women in Communications, Inc. (WICI)* in a strategy to attract more women in related communications fields and disassociate itself from the exclusivity implied by the use of Greek letters. The situation was made even more competitive when the all-male fraternal organization Sigma Delta Chi opened its doors to females in the same year and renamed itself the Society of Professional Journalists.[23]

These changes and increased competition put some pressure on the organization to update its image. One way to accomplish this would be to change its name as did Theta Sigma Phi and several other women's press organizations during this period. Official minutes from March 30, 1974, indicate that although IWPA may not have seriously considered changing its name, members indicated they opposed a renaming of the NFPW as well in a hand vote of 17 to 3. (A proposal to change NFPW's name had been made to reflect the federation's international stature after admitting a Mexican affiliate.)[24] At the same time, other NFPW affiliates had begun to admit male members; the Michigan Women's Press Club* signed up two male members, "causing a stir nationally as well as locally." It would be another decade before IWPA began to admit male members.

Some members were frustrated with these attempts to preserve the status quo. Member Fran Altman wrote an open letter attached to the minutes for May 4, 1974, urging an overhaul of the bylaws for the association's survival:

At our two previous IWPA board meetings I heard many cries that new members, new faces, etc. be put to work for IWPA. Bylaws require that members must have recorded two full years of membership before being eligible for election. We have many vibrant and creative women who come to our organization and after five or seven months have exhibited great interest as well as actively contributing to our progress. We are unable to express OUR TRUST in these newer members until WHEN? Two years down the road, provided some well meaning soul has not goofed up an initial membership. By then I would have lost interest too, wouldn't you? And moved on to that other rapidly growing women's communication group [the WICI Chicago Professional Chapter, which recorded more than 300 members during the same period].[25]

Other signs indicated the association's loss of momentum. In 1976, IWPA published its last membership directory for over a decade as the organization suffered membership stagnation, budget deficits, and continued competition from other journalism groups. It struggled to adapt its programs and activities to the changing needs of its members, beginning to meet every other month instead of monthly and changing its meeting day to Saturday to accommodate members' busy work schedules. As a result of responses to surveys of members who wanted more professionally oriented programming, IWPA adapted its meeting format to include more career-oriented workshops. It also changed its bylaws to help new members become involved in committee work more quickly.

By the 1980s, the recommitted group looked forward to its centennial with a sense of revitalized membership and prestige within the Illinois communications field. It expanded its goals in what an official history published in 1987 called "an indication of a no-nonsense attitude toward professionalism." IWPA had an active membership of more than one hundred professionals, the history reported, and, along with other NFPW state affiliates, sponsored a high school journalism contest whose intent was to "nurture future members into the medium."[26] That contest continues to be one of its notable annual events.

Although the IWPA contained the word *woman* in its title and was clearly established to promote women writers, it never had a specific policy excluding men from membership. According to past president Marlene Cook, who joined in 1973, "Male members have been invited for as long as I can remember. However, the name deters some from joining. No policy has been set that NFPW [and IWPA] was for women only. It started out that way at a time when there was no recognition for women writers."[27] This tradition eventually changed, and by 1985 the IWPA had enrolled its first male member, Dr. Eugene Vickery, a poet, medical writer, and book author who was also the husband of former IWPA president (1971–73) Millie Vickery. In 1995, Eugene Vickery was one of three members to be honored posthumously by the association when a scholarship fund was dedicated in their name.[28] Younger men have followed, and as of 1998, at least one male student was a member of the association.

ENDURING LEGACY

Unlike many other women's press organizations, the IWPA had a sense of its significance and place in history from the very beginning and sought to ensure that its role would be remembered by future generations. The association seemed to be aware of its role in women's press history and by 1899 had included a historian on its roster of officers. In 1908 it formed a standing committee to plan its twenty-fifth anniversary in 1910 and began to compile its records and files for donation to the Chicago Historical Society.[29] By the 1920s, it had begun to view itself as an organization with a history, and the nameplate of its newsletter declared it to be "the oldest organization of professional women writers in the world." That sense of history kept the association's commitment to tradition strong. In 1985, the year of its centennial when IWPA hosted the NFPW's annual convention, convention director Marlene Cook referred to that tradition in a welcoming message to the delegates: "In IWPA tradition, we have designed a program of practical value to writers, to facilate communication among women journalists, to share, support, inform and assist, and to increase the visibility of women writers."[30]

Since its founding in the 1880s, when Chicago's population swelled from 500,000 to one million in less than a decade, IWPA has given women writers a comfortable venue and a collective voice. Its membership ranks have demonstrated that women can use their talents to support themselves and help reform the world. It forged global friendships and professional affiliations as it greeted visiting writers at several world's fairs held in Chicago over four decades. By the turn of the twentieth century, it had formed a young ladies auxilliary whose modern-day equivalent is its programs devoted to mentoring student journalists and supporting the most promising through scholarships. During the twentieth century the organization witnessed both the triumph of woman suffrage in 1920 and the humiliating defeat of the Equal Rights Amendment in Illinois, a key state in the ratification movement, in the 1980s.

Amid world wars and national economic crises, IWPA members forged the foundation of the NFPW to strengthen professional standing. In bad times, IWPA sisters watched out for one another and sent those in distress flowers, condolences, even money. They celebrated each other's work with awards and messages of support and congratulations. Even when members moved out of the state or the country, they maintained professional and personal ties to the association. At the time of this writing, the venerable IWPA stands ready to witness its second fin de siècle with a firm sense of its history and steady eyes fixed on both present and future generations of communicators.

NOTES

1. *IWPA Manuals*, 1890, 1891, and 1892, p. 1, Illinois Woman's Press Association Collection (hereafter IWPA Collection), Chicago Historical Society Research Center, Chicago, Illinois; see also Marion McBride, "Report to the 1890 Convention of the National Editorial Association," *The Journalist*, 5 July 1890, p. 12.

2. *IWPA Manuals*, 1890, 1891, and 1892, p. 1.

3. Ibid.

4. Biographical information on founding members was culled from the following sources: Roselle Dean, "Our Founder and Honorary President: Julia Homes Smith, M.D.," *Pen Points*, December 1930; Caroline Huling, ed., *Prominent Women of Illinois, 1885–1932* (Chicago: IWPA, 1932); Huling's radio script aired 29 April 1933 over WCFL-Chicago, Caroline A. Huling Collection (hereafter Huling Collection), University of Illinois at Chicago Library, University of Illinois at Chicago, Chicago, Illinois; *IWPA Manuals*, 1893, 1894, and 1889–99; "The Illinois Woman's Press Association," *The Fourth Estate*, 23 May 1895; *Pen Points*, May 1935, Golden Anniversary issue; Dr. Odelia Blinn obituary, *Stylus*, February 1905, p. 2.

5. *IWPA Manual*, 1890, pp. 12–14.

6. Ibid., p. 6.

7. Ibid.

8. The expanded history of IWPA printed in its *Manual* of 1893 contains the association's first printed reference to the male-only Chicago Press Club. An October 1916 Press Club of Chicago booklet describes the history of its exclusionary membership on p. 9:

The question of Votes for Women came up in October 1880 when it was recorded by the historian of the Club William H. Freeman, that 'Blanche Roosevelt Tucker of Paris, a well-known authoress and former Chicagoan, a warm friend of President Wilkie and family and of the Club, and Joseph Hatton, of London, who had appeared for the Club at the entertainment were elected honorary members.' Some years afterwards, it is recorded, through no hostility to the female workers in the journalistic field, but simply because it was believed that the best interests of the Club and greater freedom [could be] enjoyed if women were excluded, the Constitution was amended to read "No woman shall be elected a member of this Club."

9. Mary Allen West, address on "Women in Journalism," in *Illinois Newspaper Directory: History of Illinois Press Association* (Champaign, Urbana: Illinois Press Association, 1934), p. 82.

10. *Prominent Women in Illinois*, p. 31.

11. Ibid.

12. Copy of typed radio script broadcast 29 April 1933 over WCFL-Chicago, p. 3, Huling Collection, folder 5, sec. 1: "Writing Section."

13. *IWPA Manual*, 1907, p. 11.

14. "First Annual Report of Illinois Woman's Alliance," Huling Collection, folder 39, sec. 3: "Women's Groups."

15. *Prominent Women in Illinois*, p. 13.

16. *The Stylus: A Journal for Writers*, February 1905.

17. Ibid.

18. *Pen Points*, April 1933, n.p., IWPA Collection.

19. The IWPA memorial plot was sold in 1997 to make way for suburban development, and the graves of two women buried there were moved to another part of the same cemetery. Part of the proceeds of the sale were designated for an IWPA student scholarship fund. See Margaret Bengston, "IWPA Sells Remaining Plots: Graves Moved to Make Way for Commercial Development," *Pen Points*, February 1997, p. 2; Stacey Singer, "Grave Matter Stirs Women's Press Group Association's History Unearthed in Cemetery," *Chicago Tribune*, 27 October 1996, DuPage County edition, p. 1.

20. An October 1936 *Pen Points* item (n.p.) quotes a *Rochester* (New York) *Journal* interview with Malloch about the federation movement.

21. Malloch continued to be active in IWPA until her death in 1963. She died while attending the NFPW annual meeting.

22. *Pen Points*, May 1937, p. 2, IWPA Collection.

23. Maurine H. Beasley and Sheila J. Gibbons, *Taking Their Place: A Documentary History of Women and Journalism* (Washington, D.C.: American University Press, 1993), p. 28.

24. Minutes, IWPA business meeting, 30 March 1974, IWPA Collection.

25. Undated letter addressed to all members attached to the 4 May 1974 minutes, IWPA Collection, box 2, folder 2.

26. Donna Duesel De La Torriente, *So We All Can Be Heard: An History of the Illinois Woman's Press Association, 1885–1987* (Streamwood: Illinois Woman's Press Association, 1987), p. 67.

27. Marlene Cook, e-mail correspondence with author, 18 December 1998.

28. The IWPA Memorial Scholarship honors the memory of three IWPA members: Vickery; Lynn Bermont, an artist and feature writer for newspapers, including the *Chicago Sun-Times*, and a public relations professional for Quaker Oats; and Joanna R. Cook, a former IWPA newsletter editor whose career included newspaper reporting, magazine editing, and public relations. The fund supports students and advisers in the pursuit of journalism careers and continuing education for IWPA members.

29. The IWPA Collection at the Chicago Historical Society contains information only until 1977. The collection is devoted to primary source material and did not accept a copy of the 1987 history when the association offered a copy.

30. De La Torriente, *So All Can Be Heard*.

INFORMATIONAL SOURCES

Collections

Caroline A. Huling Collection. University of Illinois at Chicago Library, University of Illinois at Chicago, Chicago, Illinois.

Chicago Press League Collection. Chicago Historical Society Research Center, Chicago, Illinois.

Illinois Woman's Press Association Collection. Chicago Historical Society Research Center, Chicago, Illinois.

Press Club of Chicago Collection. Chicago Historical Society Research Center, Chicago, Illinois.

Published Materials

Ashton, Carry May, "The Illinois Women's Press Association," *The Journalist*, 24 January 1891, p. 12.

De La Torriente, Donna Duesel. *So We All Can Be Heard: An History of The Illinois Woman's Press Association, 1885–1987*. Streamwood, Ill.: Illinois Woman's Press Association 1987.

Illinois Newspaper Directory: History of Illinois Press Association. Champaign, Urbana, Ill.: Illinois Press Association, 1934.

INSTITUTIONAL PROFILE

Illinois Woman's Press Association

Dates: Organized May 1885; reorganized January 1886; Chicago, Illinois; organized and joined National Federation of Press Women in 1937.

Newsletter: *Stylus: A Journal for Writers*, 1903–05, editor Caroline Huling; *The Quill*, 1905–7, editor Ada Barton Bogg; *Pen Points*, 1920–present (various editors held, for the most part, a one-year term).

Archives: IWPA Collection, Chicago Historical Society Research Center, Chicago Illinois; Caroline A. Huling Collection, University of Illinois at Chicago Library, University of Illinois at Chicago, Chicago, Illinois.

Contact: Peggy Grillot (president, 1998–99) IWPA, P.O. Box 59256, Schaumburg, IL 60159–0256. tel. (312) 458–9151, e-mail: <www.iwpa.org>.

11

Janet Cramer

JAWS: Journalism and Women Symposium, 1985–Present

In 1985, a group of sixteen women—journalists and journalism educators—met in the mountains of Colorado to begin an organization that would provide them, and the hundreds of women who would later join them, emotional and professional sustenance. This "camp," as these annual gatherings would come to be known, spawned the Journalism and Women Symposium (JAWS), an organization motivated as much by the need for social connections as by the recognition that women in journalism face very real professional challenges.

Driven by a mission to support "the personal growth and professional empowerment of women in newsrooms," JAWS members have also worked toward "a more accurate portrayal of the whole society." Their membership is limited to journalists (print, electronic, and full-time freelance) and college- or university-level journalism educators. Nonmembers, however, can attend the "camps," which are held annually, often in western mountain resorts, where participants hear from speakers as varied as Helena Luczywo, publisher of Poland's largest newspaper; Colorado congresswoman Patricia Schroeder; Ellen Malcolm, founder of EMILY's list; syndicated columnist Molly Ivins; and feminist author and mystery writer Carolyn Heilbrun ("Amanda Cross").

According to Jane P. Marshall, the first president of JAWS, some members "want only the annual chance to refresh and replenish," whereas others want action.[1] In addition to its social activities held each year, JAWS provides members with a wide variety of professional assistance, such as training in computer-assisted reporting; guidance regarding coverage of stories involving gays and lesbians, Native Americans, racial minorities, and legal issues such as sexual harassment and child abuse cases; and advice on how to find an agent and market a book. Although JAWS was incorporated in Colorado, its headquarters was established in 1992 at the School of Journalism at the University of Missouri at Columbia. A nonprofit, educational organization, JAWS receives foundation backing from the Ms. Foundation for Education and Communications, the Freedom Forum, the Scripps Howard Foundation, the Sister Fund, the Robert R. McCormick Tribune Foundation, and the Knight-Ridder Fund. The board works on a volunteer basis, with members providing their time and paying their own travel expenses. In 1995, a $2,500 grant from the Freedom Forum enabled JAWS to establish the Joan Cook Scholarship Fund to encourage young journalists, especially women of color, to join the organization and attend the annual camp.[2]

THE GLASS CEILING AND OTHER REALITIES

JAWS was organized by journalists and educators dissatisfied with the conditions facing women in the newsroom, particularly the lack of advancement potential and the exclusion of women, especially women of color, in news coverage and in the editorial decision-making process. Even though news organizations were hiring more women as reporters, they were not promoting women to top levels of management.[3] In 1985, a study directed by Maurine H. Beasley and issued by the University of Maryland School of Journalism described the pay inequities women journalists faced and the potential devaluation of journalism as a profession with more women entering the field.[4] Even after JAWS was organized, women's situation in journalism resisted change. In 1989, for example, two reports indicated that women were barely visible in news reports and as journalists. A study of the front pages of ten major newspapers showed that women were in bylines and photographs only about a quarter of the time. They were quoted even less, with only 11 percent of those stories featuring quotes by women.[5]

In 1990, several reports focusing on women and the media revealed that women—even women media managers—in local newspapers and broadcast stations, as well as larger media corporations, did not play a role in major decisions. Despite the fact that the majority of graduates from journalism schools were now women, their presence was not yet making an impact on the middle and upper levels of management; men still outnumbered women as media managers.[6] At the 1989 Women, Men and Media II conference in Washington, D.C., Jean Gaddy Wilson, executive director of New Directions for News—a media think tank housed in the University of Missouri School of Journalism—reported that women held fewer than 10 percent of the top decision-making jobs. Fewer than 25 percent of journalists poised for advancement within news organizations were women, whereas more than half of the entry-level positions were held by women.[7]

ORGANIZATION AND EARLY ACTIVITIES

It was because of such realities that women journalists and journalism educators decided to form an organization where they could support each other and work for change. Jean Gaddy Wilson and Tad Bartimus, a regional Associated Press reporter in Estes Park, Colorado, were the primary organizers of the first gathering of JAWS in September 1985 at the Stanley Hotel in Estes Park, Colorado, in September 1985.

The decision to hold the symposium was made at an earlier meeting of women journalists at the University of Missouri organized by Wilson in April 1985. Wilson had invited the women—all graduates of the journalism program at Missouri—to return to campus to talk about their lives and work. Bartimus, who was one of the women to attend, realized the benefits of a gathering of women journalists and suggested that the women continue to meet on an annual basis. She and Wilson organized the first meeting of JAWS that following fall to be held in Bartimus's home state of Colorado. Bartimus invited her Missouri companions and several women journalists from Colorado to the first official JAWS gathering. The sixteen women who attended that gathering, including Wilson and Bartimus, were newswomen—mostly from Colorado media, but also from papers in Fort Worth and Kansas City, Missouri—and journalism educators.[8]

The structure of the group was at first informal, without officers or a hierarchical structure. The women agreed to meet annually to socialize and discuss issues of concern to women journalists. They decided to start a newsletter. The *JAWS Newsletter*, published on a more or less quarterly basis, was first edited by Sybil Barnes with Dean Wariner providing graphics and design. The first issue, published in winter 1986, included stories about the camp gathering and articles by Dorothy Jurney, the women's section editor for the *Detroit Free Press* and *Miami Herald*, and Glenda Holste, the national-foreign editor of the *St. Paul Pioneer Press*.

According to JAWS historian Kay Mills, the organization grew by word of mouth and survived by the "hip pocket and heart" of Tad Bartimus. Organizers, such as Wilson, were concerned about the "glass ceiling" women journalists faced and attributed news organizations' loss of female readers and viewers to the lack of female leaders in media organizations.[9] Still, the most immediate need seemed to be to establish a network of collegiality and support, and annual retreats provided the opportunity for friendships and networking. As Mills writes:

The JAWS connection also started to bring dividends, in addition to friendships, for our members. Over the years, it has resulted in editors hearing about new columns to run or books to review, women finding new jobs, conference planners learning names of good speakers, members getting tips on stories or how to set up a new beat, and . . . writers finding wonderful folks with whom to stay while on research trips or book tours.[10]

The format of the first gatherings set the tone and agenda for subsequent meetings, which included reports from women who made news or who covered important stories throughout the year, plenty of networking and sharing of advice, and good times. For example, Bartimus and Edie Lederer, another Asso-

ciated Press (AP) correspondent, shared stories at the first JAWS gathering about
covering the Vietnam War. In 1990, Geneva Overholser, then editor of the *Des
Moines Register*, initiated discussion about the controversial question of identifying rape victims in news reports. And in 1989, Betty Anne Williams, of *USA
Today*, Leola Johnson, of Pennsylvania State University, and Marian Duncan,
from a Minnesota radio station, challenged the organization to bring in more
women of color. They told white journalists that they needed to interact more
with African Americans and not rely on African American women to explain
the black community to them or be the only journalists to cover stories relating
to the African American community.

In 1989, four years after its founding, JAWS leaders decided it was time to
adopt a more formal organizational structure. Jane Marshall, features editor of
the *Houston Chronicle*, was elected the first president, and a board of directors
was elected. The leadership sought nonprofit status for the organization and
drafted a mission statement and bylaws. Membership was restricted to women,
and the bylaws defined who could become voting members: journalists employed by newspapers, news services, syndicates, magazines, television, or radio
stations or other electronic disseminators of news and information programming;
college- and university-level journalism teachers; full-time freelancers in the
news field; and women who had had a career in any of the above categories.
Dues were set at $50 a year, which included a newsletter subscription.

Members adopted the mission statement: "The Journalism and Women Symposium, a national organization, supports the personal growth and professional
empowerment of women in newsrooms and works toward a more accurate portrayal of the whole society." Most members attend the annual camp, which costs
an additional $175 a year plus airfare and room and board. JAWS officers and
new board members are elected at the annual business meeting, which is the
Monday during fall camp.

The year following their adoption of a more formal structure, board members
received training in financial planning from Janet Cohen, a consultant with experience helping nonprofit groups. According to JAWS historian, Kay Mills,
"We didn't know how much money we had, what it cost to do anything or what
to do next."[11] Developing a more formal structure and financial plan led as well
to the search for permanent headquarters and a staff to handle the needs of the
growing organization. In 1991, Glenda Holste, of the *St. Paul Pioneer Press*,
succeeded Marshall as president, and she and Jane Marshall, of the *Houston
Chronicle*, explored the possibilities.

In early 1992, Holste contacted Rilla Dean Mills, the dean of the school of
journalism at the University of Missouri at Columbia, to request space. Missouri
was an ideal location, since founding member Jean Gaddy Wilson could be the
faculty sponsor and on-site executive. JAWS leaders believed the group's mission and the school's reputation would dovetail nicely. By May 1992, the organization had established its offices on campus and archived its records in the
Historical Society of Missouri.

CONTEMPORARY FOCUS

As JAWS matured, its outreach and educational efforts increased. While continuing to educate themselves, members established a scholarship fund for young journalists to become members and attend annual gatherings. Leaders emphasized technology education for women and cooperated with a number of organizations, including the National Institute for Computer-Assisted Reporting and Investigative Reporters and Editors, both located at University of Missouri at Columbia, and the Medill School of Journalism at Northwestern University, to provide training for members. Programs at the annual symposia also included sessions on technology. In 1995, Nancy Hicks Maynard, former publisher of the *Oakland Tribune*, spoke to camp attendees about how the Internet would redefine journalists' roles and responsibilities.

Meanwhile, the organization remained committed to increasing diversity and supporting women in their roles as journalists and educators. In 1998, the board urged the American Society of Newspaper Editors (ASNE) to approve a policy on diversity hires. The statement to ASNE encouraged that organization to reach parity with the national population in minority hiring—including women and racial minorities—by the year 2025. True to the sentiments that spawned their organization, JAWS leaders wrote:

Only when newsroom power is shared among men and women of all ethnic and racial groups, of all sexual orientations and ages, can the dialogue of a thriving democratic society be nurtured and our media fully serve that society. . . . Women are entering journalism in record numbers, as some 60 percent of the journalism school graduates. But the glass ceiling is a reality, especially for women journalists of color.[12]

In response, the ASNE board adopted a mission statement on newsroom diversity and stated its goal of achieving 20 percent parity by 2010.[13]

By 1999, JAWS had grown to include about four hundred members. Although the annual gatherings still provide enjoyment and recreations, these "camps"—which are held in a variety of locations, primarily in the western states—now focus more on issues and training in particular skills. They also attend to business, such as the annual election of JAWS officers and board members. Some members, however, still believe in the benefits of the camaraderie and "elbow bending" that characterized their earlier gatherings as a recent column added to their newsletter, "Wine and Whine," indicates. Thus, JAWS leaders promote their organization as "committed to the ideas of renewal, affirmation and serious examination of our professional lives."[14]

NOTES

1. Jane P. Marshall, "Jaws of Hope: Action, Yes, and Replenishment," *The Quill*, February 1990, p. 43.

2. A journalist and founding member of JAWS, Joan Cook died of breast cancer in 1995 in New York. She was a plaintiff in a class-action sex discrimination suit against the *New York Times* filed in 1974 and the first woman to lead the *New York Times* unit of the Newspaper Guild of New York.

3. Kay Mills, *A Place in the News: From the Women's Pages to the Front Page* (New York: Columbia University Press, 1990), pp. 334–40.

4. Maurine H. Beasley, *The New Majority: A Look at What the Preponderance of Women in Journalism Education Means to the Schools and to the Professions* (College Park: University of Maryland, October 1985).

5. Jean Gaddy Wilson, "At Sea in a Sea Change: Few News Organizations Have Faced up to the New Reality," *The Quill*, February 1990, p. 30.

6. Ibid., pp. 29–32.

7. Ibid.

8. The women who attended that first meeting were Jane Marshall, *Denver Post*; Carole McKelvey, *Rocky Mountain News*; Janet Chusmir, publisher of the *Boulder Daily Camera*; Judy Miller, Denver TV news producer; Pam Johnson, *Kansas City Star*; Trisha Flynn, *Denver Post*; Jennifer Gavin, Associated Press, Denver; and Harriet Simpson, *Fort Worth Star-Telegram*. Also present were Ramona Rush, University of Kentucky; Anne Banville of Washington, D.C.; Christy Bulkeley, Gannett Foundation; Lucy Conant of Sheridan, Wyoming; Susan Harlow, *Sheridan Press*; and Tay Thomas of Anchorage, Alaska.

9. Bartimus was the first woman to become a bureau chief at Associate Press and was one of only three women assigned by the Associated Press to cover the Vietnam War. Her personal papers are currently held in the Washington Press Club Oral History Project Interviews, folders 4–8.

10. Wilson, "At Sea in a Sea Change," p. 29.

11. Kay Mills, "JAWS Herstory," JAWS Web page (1998):<http://www.jaws.org>.

12. Ibid.

13. "Journalism and Women Symposium Resolution on ASNE Newsroom Diversity Policies," JAWS Web page (1998): <http://www.jaws.org>.

14. "Who We Are," JAWS Web page (1998): <http://www.jaws.org>.

INFORMATIONAL SOURCES

JAWS Archives. National Women and Media Collection, Western Historical Manuscript Collection, State Historical Society of Missouri. University of Missouri at Columbia, Columbia, Missouri.

JAWS Web page (1998): <http://www.jaws.org>.

Marshall, Jane P. "Jaws of Hope: Action, Yes, and Replenishment." *The Quill* 78, no.1 (February 1990): 43–44.

Tad Bartimus Papers. Women in Journalism Oral History Project, Records. 1987–94. Washington Press Club Foundation. Washington Press Club, Washington, D.C.

Wilson, Jean Gaddy. "At Sea in a Sea Change: Few News Organizations Have Faced up to the New Reality." *The Quill* 78, no. 1 (February 1990): 29–32.

INSTITUTIONAL PROFILE

JAWS: Journalism and Women Symposium

Dates: Founded September 1985 in Estes Park, Colorado; incorporated in Colorado and headquartered in Columbia, Missouri, May 1992.

Publication: *JAWS Newsletter*. Editors: Sybil Barnes, 1986–87; Kay Mills, 1987–89; Margaret Freivogel, Kay Mills, 1989–92; Jane Marshall, 1992–93; Lorraine Iannello, 1993–96; Karlyn Barker, 1996–present.

Papers: JAWS Archives. Western Historical Manuscript Collection, National Women and Media Collection, University of Missouri at Columbia, Columbia, Missouri.

Contact: Journalism and Women Symposium, Missouri School of Journalism, 76-G Gannett Hall, Columbia, Missouri, 65211, Web site: <http://www.jaws.org>. Contact person: Margie Meyer, tel. (573) 882–7456, e-mail: <Margie_Meyer@jmail.jour. missouri.edu>.

12

Janice R. Hume

Kansas Press Women, 1941–Present

With America on the brink of World War II and recovering from years of economic depression, women journalists in Kansas in 1941 established a state-wide community, a network of support with specific goals of encouraging a consciousness of women journalists' "power and influence" and of obtaining their "just place in the field of journalism."[1] For many women who worked at tiny newspapers scattered throughout the prairie towns of Kansas, affiliation with Kansas Press Women (KPW) would offer a sense of sorority, a chance to learn, a rare opportunity for recognition in a male-dominated field, and a way to ensure a legacy of women media practitioners through scholarships and youth competitions. Many would faithfully participate in semi-annual state meetings despite the time and the geographic and financial limitations of working for community weeklies.[2] Thus, it was that initial gathering of KPW on March 28, 1941, that established the network for rural and city women journalists that would flourish for most of the rest of the century and would serve to strengthen women's involvement in the state's strong tradition of community journalism.

ORGANIZATION

This was not the first instance of Kansas women journalists uniting. In 1891, they had established the Kansas Woman's Press Association in an effort to create a professional organization to promote the interests of women writers. A report of the fifth annual meeting of this group recounts the program, which included "a feeling and hospitable" welcoming address by Mrs. Sara B. Lynch, editor of the *Leavenworth Standard*, and a paper presentation, "What Shall We Write?" by "Becky Sharp" of the *State Journal* in Topeka. This writer suggested to her colleagues that "home news of home people and home things count most of all.

Above all write for your readers."[3] She expressed concern that there were "40–50 women actively engaged in newspaper work in Kansas who ought all to be members of this association" but apparently were not yet.[4] Further information about the Kansas Woman's Press Association has not been preserved, but the organization apparently died out after the turn of the century, as did several of the women's press organizations founded in that era.

Two other organizations were established during the twentieth century: Kansas Newspaper Women, which was established in 1928, and the Kansas Woman's Newspaper Club. These organizations, in fact, sent greetings to the women attending the first KPW meeting.[5] The creation of the Kansas Press Women was apparently seen as necessary, since it would have a national affiliation—with the National Federation of Press Women (NFPW),* founded in 1937.

Mrs. B. J. Bless, Jr., of Weston, Missouri, president of NFPW, was guest speaker at that first Kansas meeting. She encouraged the women attending to "establish an interchange of ideas and ideals for mutual benefit" and to "advance the standards of journalism for all women."[6] The first slate of officers elected that day reflect an organization that would bring together women both from tiny Kansas communities, such as Phillipsburg and Wamego, and larger ones, such as the capital city Topeka. They also reflected a range of experience and responsibilities in the journalism profession. Mamie Boyd, the president, was co-owner (with her husband Frank W. Boyd) of the *Phillips County Review* and six years later also became co-owner of the *Jewell County Record*. Other officers were Mrs. Ella Ruehmann of Wamego, first vice president; Anna Carlson of Lindsborg, secretary; Mrs. Nettie Lerrigo of Overbrook, historian; and Mrs. Ruth Rusco of Topeka, treasurer. The first program indicates an initial interest in press ethics, influence, and responsibility, and it is likely that a number of the women attending were involved in writing and production of small rural weeklies.

KPW, according to its own records, was the seventh state organization to affiliate with the NFPW. The charter list of members was held open until June 1, 1941, and the initiation fee was $1. Those invited to join were "newspaper women, editors, literary writers, authors, columnists and feature writers devoted and dedicated to their profession and all high principles of our free heritage."[7] Before the decade was out, the membership roster would reach sixty-five. It peaked in 1983 with 214 members and then gradually dropped off to 115 members in 1998.[8]

PROGRAMS AND ACTIVITIES

KPW was quick to offer an active program for its members. In its first year it hosted the NFPW convention and was soon raising funds for Kansas women studying journalism at accredited colleges or universities.[9] Many found the camaraderie offered by the organization one of its greatest attractions. In 1951,

Eulalia T. Guise, who was co-editor and co-publisher of the *Marysville Advocate* with her husband from 1946 to 1975, joined for the companionship of other women with like interests: "It was the stimulation of talking to and being with people doing what I was doing. . . . I couldn't talk about newspapering to anyone else," she recalled more than forty years later.[10] Through KPW, Guise was able to compare her writing and reporting techniques with those of other women in the state. And KPW's annual writing awards helped her and other members "become recognized as newspaperwomen, as journalists." By publishing announcements of the awards, KPW made people aware of women's accomplishments in newspaper work.[11]

Another longtime member, Marie McDonald, who joined KPW in 1947, appreciated how affiliation with the group helped members gain recognition and respect as professionals. McDonald worked for the *Wichita Eagle, Wichita Beacon*, KFDI Radio, and KARD-TV before retiring; she still wrote a column for *Active Aging*, a monthly Wichita newspaper, at the time of her death at 82. "We, in a sense, were the pioneers struggling for recognition," she said in an interview one year before her death in 1992. "In a short time we would be working for equal rights and other issues pertaining to women and children and sometimes men."[12]

KPW initially aligned itself, albeit unofficially, with the Kansas Press Association (KPA), which was organized in 1866. At first the relationship was amiable. The official KPA publication, the *Jayhawker Press*, announced the organization of KPW in a page-long article,[13] and the two groups began gathering for statewide meetings on the same weekends in the same hotels. However, by 1955, trouble was brewing over conflicts of time and space and in that year officers discussed moving the KPW convention to Sunday to avoid overlapping the KPA meeting. They suggested a change of schedules to avoid conflict: The KPW would host an informal welcoming party; the KPA would host its traditional banquet.[14]

A 1956 program indicates that KPW indeed needed its own time and space; it included papers on "News and Feature Writing," "News in Foreign Affairs," "Human Interest in the News," "News in Column Writing," and "News in Photography" all in one panel discussion moderated by Jim Reed, executive editor of the *Topeka Daily Capital*.[15] The next year, the problem of overlapping time and space became too much. The KPW "divorced" itself from the KPA and decided to hold its meetings at a separate time and place, entirely removed from KPA. Despite (or perhaps because of) this rather abrupt "divorce," KPW strengthened.[16] The group began holding separate conferences, with schedules lengthy enough to accommodate lectures by nationally prominent women journalists as well as skills-oriented workshops taught by experts, both male and female. According to Guise, "It was the beginning of a more professional organization of working newswomen other than wives of editors. Of course, in the [nineteen-] fifties that is the title and recognition we rated, whether we were on the job full time or married to the editor."[17]

In keeping with its professional interests, KPW occasionally lobbied for legislation that would directly affect women working as journalists. In the early 1990s, for example, the organization worked for open meetings laws and freedom of information in Kansas through letter-writing campaigns.[18] It also occasionally promoted broader political change. By the early 1970s, for example, KPW was ready to support a cause that might have surprised its founders. Though the effort was never unanimous,[19] the group, both collectively and as individual members, worked for women's equality, for retention of the Equal Rights Amendment (ERA) in Kansas, and for its national ratification and adoption.[20] Members participated in letter-writing campaigns, and the KPW newsletter encouraged grassroots efforts aimed at convincing Kansas legislators not to rescind their 1972 ratification of the ERA. In fact, the organization's newsletters throughout the mid-1970s reiterated KPW's stand on ERA, encouraged letters to lawmakers as well as conversations with neighbors, and asked members to write columns and editorials favoring the amendment. At least a few of these pro-ERA editorials were published.[21]

Throughout its existence, KPW fostered a supportive community for journalists who lived and worked a long way from the larger urban newspapers. Workshops in writing and editing built skills for women who might not have had the opportunity to take a journalism class but who worked as writers and editors for rural and small-town publications. In a 1956 letter, NFPW officer Bless wrote of the importance of these newspaperwomen:

Most of them (big city newspaperwomen) over the country "look down their noses" at N.F.P.W. and the state organizations. . . . Of course, one cannot be too critical when one realizes that 99% of them in the last analysis are just hirelings. . . . So while they may be "big names" because they are with a big city paper, I do not think they have the interest of the press, as a whole, at heart nearly as much as the humble little worker on a four-page weekly. That is why I am forever preaching the potentialities of the small town newspaper women.[22]

Through membership in KPW, these small-town newspaper women provided support for each other; they celebrated journalistic values and the worth of weekly, community journalism, in which the reporter-editor is a part of her community, not an outside observer.[23] A typical example of such a woman was Ruth McMillion, a KPW member who worked for the *Clark County Clipper*. In 1981 she characterized the life of a community newspaper woman as more than just news work: "It has been a short 30 years mixed with cooking for men on the farm, raising a niece and daughter, doing committee works of a small town, dabbling in paint, and baby-sitting with three grandchildren."[24]

It is not surprising, then, that finding time and funding to attend state meetings was often difficult for women who worked in media jobs in small, isolated Kansas towns. By the mid-1970s, the group had adopted a district system that allowed members unable to attend state conferences to gather regularly with other members for district meetings closer to home. Despite the difficulties, however, participation in statewide conferences was still "good," at least according to KPW literature. The strong attendance was credited to strong programs "related to practical techniques for doing one's job better, legal and ethical questions affecting professional communicators and—an increasingly important topic—women in management (everything from how to get there to how to survive once you've arrived)."[25]

Another incentive to join KPW might have been the communications contest awards, which added to women journalists' prestige and credibility. For dues-paying members, awards went to the best work in a number of categories. In the 1950s, these included the following: women's section, newspaper or magazine regularly edited by a woman (daily, weekly and trade), biographical article, fashion and home furnishing article, news story, editorial, feature, interpretive article, photography, radio and television program, and display advertising. By 1990, other categories had been added to reflect women's expanding presence in journalism, including column writing, sections and/or supplements edited by the entrant, page layout, heading, caption writing and original graphics, printed media advertising, and special series. Special student categories had been added in news writing and photography, sports, yearbook copy, and yearbook photography.[26]

Scholarships became an important part of KPW service to Kansas journalism in 1947 when Mrs. Frank Haucke was named chairman of the group's first scholarship committee, which began raising funds to present a Kansas girl a scholarship to an accredited journalism school. Charter member Mamie Boyd was an early supporter of these scholarships, "often dug into her own pocket for the necessary dollars," and later initiated her own KPW scholarship, which is still in existence.[27] Single scholarships were awarded regularly for more than twenty years. Then during the 1970s, KPW presented three scholarships at its fall meetings, and a decade later it annually awarded stipends totaling $2,000 to four communications students, one each from the University of Kansas, Kansas State University, Wichita State University, and Fort Hays State University. By 1982, fifty-two scholarships had been awarded, and a survey showed that of the thirty-four who responded, twenty-nine were working in communications. The scholarship program was still in existence in 1998, aided in part by a "patrons program" for "Kansans of worthy accomplishments who are interested in journalism and communications and have given support to Kansas Press Women."[28] The list of patrons is impressive and includes the names of former U.S. senator Nancy Landon Kassebaum and former Secretary of Transportation Elizabeth Dole.

As part of its outreach program, KPW also sponsored several youth programs as well, including high school writing contests, and joined NFPW with "On the Job with a Media Pro," a program that allowed high school students to spend a day on the job with a KPW member. The group still honors outstanding high school journalists, both male and female.[29]

KPW members were kept up to date on these activities by the organization's newsletter, which also offered tidbits about members' personal and professional lives, including job changes, promotions, and awards. Prior to March 1991 KPW's official publication had various names and an irregular schedule. The newsletter was published first as the *Kansas Press Woman*, then the *Kansas Press WomeNewsletter*, and finally, in winter 1987, as *CommuniKPW*. *CommuniKPW* still offered information about programs and awards, but it also includes features about media issues. For example, a 1994 issue featured articles on "Surfing the Net" and "A Legal Update on the First Amendment."[30]

CHALLENGES

In 1998, more than fifty years after it began, KPW included among its members more than one hundred individuals who worked full time, part time, and freelance at newspapers, magazines, radio, television, corporations, agencies, and institutions of higher education. Because of faltering participation, the semi-annual meetings were reduced in 1995 to annual spring meetings,[31] but its activities continued. Scholarships and communications awards still recognized students and journalists from Kansas communities, and the group continued to exhibit an interest in ethics and professional development, as did members at the first meeting in 1941.[32]

But there were changes in membership requirements for KPW, including the one that designated members as "women." When the group organized, of course, only women were invited to join, and the 1952 KPW constitution states that membership was limited to women. By 1974, however, that designation was changed, perhaps in an effort to attract and maintain a broader and larger membership, perhaps in an effort to adopt a more egalitarian stance. In that year, the *KPW Handbook* changed the membership designation from "any woman" to "anyone" who had worked in communications for a year. In the September 1983 *Kansas Press WomeNewsletter*, an article explains that members may "be either male or female, but must support the ideals of professional standards and the efforts of women within the profession to realize their full rights and privileges."[33] The change went unheralded in the KPW newsletters, and it was apparently not controversial.[34] Over the years, several men have joined the group and actively participated in its programs, although in 1998 there was only one male member.

"KPW is a professional organization, not a social club," states the 1998 brochure. "Our membership extends past any limitations of the 'press.' We are communicators who welcome both men and women as members."[35] In that same year, KPW president Carol Hockersmith, a freelance editor based in Manhattan, and other KPW members were working to recruit new members and strengthen the program. In a development that would seem ironic to its founders, KPW is now trying to convince "a new group of people that it's OK to be part of a women's group."[36]

"The value of belonging [to KPW] is the chance to be connected," said Hock-ersmith, echoing the sentiments of founder Eulalia Guise.[37] In the last years of the twentieth century, the biggest challenge for KPW's leaders was to promote professional development and offer networking opportunities that fit in with members' hectic 1990s lifestyles. The membership requirements might have changed, but many of the goals and projects of KPW had remained constant. The organization still provided camaraderie and professional encouragement for media workers in the prairie towns of Kansas, both large and small.

NOTES

1. Eulalia T. Guise, "Kansas Press Women, Inc., History," Program for the twentieth anniversary convention, 30 April–1 May 1966, Washington, Kansas, Kansas Press Women Papers, Manuscript Collection 223 (hereafter KPW Papers), box 9, Manuscripts Department, Kansas State Historical Society, Topeka, Kansas.

2. Kansas Press Women letters and program notes located in the KPW Papers in-dicate women did have to struggle to find time and money to attend meetings throughout the organization's history. For example, a letter postmarked 20 October 1980, noted the "trials and tribulations of a small daily newspaper" as reason for missing that year's meeting. Speaker notes from the KPW fiftieth anniversary meeting, 17 October 1991, said, "Nearly every past president remembers: We were poor; we made do. . . . Many of us recall that in the early 1970s we weren't always sure we could afford the drive to 'convention.' " KPW Papers, box 5.

3. Susie B. Junkin, "A Report of the Meeting of the Kansas Woman's Press Asso-ciation," *The Newspaper West* 4, no.5 (1896): 155.

4. Ibid.

5. Guise, "Kansas Press Women, Inc., History."

6. Ibid.

7. Ibid.

8. KPW Papers, box 2.

9. Carol Francis, former KPW historian, has put together a year-by-year history of the organization from information in the Manuscripts Department of the Kansas State Historical Society, using the organization's newsletter, *CommuniKPW*, as a primary re-source beginning in 1987. For earlier years, a decade-by-decade account was printed in the 1987 *Kansas Press Women Handbook*. Contained in the KPW Papers, box 10.

10. Eulalia T. Guise, interview with author, Marysville, Kansas, 21 February 1998.

11. Ibid.

12. "Interview Lends Insight into the Early Days in the Profession," *CommuniKPW*, September 1991, KPW Papers, box 11.

13. See "Kansas Newspaper Women Organize," *Jayhawker Press*, April 1941, KPW Papers, box 10.

14. Jane Denner to Mrs. Byron Guise, 25 October 1955, KPW Papers, box 5.

15. See the KPW convention and meeting agendas for 1956, KPW Papers, box 8.

16. Eulalia T. Guise, "Former KPW President Reflects on the Past," *Kansas Press WomeNewsletter*, spring 1982, p. 1, KPW Papers, box 11.

17. Guise interview 21 February 1998.

18. "KPW Speaks Out for Freedom of Information," *CommuniKPW*, July 1992, KPW Papers, box 11.

19. Carol Francis, telephone interview with author, 15 July 1998.

20. "Kansas Press Women, Inc., History," *Kansas Press Women Handbook*, 1987, KPW Papers, box 9.

21. See, for example, "Abzug Predicts ERA Success in Three Years," *Topeka Capital Journal*, 31 March 1979, p. 14; Kerry Barsotti, "Give ERA New Life, Fair Shake," *University Daily Kansan*, 13 July 1978, p. 4; "Equal Rights Require Constitutional Guarantee," *University Daily Kansan*, 1 July 1982, p. 4. The legislature eventually rescinded ERA in 1973 and every year from 1975 to 1979, but none of these attempts passed.

22. Mrs. B. J. Bless, Jr., to Eulalia T. Guise, 4 June 1956, KPW Papers, box 5.

23. For more about community journalism, see Jock Lauterer, *Community Journalism: The Personal Approach* (Ames: Iowa State University Press, 1995).

24. Mrs. Ruth McMillion to KPW, 4 April 1981, KPW Papers, box 5.

25. "Kansas Press Women, Inc., History," *Kansas Press Women Handbook 1987*, KPW Papers, box 5.

26. *Kansas Press Women Handbook 1987*; KPW program notes and press clippings of awards programs, KPW Papers, boxes 5 and 17.

27. See "Mamie Boyd," *Kansas Press WomeNewsletter*, December 1977, KPW Papers, box 11. The Boyd family has been long involved in community journalism in Kansas. The Huck Boyd Center for Community Journalism at Kansas State University is named for Mamie Boyd's son McDill "Huck" Boyd. For more about this charter KPW member, see her autobiographical account of pioneer life in Kansas: Mrs. Frank W. Boyd, *Rode a Heifer Calf through College* (Brooklyn: Pageant-Poseidon, 1972).

28. "Bylaw Changes," *Kansas Press WomeNewsletter*, September 1979, KPW Papers, box 11.

29. Some names of scholarship winners and lists of patrons are located in the Manuscripts Department of the Kansas State Historical Society. The contest was opened to young men as well as young women in 1975. See "NFPW Board Action," *Kansas Press WomeNewsletter*, December 1975, KPW Papers, box 11.

30. See Nancy Borst, "Surfing the Net," *CommuniKPW* 7, no.2 (1994): 4; and Sherry Pigg, "A Legal Update on the First Amendment," *CommuniKPW* 7, no.2 (1994): 5, both in KPW Papers, box 11.

31. See the report of the KPW board of directors; also see "Where Were You?" in *CommuniKPW*, May 1995, KPW Papers, box 11.

32. See the brochure for the annual spring conference, 1 and 2 May 1998, in Abilene Kansas. KPW Papers, box 5.

33. See the explanation of membership requirements, *Kansas Press WomeNewsletter*, September 1983, KPW Papers, box 11.

34. Carol Francis, telephone interview by author, 15 July 1998.

35. See the organization's current brochure, *Introducing Kansas Press Women Inc.*, KPW Papers, box 9.

36. Carol Hockersmith, telephone interview by author, 17 July 1998.

37. Ibid.

INFORMATIONAL SOURCES

Boyd, Mrs. Frank W. *Rode a Heifer Calf through College* (Brooklyn: Pageant-Poseidon, 1972).

"Guise Is Named KPW Woman of Achievement." *The Marysville Advocate*, 19 October 1989, 1B.

Junkin, Susie B. "A Report of the Meeting of the Kansas Woman's Press Association,"
    The Newspaper West 4, no. 5 (1896): 155.
Kansas Press Women Papers, Manuscript Collection 223. Manuscripts Department, Kan-
    sas State Historical Society, Topeka, Kansas.
Lauterer, Jock. *Community Journalism: The Personal Approach* (Ames: Iowa State Uni-
    versity Press, 1995).

INSTITUTIONAL PROFILE

Kansas Press Women Inc.

Dates: Organized 28 March 1941, Topeka, Kansas; affiliated with National Federation
of Press Women in 1941.

Publication: Before March 1991, the official publication of Kansas Press Women had
various names and an irregular schedule. The newsletter was published first as the
Kansas Press Woman, then the *Kansas Press WomeNewsletter*, and finally, in 1987,
as *CommuniKPW*. A partial list of editors includes Lynn Harmon, Elvira Crocker, and
Diane Lewis of Wichita; Kalen Larson of Derby; Rosie Rebek of Topeka; Martha
Elliott of Wichita; Marcia Dill of Plainville; Ruth Ann Messner of Andover; Janice
Early-Weas of Holton; and Nancy Borst of Goddard. Located in the Kansas Press
Women Papers (Collection 223), box 11, at the Kansas State Historical Society, Man-
uscripts Department.

Papers: Kansas Press Women Papers (Collection 223), Manuscripts Department, Kansas
State Historical Society, Topeka, Kansas.

Contact: Carol Hockersmith, President, 9 Argon, Goddard, Kansas 67502.

13

Willah Weddon

Michigan Press Women, 1965–Present
(Formerly Michigan Women's Press Club)

GETTING ORGANIZED

Although Michigan women journalists had organized at least two state women's press groups by the turn of the twentieth century, this had been forgotten by 1964 when Sharon Nelton of Michigan State University called a meeting to consider the formation of such an association. "I don't think any of us knew there were any earlier women's press organizations. I certainly did not know. ... We were brand new," she stated in 1998 in response to a query from this author.[1]

Nelton had decided it was time that the state's women journalists had their own organization. The Michigan Press Association, then the major press organization in the state, admitted only newspapers as members, and although women who worked for those newspapers could participate in its meetings, those who wrote as freelancers or for employers other than newspapers were excluded.[2]

Nelton, who worked in the Michigan State University (MSU) Department of Information Services, made arrangements for a luncheon meeting to be held on the MSU campus in East Lansing on October 17, 1964, in the Kellogg Center for Continuing Education. Forty-four newspaperwomen from all parts of the state responded to her invitation, and one of the first topics of discussion was who should be admitted as members. Dorothy Jurney, the women's editor at the *Detroit Free Press*, advised keeping membership to a very professional group of women "vitally interested in the newspaper business."[3] The substance of Jurney's recommendation and Nelton's plan to restrict the organization "strictly" for press women, was an echo of the debate among press women seventy-five years before this gathering. In 1892, members of the broadly defined Michigan Woman's Press Association* split off to establish the more professionally oriented Michigan Woman's Press Club.*

At the Lansing session, however, those issues took a back seat to the task of establishing the new organization. The women chose the name "Michigan Women's Press Club" (MWPC) and elected an eight-woman committee to create a constitution and make plans for the next meeting. As a result, a founders meeting was held the following February in Gaylord. Here, members named a nominating committee, decided the club should meet twice annually, and set a July date for the first meeting, which would be held in St. Joseph.

At the Gaylord meeting, the organization's objectives were defined. They were to educate members through seminars, workshops, and other means; to provide an opportunity for Michigan press women to know one another and share ideas; to recruit qualified young people into journalism through scholarships; and to conduct contests among members as a means of improving writing and newspaper-related skills.

In order to qualify as an active member, a woman had to be from the working press and to have served one year as a regularly employed staff writer or editor of a Michigan newspaper. Employees of a wire service and full-time correspondents were also eligible if they had worked for one year in the state. Associate membership was open to women who had been active for at least one year in the club but were temporarily incapacitated, unemployed, retired, working in another field, or living in another state. An associate membership could also be held by a woman whose major occupation was in a field directly related to newspapering but not directly connected with the operation of a daily or non-daily newspaper. This left the door open to women in public relations but apparently overlooked the relatively small number of women working in radio or television. To cover all bases in the future, however, eligibility in all related fields was to be determined by the executive board with recommendations from the membership. In keeping with the focus on professional concerns, it was decided that the organization would hold annual writing contests and present the awards for these contests during winter meetings. Officers were to be elected during summer meetings.

These decisions and the organization's objectives were formally adopted in the bylaws by the thirty-five women attending the first official meeting in July 1965. They also elected the first slate of officers. Luise Leismer, a Petoskey native who had recently accepted an editorial staff position with the *Royal Oak Daily Tribune*, was elected president.[4]

ISSUES AND WOMAN'S ROLE

Equal rights in employment and in the newsroom was an issue high on the agenda of these women during these years, and they spoke of it frequently at meetings of the press club. Both the discussion of these issues and the opinions individual members held on them illustrated many of the conflicts experienced by women professionals during the 1960s and 1970s. A speech given by charter member Doris M. Jarrell at the 1965 meeting provides an example of some of the conflicted views that often existed within a single individual. Jarrell, who was the Grand Rapids bureau chief for the *Detroit Free Press*, was one of the few women who had risen into management. "Women have a place in newspaper work and the first challenge each encounters is overcoming discrimination because of her sex," she advised her listeners. "Sometimes I think we newspaper women spend too much time complaining about our lot and not enough time trying to do a good job."[5]

Others, instead, assigned the responsibility for women's lack of progress in journalism to the newspaper industry rather than to the individual woman. "Although the newspaper industry is slowly beginning to accept women in areas other than Women's Pages, complete acceptance is a long time in coming," wrote Kathy Tarr, editor of the MWPC newsletter, *Banner Lines*, in its first issue.[6]

Indeed, if Tarr and the other MWPC members had been aware of the state's earlier press women's associations, they would have realized that women journalists had not made much headway during the past seventy-five years. A survey of the 1965 membership showed that the few members who held management positions were editors of women's pages and that women were also still receiving lower salaries than their male counterparts. For example, whereas the average beginning salary offered to men graduating from the MSU journalism program in 1960 was $5,244 per year, women graduates were offered only $3,564. The penalty for being a female, in this case, was $1,680 per year.[7]

One of the major goals of the MWPC was to encourage more women to enter journalism and to excel in the field. To this end, the club offered encouragement through contests in which good work would be rewarded; it also awarded scholarships to assist in the cost of a college education. During the organization's first year, it launched its writing contest, and by the time the next meeting was held in February 1966 in Jackson, the first writing contest winners were announced. A scholarship fund had also been started that year to recruit qualified students into the field of journalism.

Also in 1966, a contest was held to create a logo for the club. Ginger Sharp, a dark-room technician at the *Lansing State Journal* and the only full-time female photographer at a Michigan newspaper, created the winning logo. It depicted the image of a typewriter with the letters MWPC printed on a sheet of paper inserted in its roller.[8]

In that year, some of the MWPC members received significant promotions. Charter member and treasurer Dorothy Magee, the women's editor at the *Macomb Daily*, was named the newspaper's associate editor. Connie Reed MacLeese, a reporter for the *Jackson Citizen Patriot*, was assigned to the Washington bureau of Booth Newspapers, the first woman to be given that position.[9]

This same year, an article in *Banner Lines* described the course of these changes for women in the newspaper profession. The author, MSU professor William Haight, traced the changes he had seen in placing female journalism students in jobs up to this time:

In the late fifties, all the girls wanted to become general-assignment reporters; all the publishers wanted to hire them as society writers. This went on for years and years. Three things changed the situation in the past few years. One was the declining J-school enrollments which created a favorable balance. There just weren't enough men to go around. Next came the federal Civil Rights legislation. No one knew at first just what it meant, but it sure put a quick scare into publishers who had been buying females for the low dollar, doing the same jobs as men. . . . Recruiters began to give the full allotted 30 minutes to interviewing each female journalist when they came to campus. Finally, the Vietnam flare-up and consequent increased draft quotas drained off most of the eligible male journalists. Publishers began to sense that the draft was as great an unknown factor as the diamond ring or the blessed event; traditionally the excuse for treating all women as short-term, nonprofessional employees.[10]

Haight also pointed out that the difference between women's and men's starting salaries in journalism was shrinking somewhat; in 1966 there was only a 4 percent difference, with men starting at $6,212 a year and women at $5,923.[11]

The fact that more women were being hired by newspapers and that their salaries were improving, however, did not mean they had resolved their struggles for equality. MWPC member Peg Dawson Guthaus recalled that "the women were stuck in a corner behind a partition" when she started work at the *Kalamazoo Gazette* in 1966. Guthaus, who had graduated from the University of Missouri with a bachelor's degree in journalism in 1948, covered women's issues at first, but over the twenty-six years she spent with the *Gazette*, saw many gradual changes in positions held by women. She, for example, eventually moved from social news to education and on to covering local news beats.[12] Some other MWPC members, instead, rose quickly to influential positions. In 1968, Ann Frahm, who had founded the Almanac Publishing Company in Grand Rapids, was named the first woman to serve on the board of directors for Michigan Newspapers, Inc.

The National Federation of Press Women (NFPW)* invited MWPC to become an affiliate in 1968. After considering the advantages of belonging to the national organization, the membership voted its approval, and in June 1969 the MWPC was officially affiliated. From that time on MWPC adapted to the structure of the national body. The Michigan group sent its presidents and delegates to NFPW conventions and entered the winners of its writing contests, annual Woman of Achievement awards, and high school writing contests in the NFPW's national competitions.

Many newspapers encouraged their employees to join professional organizations such as the MWPC and the NFPW and a few even paid their expenses to attend meetings, but some apparently considered them a threat that might challenge newspaper hiring, assignment, and promotion policies. In 1970, MWPC president Arlys Derrick (of the *Benton Harbor Herald Press*) responded to these fears by emphasizing that MWPC was a professional association dedicated to promoting professional interests among women journalists through networking and not a unionized organization primarily interested in obtaining financial benefits for its members.[13] This did not mean, however, that the women were not interested in improving their salaries.

In 1970, MWPC had ninety-eight members, ninety-six of whom were active (one was a life member, one an honorary member). Many served as mentors and role models to women following them in the profession and made sure that significant news about women was disseminated. During these years, charter member Dorothy Jurney was a leader, both as an editor and as a role model, in helping qualified women achieve higher positions. In 1973, she became assistant managing editor of the *Detroit Free Press*, which she left in 1974 to become managing editor of the *Philadelphia Inquirer*. Following her retirement from the *Inquirer* in 1975, Jurney founded the Woman's Network, an executive search firm for newspapers. She became an associate member of the MWPC after leaving Michigan in 1974 and continued to play a role in the organization following her retirement.

Even as women editors and journalists began to find themselves in a position to promote women and women's issues on the women's pages and in their news columns, some began (or continued) to criticize and reject that material. In a speech during a July 1968 MWPC meeting, for example, Kurt Luedtke of the *Detroit Free Press*, told the press women, "Newspaper writing is generally pretty bad. Women's subject writing tends to be generally worse. . . . The women's pages view of women is very narrow. . . . If I was a woman and I thought this is the way you see me, I would be insulted." At the same time, some women editors were beginning to send out the message that "first" women were no longer feature material. Apparently women were gaining so much ground in so many fields that when they did earn top positions, they were no longer considered unique. In another example, this author, who established a Women's News Bureau in Lansing in 1972 to report on women's political activities at the capitol for a dozen state newspapers, was told by the male publisher of a small northern weekly that he wanted no more reports about women sent to his paper.[14] In this case, the offending stories that reported "too much" on women's news were about the most controversial "woman's" issue of the time, the contested passage of the Equal Rights Amendment.[15]

ACTIVITIES

In 1973, the MWPC hosted the NFPW convention in Dearborn. Ruth Carlton, a writer and editor for the *Detroit News*, had been named Michigan's Woman of Achievement that year and then took first place in the NFPW national competition, the only Michigan woman to win that distinction to this date. Two years later, MWPC sponsored an International Women's Year (IWY) Banquet in East Lansing. The event was planned to honor women working in communications and was held on the MSU campus. Ruth Bacon, director of the U.S. Center for International Women's Year, was guest speaker. She had brought the International Woman's Year event almost single-handedly to the United States and was determined to bring the lowly status of women around the world to the attention of all citizens She cited a series on IWY written by NFPW president Jean Wiley Huyler to illustrate what could be done by press women to help improve the conditions of women.

The number of women employed in journalism continued to rise through the 1970s, and in 1976 MSU journalism professor Mary Gardner reported that the majority of students graduating from the MSU program were now women, with sixty-four female graduates to every fifty male graduates. Recognition and promotion for MWPC members was also taking place. In 1978, three received special accolades: Marcia Van Ness, editor of the *Lansing State Journal*'s "Living Today" section, was elected the first woman president of the Central Michigan chapter of the Society of Professional Journalists, Sigma Delta Chi; MWPC founder Sharon Nelton was made one of four new vice presidents and a member of the board of *Farm Journal, Inc.*; and Marilyn Wright was named chief of the Ottaway News Service Bureau in Albany, New York.

The gender barriers that had kept women in their "proper place" for so long seemed to be coming down. Male press organizations were admitting women members, and women's organizations followed suit, though often with some hesitations. The NFPW voted to admit men to membership during its 1972 convention, but the Michigan organization did not open its doors to men until 1976. Marvin Guthaus, who was the first to join, had regularly attended meetings with his wife, Peg, from the time she became a member in 1966. During those years, he had presented several programs on computers and their potential in research. In 1994, he was chosen the organization's Communicator of Achievement, the first and only male to receive the award in Michigan. A second male member to receive acclaim was Kendall Wingrove, a journalism major at Central Michigan University, who three years later won a $1,000 NFPW scholarship. He was the first male to ever win the NFPW award, which for some years had been offered to both male and female students.

Another change came in 1984 when the MWPC became concerned that the word *club* in its title did not accurately represent the professional status of its activities or members. Thus it, like many of the other press clubs affiliated with the NFPW, changed its name to Michigan Press Women (MPW).

Although by the mid-1980s women were routinely employed by news organizations and were even being promoted to positions of authority, issues of sex discrimination and harassment were still of concern to members and still appeared on the organization's agenda. Thus, in 1985, three members employed in newspaper editorial sections presented a panel discussion on "Surviving in a Male-Dominated Profession." The interest shown in this topic served to illustrate that there was still much to be done before women gained full recognition in the workplace. Though serious, the topics of discrimination and harassment were occasionally treated with wry humor. In 1987, Carol Ankney, the senior editor of the Sturgis *Journal*, who was first-place winner in the 1988 NFPW Communication Contest Sweepstakes, reminisced on her rise in the profession. She had started her career as a proofreader and worked her way up until she became senior editor at the *Journal*. Along the way, she told her audience, she overcame discrimination by rather unusual but effective methods:

One male boss treated women like second class reporters, if that. He said we should write society news and make coffee. He also thought we should make chocolate cupcakes. And so I made them. The rest of the staff got plain ones, he got the X-Lax ones. He was busy all day as I recall. And, he never asked me to do that again.[16]

Stories like this, as well as stories of women's continuing struggles and triumphs were often the topic of meetings and workshops. In 1989, for example, one of the speakers at a workshop was Marion Marzolf, a professor at the University of Michigan and author of a text on women journalists, *Up from the Footnote*.

Meanwhile, an increasing number of Michigan women were serving in NFPW positions, ranging from elective offices to chairing committees. Not only were MPW members active within their own organization and the NFPW, but several also joined Women in Communications, Inc.* They took part in other women's associations, too. Marion Grattan, of the *Jackson Citizen Patriot*, for example, organized the first Jackson Area Chapter of the National Organization of Women in 1974 and served as the chapter's first president. Dorothy Brush, of Lansing, served as Conference Coordinator in 1976 for the Michigan International Women's Year observance and was a charter member of Michigan ERAmerica.

MPW hosted the 1992 NFPW conference in Lansing; the theme was "Promote Your Professionalism." More than 265 members of the press from across the nation attended the conference, and tours included one to the Michigan Women's Historical Center and Hall of Fame. The Hall of Fame honors, among others, Luise Leismer Mahon, MPW's first president; and Ruth Carlton, MPW's 1973 National Woman of Achievement. These women, as well as MPW charter member Virginia Baird, who in 1995 was honored with a Special Service Award by the Michigan Journalism Hall of Fame "for her many contributions in support of Michigan journalism," lent prestige and some fame to the organization, but interest began to wane after the mid-1990s.

FACING NEW CHALLENGES

By 1998, MPW membership had dropped from a high of nearly one hundred to approximately forty. Dedicated members were concerned about this loss and attributed it in part to an increase in 1992 of NFPW dues to $50. Combined with the state dues of $15, that brought the annual total for each individual membership to $65.[17] The increase had been instituted by the NFPW, which had reached a point in the 1990s when it was overspending annually and dipping into its reserve funds. The MPW soon found itself in the same financial situation.

Although other women's organizations were experiencing similar declines in membership, an objective appraisal of the MPW might suggest that it had in a sense outlived its goals. When a large enough number of women had achieved positions of comparative equality and responsibility in the workplace, it is possible they no longer felt the need for support from a woman's association. Faced with the need to balance demanding professional and family responsibilities, they might not have had enough time or incentive left to improve their professional development through membership in an organization. They certainly had less time for volunteer work, and this resulted in higher expenses for association budgets. It may also be true that human beings join together for the good of all only when facing adversity.

In an attempt to bolster its position, the MPW took several steps that broadened its appeal, on the one hand, but threatened to weaken its ties with the NFPW, on the other. In 1997, it extended membership to individuals in fields allied with journalism and offered a special $15 one-year membership rate to these recruits. In 1998, it offered some autonomy to members who might not want to pay the more expensive NFPW dues. MPW decided to allow communications contest entries by state-only members with the provision that if a first-place winner wanted to be entered in the NFPW competition, the member at that time would have to pay the NFPW dues for full membership.

The results of this strategy for the MPW are still to be determined. As for its association with the NFPW and the survival of that organization, only with an increase of membership numbers in its state affiliates will the NFPW have the resources to improve its own membership total. Clearly, as NFPW president Linn Rounds stated in 1998, "We must adapt or die."[18]

NOTES

1. See related chapters on the Michigan Woman's Press Association, founded in 1890, and the Michigan Woman's Press Club, founded in 1892.

2. The Michigan Press Association admitted newspapers as members at that time. This included publishers, editors, and staff members, but individuals of either sex were not accepted as members. The latter stipulation excluded many Michigan women journalists who were freelance writers or wrote in various capacities for employers other than newspapers. Elmer White, past executive director of the MPA, interview by the author, 17 August 1998.

3. Noreen Murphy, from notes taken while she was secretary for the founders meeting held in Gaylord, 26–28 February 1965.

4. Leismer joined the *Detroit News* staff a year later and was one of the first women in the state to be named to a sports section.

5. Excerpt from Doris Jarrell's speech at the MPWC July meeting, *Banner Lines*, 15 September 1965, p. 1.

6. Kathy Tarr, untitled editorial, *Banner Lines*, September 1965.

7. William Haight, "Women in Journalism," *Banner Lines*, April 1967, p. 3.

8. *Banner Lines*, October 1966, p. 6.

9. Ibid.

10. Haight, "Women in Journalism," p. 3.

11. Ibid.

12. Laura Zahn Pohl, "Reflecting Women's Realilty," *Michigan Women's Times*, 17 November–10 December 1994, p. 10.

13. Notes taken by the author during the 1970 MWPC business meeting in Detroit.

14. Personal files of the author, 1974.

15. The Michigan legislature approved the amendment, although it later failed to win the required approval from other states for ratification.

16. Excerpt from Ankney's acceptance speech when she was presented with the NFPW Sweepstakes Award at the Little Rock, Arkansas, 1988 NFPW conference. Quoted in Willah Weddon, *Michigan Press Women, Today and Yesterday* (Stockbridge, Mich.: Weddon Press, 1996), p. 70.

17. Membership in NFPW had also declined from more than 4,000 in 1992 to 2,085 in 1998. NFPW president Linn Rounds warned, "NFPW is at a crossroads. With increasing costs and decreasing memberships . . . NFPW cannot continue to spend beyond its income." See *NFPW AGENDA*, May/June 1998, p. 1.

18. Ibid.

INFORMATIONAL SOURCES

Banner Lines, 1965–98, passim.

Michigan Press Women Papers. State Archives of Michigan, Michigan Historical Center, Lansing, Michigan.

Press Woman, 1969–99, passim.

Weddon, Willah. *Michigan Press Women, Today and Yesterday*. Stockbridge, Mich.: Weddon Press, 1996.

INSTITUTIONAL PROFILE

Michigan Press Women

Dates: Organized 26 July 1965 in St. Joseph, Michigan as **Michigan Women's Press Club**; affiliated with National Federation of Press Women in 1969; changed name in 1984 to **Michigan Press Women**.

Newsletter: *Banner Lines*, 1965–98. Editors: Kathy Tarr, 1965; Marge Waldo, 1966; Ellen Gondeck, 1967; Margaret Demetrak, 1969; Willah Weddon, 1972; Sandra Engle, 1974; Dorothy Brush, 1976; Ardyce Czuchna-Curl, 1980; Grace Kaledo, 1982; Cheryl Higginson, 1984; Rosalyn Ridgway, 1985; and Arlys Derrick, 1987–present.

Papers: Michigan Press Women Papers, State Archives of Michigan, Michigan Historical Center, Lansing, Michigan. Papers include *Banner Lines* (1965–96), secretary's minutes, and other information.

Contacts: Patti DeAgostino (president, 1998–99), 6101 Robert Road, Traverse City, MI 49684, tel. (616) 943-3665; Cathy Stathakis (president-elect, 1998–99), Traverse City; Carole Eberly (vice president), East Lansing; Rosemary Horvath (secretary), Greenville; Naida Ayadi (treasurer), East Lansing.

14

Willah Weddon

Michigan Woman's Press Association, 1890–193(8)

ORGANIZATION

Nothing in the history of Michigan journalism created such a stir in professional circles as the organization of the Michigan Woman's Press Association (MWPA) in 1890. During the previous decade, women's organizations throughout the country had been growing in number and were devoted to a variety of interests, such as temperance and prohibition, moral reform, woman's rights and woman suffrage, culture and literature, labor reform, and the elimination of slums, poverty, and disease.[1]

Whereas women's press organizations had started to form in other states by the mid-1880s, in Michigan, it was not until 1889 that a handful of resolute newspaper women brought the subject of forming a women's press association before a meeting of the male-dominated Michigan Press Association. In response to their suggestion, "something like a groan was heard from the newspaper men," and it was obvious that the women needn't expect any help from that organization.[2]

These women were the wives (and assistants) of editors and publishers who brought them along to the meetings of the otherwise male press association. To their credit, their husbands supported these women. They worked side by side with their wives and were no doubt keenly aware of the vital role the women played in the success of their newspapers and equally aware of the importance of maintaining harmony in the workplace.

Thus, with the encouragement of their husbands, M. E. C. Bates of the *Grand Traverse Herald*, Etta Smith Wilson of the *Grand Rapids Telegram-Herald*, and Claudia Q. Murphy of the *Grand Rapids Democrat* proceeded to make plans and worked through the next year to arrange an organizational meeting for a women's press association of their own.[3]

The meeting was announced by a Detroit daily paper a few days prior to the session: "The lady newspaper men of the state will meet in Traverse City, July 22–24 [1890] to organize an association of their own."[4] This announcement, with the typical reference to women journalists as "lady newspaper men," heightened interest in the meeting. Fourteen women arrived by 9 A.M. of the first day in the parlors of the Park Place Hotel, and others soon followed. Thomas T. Bates, editor of the *Grand Traverse Herald* and E. L. Sprague, editor and publisher of the *Traverse Bay Eagle*, provided free printing of programs, notices, and circulars. The local Ladies Library Association arranged for the meeting parlors.

M.E.C. Bates, who had played a major role in planning the meeting, was delighted and surprised to find the women from all around the state were "earnest, capable women, editing departments, doing reportorial work, compiling news or helping their husbands in all around newspaper work; several, even, were found who owned and edited their papers, having come into possession of the business by inheritance or force of circumstances."[5]

By the close of the three-day meeting, the MWPA had been established and twenty-seven women from fifteen cities in the state had become charter members. Officers were elected, committees appointed, and plans laid for annual meetings. Membership was limited to "any woman regularly employed on the editorial staff of any paper published in Michigan." To qualify for membership, she was to pay the regular membership fee of $2, file an application for membership, and win the approval of a majority of those present at a regular meeting.[6]

The group elected Mrs. Frank Howard ("Aunt Frank"), editor of the Home Department of the *Detroit Tribune*, as president, M.E.C. Bates as vice president, Claudia Q. Murphy as recording secretary, Isadore Sutherland Miner of *Good Health Magazine* as corresponding secretary, and Belle MacArthur Perry of the *Charlotte Tribune* as treasurer.

Martha Rayne

One of the best known members of the MWPA was Martha Louise Woodworth Rayne of the *Detroit Free Press*, who was elected to serve on the executive committee. Rayne had been a "Sunday Writer" for the *Chicago Tribune*, written novels, and edited and published a guidebook, *Chicago and 100 Miles Around*, before moving to Michigan about 1879. She then began working for the *Free Press*, where she continued on the editorial staff until 1896.

Rayne was aware of the rising tide of feminism and a growing demand by women for careers outside the home. She had obtained information for stories that male reporters could not get and editors had begun to realize there was a place for women in their editorial departments. While writing for the *Chicago Tribune*, for example, Rayne had given a "full report" of the marriage of General Philip Sheridan, despite the fact that "all reporters were excluded and detectives placed in the house to prevent news being given out." And when all male reporters were denied access to Mrs. Abraham Lincoln, who was at that time confined in a mental institution at Batavia, Illinois, Rayne succeeded in getting an interview with the former first lady. Her story resulted in Mrs. Lincoln's release.[7]

In 1886, Rayne founded the country's first school of journalism. She was devoted to helping women enter the field of journalism (at a time when fewer than 3 percent of full-time journalists were women[8]) and dedicated to providing practical instruction for them so they would be prepared to fill opportunities when they arose. The new school, which was opened in Detroit, declared its goal to be "to cultivate a good literary style, to develop originality and fluency of expression in descriptive and creative work." It included in its course of study a wide variety of lessons, some of which were available by mail: "Preparation of manuscript. Words and how to use them. The art of saying things. Literary style. The art of taking pains. Reporting, essay writing, reviews, sketches, short stories, forms of poetry [and] novel writing."[9]

Rayne's enterprise was greeted with some skepticism—both from newsmen who typically rejected the idea of journalism schools well into the twentieth century and from those who thought it was not a woman's place to embark on such an undertaking. Only one local newspaper, the *Detroit Tribune*, reported its opening:

The new school of journalism just opened by Mrs. M. L. Rayne in the Abstract Building is attracting attention in various sections of the country. Many newspapers pooh-pooh the idea, but Mrs. Rayne is a thorough journalist, and may do the laughing herself later.[10]

According to one account, a New York editor told Rayne, "You had something very like presumption to call your institute a 'School of Journalism.' Charles Dana [of the *New York Sun*] is the only one capable of starting such an enterprise." Rayne was reported to have replied that after promoting the general idea of a journalism school, she had waited in vain for "some man to take it up." Finally, after receiving "constant letters from all over the country," she said, "I gave up waiting for Mr. Dana and started a school on such practical lines as my experience suggested."[11] With assistance from several other women in the MWPA, including her good friend Mrs. Lucy Leggett, Rayne's School of Journalism thrived against the odds until 1900.[12]

LINKS TO THE WOMAN'S MOVEMENT

Many of the members of the MWPA were involved in other women's organizations and activities and carried their messages from one to the other, providing links through this network. Rayne, for example, was also a member of the National Woman's Press Association, organized in 1885, and served as its Michigan vice president in 1886. Lucinda Hinsdale Stone of Kalamazoo, another of the charter members, started a Reading Club for women in 1844, which in 1852 became the Ladies Library Association. She wrote columns for Kalamazoo, Detroit, and Port Huron newspapers in which she urged women to further their education by joining the ladies library associations that were being established in cities throughout the state. In 1870 she had engineered the acceptance of the first woman student at the University of Michigan and, now in her seventies, played an active role in the formation of the MWPA. Her words were adopted as the association's motto at their first annual meeting, "Let us as women learn to put down self and work for a cause!"[13]

Belle Perry, who was to serve two terms as MWPA president in 1891 and 1892, was also involved in the woman's movement. An active worker in both the Women's Christian Temperance Union (WCTU) and the state and national suffrage movements, in 1889 she was the first woman in Charlotte to be elected to the school board. In 1892, she became a director for Michigan of the Association for the Advancement of Women, and in 1900, she was elected president of the Michigan State Federation of Women's Clubs.[14]

Mrs. S.E.V. Emery of Lansing, was another MWPA charter member who played a major role in other organizations. As early as 1868, when women's reform movements were in their infancy, and when a woman's sphere was still supposed to be limited to her home and family, Emery was raising questions of suffrage and temperance in her writings. She was one of the early members of the Knights of Labor as well as a member of the WCTU. In November 1892, she spoke before the national WCTU in Denver and was elected national superintendent of the department "Relation of Temperance to Labor and Capital."[15]

GOALS AND ACTIVITIES

Although a number of members were deeply involved in social issues, the emphasis of the MWPA was to improve women's standing as professional journalists rather than to bring about social changes or reform through their writings. The stated objective of the association, in fact, was the "general promotion of all matters of interest pertaining to the press, the mutual interchange of ideas and acquaintanceship for business and social purposes, and for fostering a spirit of unity and good-will among all women doing newspaper work in the State."[16]

The MWPA held its second meeting June 1891 in Battle Creek at the Battle Creek Sanitarium. The meeting was hosted by Dr. J. H. and Ella Ervilla Kellogg, who together published *Good Health Journal*. Not only did the Kelloggs make it a practice to hire women writers for their magazine, but they supported the MWPA in its formative stage and through the years. Ella was a charter member of the association and encouraged members of the staff also to join.

Ten new members were admitted into the association at this time, including

Frances C. Wood, of the *Grand Rapids Eagle*, and Emma L. Mills, of the *Grand Rapids Democrat*, who soon became central characters in a debate over the very nature and purpose of the association. The MWPA had originally defined itself as an organization for women writers who were staff members on Michigan newspapers. Now a proposal was made to open membership to any woman resident of the state who was a "literary worker," whether or not she was employed by a newspaper published within the state. Wood and Mills were staunchly opposed to broadening the membership requirement.

The controversy continued through the next year, and by the time the third annual meeting was held July 1892 at Bay View, it had come to a head. Members revised the bylaws to open membership to any woman resident of Michigan who wrote for any paper or magazine within the United States. In response, several members, including Mills and Wood, withdrew in protest and formed a separate organization, the Michigan Woman's Press Club (MWPC).* Most, however, continued their membership in MWPA. A few, in fact, retained their membership in MWPA, joined the newly formed MWPC, and were active in both groups. By 1896 there were one hundred members in MWPA, including general writers, magazine editors and authors.[17]

During subsequent years, annual meetings were held in various sites throughout the state and membership consisted of active, associate, honorary, and auxiliary categories. The principle goals of the association were illustrated in its conference programs: to give help and inspiration to those new in the profession; to provide lively round table discussions; to arrange lectures by prominent writers; and to stimulate social contacts among Michigan writers.[18]

News about these meetings and activities was disseminated through *The Interchange*, a newsletter published for nearly a decade, from 1893 to 1902. The monthly newsletter was edited by Belle Perry, whose husband was the publisher of the *Charlotte Tribune*. *The Interchange* ceased publication when Perry apparently became caught up in other projects, including the publication of a biography of MWPA founder Lucinda Stone.[19]

MWPA remained active until shortly before World War I, when competing interests, responsibilities, and circumstances led to a gradual reduction of its activities.[20] Ironically, the association's motto, "Let us, as women, learn to put down self, and work for a cause," may have been its undoing. When the United States entered the war, women journalists, many of whom were already active in social movements such as suffrage and prohibition, became even more involved when they joined in patriotic work such as the Red Cross in addition to their regular duties. This left them little time for attending professional meetings. The situation worsened in 1918, when gatherings of any type, including church services, were banned because of the nationwide influenza epidemic. MWPA meetings were discontinued.

The MWPA did not surface again until 1937, when the Illinois Woman's Press Association* held an organizational meeting to create a National Federation of Press Women (NFPW).* Fannie Sprague Talbot and Grace Greenwood

Browne, who had been active members of the MWPA until it ceased to meet shortly before World War I, were invited to attend as Michigan representatives. Talbot was appointed to act as a liaison for the state, and it was decided that Michigan would be approved as a founding member, contingent on its vote to affiliate later in the year.

Returning home, Talbot called a reorganizational meeting of the MWPA on September 3, 1937, at the Battle Creek Sanitarium. Margaret Y. Smith, editor and publisher of the *Tuscola County Pioneer Times*, was elected president; and Browne, who was living in Chicago, honorary president. Talbot was elected second vice president, and Marie Jay Cady, of Grand Rapids, third vice president.

Fourteen women attended the reorganizational meeting and apparently voted to affiliate with the NFPW because records of the 1938 NFPW convention in Chicago show that Michigan was accepted as a charter member. During this convention, Michigan's Smith was elected a regional vice president and Cady elected NFPW treasurer.

Another Michigan woman, Martha Moll, was elected a vice president for affiliates during the 1939 NFPW convention held in New York. But five years later, Fannie Talbot was still the NFPW representative-at-large for Michigan; apparently the Michigan group had failed to gather sufficient support to become a full-fledged NFPW affiliate. The MWPA had gradually disintegrated, and Talbot's attempts to revive the association failed.[21]

NOTES

1. Eleanor Flexner, *Century of Struggle: The Woman's Rights Movement in the United States*, rev. ed. (Cambridge, Mass.: Belknap Press of Harvard University, 1975), pp. 182–96.

2. *The Journalist*, August 1890, p. 11

3. Whenever possible, the author will use the Christian name of the women cited in this chapter. Because it was the frequent custom during this period for married women to use their husband's names, however, this is not always possible. In addition, some women, whether married or single, used only their initials in their newspaper work because it was easier to get their work published if it was not obvious they were a woman. Mabel Thayer Rouse, for example, "had poems published over the name M. Thayer Rouse, supposed, of course, to be a masculine hand," according to *The Literary Century*, May 1893, p. 413. Also, all cities and newspapers named are located in Michigan unless otherwise noted.

4. *The Literary Century*, May 1893, p. 384.

5. Ibid. M.E.C. Bates (her full name is never provided in references about her) was married to Thomas Bates, editor of the *Herald*. Her daughter, Mabel Bates, also worked at the *Herald*.

6. Michigan Woman's Press Association, *Proceedings of the Second Annual Session* (Battle Creek, Mich.: Wm C. Gage and Sons, 1982), p. 11.

7. *Leaves from Our Lives: Michigan Woman's Press Club* (Grand Rapids, Mich.: Dean Printing and Publishing Co., 1894), p. 11.

8. U.S. Census Office, *Compendium of the Eleventh Census, Part III* (Washington, D.C.: Government Printing Office, 1897), p. 516.

9. Undated handbill, quoted in James S. Bradshaw, "Mrs. Rayne's School of Journalism," *Journalism Quarterly*, 60, no. 3 (autumn 1983): 517.

10. "The City," *Detroit Tribune*, September 17, 1886, p. 4.

11. Cora S. Wheeler, "Mrs. M. L. Rayne," *The Journalist*, 24 February 1891, p. 1.

12. Rayne returned to Chicago during the 1890s, and Leggett continued the school until about 1900.

13. *Proceedings of the Second Annual Session*, p. 23. Lucinda Hinsdale Stone was known in Michigan as "The Mother of the Women's Club Movement."

14. Fran Harris, *Focus: Michigan Women, 1701–1977* (Michigan Coordinating Committee of the National Commission on the Observance of Women's Year, 1977), p. 47.

15. *The Literary Century*, May 1893, p. 415.

16. *Proceedings of the Second Annual Session*, p. 11.

17. Grace Greenwood Browne, "Michigan Woman's Press Association," *Michigan History Magazine* 34 (summer 1940); 311.

18. Ibid.

19. This is based on information obtained from the Library of Michigan, Lansing, where copies of *Interchange*, vols. 4–8 (1897–1902) had been cataloged but are now missing. The biography of Stone, published in 1902, is *Lucinda Hinsdale Stone: Her Life Story and Reminiscence*.

20. One of the association's last meetings was held in Detroit 27–29 May 1913.

21. "Mainly about Folks," *Battle Creek Enquirer and News*, 24 September 1944, p. 24.

INFORMATIONAL SOURCES

Bradshaw, James S. "Mrs. Rayne's School of Journalism." *Journalism Quarterly* 60, no. 3 (autumn 1983): 513–17.

Doll, Louis W. *A History of the Newspapers of Ann Arbor, 1829–1920*. Detroit: Wayne State University Press, 1959.

Harris, Fran. *Focus: Michigan Women, 1701–1977*. Michigan Coordinating Committee of the National Commission on the Observance of Women's Year, 1977.

The Literary Century, 1893, passim.

Michigan Woman's Press Association. *Proceedings of the Second Annual Session*. Battle Creek, Mich.: Wm C. Gage and Sons, 1892.

Michigan Woman's Press Club. *Leaves from Our Lives*. Grand Rapids, Mich.: Dean Printing and Publishing Company, 1894.

Weddon, Willah. *Michigan Press Women, Today and Yesterday*. Stockbridge, Mich.: Weddon Press, 1996.

Wheeler, Cora. "Mrs. M. L. Rayne." *The Journalist*, 24 February 1891, p. 1.

INSTITUTIONAL PROFILE

Michigan Woman's Press Association

Dates: Founded in Traverse City, 1890; became inactive ca. 1918; reorganized 1937–38; charter member NFPW 1938; ceased ca. 1940.

Newsletter: *The Interchange*. Published in Charlotte, Michigan, 1892–1902, Belle M. Perry, editor. Volumes 4–8 (1897–1902), cataloged in the Michigan State Library, Lansing. Holdings had disappeared by 1998.

Publication: Profiles of members are included in *The Literary Century*, edited and published by E. Cora DePuy, Ann Arbor, Michigan, May 1893, pp. 384–422. Available in the Michigan Historical Collections, Bentley Historical Library, University of Michigan, Ann Arbor, Michigan. Proceedings of the Second Annual Session of the Michigan Woman's Press Association are also located in the Bentley Historical Library.

15

Willah Weddon

Michigan Woman's Press Club, 1892–19(14)

ORGANIZATION

For women journalists organizing in Michigan toward the end of the nineteenth century, the issue of who should be allowed as a member quickly became divisive. When the Michigan Woman's Press Association (MWPA),* which was founded in 1890 by and for women on the staffs of Michigan newspapers, considered expanding its qualifications to admit any Michigan woman who published in any newspaper or magazine published in the United States, a few women disagreed strongly with the proposed changes. They disagreed so strongly, in fact, that in 1892 they withdrew their membership and created a separate organization, the Michigan Woman's Press Club (MWPC).

Another disagreement over MWPA policy led to the creation of the MWPC. Many of the women in the MWPA were active in social issues such as suffrage, temperance, and education reform, but the association's policy did not include working through the press to promote these goals. Rather, its primary concern was to improve and extend good journalism among women in the press so they would be accorded respect by the entire profession.

After considerable debate over these two issues at the MWPA's second annual meeting in 1891, Frances C. Taylor Wood of the *Grand Rapids Eagle* arranged for a meeting with several members from the Grand Rapids newspapers and the *Detroit Free Press*. They convened January 7, 1892, in the parlors of the Grand Rapids Press Club to form their own organization, the Michigan Woman's Press Club.

Wood and her colleagues adopted a constitution that strictly limited membership to "any woman, resident in Michigan, connected as a professional writer, manager or publisher with any reputable newspaper or magazine, or on the staff of such periodical." As for their objectives, they were modeled on those of the New England Woman's Press Association,* founded in 1885, "to promote acquaintance and good fellowship among newspaper women; to elevate the work and the workers; and to forward by concerted action through the press such good objects in social, philanthropic and reformatory lines as may from time to time present themselves."[1]

Annual dues were set at $2 for active membership with a $1 initiation fee. The bylaws also specified that visitors should not be admitted to the business meetings of the club, although social meetings could be public.

EARLY MEMBERS AND THEIR NETWORKS

Although Wood was credited with the idea of establishing the MWPC, it was Etta Smith Wilson of the *Grand Rapids Herald* who was elected president. Martha Louise Woodworth Rayne, of the *Detroit Free Press*, was elected vice president, Wood was elected secretary, and Jennie F. Patten of the *Grand Rapids Morning Press* was elected treasurer. Of the four officers, Wood, Wilson, and Rayne had been members of MWPA; Wilson and Rayne had both been charter members and had served in elective positions.

An examination of the early roster of the MWPC clearly indicates the connections it had to the older press association. Several members of the executive board, like Emma Louise Hammond Mills of the *Grand Rapids Democrat*, Alice M. Hitchcock Miller of the *Muskegon News*, and Jenny O. Starkey of the *Detroit Free Press*, had previously belonged to the MWPA but severed their ties to that organization when they joined the MWPC. Others, like Rayne, instead continued to remain active in the MWPA, although they joined MWPC in 1892 as charter members. Yet others, like S. Isadore Sutherland Miner of Battle Creek's *Good Health* magazine and Hattie G. Sleeper of the *Port Huron Daily Times*, dropped their MWPA membership and became associate members in the MWPC when they moved from the state.[2]

The MWPC occasionally bent its membership rules to accommodate individual situations. Agnes d'Arcambal, of Kalamazoo, who was an honorary member of the MWPA, became a full member of the MWPC in 1894. Here, the club apparently bent its rules because d'Arcambal satisfied the club's objective of working for social reform. Although she apparently did not write or work for the press, d'Arcambal had devoted her life to reforming the treatment of prisoners, during and after confinement in jails, and gave public lectures describing her work. The connection was no doubt mutually beneficial—her membership in the MWPC provided members with provocative ideas and at the same time provided her with an audience that could give those ideas an airing in the press. The connection had clearly born fruit in 1891 when MWPA member E. Cora DePuy published a book, *Pebbles and Pearls*, about d'Arcambal's work.[3]

The importance of the networks provided by membership in the MWPC is apparent in the lives of other women, who were clearly struggling to survive in an anti-feminist environment. This assistance was especially important at this time, since there were few women in a position to offer work to other women writers. According to the Michigan Census reports of 1890, only 130 women were listed as full-time editors, reporters, authors, and lecturers. Until this time, because Michigan women writing for publication had done so either as correspondents or as poetry writers who worked in their homes, they were not counted by the census. Only a few women actually worked in newspaper offices at this time, and before the 1890s, these were almost always wives of the publishers or editors.

There were a few exceptions. In 1893, five Michigan women owned, edited, and personally managed their own newspapers. Two of these women were charter members of MWPC. Harriet Sinclair Applegate became owner and editor of the *Adrian Weekly Times and Expositor* in 1891, after the death of her husband, and Maggie L. Smith established her own paper in 1892. Their success was considered extraordinary for the times. Smith had written for the *Otsego Union* for three years and then started her own paper, the *Otsego Nerve*. An active WCTU worker, Smith gained a circulation of eight hundred subscribers before selling the *Nerve* to the *Otsego Union* and becoming the editor of that paper.[4]

In 1894, the MWPC elected a new slate of officers. They were Jennie O. Starkey of the *Detroit Free Press* as president, Rayne for the second time as vice president, Harriet Sinclair Applegate of the *Adrian Weekly Times and Expositor* as secretary, and Jennie F. Patten of the *Grand Rapids Morning Press* as treasurer.

PROMOTING WOMEN'S PROGRESS

Woman's rights, woman suffrage, and temperance were issues of the day, and many women journalists were convinced they should their use writings to influence the progress of these reforms. For most of the nineteenth century, "meddling in politics" had been considered inappropriate for women, who were often prohibited by law from addressing mixed audiences.[5] But these presswomen were independent thinkers, and this did not stop them from crossing gender lines and participating in various issues of the day. Woman's rights, woman suffrage, and temperance were among the reforms they were convinced they should promote through their writings. Many felt that suffrage was the key to obtaining progress in all the other fields.

Harriet Sinclair Applegate's newspaper career illustrates what one woman could and did do to assist the woman's movement during this time. Applegate took over the *Weekly Times and Expositor* at the time of her husband's death in 1891, though she had no experience in the newspaper business. According to one historian, Tom Applegate had "given little or no editorial support to the women's rights movement and maintained a slightly hostile attitude toward their attempts at social reform."[6] When his widow took control of the paper, however, she made a complete change in its editorial position. She supported the prohibition movement, woman suffrage, higher education for women, equal employment opportunities for women, and social reform policies. She devoted space to reports on women's activities in the community and in 1892 began a column, "Woman and Her Ways," that promoted woman suffrage leaders and equal rights for women.

Applegate was a member of several important women's organizations, including the Woman's Relief Corps and the MWPA as well as the MWPC. Although she was not known to be an active member of the state suffrage association or the WCTU, she gave them increased editorial support. She followed activities of the Federated Woman's Clubs of Michigan, the Women's National Council, the Working Girls' Clubs, and the New York Consumer's League and carried reports of their meetings in the Adrian paper. She provided Adrian residents with information on the progress of the woman's rights movement and gave favorable support to their reform efforts.

Although Applegate lacked experience in the newspaper business, she quickly learned how to manage after she succeeded her husband as owner-editor of the *Weekly Times and Expositor*. She also became adept at presenting her opinions in her editorials, which she did passionately. When, in 1893, the Michigan legislature dropped suffrage legislation following a Supreme Court ruling that a law allowing women to vote in municipal elections was unconstitutional, Applegate was outraged. She wrote: "Thanks to the stupidity of a Republican Legislature, and the vigorous hostility of the state Democrats, the advanced movement in the direction of woman suffrage in the great and progressive commonwealth of Michigan has become a dead letter."[7]

An exceptional woman, Applegate was able to present her case for woman's rights in conjunction with support for community improvements so that her paper was a business success despite anti-feminist attitudes prevalent at that time. She was widely respected not only in Adrian and in the MWPC but also in the mixed-sex newspaper organizations to which she belonged, such as the Michigan Newspaper Association and the National Editorial Association (NEA), and she used her position to promote women's position in newspapers. While speaking to the NEA in 1897, Applegate illustrated the progress being made by women in the field of journalism. "Fifty years ago, it was generally held that no woman was intelligent enough to think, let alone manage a newspaper," she said, adding that now women were in every department of newspaper work and "winning respect and a cordial welcome from their masculine competitors."[8] Applegate also pointed out that through their influence, women had by 1897 contributed a great deal to widening the scope of newspapers, as they had added domestic and social topics to their content.

Although there is no record that the MWPC officially joined other groups in their drive for social reforms, it is clear that individual members like Applegate were aware of the need for improvement in the lives of women. They did not hesitate to use their influence in promoting equality for women. Ironically, this activism, as well as increased professional responsibilities, gradually drained energy and membership from the MWPC. By the beginning of World War I, the MPWC, like its sister organization, the MWPA, was dying out. There is no known record of an attempt to revive the organization.

NOTES

1. Michigan Woman's Press Club, *Leaves from Our Lives* (Grand Rapids, Mich.: Dean Printing and Publishing Company, 1894), p. 4.

2. Miner and Sleeper moved from Michigan to Toledo, Ohio, in 1890. Miner moved to a job on the *Toledo Commercial* and Sleeper to the *Toledo Blade*. The club apparently relaxed its own membership requirements to accommodate out-of-state residents who had previously been full members of MWPA.

3. M.E.C. Bates, "Michigan Woman's Press Association," *The Literary Century*, May 1893, p. 422.

4. *Leaves from Our Lives*, p. 19.

5. Frank J. Sulloway, *Born to Rebel* (New York: Pantheon Books, 1996), p. 555.

6. Claudia Cepac, "A Historical View: The Editorial Perspective of a 19th Century Woman Newspaper Editor" (unpublished research paper, University of Michigan School of Journalism, 1972), p. 14.

7. *Adrian Weekly Times and Expositor*, 19 February 1897.

8. *Leaves from Our Lives*, p. 21

INFORMATIONAL SOURCES

Beakes, S. W. *Past and Present of Washtenaw County, Michigan.* Chicago: S. J. Clarke Publishing Co., 1906.

Cepac, Claudia. "A Historical View: The Editorial Perspective of a 19th Century Woman Newspaper Editor." Unpublished research paper, University of Michigan School of Journalism, 1972.

Chapman Brothers, eds. *Portrait and Biographical Album of Lenawee County, Michigan.* Chicago: Chapman Brothers, 1888.

Doll, Louis W. *A History of the Newspapers of Ann Arbor, 1829–1920.* Detroit: Wayne State University Press, 1959.

Knapp, John I., and R. I. Bonner. *Illustrated History and Biographical Record of Lenawee County, Michigan.* Adrian, Mich.: Times Printing Company, 1903.

Michigan Woman's Press Club. *Leaves from Our Lives.* Grand Rapids, Mich.: Dean Printing and Publishing Company, 1894.

Sulloway, Frank J. *Born to Rebel.* New York: Pantheon Books, 1996.

Weddon, Willah. *Michigan Press Women, Today and Yesterday.* Stockbridge, Mich.: Weddon Press, 1996.

INSTITUTIONAL PROFILE

Michigan Woman's Press Club

Dates: Organized 7 January 1892 in Grand Rapids, Michigan; became inactive by 1914.

Publication: A record of the formation of the club and profiles of members were published in *Leaves from Our Lives* (Grand Rapids, Mich.: Dean Printing and Publishing Company, 1894).

16

Patricia L. Dooley

Minnesota Press Women, 1940–1982

INTRODUCTION

In fall 1940, Geraldine Rasmussen, co-publisher and business manager of the *Austin Daily Herald*, parleyed a small group of independent-minded women journalists attending a meeting of the Minnesota Editors of the First District. Under discussion was whether Minnesota women journalists should organize a press club of their own. Since Minnesota's only other women's press club, the Minnesota Woman's Press Association, formed in the late nineteenth century, had disbanded, the state's women journalists were without a formal organization whose mission it was to address their special concerns. Rasmussen invited a guest speaker, National Federation of Press Women (NFPW)* President Bertha Bless, of Weston, Missouri. Bless stressed how important it was for women to have their own organization apart from male-oriented press organizations, explained the goals and objectives of the national federation, and provided guidance on how to organize a state group. Pro tem officers were appointed, and a date was established for a program.[1]

Rasmussen's and Bless's efforts paved the way for the formal organization of Minnesota Press Women (MPW) in Minneapolis in January 1941. Twenty-five Minnesota women attended the organization's first meeting. Of this group, eight would become MPW charter members. The new organization voted to become a chapter of the NFPW,* establishing a relationship that would continue until 1961, when its members declared their independence from the national association. In 1982, MPW's members voted to disband.[2]

Although a second organization, Press Women of Minnesota, would be created in 1978, this chapter focuses largely on the history of the older group,[3] whose creation signals the more central role women journalists were playing in journalism during the years before the country's entry into World War II.

Throughout MPW's forty-year history, the organization would become an agent of further professionalization among women journalists, and its programs and networking opportunities would became springboards for those within its ranks with higher ambitions.

BACKGROUND

Since even before Minnesota became a state in 1858, women played important but largely invisible roles in journalism. Whereas some were overshadowed by the journalist fathers, brothers, and husbands with whom they worked, others would come to assume more prominent journalistic positions within their communities. One early example is Jane Grey Swisshelm, the well-known feminist and abolitionist who moved to Minnesota Territory in 1857. Seeking to start a new life for herself and her six-year-old daughter, she agreed not long after her arrival to serve as editor of the *St. Cloud Visiter* [*sic*]. Swisshelm would thus go on to rock early state politics and leave her journalistic mark long after she moved on in 1863 to other localities.[4]

Although not as well known as Swisshelm, Julia A. S. Wood would also serve among the ranks of the state's earliest journalists. After settling in Minnesota Territory in 1851, Wood edited a Sauk Rapids paper, *The New Era*, from 1859 to 1863. She would later publish numerous articles, poems, and stories, some of them written under the pen name "Minnie Mary Lee."[5]

Another pioneer woman journalist was Eva McDonald Valesh, born in Orono, Maine, in 1866. Eva moved with her parents to Stillwater, Minnesota, in the mid-1870s. As a teenager, she worked as a typesetter and proofreader for the *Minneapolis Saturday Evening Spectator*. Earning $6 a week, she eventually joined the typographers union. In 1888, under the pen name "Eva Gay," she wrote a series of articles for the *St. Paul Globe* on women workers in the Twin Cities. Ultimately Valesh would become a champion of labor and write for and edit a variety of papers and magazines, including the *Minneapolis Tribune, New York Journal, American Federationist* and *American Club Woman*.[6]

Minnesota women slowly made inroads into the male domain of journalism. Educator and suffragist Keith Clark wrote editorials for the *St. Paul Dispatch* from 1898 to 1917.[7] After serving early in the century as publisher and editor of her family's paper, the *Le Sueur Sentinel*, Elizabeth McLeod Jones held jobs as a reporter, editor, and publisher for newspapers across Minnesota and South Dakota.[8] And Dorothy Leicht, of Winona, from 1926 to 1941 carried on a family publishing tradition by serving as vice president of National Weeklies, Inc., treasurer of the Leicht Press, and editor and co-publisher of *Midwest Review*.[9]

Swisshelm, Wood, Valesh, Jones, Leicht and the many other women who practiced journalism in Minnesota during the nineteenth and early twentieth centuries helped pave the way toward better working conditions for women in the field. In addition, the many women's press organizations established throughout the country during the last two decades of the nineteenth century also made notable contributions. Such associations were part of the women's club movement and of a more generalized professionalization process underway in the broader journalistic occupation.[10]

But as America grew closer to war in 1941, women journalists faced new challenges. Increasingly called on to fill journalistic positions vacated by male journalists who had accepted war-related posts, women sought to capitalize on their newly found prominence in the field.[11] Recognizing this, the NFPW, established in 1937, traveled to states like Minnesota to encourage the formation of local chapters. Three of the national federation's charter members were Minnesotans who worked for Minnesota papers: Elsye D. Drewe, of the *Truman* (Minnesota) *Tribune*, Harriet Sitz of the *Grand Rapids Herald-Review*, and Catherine M. Sheire, editor of the *Fairfax Standard*.

Some of the enthusiasm felt by Minnesota's women journalists for the establishment of their own press organization likely came from concerns about whether their interests were being well served by the Minnesota Newspaper Association (MNA). Established in 1867, the MNA invited newspapers, rather than individual journalists, to become members. Thus, although women journalists were not specifically barred from participating in the association's programs, relatively few did until the 1960s. Decades would pass before women would be appointed to positions of leadership in the MNA, and it wasn't until 1983 that it swore in its first woman president, Carole Larson, of the *Osseo-Maple Grove Press*, and appointed former school teacher Linda Falkman to serve as its first female executive director.[12]

MISSION AND MEMBERSHIP

That Minnesota Press Women's eight charter members grasped the importance of their newly minted organization is reflected in the words of a poem written in 1946 to commemorate the group's founding:

> Where mighty river waters roar,
> And far-flung lakes with verdant shore
> Lie dreaming in the summer sun,
> There gathered for earnest discussion
> A small group of Press Women, who
> Believed that, without more ado
> They must let the wide world know
> A Distaff Press exists—and so
> They went into action—and now
> They've proved it, we think you'll allow.

> This little brochure, penned with care,
> Will show you what women will dare.
> Not fearing scorn or ridicule,

Plunging in the sphere of man's rule,
To attain their place in the world,
Where most dangerous quick sands whirled,
Where problems of survival piled
Like alpine snows, and tempers riled
More oft than 'tis seemly to tell.
Now the task is done—all is well![13]

These members of the "distaff press" faced a formidable task in bringing together their sisters. In 1940, the journalists who worked at Minnesota's 500 newspapers (36 dailies, 464 weeklies) were scattered throughout its eighty-seven counties. U.S. Census records indicate 25 percent of the state's reporters and editors were women. Devising plans that would successfully attract a large membership from throughout Minnesota's vast regions of "mighty rivers" and "far-flung lakes" would thus prove to be a challenge throughout the organization's history. Ranking eleventh in size among the states in 1940, Minnesota measured 380 miles north to south and 183 miles east to west. The state's 1935 population of approximately 2,627,000 was roughly half rural and urban. The urban population lived largely in Minneapolis and St. Paul, cities located at the confluence of the Minnesota and Mississippi rivers near the state's eastern border with Wisconsin. Geographically, the state is divided into two areas: its northern lake, timber, and iron ore region, and its southern plains and prairie areas. In the 1940s, northern Minnesota was a center for lumbering, mining, and tourism; the southern part of the state was largely a farming and manufacturing region.[14]

Despite the obstacles inherent in attracting members from throughout such a large and diverse state, MPW's small group of charter members solicited women from throughout the state's regions to fill the organization's active, associate, and honorary categories. To be eligible for membership in the active category, according to the organization's bylaws, individuals were required to be residents of Minnesota who had been engaged in a journalistic professional capacity for at least one year. Positions deemed "journalistic" were those at news press wire services or in the editorial or business departments of newspapers, magazines, and journals with bona fide subscriptions.

MPW grew slowly. In April 1943, its membership rolls tallied thirty-one members; in 1946, fifty-six; in 1949, sixty-five; and in 1955, eighty-five. The organization's leaders occasionally announced formal membership drives, but any increases were hard won. From membership reports published in MPW's newsletter, *Gopher Tidings*, it appears the group never totaled more than one hundred. Most MPW members, especially in the years following its establishment, were from the state's more heavily populated southern and central areas.

MPW charter members established four goals: to secure for Minnesota women journalists the benefits of organized effort; to foster mutual improvement through association; to make possible the expression of a common voice in matters of interest to press women; and to promote the highest ideals of American journalism.

ACTIVITIES

In order to achieve such ideals, MPW's leadership established a variety of activities meant to serve a blend of organizational, social, professional, educational, and civic-related functions. The group held summer and winter organizational meetings. In addition, it sponsored a variety of programs and other activities, including an annual journalism contest, vocational and professional training workshops, the monthly publication of *Gopher Tidings*, a legislative lobbying committee, and a series of scholarships for women university and college students majoring in journalism.

MPW officers held the organization's annual winter meetings in the Twin Cities and its summer meetings in diverse locations throughout the state in an effort to serve the group's widely dispersed membership. Summer gatherings were occasionally held in locations ideal for sightseeing and vacation activities. In June 1947, for example, *Gopher Tidings* reported that the group's summer meeting had been held at Alexandria, located in the heart of one of the state's northern lake resort areas. An editor of the *Park Region Echo* welcomed the group on behalf of Alexandria's newspapers, and the meeting's luncheon speaker, Minnesota attorney general Keith L. Wallace, spoke on the history of communism. Following lunch, the group dispersed for shopping and a tour of the city and the area's lakes. That evening, there were more social and dinner gatherings, and the next morning the group held its organizational business meeting.

Although MPW's membership remained relatively small, its influence was significant. Through its programs, scholarships, contests, and networking opportunities, many of the group's members not only advanced in their own careers but also became role models for a younger generation of women entering the profession. In addition, not only would MPW members become leaders in the state's press community, but a number of them would assume prominent positions in press circles outside their home state as well. From her position as MPW's fourth president (1947–49), Irene Bedard, the business and advertising manager of the *Hibbing Daily Tribune*, graduated to the NFPW presidency in 1949, and in 1959 she became the first woman board member of the Northwest Daily Press Association. For Bedard, like many other MPW members, community involvement would become a way of life. After joining the staff of the *Daily Tribune* in 1921, she became active in a number of other civic activities and in 1952 was named Woman of the Year by the city of Hibbing.[15]

Charter member Geraldine Rasmussen, who together with her husband published the *Austin Daily Herald*, was another civic leader who would strive to improve the lot of women journalists both in Minnesota and across the nation.

Rasmussen became MPW's second president (1943–45) and went on to a number of influential posts at regional and national levels. For example, in addition to serving in various positions with the NFPW, Rasmussen would become the first woman to serve as president of the Northwest Daily Press Association and treasurer of the American National Publishers Association.[16]

MPW's third president (1945–47), Marion Johnson, of the *Blue Earth County Post*, was elected treasurer of the International Press Club. And the group's fifth president (1948–51), Carol Marx, editor and publisher of the *Owatonna Photo News*, became the first woman president of the First District Editorial Association and served as an officer in state and national associations both in the areas of journalism and broader civic-affairs.[17]

Marx's tenure as MPW's president was an especially notable one. From early on, Marx was a leader. After graduating with honors from the University of Minnesota School of Journalism in 1931, she worked for a short time in Elk River, Minnesota, and then went to Owatonna, where she would remain throughout the rest of her career.[18] Not only did she challenge the group's members to contribute to the welfare of the state's press women, but she set goals for the organization that went beyond its members' press- and career-related concerns. Marx was especially interested in press women's involvement in civic and community activities. In her 1949 presidential inaugural message, she laid out what she expected from the group's members: "The Minnesota Press Women, no matter how large or great they become, can never be the organization we hope for without tangible proof of civic service."[19]

Of particular interest to Marx were the state's mental hospitals, which she urged members to visit and report on in their newspapers. Spurred on by a recent governor's report on the deplorable conditions at such institutions, Marx stated, "Let us lend the strength and confidence which our readers have in their 'hometown newspapers' to the full, complete and TRUE story of the needs existing in our mental institutions today."[20]

Marx also pushed MPW to lobby against gender-related job discrimination. In response to the proposal of a 1949 legislative bill that would limit the hours Minnesota women could legally work to forty-eight, she wrote: "If you uphold discrimination, of course you will support the bill. If you resent discriminations against you because of sex and which destroy our freedom of opportunity to contract for labor upon your own terms, you will of course use your influence to defeat the measure."[21]

As the organization's influence grew, its leaders were asked by the NFPW for help in organizing chapters in other states. Early in 1948, several Minnesota Press Women traveled to Aberdeen, South Dakota, to help establish a National Federation chapter in that state. Former MPW president Marion D. Johnson spoke on the "Mechanics of the Federation," as well as on her view of the world's current state of affairs and the role of women. According to Johnson, the world had never faced such critical events, and the need was great for women to get together and "do something about it."[22] In addition, MPW's sitting president, Irene R. Bedard, presented information on MPW activities and extended an invitation to South Dakota women to become active members of the national federation. Seventeen South Dakota women became charter members of South Dakota's new NFPW affiliate.

ORGANIZATIONAL HISTORY

Minnesota Press Women's history can be divided into two periods: 1941 to 1961, when it was affiliated with the NFPW; and 1961 to 1982, after it dissolved its bond with the national organization. During the early era, the organization was formally affiliated with the NFPW, meaning that its members paid annual dues to both the state chapter and national federation. In exchange, MPW members received copies of the national group's newsletter, *Press Woman*, were invited to send delegates and members-at-large to its annual national conventions, and were eligible for election to positions on the national board of directors.

For twenty years, the bond between the Minnesota group and the NFPW was a strong one. Hundreds of Minnesota women attended the national group's annual conventions, which were held each summer in various cities across the country. In 1943, for example, eight MPW members attended the national convention in Des Moines, and several were elected to positions on the national board. And in 1948, MPW hosted the federation's annual convention in St. Paul. Nearly one hundred press women—thirty-six of them Minnesotans—attended the series of meetings, workshops, and sightseeing events scheduled in the Twin Cities.[23]

The relationship between the Minnesota Press Women and the national organization dissolved in 1961 when three controversial initiatives were approved by the state group's members: They severed the organization's ties with the NFPW, voted to hold their annual meetings in conjunction with the Minnesota Newspaper Association, and moved to schedule the organization's annual summer and fall conferences at the University of Minnesota. Such changes would usher in a new era for the organization, one marked by a general withdrawal from involvement in national activities and closer coordination among Minnesota Press Women, the Minnesota Newspaper Association, and journalism faculty at the University of Minnesota.[24]

These changes were precipitated by several concerns. Not only were MPW members critical of the financial obligations involved in maintaining a formal relationship with the national federation, but some believed the NFPW membership qualifications and programs no longer reflected their interests. Some members regretted the national group's active solicitation of new members from the broadcasting and public relations fields, arguing that such initiatives were diluting the organization's former newspaper journalism emphasis.

After withdrawing from the NFPW umbrella, the Minnesota group carried on its tradition as an active and viable organization for another twenty years. But in 1982, the organization's members voted to formally disband.[25] The group's dissolution was in part tied to competition from a new state chapter of the NFPW established in 1978.[26] The new organization, Press Women of Minnesota, extended membership to all women mass communicators, not primarily newspaperwomen, as did the MPW. In addition, the new organization's officers were especially concerned about the "special needs of its increasing numbers of self-employed members."[27]

Thus the new organization attracted members who might have joined Minnesota Press Women had its programs been more appealing to women who worked in mass communication fields such as public relations and advertising. In addition, some women may have been interested in the national affiliation Press Women of Minnesota offered and broader opportunities for networking with women in the communication industry.

Margaret Lee, who attended the meeting that led to MPW's dissolution, said some in the group thought it was time for them to throw the group's support to Press Women of Minnesota. Lee, who edited *Gopher Tidings* for more than twenty years and served as MPW president (1957–59), recalled how difficult it was for the group to dissolve. "Minnesota Press Women gave me a wonderful education through its programs," she said.[28]

Lee and other former MPW members joined Press Women of Minnesota, which remained active until 1992, when its members voted to disband after the group's membership and participation declined. In 1998 the NFPW announced that it was planning to reestablish a chapter of Minnesota women communicators.[29]

NOTES

1. This information, as well as much of what follows, is taken from two sources: Catherine M. Sheire, *History of Minnesota Press Women, 1940–1946*, published by MPW circa 1946; and *Gopher Tidings*, MPW's newsletter, which was published monthly, and at times bimonthly, from 1941 until the early 1970s.

2. Margaret Lee, telephone interview by author, 28 August 1998.

3. Peggyann Hutchinson, NFPW historian, telephone interview by author, 4 September 1998. After Minnesota Press Women severed its ties with the NFPW in 1961, the national group sought to reestablish a group in the state and succeeded in 1978 with the establishment of Press Women of Minnesota. The history of Press Women of Minnesota can be compiled by examining the national federation's annual membership directories and periodic histories. Such records are part of a collection of the organization's records at the Missouri Historical Society.

4. Abigail McCarthy, "Jane Grey Swisshelm: Marriage and Slavery," in *Women of Minnesota: Selected Biographical Essays*, ed. Barbara Stuhler and Gretchen Kreuter (St. Paul: Minnesota Historical Society Press, 1977), pp. 34–54.

5. Ibid., p. 343.

6. Ibid., pp. 56–58.

7. Ibid., p. 328.

8. Jones, who is discussed briefly in *Women of Minnesota*, on p. 333, wrote an unpublished autobiography, *Ink on Her Fingers*, which is in the collections of the Minnesota Historical Society.

9. For a biographical sketch of Leicht, see Patricia L. Dooley, "Minnesota Journalists as Elected Officials, 1923–1938: An Historical Study of an Ethical/Conflict of Interest Question" (M.A. thesis, University of Minnesota, 1985), pp. 75–76.

10. Historians who have written about these developments include Maurine Beasley, "The Women's National Press Club: A Case Study of Professional Aspirations," *Journalism History* 15, no. 4 (winter 1988): 112–21; Elizabeth V. Burt, "A Bid for Legitimacy: The Woman's Press Club Movement, 1881–1900," *Journalism History* 23, no. 2 (summer 1997): 72–84; Agnes Hooper Gottlieb, "Networking in the Nineteenth Century: Founding of the Woman's Press Club of New York City," *Journalism History* 21, no. 4 (winter 1995): 156–63.

11. Patricia L. Dooley, "Minnesota Women Journalists during World War II," *Roots* 17, no. 2 (winter 1989): 22–26.

12. When originally established, the organization's name was Minnesota Editors' and Publishers' Association. In 1900, the group renamed itself Minnesota Editorial Association, and in 1960, the Minnesota Newspaper Association. For a history of the organization, see George S. Hage, *Minnesota Newspaper Association: 125 Years of Service to Minnesota, its People and to Journalism* (Minneapolis: Minnesota Newspaper Association, 1992).

13. Sheire, *History of Minnesota Press Women*, p. 1.

14. J. Percy H. Johnson, ed., *N. W. Ayer & Son's 1940 Directory of Newspapers and Periodicals* (Philadelphia: N. W. Ayer & Son, 1940), p. 446.

15. Biographical information on Bedard is scattered throughout *Gopher Tidings*. See particularly the following issues: 15 May 1943, p. 2; March–April 1946, p. 2; April 1949, p. 1. In addition, see *Women in Minnesota*, p. 326, and her obituary published in *Minnesota Press*, February 1959, p. 7.

16. Information on Rasmussen is contained throughout the pages of *Gopher Tidings*. See especially 15 July 1943, p. 4. See also *Minnesota Newspaper Association Bulletin*, 18 August 1987, p. 6.

17. For biographical information on Johnson, see *Gopher Tidings*, 15 October 1943, p. 1, and 15 February 1945, p. 1. For information on Marx, see *Gopher Tidings*, which extensively covered her activities from 1943 until her death in January 1956. See, for example, the following issues: 15 July 1943, p. 1; 15 August 1943, pp. 1–2; 15 January 1944, p. 1; February 1949, p. 3; and January–February 1956, p. 2. Also see her obituary, published on page one of the paper she published and edited, the *Owatonna Photo News*, on 25 January 1956.

18. *Owatonna Photo News*, 25 January 1956, p. 1

19. *Gopher Tidings*, February 1949, p. 1.

20. Ibid., p. 4.

21. Ibid.

22. *Gopher Tidings*, March 1948, p. 4.

23. *Gopher Tidings*, July, 1948, p. 1.

24. *Gopher Tidings*, March 1961, p. 1.

25. Lee interview.

26. After MPW severed ties with the NFPW in 1961, the national group sought to

reestablish a group in the state. It succeeded in 1978 with the establishment of Press
Women of Minnesota (PWM), which was chartered on 6 May 1978 at St. Cloud.

27. *Press Women*, April 1987.

28. Lee interview.

29. NFPW's Sixtieth Anniversary Membership Directory and Information Guide, p. 3.

INFORMATIONAL SOURCES

Primary Sources

Constitution of the Minnesota Press Women. ca. 1941.

Gopher Tidings. 1943–69, passim.

Jones, Elizabeth McLeod. "Ink on Her Fingers." Unpublished autobiography in the collections of the Minnesota Historical Society.

National Federation of Press Women Membership Directory and Information Guides,
1983–95 and 1998.

Published Material

Dooley, Patricia L. "Minnesota Women Journalists during World War II." *Roots*, 17, no.
2 (winter 1989): 22–26.

Hage, George S. *Minnesota Newspaper Association.* Minneapolis: Minnesota Newspaper
Association, 1992.

Sheire, Catherine M. *History of Minnesota Press Women, 1940–1946.* Minnesota Press
Women, ca. 1946.

Stuhler, Barbara, and Gretchen Kreuter, eds. *Women of Minnesota: Selected Biographical
Essays.* St. Paul: Minnesota Historical Society Press, 1977.

INSTITUTIONAL PROFILE

Minnesota Press Women

Dates: Organized January 1941; affiliated with National Federation of Press Women,
1941–61; disbanded in 1982.

Newsletter: *Gopher Tidings.* Issues published from 1943 to October–November 1969 are
available at the Minnesota History Center, St. Paul, Minnesota. Several additional
issues published in 1970 are held by the Minnesota Newspaper Association, Minneapolis, Minnesota.

17

Tina Lesher

National Federation of Press Women, 1937–Present

INTRODUCTION

In the more than six decades since its founding, the National Federation of Press Women (NFPW) has extended its identity far beyond its initial professional base.

The NFPW was organized in 1937, a time when women were barred from many press clubs. The thirty-nine women who met in Chicago in 1937 approved a constitution that called the group "an organization for professional women writers" and defined "professional" as participation in journalistic or literary service for remuneration.[1] NFPW brought together existing women's press groups and encouraged the formation of new groups across the country as affiliates. These affiliates were to remain autonomous, with their own officers and bylaws. The national federation became a resource for mutual support, networking, and learning for women in print journalism.

In the intervening years, the NFPW has grown to include male members and to welcome those whose specialties include public relations, advertising, broadcasting, and new media. As the decades have unfolded, though, so has the need for radical changes within the NFPW. In the late 1990s, the NFPW's leadership began to reposition the organization by cutting programs that had failed to attract support and by establishing a new headquarters operated by a professional management firm. Membership, which had peaked at close to five thousand in the mid-1970s, declined to half that, and the number of state affiliates dropped to forty-two. The organization's officers undertook an extensive repositioning study, which culminated in "Blueprint for 2000," a report on reorganization and recommendations for change. The report indicated that the leaders themselves were unsure if the organization could remain viable:

Indeed, NFPW leaders have been the first to declare that if it cannot meet a need, NFPW should be closed. Sadly, but realistically, the leadership contemplated that possibility and asked itself in sincerity whether a need for NFPW existed. It posed that question to its task forces, who discussed the future with local members. The resounding response to the question was "YES." NFPW has a mission to perform. Its mission is threefold: professional development for all communicators, encouragement and direction of professional women and support of youth, through the NFPW Education Fund.[2]

Some of the recommendations were implemented immediately; others took effect after bylaw changes at the NFPW conference in Nashville in June 1999.

ORGANIZATION

The roots of NFPW extend back to 1885, when *Boston Post* staffer Marion MacBride served as press commissioner for the World's Industrial and Cotton Exposition in New Orleans.[3] In a time of a failing economy, women journalists had few opportunities for advancement and working conditions were considered to be poor. In discussions with other newspaperwomen at the exposition, MacBride shared her dream of a national association of women journalists. The women organized the National Woman's Press Association, which soon spawned state and regional associations in more than a dozen states. By the 1930s, however, many of the women's press organizations founded in the nineteenth century had died out, lost their viability, or lost their ties with organizations in other states. One that survived was the Illinois Woman's Press Association,* founded in 1886. It was the president of that organization, Helen Miller Malloch, who in 1937 convened a Chicago meeting with the intention of federating press women from a number of existing state organizations.[4] Thirty-nine women from the District of Columbia and six states—Illinois, Indiana, Michigan, New York, Ohio, and Oregon—attended that meeting and agreed to establish the NFPW.[5] It was decided that each affiliate would be allotted a vote for every fifty members and would be levied a twenty-five-cent annual per capita fee for membership in the national organization.[6]

The federation objectives were spelled out. They were to promote the highest ideals in journalism, to provide exchange of journalistic ideas and experiences, and to coordinate editorial opinions on matters of national interest to women. A half-century later, a NFPW member argued that "the commitment of NFPW's leaders remains constant . . . and unchanged. The purpose of NFPW when founded in Chicago is still the same today."[7]

Malloch was elected president, and six vice presidents were chosen. They were Harriet Bishop Christie of New York, Marion Reeder of Ohio, Vera Hall of Indiana, Bernadine Bailey of Illinois, Bernie Bless of Missouri, and Beatrice Locke of Oregon.[8]

As part of a day-long agenda at the Chicago conference, charter members toured the *Chicago Tribune* on May 6, 1937. Louise Eleanor Ross of Indiana, the newly elected recording secretary, headed to the *Tribune* newsroom to type a scheduled front-page story about the organization of NFPW. As she worked, the wires brought the story of the crash of the German zeppelin *Hindenburg*. In classic journalistic fashion, that breaking news took precedence, and only the lead of the NFPW story made it to print.

GROWTH

Within the first year, additional affiliates were formed in Michigan, Pennsylvania, New England, Iowa, and Washington, D.C. Under the umbrella of autonomy, members joined local affiliates (if they were in existence) and part of their dues was designated for operation of the national federation. Those who resided in areas where there were no affiliates became members-at-large. For the NFPW to survive in its early days, a number of officers spent personal monies to fund mailings and other operating costs.

At the second NFPW convention in 1938 in Chicago, it was reported that NFPW had 451 members—363 from the affiliated organizations and 88 members-at-large. Malloch told delegates that NFPW "should be a source of inspiration for actual working, writing women. I hope it will not be used for personal purposes. We want it to be above reproach."[9] The requirement that members work for money was dropped, since it was pointed out that many women were staff members of publications owned by their spouses and did not receive regular salaries. At the time, pay for press women at large newspapers was approximately $20 a week, with those on weekly newspapers being paid as little as $5 per week. Few received benefits of any type.

The NFPW conventions became a major event for newspaperwomen. The 1939 convention, which was held in New York to coincide with the World's Fair, was attended by more than forty delegates and many other members. The prime event, a formal banquet at the Waldorf-Astoria, drew seven hundred people, including two hundred press women. Here, the NFPW honored outstanding women in journalism, including Anne O'Hare McCormick of the *New York Times*, Dorothy Thompson of the *New York Herald-Tribune*, and Oveta Culp Hobby of the *Houston Post*.

For most of its history, NFPW has been an organization run by volunteers with a board of directors setting federation policies. For years, it lacked an official headquarters, with the incumbent president usually working from her home or a nearby office. National officers met periodically to plan NFPW activities and discuss the future of the federation. In 1969, Missouri member Lois Lauer Wolfe became editor of *Press Woman*, the NFPW publication that had debuted almost two decades earlier. By the 1980s, Wolfe also assumed the post of executive director under a contract with the federation. But volunteers and affiliates continued to help organize the national conference and oversee many NFPW activities.

By 1999, many of these tasks had been assumed by the professional managers at national headquarters. As "Blueprint for 2000" notes: "The phenomenon of shifting away from volunteer-driven projects was seen as an inevitable result of demographic changes as women have assumed more demanding professional careers and the time available for volunteer projects has diminished."[10]

ACTIVITIES AND ISSUES

The onslaught of World War II brought changes to the American employment scene and the news industry was no exception. As author Nan Robertson wrote, "A whole generation of women entered the newspaper business during the 1940s; they filled the city rooms."[11] NFPW members proved especially supportive of the war effort. Eloise Davison of the *New York Herald-Tribune* was loaned by her paper to the Civilian Defense Council for $1 a year. Gertrude Dracken, a Massachusetts writer, resigned as editor of *Press Woman*, and joined the WACs. At one point, a quarter of the members worked in men's jobs. At war's end, however, most of these women were replaced or demoted and many were forced to retire from the profession.[12]

NFPW became active in its support of women's issues, especially as they would affect women in the news industry. During the war, it officially supported an Equal Rights for Women Amendment (ERA), citing the realization that many women journalists would lose their posts at the conclusion of the war. This position was not unanimous among the membership, however, and sparked some debate. Former NFPW president Octavia Goodbar, for example, disagreed. An associate editor of the magazine *America First*, Goodbar "was among those who felt passage of the amendment would strike 'protective legislation' from the books."[13] ERA considerations remained vital within the fold; in 1969, delegates at the national conference in Montana passed resolutions to improve the status of women and remedy inequalities by whatever legal means necessary. A year later, with the ERA awaiting ratification by the states, the Nebraska affiliate (Nebraska Press Women) hosted a discussion on working women and equal rights. Guest speaker Nebraska state senator Fern Hubbard Orme, in discussing lower salaries usually given to women, said:

We are going to have to work very hard to convince people we like to eat and we like a new dress once in a while. We are very, very tired of having people pat us on the back and saying "you have come a long way, just be patient about it, [equality] will arrive." It isn't going to until we push for it.[14]

In line with its support of equal rights, NFPW increased legislative activity and in 1972 admitted men to membership. The organization's name was not changed to reflect that move, even though discussions on the topic over the years have yielded such name suggestions as National Federation of Professional Communicators and National Media Professionals. In 1996, 60 percent of the membership responded to the most recent survey on this issue. In the opinion of many members, the name the organization had chosen nearly sixty years earlier had strong historical ties to the commitment of its founders. No change resulted.[15]

An important tool used by the NFPW to keep its membership up to date on these activities and issues was its newsletter, *Press Woman*, first published in 1940. The initial issue was numbered volume 4, reportedly to give precedence to the occasional bulletins published by the organization in earlier years. *Press Woman* remained the NFPW's main vehicle for information until 1989, when the federation decided to begin publishing a new "tab" paper, *Agenda*, which would cover the organization's news. *Press Woman*, instead, would publish substantive articles related to the media and focus on varied professional issues of interest. A 1992 edition, for example, was devoted to journalism education and featured articles by college professors. *Press Woman* and *Agenda* were published in alternate months until the former ceased publication in 1995. Today, the bimonthly *Agenda* remains as the official publication of NFPW. The federation also publishes an annual membership directory and information guide and a Web site that is updated periodically to provide general information about the organization, names of officers and affiliates, and information about its annual convention.

Another important activity has been the NFPW's leadership training program started in the early 1970s. It became an integral part of the organization's strategy to ensure that its officers understood the importance of guiding the national organization and its affiliates, and to allow members a chance to build leadership qualities for their respective careers. A comprehensive leadership manual was published and workshops set up at affiliate and national conclaves. The efforts continue until the present, with "Blueprint for 2000" clearly noting the organization's need to provide such training.

One of the most active programs in NFPW is its annual communications contest, initiated in 1938. Today, affiliates sponsor contests in close to one hundred categories, from traditional newspaper pieces to broadcast reporting to new media works. First-place winners in the affiliate competitions become eligible for the national contests, and awards are presented at the NFPW annual conference. A youth writing contest, developed in the 1970s, attracts thousands of entries from high school journalism students, with winners also honored at the annual conference.

The federation's highest honor is its annual Communicator of Achievement Award, which it launched in 1957 as the Woman of Achievement Award. It is presented to a member who has made national contributions in journalism. The first to receive the award was Washington Press Woman Charlotte Paul, a weekly newspaper publisher in Snoqualmie, Washington, and the author of several novels. Katharine Graham, publisher of the *Washington Post* and a member of the Virginia affiliate, was a 1974 recipient. Upon receiving the award, Graham said she "was especially pleased because it was given by a group of highly distinguished women journalists from all over the United States who have contributed greatly to the profession of journalism."[16]

Periodically since 1982, the NFPW president has presented a President's Award to recognize an individual of national stature; the honoree need not be a NFPW member. Recipients have included syndicated columnist Sarah McClendon; Nancy Woodhull, the founding editor of *USA Today*; and United Press International (UPI) White House correspondent Helen Thomas.

These award ceremonies are a highlight of the NFPW's annual conferences, but another important element of the conferences are workshops and talks by well-known personalities. The 1998 conference in Washington, D.C., gave attendees a chance to meet Attorney General Janet Reno at a press conference and to hear NBC legal correspondent Peter Williams and others debate issues related to the Internet. Many of the annual conferences include optional trips before and/or after the conference.

CHALLENGES

Membership in NFPW grew steadily during the organization's first four decades. From fourteen affiliates in 1942, the federation grew to thirty-nine by the mid-1970s, when membership peaked at nearly five thousand. By 1984, all fifty states were represented in the membership. But in the late 1980s, NFPW began to wrestle with declining membership in affiliate groups. Cited for the drop were the unsettled economic climate and the closing of many community papers that employed members. Ironically, it was during the 1980s that NFPW took "giant steps forward" to move into the realm of a professional support organization by providing credit cards, insurance, mail-order prescriptions, and job listing services.[17] The organization observed its fiftieth anniversary at a highly touted conference in Williamsburg in 1987. Literacy-related projects were instituted, and steps were taken to help reorganization of affiliates that appeared to be struggling to stay alive.

With membership declining, financial stability proved difficult to achieve. Marj Carpenter, a news service director for the Presbyterian Church, ascended to the presidency in 1991 and quickly discovered a budget crisis: "They had been telling us for the last four years that our reserve was going fast and that we were going to be broke and that we [were] nearly broke. When I got there, they told me we were broke," she wrote in 1997.[18] Carpenter cut the budget 10 percent in every category and fought for a doubling of national dues to $50. (Members also paid affiliate dues in the $15 or $20 range per year.) After much debate at the 1992 convention in Lansing, Michigan, the proposal was passed by delegates.

Many members failed to maintain their affiliation as the annual fees increased. Membership continued to decline in the mid-1990s to the point that an "Adopt-a-Member" program was instituted to help those who had lost jobs and could not spare the funds needed to join NFPW or remain members. Many affiliates reduced the frequency of meetings because they lacked sufficient members to attend these events.

In 1995 NFPW chose a new executive director, Pris Chansky, a member of Kansas Press Women.* Two years later NFPW moved its headquarters to Arlington, Virginia, where it would be managed by American Pressworks. The federation's records and historical files were also moved to this location.

CONCLUSION

Throughout its history, NFPW has attracted dedicated, often highly educated members, including many freelancers and public relations specialists. While most do not fall into the realm of famous personages, the membership has included publisher Katharine Graham, first lady Eleanor Roosevelt, and UPI reporter Helen Thomas.[19]

What has set the NFPW apart from many press-related organizations is its strong networking environment wherein members support each other and establish close friendships. In fact, according to "Blueprint for 2000," "the number one reason members have given for joining the organization has been 'networking' or 'making new friends.' " The report acknowledges the benefits therein but adds that "the ability to network and mentor does not require a national organization. Luncheons, dinners, workshops and idea sharing can occur more effectively on a local or state level than on a national level, where the expense of travel will always be an inhibition for many members."[20]

Members dropped out, it was reported, because they believed NFPW did not provide enough opportunity or services for their needs. With that in mind, eight task forces were established in spring 1998 to study NFPW and to position it for growth in the new century. Looking to the next century was not a new development for the national organization. In the late 1980s, a 21st Century Committee of member volunteers identified objectives that resulted in establishing more professional workshops and identifying needs for better affiliate relationships. A Strategic Development Committee replaced the 21st Century Group in 1993. The latest organization group, consisting of national executive committee members, worked closely with lawyer Tonda Rush, president of American Press Works, to prepare "Blueprint for 2000." The document clearly elucidated ways in which NFPW could remain viable:

The reorganization architects arrived at two answers: It must cut operational costs so that revenues can be directed to programs. It must focus upon two or three core programs that will benefit members and let go of some programs that may have been important but do not necessarily provide momentum for the core missions.[21]

Emphasis was to be placed on professional development, with the NFPW and affiliates potentially sponsoring short courses in life and leadership skills not usually taught in professional schools. Suggestions included financial management, consensus building, and meeting management. In addition, the NFPW planned to develop a leadership manual, make additions to its Web site, study fund-raising needs, and streamline some programs. The Communicator of Achievement recognition, for example, was to be moved from an annual to a biennial event. The NFPW also planned to continue its longstanding support for education through its Education Fund, which offers scholarships to college and graduate students, as well as mini-grants for members to undertake research or attend seminars.

The bid to implement sound fiscal and management practices, coupled with the move to more professional development training, quickly contributed to an upswing in membership. When the reorganization team began its work in mid-1998, membership was 1,925; by June 1999, that had increased to nearly 2,100.

At the 1999 Nashville conference, delegates voted for new bylaws that listed a series of organizational objectives, including the advancement of "the professional development of women communicators." Although men remain eligible for membership, the NFPW delegates overwhelmingly agreed that the federation is committed to helping further the work of women in the new millennium.[22]

NOTES

1. "Helen Malloch's Vision," *Press Woman*, June 1976, p. 2. Much of the information provided here about the organization of the federation came from this article.

2. National Federation of Press Women, Inc., "Blueprint for 2000," 1998, p. 3.

3. Editors note: The spelling of the name MacBride differs according to the source. Elsewhere in this volume she is referred to as Marion McBride.

4. Malloch had worked for newspapers and then as managing editor for the David Cook Publishing Company. She quit in 1935 when she married, then went back to work in 1938 as editor for some magazines, including the *American Osteopathic Magazine*.

5. These were the Illinois Woman's Press Association,* the Woman's Press Club of Indiana,* the Woman's Press Club of New York City,* the Michigan Woman's Press Association,* the Ohio Newspaper Women's Association,* the Portland (Oregon) Press Women, and the National Women's Press Club, located in Washington D.C. All except the Washington club became charter members; in addition the New England Woman's Press Association* and the Missouri Woman's Press Club* became charter members.

6. "Helen Malloch's Vision."

7. Betty G. Spencer, "Moving Confidently into the Second Half-Century," *Press Woman*, July 1988, p. 13.

8. "Helen Malloch's Vision."

9. Ibid., p. 3.

10. "Blueprint for 2000," p. 2.

11. Nan Robertson, *The Girls in the Balcony* (New York: Random House, 1990), p. 63.

12. *Press Woman*, October 1970, p. 4.

13. "Helen Malloch's Vision," p. 5.

14. "Nebraska Press Women Discuss Working Women, Equal Rights," *Press Woman*, October 1970, p. 6.

15. "60 Years of Excellence," NFPW, summer 1997, p. 2.

16. "Honored by Award," *Press Woman*, June 1976, p. 27.

17. Spencer, p. 13.

18. "60 Years of Excellence," p. 5.

19. Roosevelt wrote a syndicated newspaper column, "My Day," from 1936 until her death in 1962; she also had a radio program.

20. "Blueprint for 2000," p. 3

21. Ibid.

22. Author's notes, annual business meeting, NFPW convention, Nashville, 24 June 1999.

INFORMATIONAL SOURCES

Agenda, 1987–98, passim.

"Helen Malloch's Vision." *Press Woman*, June 1976.

"NFPW: 60 Years of Excellence." Special edition of *Agenda*, 1997.

Press Woman, 1970–94, passim.

Robertson, Nan. *The Girls in the Balcony*, New York: Random House, 1992.

INSTITUTIONAL PROFILE

National Federation of Press Women

Dates: Organized 1937, Chicago, Illinois; management assumed by American Pressworks, Arlington, Virginia, in 1997.

Publications: *Agenda*, bimonthly, 1989–present; *Press Woman*, 1940–95 (published monthly 1940–89, bimonthly 1989–present).

Papers: National Federation of Press Women Papers, American Pressworks, Arlington, Virginia. Documents and correspondence from the early years are located in the Illinois Woman's Press Association Collection, Chicago Historical Society, Chicago, Illinois.

Contact: Carol Pierce, Executive Director, NFPW, P.O. Box 5556, Arlington, VA 22205, tel. (800) 780–2715; e-mail: <presswomen@aol.com>.

18

Agnes Hooper Gottlieb

National League of American Pen Women, 1897–Present

(Formerly League of American Pen Women)

ORGANIZATION

Women were rankled by their exclusion from all-male press clubs when three newspaper contributors organized a meeting of seventeen women in Washington, D.C., on June 26, 1897. The idea was originated by Marian Longfellow O'Donoghue, who contributed poetry and prose to newspapers in Boston and Washington, D.C. She sought the assistance of Margaret Sullivan Burke and Anna Sanborn Hamilton. Burke covered the capital for many newspapers as the first regularly accredited woman telegraphic correspondent admitted to the congressional Press Gallery; Hamilton was the social editor at the *Washington Post* and also worked as a proofreader for the federal government.

O'Donoghue was not the first woman writer in the nation's capital to think of organizing. A Ladies' Press Club had, in fact, been established some sixteen years earlier in Washington, and this had been succeeded by the Woman's National Press Association, which still existed, but these three women decided it was time to establish an organization of their own.[1] The triumvirate, later referred to fondly within the organization as the "Dauntless Three," agreed that rather than limit the group to newspaper women, they would try "bringing together women journalists, authors, and illustrators for mutual benefit and the strength that comes with union."[2] That definition was soon expanded to include musicians and composers.

With high hopes of removing discrimination and prejudice against women in the professions, Burke and Longfellow each suggested the names of six possible members while Hamilton contacted five. Seventeen women showed up for the organizational meeting—all but one were writers. They met at the home of novelist Mary Andrews Denison. Hamilton, who presided at the meeting, outlined the trio's plan for an organization that could help them with problems specific to their careers, including "such matters as the libel law, better copyright laws, plagiarism, and for inspiration and mutual aid."[3] The women agreed.

When O'Donoghue and Hamilton declined offers for the presidency, Burke was elected unanimously. Hamilton was elected corresponding secretary. In addition to the three founders, charter members included women who identified themselves in a variety of writing specialties. Newspaper writers included Belle Vane Sherwood and Margaret Wade; Virginia King Frye was a magazine writer; and Nannie M. Lancaster identified herself as a journalist. Writers who identified themselves in specialties were Tillie Orr Hays, advertising writer; Emma V. Triepel, technical and scientific writer; and Jennie S. Campbell, education writer and teacher. Four members—Mary Temple Bayard, Abbie Gunn Baker, Mattie Hamilton Flick, and Ada Tower Cable—simply identified themselves as "writer." Anna B. Patten was a poet, and Alice R. Morgan, instead, identified herself as "artist."

The charter members approved the name League of American Pen Women, which had been proposed by the planning trio, as well as the constitution and bylaws, written by O'Donoghue. Although today it might seem odd that the women would seek inspiration from the writings of two men, they agreed to the motto "All for one, one for all," derived from both Alexander Dumas's *The Three Musketeers* and William Shakespeare's *The Rape of Lucrece*. Patriotic red, white, and blue were selected for the club colors, and the club insignia was designed by the only artist among the charter members, Alice R. Morgan. The insignia of an owl (symbolizing wisdom) perched on a triangle formed by a pen, a pencil, and an artist's brush was then crafted into a pin by a Philadelphia jeweler.

Dues, originally set at $1 a year, were raised to $2 in 1905. Although the club was based in Washington, the organizers envisioned a national network of women writers, artists, and composers. By the end of the first year, membership had grown to fifty women from locations as far afield as Texas, California, New York, and Maine. In 1898, the organization was admitted into the International League of Press Clubs.

GROWTH AND ACTIVITIES

The League of American Pen Women grew steadily and, in 1921, changed its name to the National League of American Pen Women to reflect its influence. By this time, local branches had been established around the country. Los Angeles was organized in 1915; Texas in 1916. By 1921, when the first national convention was held, thirty-five separate branches had been established, including the District of Columbia, Hawaii, and the Philippines.

At the national headquarters in Washington, regular meetings were first held in the living rooms of club members, but as the League grew, it became clear that separate club headquarters were imperative. After World War I, using

$1,500 in profits from an Authors' Carnival Ball, a masquerade party in which the women dressed as literary characters, the club rented a house at 1722 H Street NW. The League used the rooms on the first floor for its offices and meetings, rented rooms on other floors to writers, and established the "Hoot O' the Owl Coffee House" in the basement for club luncheons and dinners. Although some members wanted the cafe to expand its hours and become more publicly accessible, the idea was abandoned because, according to one member, "certain conservative members of the League gathered their classic skirts about them and deplored the League's 'going into trade.' "[4]

Whereas proceeds from the first ball funded the club house, profits from the second carnival ball were used to support a League journal. *The Pen Woman* was first published as a quarterly magazine in April 1920. Prior to its appearance, the headquarters communicated with membership through the *LAPW Bulletin*, which began publication in 1915. The bulletin was used as a networking vehicle so the women would be alerted to writing and poetry contests and activities of other members throughout the United States. More important, perhaps, the League magazine provided a publishing outlet for its members, and branch meetings gave women the chance to read their offerings publicly. "As an added incentive the League guarantees its poets, budding and full-blown, an audience. Could a mother do more for her children?" asked a magazine article about the organization in 1928.[5] The League's journal attracted other readers as well; a third of the subscribers to *The Pen Woman*, which sold for thirty-five cents a copy or $1 a year, were not members of the League.

The League discovered, as did other women's organizations such as the General Federation of Women's Clubs, that the journal, however vital to the networking ability of its membership, was not profitable. In 1923, *The Pen Woman* was replaced by *The Official Bulletin*, which was published until 1940. In that year, the publication of *The Pen Woman* was resumed—first as a monthly, then as a bimonthly—and continues today as a vital voice for the organization. Its importance was underscored during the 1970s in an article reprinted in *The Pen Woman*'s centennial edition:

Keeping our lines of communication open is a big task, and has to be a labor of love for all who have served the League in this capacity. Keeping our lines of communication open is an important task because the right hands need to know what the left hands are doing. Keeping our lines of communication open is breathing life into the official voice of the League.[6]

The League also provided opportunities for publicity and advancement to its artistic members. Individual artists were allowed to exhibit their work at one-woman shows in the national headquarters until the 1920s, when art membership swelled sufficiently to warrant sponsoring the first League Art Show.

In the 1920s, the League had about 1,350 members and the women decided it had grown large enough to begin sponsoring national conventions. The first was held in Washington, D.C., April 13–16, 1921, and attracted three hundred women. After that success, the League began sponsoring biennial conventions. At these gatherings, workshops were held on suitable topics. From the first convention, when the women were received at the White House by President Warren G. Harding and his wife, a visit with the president became a regular feature of the conventions that has survived to the present. The dour Calvin Coolidge, however, refused requests for a tea with League members, but he did pose for a photo with the hundreds of League representatives on the White House lawn.

First ladies who have written books and articles, beginning with Edith Bolling Wilson and including Hillary Rodham Clinton, have been honorary members of the League. Eleanor Roosevelt, who wrote a syndicated newspaper column, "My Day," during her long tenure as first lady, was an active member of the League beginning in 1933. National honorary members have included authors Pearl S. Buck and Anne Tyler, artist Georgia O'Keefe, actress Helen Hayes, syndicated columnist Erma Bombeck, and United Press International reporter Helen Thomas.

In 1951, the League's president, Dorothy Betts Marvin, convinced her executive board to buy an historic house at 1300 17th Street, NW. A new headquarters had been a necessity for some time because the former meeting place had been torn down and meetings had been held in various locations around the city for some time. The new building cost $65,000 and needed about $14,000 in renovations before the women could move in. Through fund-raisers and donations, however, the mortgage was paid off before Marvin completed her tenure as president in 1958. The Pen Arts Building, as it was named, had been built in 1887 for opera star Sarah Adams Whittemore and was later the home of Robert Todd Lincoln and his wife for a year.[7] Now a historical landmark, the mansion contains a library of more than two thousand books written by League members, meeting rooms, and bedrooms where members visiting Washington may stay for a small fee.

Like other women's press organizations, the League has been criticized or disregarded as unimportant and its members accused of dabbling in the arts rather than dedicating themselves to careers. "Certain over-sophisticated souls, who are forever taking the joy out of life by making cutting remarks, have spread the gossip that the Pen Women spend nearly all their time running around to tea parties, bridge games, luncheons or literary meetings," one magazine article noted in 1928. But it then squelched those ugly rumors by adding: "It is true, and the Leaguers freely admit it is true, that they do have parties; they play bridge a great deal, and they have luncheons and literary meetings—oodles of them. But over and above their manifold social functions, the ladies work very hard and very seriously."[8]

Indeed, some of the League's active members included women who began writing or painting well into their middle age after their children had grown and left home (which did not mean, however, that they were necessarily "dabblers"), but others were often committed career women who turned to the League for support and fellowship. Ida Tarbell, the muckraker who exposed the Standard Oil monopoly in 1901 with her articles in *McClure's Magazine*, was an early member, and actress Mary Pickford was an active participant in the Los Angeles branch. And, in the 1930s, when several New York newspapers and the *Literary Digest* debated who were the "Twelve Greatest Living American Women," the names of ten members of the League were mentioned.

THE PRESENT-DAY LEAGUE

By 1999, the League had more than five thousand members with more than two hundred branches in the United States and the Panama Canal Zone. Members are admitted to the League in at least one of three main areas: letters, music, or art. The number and variety of subcategories within each of the three categories attest to how much professional employment and careers had opened up to women since the League was established in 1897. A member in the letters category, for example, may be an author, journalist, poet, dramatist, editor, sales promotion or advertising copywriter, researcher, scriptwriter, lecturer, or genealogist. Membership in the music category is available to published composers or arrangers, and in the art category, to architects, cartoonists, choreographers, craftsmen, designers, interior designers, graphic artists, painters, photographers, sculptors, and illustrators. All the categories require proof that the prospective member is indeed engaged professionally in her chosen field. Writers must submit samples of their published work; artists must show that they have sold work or been accepted in exhibitions or published in magazines within the last five years. Members must also be American citizens.

One hundred years after it was established, the League sees itself as a support system that encourages women to flourish in their creative professions. It has survived far longer than many women's press organizations established at the end of the nineteenth century, but members in recent years have expressed concern that the club's population is aging and not being renewed with fresh, younger blood. "As long as books and paintings are higher valued when signed with a man's name, our League is still needed. But we must attract the younger generation," observed Marty Ouwehand-Hartree of the Palm Beach, Florida, branch, in a 1997 article in *The Pen Woman*.[9] She suggested opening membership to a new category in "computer creativity" as a way of luring younger members. Other members have advocated a name change to something more modern than the image of a pen, and still others have proposed the creation of a public relations campaign to revitalize the organization.

Despite these concerns, the League has continued its tradition of workshops, contests, and social activities, and it continues to sponsor creative writing conferences and workshops to nurture novices and give women opportunities to meet and learn from accomplished artists and authors. Members find this support and encouragement irreplaceable. One member who joined the League in Jacksonville, Florida, in 1957 reminisced about her first meeting: "When I entered that room of creative and accomplished women, several of them civic and social leaders in Jacksonville, I was inspired and thrilled to join them."[10]

Mary Manning, a United Press International reporter who later became president of the League's Nevada State Association, said she joined the League because she was barred from the National Press Club when she worked in Washington, D.C. "As a member of the Pen Women, however, I got the support, the lively discussions, the ideas, and the perseverance to keep working at writing—and not only journalism, but hidden talents neglected by the daily grind—such as writing poetry and learning calligraphy."[11] Manning argued in 1997 that women journalists and writers were still in need of the networking, support, and education provided by the League. "The issues for women reporters and editors today are strangely the same as they were when our Pen Women founders gathered in June of 1897 at the nation's Capital to gather their strengths in numbers," she asserted. "A century ago the seventeen women who hatched the idea of the League faced discrimination, vague copyright laws, plagiarism and labor laws. Sounds familiar, doesn't it?"[12]

The National Press Club eventually admitted women members in 1971.[13] When this happened, Manning became a card-carrying member, but she said the co-ed club could never replace the strength she drew from the League. "The real treasure lies in the friendship and support of belonging to Pen Women. And you don't need a gold card to get respect."[14]

Other members have attested to the importance of the League in providing a support system and professional guidance. "To be able to compare markets, editors, techniques, experiences, helps tremendously," wrote Elizabeth Shafer of the Colorado Springs branch in 1975. "To hear a colleague say, 'Yes, I know the problems facing you—I've been through that myself,' can be of enormous comfort."[15]

NOTES

1. The Woman's National Press Association existed until the 1920s.

2. Claracy Lee M. Waldrop, "We Make History," *The Pen Woman* (June/July/August 1997), p. 11.

3. Ibid., p. 11.

4. Ibid., p. 15.

5. Margaret Cobb, "Gifted Gals," *American Mercury*, June 1928, p. 203.

6. Claracy Lee M. Waldrop, "The Communication Line," *The Pen Woman* (June/July/August 1997), p. 18.

7. "The National League of American Pen Women Pen Arts Building" pamphlet, p. 1.

8. Cobb, "Gifted Gals," p. 203.

9. Mary Ouwehand-Hartree, " 'C' is for Computer," *The Pen Woman* 76 (June/July/August 1997), p. 64.

10. Paula Ferrell Harding, "My Forty Years as a Pen Woman," *The Pen Woman* 76 (June/July/August 1997), pp. 33–34.

11. Mary Manning, "One Woman's Adventures in Journalism," *The Pen Woman* 76 (June/July/August 1997), p. 38.

12. Ibid.

13. Nan Robertson, *The Girls in the Balcony: Women, Men, and the "New York Times"* (New York: Random House, 1992), p. 99.

14. Manning, "One Woman's Adventures," p. 51.

15. Quoted in Elizabeth Shafter, "The Value of Being a Member of the National League of American Pen Women," *The Pen Woman* 76 (June/July/August 1997), p. 42.

INFORMATIONAL SOURCES

Beasley, Maurine H., and Sheila J. Gibbons. *Taking Their Place: A Documentary History of Women and Journalism.* Washington, D.C.: American University Press, 1993.

"Centennial Celebration, 1887–1997." *The Pen Woman* 76 (June/July/August 1997).

Cobb, Margaret. "Gifted Gals." *American Mercury* 14 (June 1928): 199–207.

Robertson, Nan. *The Girls in the Balcony: Women, Men and the "New York Times."* New York: Random House, 1992.

INSTITUTIONAL PROFILE

National League of American Pen Women

Dates: Organized 26 June 1897, as the **League of American Pen Women** in Washington, D.C.; name changed unofficially in 1921 and legally in 1926 to the **National League of American Pen Women**.

Publications: *LAPW Bulletin*, 1915–20, Theodora B. Cunningham, editor; *The Pen Woman*, April 1920–23, Edna M. Colman, editor; *The Official Bulletin*, editors Elizabeth Burgess Hughes (1925–28), Nina Reed (1928–30), Patricia Poe Bennett Dimitriu (1930–32); *The Pen Woman*, 1940–present. *The Pen Woman* currently is published bimonthly and is edited by Jill Chambers and Judith La Fourest.

Contact: National League of American Pen Women, Inc., 1300 17th St. N.W., Washington, DC 20036–1973.

19

Elizabeth V. Burt

New England Woman's Press Association, 1885–1982

INTRODUCTION

When Sallie Joy White started work as a newspaper reporter for the *Boston Post* in 1870, she was the first woman to be hired full time on the staff of a Boston newspaper. She was received by her male colleagues with mixed feelings. White enjoyed her novelty as "the charming girl reporter," but the isolation she experienced among her male colleagues must have been crushing at times.[1] By 1885, White was no longer the only full-time woman reporter in town, but the number of women in that position could be counted on one hand. At the same time, the number of women pursuing an uncertain career as part-time newspaper correspondents and contributors had grown to several score. Despite the growing market for their work in women's magazines and newly established women's columns and sections in newspapers, they faced limited career opportunities, professional isolation, and frequent hostility and ridicule from male colleagues.[2]

It was in this climate that Marion McBride, a special editorial writer for the *Boston Post*, sent out a call to other Boston newspaperwomen to establish a women's press association. The six women who responded quickly agreed to establish the New England Woman's Press Association (NEWPA). Within fourteen months they had attracted several dozen members and approved a constitution that was to serve as a model for many of the women's press organizations established in the next twenty years.[3] It embraced goals that were social, professional, and benevolent:

For the purpose of promoting acquaintance and good fellowship among newspaper women; elevating the work and the workers; and forwarding by concerted action through the Press such good objects in social, philanthropic and reformatory lines as may from time to time present themselves.[4]

Growing to more than 150 members by the turn of the century, NEWPA provided regular meetings and events where women writers could share experience and advice and could meet political, social, and cultural leaders. It provided its members with professional assistance and recognition. Part of the woman's club movement, it occasionally became politically involved, promoting both professional and social issues.

NEWPA's prominence began to fade after the early 1970s. In the face of growing competition from other organizations such as American Women in Radio and Television (AWRT),* Women in Communications, Inc. (WICI),* and the Society of Professional Journalists (SPJ), it failed to attract new members and sustain itself. The association held its last annual meeting in 1982. After that, it disappears from the record.[5]

ORGANIZATION

When Marion McBride sent out her call to Boston newspaperwomen in November 1885, she had already participated in the creation of at least two other women's press organizations earlier that year—the National Woman's Press Association and the Illinois Woman's Press Association.*[6] Boston was a fertile location for such an organization. In 1885, it was the home of nine flourishing dailies, nineteen weeklies, and a variety of religious, trade, and special interest publications, equaling a grand total of 193 publications. Surrounding cities and towns also boasted a full complement of daily, weekly, and miscellaneous publications, making the Boston area one of the richest media centers in the country at that time.[7]

But it was a media center dominated by men, and few of these newspapers employed women as full-time staff members. They did, however, fill their pages with material submitted by women correspondents, "specials," and contributors. These women were usually middle class, with a modest education, and few, if any, professional connections. What many did have, though, were connections to women's organizations such as reading clubs, philanthropic societies, temperance organizations, and suffrage groups. McBride hoped the women who responded to her call would be able to tap into this network, sort out the newspaperwomen, and bring them together for a common purpose.

The six women who met to create NEWPA were McBride; White, who by now was a reporter and columnist for the *Boston Herald*; Estelle M. Hatch ("Jean Kincaid"), who wrote the "Housekeeper's Column" for the *Boston Globe*; Helen M. Winslow ("Trebor Ohl") of the *Boston Advertiser*; Grace Weld Soper of the *Boston Journal*; and Cora Stuart Wheeler, a freelancer for the *Boston Record* and *Boston Advertiser*. They chose White as president and Hatch as secretary. During the next year they recruited as many newspaperwomen as possible, and a second meeting held in December 1886 was attended by a score of New England press women. Alice Stone Blackwell of the *Woman's Journal* was empowered to head a constitutional committee, and a month later, the resulting constitution and bylaws were adopted. To distinguish NEWPA from a purely social club, membership was restricted to women residents in New England who were "regularly and professionally connected with the press of New England, either as writers, editors, business managers, or correspondents—all, in short, for whom work on the press is a vocation, and not an avocation, a breadwinning occupation, and not an amusement."[8] In 1891, a category of associate membership was added, which allowed a broader membership base, but reserved voting privileges for active members.[9]

NEWPA announced its meetings and activities in the women's and society columns of the Boston newspapers, in *The Journalist*, the national trade journal published in New York City, and in the national suffrage publication, the *Woman's Journal*. This publicity, combined with word of mouth and continued recruiting efforts, quickly increased the number of members so that by the time NEWPA incorporated in September 1890, it claimed nearly one hundred. Most were from the Boston area, but there were also representatives from Rhode Island, Maine, New Hampshire, Vermont, and even Nova Scotia.[10]

These women represented a wide variety and range of experience. There were a few newspaper proprietors, including Fannie K. Hamilton, who published the *Old Orchard Rambler* in Biddeford, Maine; Mrs. A. B. Cowell, who inherited the *Winthrop* (Masachusetts) *Visitor* from her husband and published it with the assistance of her mother, Mrs. Hittie Pond; and Alice Weld Whitaker, who with her husband published the *Southbridge Journal*, the *New England Farmer*, and *Our Grange Homes*. Several members were editors for newspaper sections (usually the "household," "at home," literature, or art departments), and some were department editors for several newspapers at the same time. Frances C. Mixter, for example, was the household editor for the *Athol* (Massachusetts) *Chronicle* and the *Templeton* (Massachusetts) *Recorder* as well as the editor of "The Easy Chair" for the *Woman's News*, published in Indianapolis. The majority of NEWPA members, however, were correspondents or special writers who published their work in as many as a dozen newspapers and magazines in as many years. Lucille Lovelle of Taunton, Massachusetts, for example, reported that between 1886 and 1889 she had published her work regularly in more than eight newspapers: the *Boston Post*, the *Boston Daily Globe*, the *Boston Herald*, the *Bristol Country Republican*, the *New York Herald*, the *New York Telegram*, and "other New York papers."[11]

By its second year, the association had established a regular schedule, meeting twice a month between October and May and alternating business with literary meetings. It held annual elections each November, an annual outing each spring, and a "Gentlemen's Night" each February.[12] In addition to these regular meetings and events, NEWPA often held special events—authors' readings, teas, receptions, benefits, and fund-raisers. In 1903, it started holding an annual breakfast each May. With as many as two or three events a week during particularly busy seasons, the association provided its members, even those living at a distance, ample opportunity to participate.

EARLY ACTIVITIES

NEWPA served its members' professional interests through lectures, workshops, special projects, and networking. At its monthly literary meetings, members read papers on topics dealing with the various aspects of writing and publishing, such as "Seeking Employment," "Some Obstacles to the Success of Women in Journalism," "The Sense of Proportion in Journalistic Work," and "The Business End of a Newspaper."[13] Prominent authors or newspaperwomen were frequently invited to speak about their own work. In June 1887, for example, NEWPA gave a banquet in honor of Jane Cunningham Croly, the veteran New York newspaperwoman who wrote under the byline of "Jennie June."[14]

To assist members in finding work, NEWPA established the Woman's Press Bureau in 1888. The Bureau served as both a clearinghouse and an employment agency, its goal being to bring NEWPA members and their work to the attention of the city's editors. In 1894, the association brought its members' work to the attention of the entire city when it put out the February 11 edition of the *Boston Post*. The *Woman's Post*, "written, edited, and put out entirely by women," was heralded in advance, hawked on the streets, and written up in *The Journalist*. It sparked a nationwide fad of "women's editions" for the next two years.[15]

NEWPA also promoted itself by establishing ties with other organizations and in 1889 created a committee dedicated specifically to that task.[16] It developed close ties with other women's press organizations that had been created in its wake. It frequently hosted visiting representatives of sister organizations and encouraged traveling NEWPA members to attend activities sponsored by these organizations. In 1891, NEWPA became a charter member of the International Federation of Women's Press Clubs and sponsored the federation's first convention in Boston that November.

NEWPA also maintained friendly relations with those male press organizations willing to work with or open their doors to women. The association cosponsored a number of events with the Boston Press Club (a male-only organization) and frequently invited its members to receptions and its annual "Gentlemen's Night." It sent delegates to the annual conventions of the National Editorial Association and in 1891 became a member of the International League of Press Clubs.[17]

Topics raised at NEWPA meetings occasionally led to political action. In March 1889, following a debate on international copyright law, the association petitioned Congress to pass such a law. Signed by all the officers and twenty-four members, the petition argued that the lack of a copyright law was "an obstacle to the path of every literary woman, whether author or journalist."[18] At the turn of the century, the association became active in the campaign for clean journalism. It hosted speakers on the topic, sponsored a meeting open to the public on the issue, and petitioned newspapers to halt their descent into sensational journalism.

Very much a part of the woman's club movement, NEWPA sponsored benevolent activities. During the economic recession of 1893, it established a benefit society, "Samaritana," and in the following winter raised $1,100 for the poor at an authors' reading at the Hollis Street Theater. A portion of the proceeds established a reserve fund "for the relief of suffering men and women journalists." NEWPA added to the Journalist's Fund, which was still in existence in 1982, through further authors' readings, auctions, subscription drives, newspaper and book sales, and occasional gifts and bequests. In 1915, a portion of the fund was diverted to endow a hospital bed for women writers at the Lynn Hospital, an arrangement that continued until 1929.[19]

NEWPA also participated in many of the broader activities of the woman's club movement at the turn of the century, becoming a charter member of both the General Federation of Women's Clubs (in 1890) and the Massachusetts State Federation of Women's Clubs (in 1893). In 1892, it sent seven representatives to the World's Fair in Chicago to participate in the Congress of Literary Women in the Woman's Building, and in 1895, it sent twenty members to participate in the Woman's Congress at the Cotton State Exposition in Atlanta.

Many NEWPA members were active in the suffrage movement; indeed, during its first years, the association met in the offices of the *Woman's Journal*. Votes for women was frequently a topic on the agenda, and as the suffrage campaign heated up during the 1910s and suffragists took to the streets, so did the normally staid NEWPA. In 1914, a delegation joined the Writers' League for Suffrage in the May 2 Boston suffrage parade, and in March 1919, NEWPA delegated member Grace E. Cross to participate in the National Woman's Party demonstration in Washington, D.C.[20]

CHANGING WITH THE TIMES

By 1915, many of NEWPA's founders had died, but because of continued recruiting over the years, younger women had taken their places at the helm. The association's awareness of the need to constantly revitalize itself was apparent in a 1917 address by its president, Grace M. Burt. She pledged to "make the Association of more vital interest and value to members at a distance from Boston, to emphasize the fact that it really is a New England and not a local organization, [and] to make it equally attractive to the young, active newspaper women on the city dailies as to the women writers of greater leisure." Burt made this pledge at a time when other women's press organizations were faltering, perhaps because of women's greater career opportunities (and therefore greater responsibilities), perhaps because of their involvement in the war relief effort. She wisely decided to suspend the association's frequent teas and banquets in a spirit of wartime sacrifice, but she retained the essential business and literary meetings each month "lest the intimate, friendly touch of member with member . . . and the good fellowship for which we were organized, should be lost."

Whereas other women's organizations became involved in war relief work and NEWPA members might certainly participate in them, Burt decided that NEWPA's focus should remain those of a "technical organization."[21]

NEWPA maintained an average membership of more than 120 well into the 1940s and did so through special efforts to encourage young women entering the profession.[22] In April 1918, for example, the association sponsored a "Newspaper Day" to which it invited "a number of the younger newspaper women on the Boston dailies." It took another step toward attracting younger members in 1927, when president Helena B. Shipman organized the Junior Pen Writers as an auxiliary. And twenty-three years later, NEWPA member Roberta B. Brown became the liaison to women journalism students at Boston University when she became the faculty adviser to Etaoin Shrdlu (the Women's Journalism Society of Boston University).[23]

NEWPA also took into account the growing number of writing opportunities open to women and the new communication technology of radio. In the early 1920s, it amended its constitution so that instead of being devoted only to "newspaper women," it included the larger population of "newspaper and kindred women writers." NEWPA's interpretation of "kindred women writers" eventually came to include magazine writers, poets, authors, playwrights, publicity and public relations writers, and, by the late 1920s, radio script writers.[24] Radio, in fact, became a topic of fascination as well as a window of opportunity for the association. Women and men in the industry were invited to meetings to speak on the various aspects of the new technology, and during the 1930s and 1940s, NEWPA broadcast regular shows on WEEI-Boston and WORL-Boston that featured women's interests and their achievements in specific fields.[25]

NEWPA had long relied on the society and club columns in local newspapers to announce the programs for its upcoming meetings, but in the early 1930s, it began publishing a monthly bulletin. The bulletin, which was published from September to May during the association's "active" season, was mailed to NEWPA members as well as women's department editors. It presented the program for upcoming meetings, the names of officers and new members, profiles on guests and speakers, items concerning upcoming issues, and poems.[26] By the mid-1940s, the bulletin had begun to announce an annual workshop, which was designed to assist members and attract new ones. Though these workshops often offered standard fare, such as "Writing a Feature Column" and "Ask the Society Editor," they occasionally broke new ground. In 1948, for example, sessions were offered on "Editing Winter Sports" and "Photography Afield."[27]

Another publicity and recruiting tool was an annual awards competition, established in 1946. The competition was open to any woman's work published in a magazine or a New England daily or weekly newspaper. As the years went by, additions and changes to the list of awards reflected women's growing opportunities in the periodical industry. Initially, awards were given for the top stories in a number of categories, including news story, feature story, and "article or column of special interest to women." In 1951, the contest added a "New England Newspaper Woman of the Year" award, which made the awards ceremony a media event widely covered by New England papers. During the 1970s, the association added three more awards: best student journalist, best series by a woman, and best woman columnist. By 1982, awards for best sportswriter and magazine journalist had been added and the contest was open to "all New England Journalists," which allowed men to participate. Recipients for the top award included Catherine Coyne (Hudson) of the *Boston Herald* (1947 and 1949), Mary Handy of the *Christian Science Monitor* (1952, 1953, and 1955), Mary Crewmen of the *Boston Globe* (1960), Kay Maxwell of the *Hartford Times* (1963), and Karen J. Sherbin of the *Hartford Courant* (1982). In the association's last awards ceremony in 1982, two men received awards: Bruce Butterfield of the *Providence Journal-Bulletin* won the Best Series Award; Mark Muro of Harvard University was a finalist in the Student Journalist Award.[28]

LAST YEARS

For nine decades, NEWPA remained a vital organization for women in the print media. In the early 1970s, it followed the lead of other women's press organizations such as the Women's National Press Club* and WICI by opening membership to men. But the decision was reached only after some spirited resistance from members who wanted to keep the organization a women's group.[29] Despite the change, membership dropped, attendance shrank, and the number of meetings was reduced to four a year. Eventually, in the early 1980s, NEWPA simply "faded away," in the words of one former president.[30]

It is ironic that it was during the years of "women's liberation" that the association lost its impetus. Unlike its founders, who engaged NEWPA in suffrage activism at the beginning of the century, the association's leaders in the 1960s and 1970s were reluctant to take similar action for women's rights. Programs during its last years occasionally included "topics such as the ERA [Equal Rights Amendment],"[31] but no formal position was taken on the amendment, no representatives were sent to demonstrations, and no resolutions, petitions, or calls for action were issued.[32] Former president Muriel Knight (1972–73), who in the mid-1960s became the association's first African American member and was its only African American officer, said she believed women were simply too busy "working and making ends meet" to get involved in much activism.[33] Former president Evelena Hudson (1973–74) said she believed the leadership was too "conservative and traditional" to become politically active.[34]

Hudson also traced NEWPA's demise to increasing competition from other professional organizations such as SPJ, which had opened membership to women in the early 1970s, AWRT, and WICI. In an attempt to retain members and work with other women's organizations rather than compete with them, Hudson organized a few joint meetings with AWRT and WICI in 1974 and tried opening NEWPA meetings to members of the other groups. But "the other groups were newer and more appealing for some of our younger members," she said. "They offered something we couldn't—attention to broadcast on one hand, and to wider fields in communication on the other. Some women just began to see us as too restricted. Too 'old.' " Hudson also believes NEWPA's decision to restrict its annual awards to individuals in print journalism discouraged those in other fields of communication from joining.[35]

Another reason for NEWPA's demise is that by 1980, the organization was no longer actively recruiting new members, as it had done in earlier years and as its rivals were now doing. For example, whereas both SPJ and WICI had chapters that actively engaged students in Boston University's School of Communication, NEWPA no longer made the attempt.[36] "There was no one to come along and carry the torch," said Knight.[37]

CONTRIBUTIONS

Despite its quiet end, NEWPA was a vital resource for hundreds of New England women in newspaper and magazine work for more than nine decades. It provided a podium at which they could voice their concerns and interests about their role in American society and in the newspaper profession at a time when they were far from welcome among their male colleagues. It allowed them to state their ambitions without fear of ridicule, and it opened new avenues where they could publish their work. Through its affiliations with other press organizations, NEWPA created a sense of legitimacy for its members within the press community. Through activities like the *Woman's Post* of 1894, its radio shows of the 1930s and 1940s, and its annual awards from 1946 to 1982, it promoted that legitimacy to the general public.

After traveling through uncharted and often hostile territory, the women journalists who joined NEWPA found it a haven. Founder Sallie Joy White noted this when she spoke of the need for women's press organizations in her public lectures and newspaper columns. Mary Sarah King, who entered journalism in the early 1930s with no more than a high school education and the ambition to succeed, noted this when she said, "The men didn't like women in the business at all. . . . You had to be tough. . . . You had to keep on your toes all the time. We could talk about that at NEWPA."[38] And Muriel Knight, who had encountered professional discrimination both as a woman and as an African American, said membership provided a form of recognition. "The playing field wasn't level. We were 'supposed' to go only so high," she said. "We needed an organization like NEWPA to make sure we would get parity."[39]

Although Knight moved on to other activities and organizations after 1982, she believed NEWPA's cessation was premature. Women had made great strides in journalism, with increasing numbers attending journalism school, getting college degrees, and securing jobs and noteworthy promotions in the news and communications industry. But the playing field had not yet been leveled. After 1982, New England women who wanted to achieve parity would have to do it on their own or with the support of the remaining and more competitive organizations.

NOTES

1. White began work as Sarah Elizabeth Joy; she became Sallie Joy White after her marriage in 1874. Hired by the *Post* to cover woman suffrage, she quickly branched out to cover cultural, social, and women's news. Elizabeth V. Burt, "Pioneering for Women Journalists: Sallie Joy White, 1870–1909" (unpublished paper presented to the national convention of the Association for Education in Journalism and Mass Communication, Baltimore, August 1998).

2. S. D. Fry, "Newspaper Women," *Philadelphia Herald*, n.d., quoted in "Newspaper Women," *The Journalist*, 19 November 1892, p. 10.

3. Major sources for the material presented in this chapter are Myra B. Lord, *History of the New England Woman's Press Association* (Newton, Mass.: Graphic Press, 1932); *The Journalist*, 1885–1905, passim; New England Woman's Press Association Papers (hereafter NEWPA Papers), Massachusetts Historical Society, Boston, Massachusetts; and interviews with former NEWPA presidents Evelena Hudson, Muriel Knight, and Laura White.

4. Jean Kincaid (Estelle M. Hatch), "New England Woman's Press Association," *The Journalist*, 26 January 1889, p. 7.

5. Evelena Hudson (NEWPA president, 1973–74), telephone interview by author, 4 June 1999.

6. McBride suggested the creation of the national association in discussions with Eliza Nicholson, editor of the *New Orleans Picayune*, while she was in New Orleans as assistant press commissioner of the 1885 North, South and Central American Exposition. A contributor to a number of newspapers and magazines in addition to the *Post*, McBride combined her work as a newspaperwoman with her promotion of charitable and industrial enterprises. "Mrs. Marion A. McBride," obituary, *Boston Transcript*, 17 September 1909.

7. In 1886, 551 periodicals were published in Massachusetts. Of these, 48 were daily and 375 weekly newspapers. N. W. Ayer and Son, *American Newspaper Annual, 1886* (Philadelphia: N. W. Ayer & Son, 1886), pp. 28–32.

8. Jean Kincaid, "New England Woman's Press Association," p. 7.

9. Lord, *History*, p. 51.

10. Boston newspaperwomen dominated the association until the 1970s, when women from the Massachusetts north and south shores started to challenge the leadership. Evelena Hudson, correspondence with author, 18 June 1999.

11. *The Journalist*, 26 January 1889, pp. 7–11.

12. In 1906, the annual meeting was moved to May to conform to the annual schedule of the General Federation of Women's Clubs, which it had joined in 1890.

13. Lord, *History*, pp. 23, 28, 65.

14. "Banquet to 'Jennie June,' " *Boston Post*, 21 June 1887.

15. Burt, "Bid for Legitimacy," pp. 77–78; Ann Mauger Colbert, "Philanthropy in the Newsroom: Women's Editions of Newspapers, 1894–1896," *Journalism History* 22 (autumn 1996): 91–99.

16. Lord, *History*, p. 37.

17. Ibid., pp. 79–80.

18. The copyright bill was eventually signed by President Harrison. Lord, *History*, pp. 27–28.

19. One benefactor was *Christian Science Monitor* publisher Mary Baker Eddy, who donated $500 in 1909. Lord, *History*, pp. 258, 363.

20. Lord, *History*, p. 305.

21. Ibid., pp. 286, 304.

22. *NEWPA Year-Book, 1946* and "Treasurer's Report, 1939–40," both in NEWPA Papers.

23. Lord, *History*, pp. 287, 289; *NEWPA Bulletin*, May 1950, NEWPA Papers.

24. "Constitution," *NEWPA Year-Book, 1946*, NEWPA Papers.

25. "Tuning in on Radio," *NEWPA Bulletin*, February 1939; Lord, *History*, p. 352; *NEWPA Bulletin*, 1934–36, passim. All in NEWPA Papers.

26. It is unclear when publication of the bulletin began or ceased, since the available issues are dated but not numbered. The only copies the author could locate were contained in the NEWPA Papers at the Massachusetts Historical Association. These were dated from 1934 to 1953.

27. "NEWPA's Workshop Program," *NEWPA Bulletin*, October 1948.

28. "NEWPA Awards," *NEWPA Yearbook, 1965*, pp. 6–7; "Entry Form," 1982 Awards, NEWPA; and "Program," NEWPA Thirty-seventh Annual Awards Dinner, 3 June 1982, all in the possession of Muriel Knight; Evelena Hudson, correspondence with author, 18 June 1999.

29. Laura White, telephone interview by author, 25 June 1999. White successfully brought a male journalist into the organization over the resistance of some members who wanted to keep NEWPA a women's organization. Hudson, who followed her as president in 1973, remembers that another male nominee was rejected. Evelena Hudson, telephone interview by author, 17 January 1999.

30. Hudson, telephone interview by author, 17 January 1999.

31. NEWPA membership application, in possession of Muriel Knight.

32. Evelena Hudson, telephone interview by author, 17 January 1999.

33. Muriel Knight, interview by author, Boston, Massachusetts, 19 February 1999.

34. Hudson, telephone interview by author, 17 January 1999.

35. Ibid.

36. The author was a student at the Boston University School of Communication in 1980 and worked at newspapers in the Boston area until 1988. She was never contacted by NEWPA and never heard of the association until she began research on women's press organizations in 1994.

37. Muriel Knight, interview by author.

38. Mary Sarah King, telephone interview by author, 12 January 1999.

39. Knight was a reporter for WILD Radio, the city's only African American radio station, and the *Roxbury City News*, an African American community paper. She entered the doctoral program in educational administration at Northeastern University and received her Ed. D. in 1988 at the age of sixty-five. Muriel Knight, interview by author, 19 February 1999.

INFORMATIONAL SOURCES

The Journalist, 1885–1904, passim.

Lord, Myra B. *History of the New England Woman's Press Association*. Newton, Mass.: Graphic Press, 1932.

New England Woman's Press Association Papers. Massachusetts Historical Society, Boston, Massachusetts.

Sallie Joy White Papers. Schlesinger Library, Radcliffe College, Cambridge, Massachusetts.

Weltman, Janie Gordon. *Our First 50 Years, 1885–1935*. Malden, Mass.: Maplewood Press, 1936.

INSTITUTIONAL PROFILE

New England Woman's Press Association

Dates: Established in Boston, Massachusetts, 15 November 1885; incorporated 15 September 1890; charter member General Federation of Women's Clubs, 1890; charter member Massachusetts Federation of Women's Clubs, 1895; charter member National Federation of Press Women, 1938; ceased after May 1982.

Newsletter: A bulletin was published approximately nine times a year between 1934 and 1953; initial and final publication dates are unknown by the author. Copies available in New England Woman's Press Association Papers, Massachusetts Historical Society, Boston, Massachusetts.

Papers: New England Woman's Press Association Papers, Massachusetts Historical Society, Boston, Massachusetts. Some papers pertaining to the association are contained in collections in the Schlesinger Library, Cambridge, Massachusetts, including the Sallie Joy White Papers, the New England Woman's Club Papers, and the Estelle Hatch Merrill Vertical File.

20

Linda Steiner

The *New York Times* Women's Caucus, 1972–Present

ORGANIZATION

The *New York Times* Women's Caucus emerged in 1972 from the concerns of women working at the *New York Times* that, relative to men, they were underemployed and underpaid. From the outset the group committed itself to representing the interests of women on both editorial and business sides of the paper, especially getting women promoted, including into the highest ranks of *Times* management. Although the Women's Caucus was primarily inspired and led by reporters, it was open to all women at the *Times*. For example, attending one of its early meetings with publisher Arthur Ochs Sulzberger and some of his top executives were not only reporters but also a picture researcher who had started as a secretary; and a group of secretaries eventually joined the Women's Caucus.

The group of women that founded the Women's Caucus gathered at a luncheon at an out-of-the-way restaurant. They chose Betsy Wade as their first leader. Wade, who had been hired in 1956 as the *Times*'s first woman copyreader, was then the chief copyeditor on the newspaper's foreign desk. She was the sole woman at the *Times* holding a title usually reserved for men; the only other two women in top editorial positions at the paper, the editor and the deputy editor of the family department, held positions traditionally held by women.[1] Indeed, of the forty women reporters (out of a total of 425 reporters) at the *Times*, eleven were in the family and style department.

One of the Caucus's earliest acts was to send a five-page letter to Sulzberger and his sisters and mother, as directors of the New York Times Company, and to a few editors. This letter outlined the statistical evidence, obtained from the Newspaper Guild, for the women's claim that the paper was stubbornly relegating women to its lower-paying, lower-ranking jobs. Furthermore, the letter showed, women with comparable education, ability, and experience were paid less than men for the same work. At the level of general assignment reporters, for example, the wage gap was $59 a week. Noting that none of the twenty-one names on the masthead was that of a woman, the letter stated, "*The Times* is and always has been remiss in seeing that women employees reach positions in the vital decision-making areas of the paper."[2] The letter, signed by fifty women, called for an affirmative action program at the paper in accordance with the Civil Rights Act of 1964.

The formation of the Caucus needs to be put in the context of both the *New York Times* and the times. It followed not only changes in the law that barred employment discrimination but also the formation of all kinds of feminist organizations and consciousness-raising groups, including the National Organization for Women (NOW) and the National Women's Political Caucus. According to founding member Nan Robertson, "The momentum everywhere in the country was irresistible."[3] Yet, although the Caucus certainly was aware of the organizing and legal actions of women at other media institutions (including *Newsweek* and *Reader's Digest*, as well as newspapers and wire services), it did not make contact with feminist and activist groups.

In addition to Wade, the moral and intellectual leaders and organizers of the Caucus were Grace Glueck, a reporter on the culture desk, and Joan Cook, who had begun as a woman's page reporter in 1959. Other prominent members were Grace Lichtenstein, a cityside reporter who had been fighting for permission to cover the women's movement; Eileen Shanahan, a top economics reporter; and Judy Klemesrud, a reporter for the family and style page. These women represented a distinct minority among female employees. In 1972, approximately 10 percent of the entire *Times* workforce (from cleaning ladies to editors) was female; and only about 10 percent of those women joined the Caucus. According to Robertson, conspicuous by their absence were society reporter Charlotte Curtis and architecture critic Ada Louise Huxtable; their lack of support may have somewhat undermined the strength of the Caucus.

Soon after sending out its letter to the Sulzbergers, the Caucus began a period of rapid growth. After six months of active recruiting, eighty-four Caucus members had filed individual complaints against the *Times*.

LEGAL ACTION

Regardless of the numbers of women who did or did not sign on with the Caucus, the organization met with some preliminary success. Shortly after the Caucus's meeting with *Times* executives, Flora Lewis was named as chief of the Paris bureau, where Robertson herself was also sent for three years. Lewis and Robertson both gave credit to the Caucus for these plum assignments. Other immediate results were "equalization raises" for fourteen women reporters. Sulzberger sent a memo to the entire staff promising both equal pay for equal work and full use of the talent of women employees. He promised to hire, train, and promote women. In 1973, 47 percent of the newly hired reporters and editors were women.

Yet, even by the account of John Mortimer, vice president for industrial relations, progress on certain fronts was "glacial."[4] When, more than a year after the initial meeting with the Sulzbergers, the glass ceiling remained intact, the Caucus acted again. Betsy Wade made a formal statement at the April 1974 board meeting of the *Times* stockholders and the Caucus leaders sent a letter to all women working for the *Times* noting that the gap between women's and men's average salaries had actually increased since their initial complaint. The Caucus eventually decided to get a lawyer, choosing Harriet Schaffer Rabb, of the Employment Rights Project at Columbia Law School. Rabb's clinic also represented women working for some other news organizations. The *Times* women were cautious about suing, however, perhaps because their "love affair was stronger than [their] anger," as Joan Cook put it.[5]

Finally, in November 1974, six members of the Caucus sued the *Times* for sex discrimination. Because Wade used her legal married name, Boylan, her name came first alphabetically and the suit became known as *Elizabeth Boylan, et al., Plaintiffs v. The New York Times Company, Defendant*. The other plaintiffs were Louise Carini, an accountant; Andrea Skinner, a Sunday magazine news clerk and children's fashion editor, and one of the paper's few women of color; Nancy Davis, a telephone advertising solicitor; Grace Glueck; and Joan Cook. Two years later, Eileen Shanahan, who was still covering economics from the Washington bureau, joined the suit, although she soon quit the *Times* to take a job as the press officer for the Department of Health, Education, and Welfare.

In 1977, on the basis of documents filed by Harriet Rabb and her colleagues, a judge approved a petition to declare *Boylan v. The New York Times* a class-action suit. That is, the plaintiffs were seen as representing all women under Guild jurisdiction as well as women who were management secretaries. Since the *Times* declared that it would never settle with the women, the case moved toward trial. There were months of interviewing of potential witnesses and taking of depositions—processes that were, not surprisingly, highly acrimonious and divisive. Rabb told the Caucus that the *Times* had vowed not to give the women "even a peppercorn in back pay."[6]

On October 6, 1978, however, the *Times* settled for $350,000. Of this amount, $233,500 was back pay (which the *Times* called annuities) for 550 women. Distribution of specific amounts was determined by seniority. Some of the remaining money went to the named plaintiffs and to cover the lawyers' fees and expenses (these fees were used to fund the training of law students). The *Times* agreed to a four-year affirmative action plan and was ordered to make yearly reports until the end of 1982.

The Caucus itself received $1,500 to defray the costs of enforcing the court decree, that is, to monitor the paper's compliance. The Caucus continued in other ways, under the leadership of *Times* mapmaker Emily Weiner, who was hired shortly after the suit was settled.

Assessments of the success of the Caucus and of the suit are "mixed," especially when compared, for example, to the suit filed by women against the Associated Press in 1978 and settled in 1983. Weiner described the paper's compliance "woefully inadequate," at least regarding issues of status and power.[7] Kay Mills, of the *Los Angeles Times*, notes that some people believe the *New York Times* was able to avoid honoring its promises because the settlement decree was insufficiently monitored.[8] Whether this was a way of criticizing the Caucus is not clear, but Margaret Hayden, Rabb's successor as the attorney for the Caucus, did send a letter to the magistrate supervising the decree in which she complained that the paper was essentially ignoring the employment goals that had been set out in 1978. Other evidence of the *Times*'s failure to live up to the agreement can be found in a study of ten elite newspapers conducted in 1985 by NOW's Women's Media Project. Counting the number and percentage of female bylines in each of the newspapers, the study rated the *New York Times* the worst in the group. (*USA Today* was rated best.)[9]

Certainly, the named plaintiffs did not do well. According to Wade, the result of the settlement was "neither the extreme of seeing scales fall from management's eyes nor a purgatory of corporate revenge."[10] Yet, Wade was derailed to writing the "Practical Traveler" column for the *Times* travel section, where she continues still. Since 1978 she has received only union or mandated raises. By Wade's account, Joan Cook, who was shifted to day rewrite, was "the most punished." Andrea Skinner continued with the same job until her retirement. Having disliked editing, Grace Glueck returned to working as an arts news reporter; now retired, she writes for the *Times* on contract. The other women left the paper. Ironically, in 1991, when the *Times* bought out several employees covered by the Newspaper Guild, including Cook, Glueck, and Skinner, it required that those employees promise not to sue on the basis of age discrimination.[11] The gap between men's and women's salaries did not widen in the four years of the court-enforced affirmative action program. Later, however, examining Newspaper Guild statistics, the Caucus found that this gap had again widened significantly, especially at the higher ranks of reporters. According to Wade, because the Caucus had little power to reach newly hired women, these women were "shortchanged on arrival" and never managed to catch up.[12]

In contrast, in the years after the settlement, the *Times* hired and promoted a number of talented women on both the business and news sides, the latter ranging from foreign reporting to sports. Many of those newcomers hired in the 1980s acknowledged their debt to the Caucus. In 1987, at the tenth anniversary celebration of the suit's settlement, several of the new women acknowledged the importance of the Caucus as a support group, as a voice for advocating child care, flextime, and promotions, and as a teaching arm—for retraining men to think differently about women. Leaders of the Caucus could and did go to management on behalf of individual women who may not have enjoyed as much credibility or who may not have wanted to "engage in hand-to-hand combat."[13] It might also be noted that Charlotte Curtis, among others, long a nemesis of the Caucus, also enjoyed the benefits of the settlement; in 1974, she was promoted to editor of the Op-Ed page. According to Robertson, however, the higher Curtis rose in rank, the less clout she wielded.[14]

AFTER THE SETTLEMENT

During the years following the settlement, the Caucus continued to represent the interests of the women at the *New York Times* through a variety of activities. It intermittently published a newsletter that was generally taken outside the company to be typeset. The newsletter was mostly taken up with notices about meetings and other routine business, but it occasionally carried a longer article, such as a profile of a newly hired female security guard. The Caucus also put together a booklet on how to organize a women's caucus that it made available to other journalists through the Women's Institute for Freedom of the Press in Washington, D.C.*[15]

In 1990, the Caucus took on management again, in response to sexist remarks *Times* executive editor Max Frankel made in an interview published in the *Washington Post*. Frankel was trying to defend the *Times* against the criticism that it ran fewer front-page stories by and about women than did other major papers. The *Washington Post* quoted him as saying, "If you are covering local teas, you've got more women than the *Wall Street Journal*." The day after the *Post* story appeared, many *Times* employees arrived at work wearing tea bags on their lapels. The Caucus protested in writing, and Frankel soon apologized for his sexist remark.

In 1991 the Caucus protested again when Frankel allowed a profile to run in the *Times* that named the woman who had accused William Kennedy Smith of rape. By mentioning details of the accuser's life, such as bar-hopping, her illegitimate child, her poor record in school, and other incidents allegedly indicating her "wild streak," the *Times* profile essentially portrayed the woman as a slut. When the *Times* coverage was criticized as sexist and insensitive, Frankel at first defended his position. In this case, Caucus members were not alone in complaining about the insensitivity of their paper. Some 250 *Times* staffers, about half of them men, joined the fifty members of the Caucus in a public meeting to object. Frankel was compelled to retract his defense of the story. This, in combination with the result of the earlier case, appeared to some to be a sign of a cultural-political shift at the *Times*. To others, instead, the fact that Frankel had said what he had said in the first place was a sign that there had *not* been much of a shift.

The last event sponsored by the Caucus was in 1994, when Joan Cook, just months before her death, organized a showing at a nearby union hall of a documentary about women imprisoned for killing their abusive lovers or husbands.

The event was co-sponsored with the Citywide Newswomen's Caucus (which involved women from *Newsday*, the *New York Post*, the *Daily News*, and the *Wall Street Journal*). Since then, the Caucus's glass-covered bulletin board has been empty and the Caucus has been inactive, even though Shelly Freierman is its official head.

Although women hired at the *Times* during the 1990s may not know of the Caucus, its success in forcing a landmark settlement with the newspaper, or the changes it sought to bring about, veterans of the 1970s remember it well. Robertson, who worked in New York for the paper from 1975 to 1988 and moved on to teach journalism at the University of Maryland, calls the Caucus "one of the great experiences of my life. . . . [The Caucus showed] that in unity and organization there really is strength. . . . One thing that really works is a show of strength—of banding together. . . . No one representing the status quo will give away power. Management had to be pushed and the Caucus did that."[16]

Robertson also believes the Caucus was a victim of its own success. When Arthur Ochs Sulzberger, Jr., became publisher, he made it clear that "the old ways [wouldn't] wash any more." By 1998, the salary gap between men and women at the *Times* had virtually closed. Furthermore, Robertson attributes some of the disinterest in the Caucus to the general "mindset" of reporters and editors to avoid organizations. "Journalists are not likely to be strong unionists—or feminists," she says.[17]

Wade attributes the quiescence of the Caucus during the 1990s to the fact that no one has the time and energy to move it into action. About the organization's achievements she has written: "We remain proud. Though we may walk invisible among our legatees, we know that we opened doors for a new generation that may not know they were ever closed."[18] Meanwhile, she adds, "the Caucus always needs to be there . . . for the next time that things go haywire."[19]

NOTES

1. Nan Robertson, *The Girls in the Balcony: Women, Men, and the "New York Times"* (New York: Random House, 1992), p. 7.

2. Quoted in Robertson, *Girls in the Balcony*, p. 145.

3. Ibid., p. 131.

4. Ibid., p. 157.

5. Joan Cook and Betsy Wade, "One Shot at History," audiotape of talk at the Schlesinger Library, Radcliffe College, 1 May 1986.

6. Robertson, *Girls in the Balcony*, p. 204.

7. Ibid., p. 211.

8. Kay Mills, *A Place in the News: From the Women's Pages to the Front Page* (New York: Dodd Mead, 1988), p. 164.

9. Ibid., pp. 280–81. The name of the study was the Women's Media Project of the National Organizations of Women's Legal Defense and Education Fund.

10. Betsy Wade, "Surviving Being a Survivor, Or, Whatever Became of What's Her Name?" *Media Studies Journal* 9 (1995): 33.

11. Ibid.

12. Ibid., p. 43.

13. Betsy Wade Boylan, conversation with the author, 4 September 1998.

14. Robertson, *The Girls in the Balcony*.

15. The Women's Institute for Freedom of the Press published *Media Report to Women*, which provided the most complete coverage of the suit and settlement. Since the *Times* and other New York papers were on strike at the time of the settlement, *Media Report to Women* was all the more valuable.

16. Nan Robertson, interview by author, 9 September 1998.

17. Ibid.

18. Wade, "Surviving Being a Survivor," p. 33.

19. Wade, interview by the author, 4 September 1998.

INFORMATIONAL SOURCES

Cook, Joan, and Betsy Wade. "One Shot at History." Tape of talk at the Schlesinger Library, Radcliffe College, Cambridge, Massachusetts, 1 May 1986.

Media Report to Women, 1972–present, passim.

Mills, Kay. *A Place in the News: From the Women's Pages to the Front Page*. New York: Dodd Mead, 1988.

Robertson, Nan. *The Girls in the Balcony: Women, Men, and the New York Times*. New York: Random House, 1992.

Wade, Betsy. "Surviving Being a Survivor, Or, Whatever Became of What's Her Name?" *Media Studies Journal* 9 (1995): 32–43.

INSTITUTIONAL PROFILE

New York Times Women's Caucus

Dates: Founded 1972; reached settlement with the *New York Times*, 6 October 1978.

First leader: Betsy Wade; current head, Sheila Freierman, the *New York Times*.

Beverly G. Merrick

Newswomen's Club of New York, 1922–Present

(Formerly New York Newspaper Women's Club)

INTRODUCTION

The New York Newspaper Women's Club was founded in 1922 by New York City newspaperwomen who had walked with and written about the suffragists. These news reporters had apparently begun to believe the words of the crusading women they covered: A woman was fully capable of holding any job held by a man. Several of these women were given the opportunity to prove this to be true during World War I, when the men left the newsroom to fight the war. They stepped into their positions, some hesitantly, others boldly. After the war, when the men returned to take back their jobs, many women decided to remain, although not all were invited to stay on. And those who were invited to remain were often kept on grudgingly and at lower pay.

These were exceptional women because only the very capable were allowed to keep their positions in this highly competitive profession. Their ability was not always acknowledged; their occasional male supporters were at times bemused and at other times just barely tolerant of this new creature in the newsroom. Most newsmen, however, were intolerant, convinced that a mere woman could not actually cut the mustard in the long term—that is, do as good a job as a man. Thus, they often ignored her or were openly hostile. Even when women journalists demonstrated they could do the job, few of their male colleagues cared to record for history their contributions or crusading spirit.[1]

Although there was already another women's press club in New York, the Woman's Press Club of New York City,* established in 1889, these women apparently felt the need for an organization devoted specifically to newspaperwomen.[2] The organization originally stressed that its members must be women who worked for newspapers on a regular basis, not transients or temporary stars who contributed only briefly or sporadically to the quality of newspaper work.[3] As the decades passed, the club changed with the times and came to welcome, first, women working for magazines and, later, those in radio and television. In 1972, in order to reflect these changes, the organization changed its name to the Newswomen's Club of New York, and women across the media professions of the greater metropolitan area joined.[4]

FOUNDING

The New York Newspaper Women's Club was founded by thirty-two news-paperwomen at the Hotel Vanderbilt on March 8, 1922. The founders had marched with the suffragists, reporting on the exploits of such women as Emmeline Pankhurst and Alice Paul. The organization was, in fact, to a large degree a result of women's networking during the suffrage movement, according to an article published in the club's newsletter some thirty years later: "Martha Coman and other ladies of the press, assigned to cover suffrage meetings, would gather after the meetings for tea and talk, and so the idea for a club for newspaper-women was born."[5]

The founders and first officers all had impressive credentials. Martha Coman of the New York Herald was the club's first president. A graduate of Stamford University, Coman had been hired as a reporter by Frank Munsey during his short stint as the *Herald*'s publisher and was among the first women reporters to receive a byline.[6] Other officers were Jane Dixon, of the *Evening Telegram*, vice president; Theodora Bean, of the *Morning Telegraph*, vice president; Ann Dunlap, of the *American*, corresponding secretary; and Emma Bugbee, of the *Tribune*, recording secretary. Jane Grant of the *New York Times* was committee chairwoman, and Josephine Ober of the *World*, Louella Parsons of the *Morning Telegraph*, and Esther Coster of the *Brooklyn Eagle* were elected to the board of directors. Each one of them would play a significant part in the ensuing history of the organization.[7] Other significant women to attend the first meeting were Ishbel Ross, the first woman to actually work for the front page of the *Tribune* and who later published the first history of women journalists, and Mary Margaret McBride, who was to become the first woman radio talk show host.

At the first meeting, it was agreed that membership would be limited to women who made newspaper work their profession. In order to be active members, they had to be regularly employed on salary or guarantee on the editorial staff of a New York newspaper. Former newspaperwomen who lived in New York City or nonresidents who had been formerly employed by a New York newspaper could join as associate members. Annual dues were $25, a week's pay for many of the newswomen.[8] This restrictive policy was intentional. As Helen Rowland of *King Features* said at the group's first annual meeting, "Make the club exclusive rather than inclusive, and then it will serve a purpose. Don't take in anybody at all, as does the Author's Club, and kindred organizations."[9]

Signing the charter of the New York Newspaper Women's Club within a few short seasons were Martha Coman, Emma Bugbee, Theodora Bean, Jane Dixon, Mary Margaret McBride, Winifred Van Duzer, who had all attended that first meeting in 1922, and Lillian Lauferty, of the *American*. The first recorded meeting and election of officers following the signing of the charter was held the first Monday of May in 1924, an event which attracted the attention of the press, including the *New York Times*.[10]

EARLY ACTIVITIES

In April 1922, the newswomen started a tradition of an annual celebration, which grew from a social event featuring a dinner and a ball into an event honoring newswomen. At the first dinner, held at the elegant Hotel Vanderbilt, a congratulatory letter from Mrs. Warren G. Harding was read. The first lady, the former business manager of the *Marion* (Ohio) *Star*, expressed solidarity with the group, writing, "I have always looked upon myself quite as a newspaperwoman." She was invited to become the club's first honorary president. The first lady's letter, or perhaps the social significance of the ball, made the event newsworthy. It was covered by at least one newspaper.[11]

Coman, who would later become the organization's second honorary president, outlined the purpose of the organization and the requirements for membership. She explained that the club was meant to be primarily social. "The purpose is merely to get together socially," she said. "That's why we are going to have no programs. I have been told that unless we have speakers to keep us entertained, we shall become very tired of each other; but I do not believe so. Anyway, we shan't have speakers until we are tired of each other."[12]

In their hearts, however, the newspaperwomen knew they wanted more than a social club, and they quickly suggested ways in which the organization could assist members professionally. Anne O'Hagen Shinn, of the *New York World*, recommended that the organization should provide to potential employers a list of names of those members who would be eligible for job interviews upon short notice. Mrs. M. Ryan, of Northcliffe Publications (London), suggested that the organization should affiliate with English and French newspapers, which were just beginning to employ women in many departments.[13]

During the next few years the Newspaper Women's Club attempted to locate a satisfactory site for its headquarters and began to raise funds for the move. Initially, the club had headquarters at the Vanderbilt. Then in 1924, Coman signed a lease for its first permanent headquarters, the parlor floor of 53 West 47th Street.[14] When the lease proved unsatisfactory, the members continued to seek a more permanent site, and Jean Dixon was appointed the head of a committee to organize an annual ball for the purpose of raising money for permanent headquarters.[15] The first ball was held March 21, 1924, at the Hotel Astor, and over the years this highly visible social event would place newspaperwomen on the political and professional agenda in many quarters.[16]

In 1925, the newswomen used the ball to bring together journalists from across New York and to promote the status of women in the profession. That is, the ball would serve as a kind of an "atta girl" network, with newspaper women being recognized for their accomplishments at a banquet and ball before their peers, their male counterparts, and the greater professional communities of the region. That second annual ball was held on the roof garden of the Waldorf Astoria and featured Emma Haig and George Hale of the Three Hundred Club.[17] Dan Smith of the *New York World* developed a club logo, which depicted a woman astride Pegasus, for the masthead of all bulletins, programs, and correspondence promoting the event. Margaret Mara of the *Brooklyn Eagle* noted in the club's newsletter that Smith had depicted the newspaperwoman riding astride rather than side saddle: "Had he compromised on a side-saddle rider, I'm sure all of us to follow would have resented the compromise. However the lady, you will note, wields an ink-dripping quill pen in lieu of a riding crop; a quaint and ladylike touch."[18] In later years this image took on a more daring (and modern) look. The club's logo designed by illustrator Tony Sarg several years later depicted the newswoman astride a bucking bronco. The image now incorporated a more contemporary technology in newswriting, the typewriter.[19]

The newswomen's ball became one of the social events of the year. One thousand attended the 1927 ball, including newspaper women and men, artists, and guests. Among the guests that year were New York City Mayor James Walker, Major General Charles P. Summerall, Major General James H. McRae, and Rear Admiral Charles P. Plunkett, all of whom made short speeches. Among the wealthy socialites who attended were some of the elite of newspaper circles, such as Mr. and Mrs. Cyrus H. K. McCormick, Mrs. William R. Hearst, Mr. and Mrs. Roy Howard, Mr. and Mrs. Adolph Ochs, Mr. and Mrs. Joseph Patterson, Mr. and Mrs. Ogden Reid, and Ralph Pulitzer.[20]

The Newspaper Women's Club occasionally took positions or action on social or feminist issues, being connected through its members to groups that played more active roles. In 1927, for example, several members were active in the Lucy Stone League, an organization devoted to the fairly revolutionary concept of women legally keeping their maiden names after marriage. One of the founders was Jane Grant, a charter member of the newswomen's organization who in 1925 had established the *New Yorker* with her husband, Harold Ross. Other active members of the Newspaper Women's Club who were also members of the Lucy Stone League were Doris Fleischman, Ethyl Lloyd Patterson, Mary Margaret McBride, Hannah Mitchell, and Helen Rogers Reid.[21]

During the club's early years, it sponsored a tea to honor women journalists of the senior class at Columbia University, launching a tradition of professional support that has continued to the present.[22] The club also occasionally became involved in social service activities. During the Depression and World War II, for example, it was involved in an extensive relief effort for young unemployed newspaperwomen, providing them with nominal funds as they sought employment. It also sponsored a similar program for servicemen during World War II.

SOME PROMINENT MEMBERS

Many of the members of the New York Newspaper Women's Club became prominent because of the influential news organizations for which they worked, the excellence of their contributions to the field, and their pathbreaking for women journalists. Emma Bugbee, who served as the club's president from 1926 to 1929, and again from 1934 to 1935, was such a woman. When Bugbee was hired by the *New York Tribune* in 1911 to report on the suffrage movement, she was given a desk in the hallway outside the newsroom because women working at the *Tribune* were not granted a place in the newsroom. And there she stayed—in the hall—until 1919, when Ishbel Ross was hired to work on the city desk. Only then was Bugbee was brought into the newsroom, along with Ross.[23] Bugbee was active in the club for five decades. An archivist at heart, she preserved much of its history, including records of the top prizes it awarded women journalists and books published by club members. Other early members who would contribute greatly to the organization were Josephine Robb Ober of the *New York World*, Helen Rowland of King Features, and Jane Dixon, who once sold more than $1,000 in tickets to an early ball, and who was awarded a prize for her efforts.[24]

Over the years, the club's presidents were among the most noted women journalists in New York. The most notable were Kathryn McLaughlin of the *New York Times* (1939–41); Virginia Pope of the *Herald Tribune*, the *New York Times*, and *Parade* (1953–55); Joan O'Sullivan (Vassiliadias) of King Features (1958–60, 1984–86); and Sylvia Carter of *Newsday* (1990–92). Two of the club's more flamboyant presidents were Louella Parsons of the *Morning Telegraph*, the *American*, International News Service, and Hearst Publications (1924–26), and Edith Evans Asbury of the *World-Telegram* and the *New York Times* (1952–53). Parsons and Asbury took risks in coverage and were outspoken in broadcasting the new ground they had covered in the profession.

CONTRIBUTIONS

Over the years, the club has offered a professional program for aspiring and veteran newswomen alike. In fall 1941, for instance, it conducted a forum about the role of the press in wartime at which newsmen and newswomen shared their perspectives. During that same year it set up a networking workshop at which members could meet with some of the club's more prominent news women: Mary King of the *Sun; New York Times* columnist Anne O'Hare McCormick; *Herald Tribune* publisher Helen Rogers Reid; syndicated columnist Dorothy Thompson; and talk show host Mary Margaret McBride.

The annual workshops proved to be popular events. In 1954, for instance, the organization sponsored a lecture series entitled "The Working Press—Today," which featured top newspaper talent. Speakers were John Chapman, drama critic of the *Daily News*, and a TV panel comprised of Harriet Van Horne, Jay Nelson Tuck, and Val Adams. In a 1991 workshop, members met with a book editor, who walked members through the steps of publishing a manuscript.

The club created another effective networking tool with its newsletter, the *New York Newspaper Women's Club Bulletin*, which tracked the professional progress of its members and supplied them with information about job openings and publishing opportunities. In additon to recording the progress of its members, the club on occasion attempted to evaluate and record the status of women journalists. In 1934, at Coman's suggestion, it conducted a survey on the status of newspaperwomen in New York City. The results were encouraging, showing that editors and publishers were beginning to use the club for job placements, an idea the members had hoped for in planning their social and professional networking activities.[25]

One of the club's early activities was to provide mentors and encouragement to women entering news work. In 1959, the club took this a step further by establishing a scholarship for women college students pursuing a journalism degree. The scholarship received its first endowment, in the amount of $500, from the estate of Martha Coman, who died of pneumonia in 1959. The scholarship was named after Anne O'Hare McCormick, who received the 1937 Pulitzer Prize for her editorial correspondence for the *New York Times*.[26]

Although one of the club's earliest goals was to establish its own clubhouse and many of its events were organized to create funds for that purpose, the club never achieved this goal. For a while the headquarters were at 47 West 44th Street, and in 1960 there were hopes to establish headquarters in the Overseas Press Club.[27] When that building proved unavailable, the organization, which had grown to two hundred members, sought other quarters.[28] Eventually, the club, renamed the New York Newswomen's Club in 1972, settled into its current offices at the National Arts Club, 15 Gramercy Park, New York City.

Since then, fund-raising activities have been focused on providing scholarships to young women to continue their journalism education at Columbia University School of Journalism, worthwhile projects to help the status of women in the profession, and workshops to help members become more proficient in news gathering and reporting. Another endowment administered by the club is the Eleanor Roosevelt Newspaper Women's Fund, established in 1963 to encourage practicing newswomen with interest in international reporting. The Mary E. Watts Award provides funding as well for worthwhile projects.

NOTES

1. Ishbel Ross, *Ladies of the Press* (New York: Harper & Brothers, 1936); Marion Marzolf, *Up from the Footnote* (New York: Hastings House, 1977); Maurine H. Beasley and Sheila J. Gibbons, eds., *Taking Their Place: A Documentary History of Women and Journalism* (Washington, D.C.: American University Press, 1993).

2. Ross, *Ladies of the Press*, pp. 20–25.

3. Jean Lyon, memorandum on prize story award, 22 April 1946, Newswomen's Club of New York Papers (hereafter NCNY Papers), Newswomen's Club of New York, National Arts Club Building, New York City.

4. The author has conducted interviews with many of the past and present members of the club; she would like to thank Joan O'Sullivan, Sylvia Carter, Judith Crist, Edith Asbury, Emily Nathan, Mildred Faulk Branham, Guin Hall, Maggie Bartel Kivel, Patricia Failla, Charlotte Leyden, Romola Metzner, Gay Pauley, Ruth Preston Peskin, Lily Singer, and Theo Wilson.

5. Joan O'Sullivan, "Martha Coman, Founder of Club, Dies," *New York Newspaper Women's Club Bulletin* (November–December 1959), NCNY Papers.

6. Ibid. Coman became the dean of women reporters on the newspaper. She was sent to Europe as a correspondent. She was an early sports reporter, covering football, baseball, and world championship fights from a woman's angle. She left the *Herald* in 1924, when it merged with the *New York Tribune*, to work as publicity director for Smith College for five years. She then worked as a reporter for the *Scarsdale* (New York) *Enquirer* until 1955.

7. "New York Newspaper Women's Club Minutes," *New York Tribune*, 24 November 1922.

8. Emma Bugbee, minutes, 22 March 1922, NCNY Papers. The spelling of the club's name varied, it was also referred to as the "Newspaperwomen's" (one word) Club. Here the author shall refer to it as the Newspaper Women's Club.

9. "Mrs. Harding Hails Newspaper Women," *Brooklyn Eagle*, 10 April 1922.

10. "Favors Club Charter," *New York Times*, 19 April 1924.

11. "Mrs. Harding Hails Newspaper Women."

12. Ibid.

13. Ibid.

14. NYNC Minutes, 18 January 1924, NYNC Papers.

15. NYNC Minutes, 15 February 1924, NYNC Papers.

16. NYNC Minutes, 22 February 1924, NYNC Papers.

17. "Newspaper Women's Dance," *New York Herald-Tribune*, 14 June 1925; "Dance of Women Writers," *New York Times*, 11 June 1925.

18. *Monthly Bulletin of New York Newspaper Women's Club*, September 1950.

19. Ibid.

20. "1,000 Attend Dance of Newspaper Women," *New York Times*, 12 March 1927.

21. "Annual Ball Is to Be Held on March 11 This Month; Committees Are Announced," *New York Times*, 13 February 1957.

22. "Newspaper Women Elect," *New York Times*, 8 May 1927.

23. Ross, *Ladies of the Press*, p. 125.

24. "Newspaper Women Elect," *New York Times*, 3 May 1928.

25. "Miss Coman, Led Newspaper Women's Club," *New York Herald Tribune*, 28 November 1959.

26. Court document, "In the matter of the estate of Martha D. Coman," signed by Joan O'Sullivan, president (28 April 1960), filed by Alfred C. Turino, NYNC Papers. McCormick covered World War II and the Korean Conflict for the *Times*. She died in 1954.

27. Martha Coman to Joan O'Sullivan, Hotel Van Rensselaer, 15 East 11th Street, New York, 10 September 1959; Joan O'Sullivan to Martha Coman, 25 August 1959, both in NYNC Papers.

28. Joan O'Sullivan to John H. Fulweiler, 366 Madison Avenue, New York, 25 August 1959, NYNC Papers.

INFORMATIONAL SOURCES

Newspaperwomen's Club of New York Papers. Newswomen's Club of New York, National Arts Building, 15 Gramercy Park, New York.
New York Newspaper Women's Club Bulletin, 1924 to present, passim.
Ross, Ishbel. *Ladies of the Press*. New York: Harper & Brothers, 1936.

INSTITUTIONAL PROFILE

Newswomen's Club of New York

Dates: Established as **New York Newspaper Women's Club**, 1922, in New York City; name changed to **Newswomen's Club of New York**, 1972.

Newsletter: *New York Newspaper Women's Club Bulletin*, 1924 to date.

Papers: Records, minutes, and correspondence are held at its offices: Newswomen's Club of New York, National Arts Club Building, 15 Gramercy Park, New York, New York, tel. (212) 777–1610.

22

Therese L. Lueck

Ohio Newspaper Women's Association, 1902–Present

The Ohio Newspaper Women's Association (ONWA) was founded in Toledo, Ohio, in 1902 as the Women's Centennial Press Association by a self-described group of "pencil pushers." Toledo was the convention site that autumn of the Ohio Federation of Women's Clubs, and newspaperwomen who had come from throughout the state to cover the convention "went into a huddle and decided it was just about time Ohio women reporters had an association of their own. They held an organization meeting at once on October 24, 1902, at which Kate Brownlee Sherwood, an editor at the *Toledo Journal*, was elected president and Delia Amos, managing editor of the *Sidney Daily News*, vice president."[1]

The organizers borrowed the manager's office at Toledo's Valentine Theater for that first meeting.[2] After changing its name to the Ohio Newspaper Women's Association (ONWA) in 1903, the group met during the annual convention of the Ohio Federation until 1912. At that time, ONWA decided it "could best attain its aims as a separate and distinct body" and that it should be convened "at a time when its members would not be on duty reporting the deliberation of some other organization." The next and first solo meeting was set for the following October in Columbus.[3]

ACTIVITIES

One of ONWA's major activities since its founding has been its annual convention, whose purpose is to "give members an opportunity to exchange ideas and professional experiences."[4] The convention has been funded by various means over the years, including registration fees and newspaper donations. It is held in a different location each year, and the chair from the host city coordinates the event and raises funds by whatever means necessary. One Depression era convention chair recounted her experiences in a 1932 program replete with advertising. "We did everything to make money except sell angel food cakes and crochet baby booties . . . [and] we even considered sponsoring a prize fight—Heaven forbid! And then we thought of this advertising program."[5] Occasionally the annual meetings have been supported by local media, as in 1941, when it was hosted by John S. Knight, publisher of the *Akron Beacon Journal*.

The annual meetings often feature celebrity speakers or local figures who claim national recognition. In 1970, for example, when the annual meeting was held in Toledo, feminist Gloria Steinem, a native of that city, addressed the association. In 1981, John R. Block, whose family owned the *Toledo Blade* spoke as a Washington-based correspondent; in 1989, after he had become the *Blade*'s executive editor, he spoke before the newspaperwomen again.[6] Other speakers have included newspaper columnists from Ann Landers to Clarence Page.[7]

Another high point of the annual convention has been its writing and design contest, initiated in 1923 by ONWA president Ruth Neely France "after she convinced her boss, *Cincinnati Times-Star* owner Charles P. Taft, to donate two cash prizes."[8] Donations from media companies were a major source for the contest prizes until 1990, when the largest contributor, Gannett, pulled out its regular $1,000 donation. In response ONWA raised dues and entry fees in an effort to make the contest self-supporting.[9] A few years later, a needed financial boost came when, prompted by an affiliated member, Sprint-United telephone stepped forward as an annual contest sponsor.[10]

Although the membership was distributed throughout the state and communication among members was not always easy, the association did not begin to publish a newsletter until the 1950s. The first editor, Helen Geib Fry, was made executive secretary primarily to edit the newsletter, which she put out monthly, with contest, convention, and member news. After that, the task of editing the newsletter often fell to the association's presidents during their terms of office. Some of these president-editors include Margaret E. Grube of the *Fairborn Daily Herald* and Jo-Ann Huff Albers of the *Cincinnati Enquirer* during the 1970s, and Melody Snure of the *Wooster Daily Record* during the 1980s. When Snure, "a confessed newsletter junkie," stepped down as president, she volunteered to continue editing the newsletter in order to keep members connected during the year-long stretches between conventions.[11]

ORGANIZATION AND MEMBERSHIP

Officers—the president, vice president (who is membership chair and not necessarily the next president), secretary, and treasurer—are elected biennially at the convention. They, along with the past president and committee chairs, constitute the executive board, which meets throughout the year to govern the organization. How the organization defines active membership has shifted over the years to account for changes in women's opportunities in newspaper work, but generally the definition has included working professionals current on their dues, along with those who have bought lifetime memberships. New members apply each year, and old ones lapse on their dues, but counts in the 1940s and 1950s typically showed between 100 and 250 active members. In the 1970s, membership regularly reached 350, whereas the 1980s and 1990s have seen a slight drop, with membership ranging from 250 to 350.[12] Members come from all parts of the state, and from the beginning, state boundaries have formed the parameters of the association's membership. Founders were "Ohio women by birth and residence," but eventually women working on Ohio newspapers who lived in neighboring states were allowed to join.[13]

The character of the association has been forged by a legacy of working journalists. Some early members, like Amos, whose family was in the newspaper business, were "reared on printers' ink."[14] A survey of the members in the late 1960s showed that this heritage still held true for two members on weekly papers, with two others noting that their mothers were newspaperwomen.[15] Members had to work on the editorial—as opposed to the business—side of a publication. The association's broadening definition of "editorial" has mirrored a century of women's progress in the profession; by the 1990s, members could be "engaged in editing, reporting and/or pictorial work, of the editorial staff of an Ohio newspaper . . . ; of a news wire service bureau in the state of Ohio; or as a syndicated columnist whose column appears regularly in one or more Ohio newspaper."[16] The association further distinguishes editorial work from the purely promotional, by stating in its bylaws that "the term 'newspapers' [is] to be defined as a daily or weekly publication, the primary purpose of which is to disperse general news—not a sales promotion sheet or special business organ."[17]

WOMEN'S INTERESTS

With the first years of the association so closely tied to the activities of the Ohio Federation of Women's Clubs, it is not surprising that ONWA shared more traits with its club sisters than just an annual meeting and an organizational structure. Traditional female influence is evident in those journalists' philosophy: "Their fine sounding . . . purpose . . . was to 'raise the educational, cultural and economic standards of women in the home, the family and the state,' by un-trammeled accounts of women's activities."[18] After nearly a century, the group maintains its high-minded mission "to encourage thought and action among the newspaperwomen of the state, to elevate the standards of the profession through educational programs and interchange of methods and experience."[19]

Participation in the association is closely tied to this philosophy, with membership carrying "definite obligation and definite responsibility. The obligation is that of personal and professional integrity; the responsibility is for conduct such as will uphold the ethics of the newspaper profession." And this policy is not without teeth: "Violation of this code of ethics shall constitute reason for withdrawal of membership subject to action of the board."[20]

As with many of the women's press organizations founded in the early part of the century, debates over membership qualifications have reflected broader societal and professional changes. Debates over the name of the organization and the language of its constitution and bylaws in recent years have centered on their female designation. Early documents specified that members be women because "[n]o one ever dreamed men wanted to join," but over the years wording had shifted from "women residents" to "any resident of Ohio," which opened the door to male members.[21] In 1969, the male editor of the *Cleveland Plain Dealer*'s women's pages took advantage of this language to join.[22] He was followed shortly by four newsmen from Dayton. These inductions spurred delegates at the 1971 convention to propose reinstating the earlier restrictive wording, but many women thought that intentionally limiting membership by sex (to exclude male members) "would be a backward step," and the amendment did not pass. Membership chair Jo-Ann Albers, who would be elected president at that meeting, argued that the association should welcome men "as long as men members agree to the ONWA objectives."[23]

Once the association began to admit male members, its name became a matter of discussion. Whether its name should be "changed [from Ohio Newspaper Women's Association] to Ohio Newspaper Writers Association or some other name with which prospective male members might feel more comfortable" was discussed "extensively" at the 1985 convention.[24] Although members left the convention "divided" over the issue, they "chose not to discuss changing the name of the organization" at the 1986 convention.[25] However, the executive board continued to debate whether there was "still a need for a women's journalism organization in Ohio" and set up a regional panel in 1988 to address the question: "Is there a need for an exclusively women's newspaper organization?"[26] After this panel reached its conclusions, the president commented that the association's object was not "an apology; it's a goal."[27] The consensus was that "ONWA does not need a new name. We need to do a better job living up to the one we have."[28]

Several years of discussions and the work of the panel had brought the focus around to the status of women in news. In 1988, an article reporting on the panel's activities in the newsletter assessed women's position in the news industry and found it problematic. It rededicated the association to the objective of improving newspaperwomen's lot:

Though women have, since the mid-'70s, constituted a majority of journalism school graduates, women still are underrepresented in newsrooms and are far underrepresented in editing and management positions. Because of these realities and issues of general social inequality for women, newspaper women still have specific needs that must be served. ONWA must more clearly address the needs of its members as women who are professional journalists. ONWA must keep issues important to women journalists in the minds of all journalists in the state.[29]

Although the association did not remove the word *women's* from its name, it did, in 1994, adopt gender-neutral language such as *chairperson* for use in its documents.[30]

Thus, the association clarified its stance that any Ohio journalist, female or male, dedicated to promoting the cause of women in journalism could apply for membership. Male members in a women's group, however, faced unmentionable peril, especially when it came to door prizes. For example, in 1971, "the blushing husband of Ruth Meyers, of the Dayton Journal *Herald*, heard his name called out as the first winner of a pair of panties."[31] A male member from Wooster who admitted to having been a member of the association for "a number of years" finally found enough courage to attend a convention in 1988. After experiencing the "collective feeling of confidence" there, he wrote, "I am discovering that when new experiences pop into your life, the anxiety level is proportional to the stupidity of your perceptions."[32] Such hazards and trepidation notwithstanding, by 1998, twenty-six men had dared to join the association.[33]

ONWA AND "WOMAN'S LOT"

A certain realism that pervades the group's latter-twentieth-century outlook can be seen as early as the late 1930s in the writings of ONWA president Dorothy Todd Foster of the *Columbus Dispatch*, who commented on the status of women in journalism:

Women must be credited, undoubtedly, with developing the modern newspaper along lines of constructive human service. But they must also carry their share of responsibility for the ills to which the newspaper, like all imperfect human institutions, is still heir. . . . Newspaper women certainly did not start these appeals to the lowest forms of 'human interest.' But they do not seem to have lessened them a bit.[34]

In 1969, the newspaper woman of Ohio was an "educated, idealistic woman who loves to write and likes people," according to an ONWA profile drawn from a survey of its members. More than half of those who responded to the survey had been homemakers, with that "interlude in their careers, varying from three months to 30 years."[35] That description of staying at home as an "interlude" was a shift in perspective from a decade earlier, when women considered reentering the workforce a separate career and worried that they were "not executive material" until their second newspaper stint—after marriage and when children are old enough to leave under other supervision at home."[36]

Despite changes such as this in members' perspectives, women's professional opportunities in 1969 were still clustered in low-prestige positions in the news industry. Nearly half the respondents to the survey worked in women's departments, where they "evidenced more participation in decision-making and held more administrative responsibilities" than those who worked in news departments. With regard to salaries, women on weeklies seem to fare better. By the late 1960s, women saw salary linked to a larger problem of perception. "The biggest change necessary to bring equality in salaries will be a change in the attitude of men towards women in the field."[37] This echoed a call that had been published in the newsletter a decade earlier: "Remove the eternal masculine prejudice from the minds of editors and men reporters, also from [those of] journalism professors."[38]

"Overwhelmingly, women want equal pay for equal work," the 1969 profile noted.[39] This was not a new cry but, rather, a lingering situation. A 1958 survey had cited, "The biggest sore spot turned up in the poll is a widespread difference in pay between men and women,"[40] and a member had commented, "Give women . . . equal pay for equal work."[41] Although the 1950s had brought new jobs, there was "less future for women city-side and in executive positions."[42] By 1969, this lack was labeled discrimination, with more than 80 percent of those responding to the survey saying that women did not have "equal opportunity for career advancement with men in news media." Newspaperwomen said they were "discriminated against both in equality of salary and advancement to administrative positions by comparison to men in the field." One member wrote that her paper "preferred to bring in someone from the outside rather than promote a woman 'higher than the society desk.' "[43]

These continuing concerns politicized the membership. At the 1972 convention, ONWA endorsed passage of the Equal Rights Amendment (ERA) and established a committee to help secure Ohio ratification of the ERA.[44] Such feminist activism coming from the bulging membership rosters indicates a particularly strong ONWA in the 1970s.

CONTINUED TRADITIONS AND NEW CHALLENGES

Over the years, ONWA established various programs to encourage students to join the association and to support journalism education. During the 1950s, it began awarding scholarships as part of its commitment to journalism education. During the 1960s, the group sponsored "cub days," or opportunities for students to shadow professionals.[45] During the 1970s, it sponsored an internship program with Ohio newspapers and funded a course on women in journalism at Ohio State University.[46] In 1989, it presented a "New Directions for News" program at the annual convention.[47]

In the mid-1990s, membership was extended to college students.[48] President Laurie Denger, of the *Dayton Daily News*, noted in 1996 that ONWA was "adding student members, adding a student category in our annual contest and adding a minority scholarship."[49] Encouraging student involvement was a natural consequence of the association's efforts to involve a new generation of journalists in its activities, but it was also probably in part motivated by an effort to boost a dwindling membership and lagging attendance at conventions.[50] Like other women's organizations, ONWA has been affected negatively by the "time and responsibility" crunch experienced by working women. In a survey conducted in 1994, members reported that they simply had "no time."[51]

ONWA's independent and transient nature, which is evident from its inception, has served to sustain it in its role as a statewide organization. Without an established headquarters, ONWA passes its gavel, and more literally its "crates" of records,[52] from president to president, to whatever Ohio city with which she is affiliated. From Cleveland to Cincinnati, from Findlay to New Philadelphia, annual conventions pass from large city to small, encouraging members to trek the heart-shaped state. Their myriad routes have become the sinews that bond Ohio newspaperwomen to their profession and to each other. In keeping with this defining nature, the association plans a traveling exhibit on the history and significance of Ohio's women journalists to commemorate its centennial in 2002.[53]

NOTES

1. Ruth Neely France, "Toledo Press Club Launched State Organization of Scribes," Ohio Newspaper Women's Association convention program, 1932, p. 10, Ohio Newspaper Women's Association Records, Manuscript Collection 773 (hereafter ONWA Records), box 1, Ohio Historical Society (hereafter OHS), Columbus, Ohio; "About the ONWA," attachment, Constitution and Bylaws, as amended 1944, ONWA Records, box 1; Dorothy Todd Foster, "Women in Journalism, in Publicity and in Radio," in Ruth Neely, ed., *Women of Ohio: A Record of Their Achievements in the History of the State* (Cincinnati: S. J. Clarke, ca. 1939), p. 1145. Amos served as acting president for Sherwood, who was not able to serve, and then was elected president herself. These women were seemingly ignorant of the fact an organization for Ohio newspaperwomen already existed, the Ohio Woman's Press Association (founded in 1889), which was still active in 1902 (see related chapter).

2. France, "Club Launched State Organization of Scribes."

3. Transcript of the 1921 convention program, ONWA Records, box 2.

4. ONWA Constitution, as amended 1988, Pamphlet Collection, OHS.

5. Jane Williams, "In Which We Headline Ourselves," Ohio Newspaper Women's Association convention program, 1932, p. 20, ONWA Records, box 1.

6. Ohio Newspaper Women's Association convention program, 1941, ONWA Records, box 1; "Happy New Year," Ohio Newspaper Women's Association newsletter (hereafter ONWA newsletter), December 1986, p. 4; "Toledo in October, Ole!" ONWA newsletter, summer 1981, p. 1; 1989 convention program. The author would like to thank Melody Snure, past ONWA president, for providing access to her collection of ONWA's newsletter for this project.

7. Jane Williams, "Famous Speakers at ONWA Banquets," ONWA Records, box 2; 1991 convention registration flier, personal holdings, Melody Snure, past president and former newsletter editor (hereafter Snure Holdings).

8. "Ruth Neely France Was Big Booster of ONWA," ONWA newsletter, May 1988, p. 3.

9. Sylvia Krupp, "The Word from the Top: Board Will Review Future of Contest Funding," ONWA newsletter, September 1990, p. 1; Krupp, "The Word from the Top:

ONWA Needs to Make Contest Self-Supporting," ONWA newsletter, February 1991, p. 1.

10. Lynn Hulsey, "The Word from the Top: Sprint/United to Sponsor Triple Entry," ONWA newsletter, September 1995, p. 1.

11. Michele Toney, "The Word from the Top: Newsletter Is Our Major Member Link," ONWA newsletter, March 1988, p. 1.

12. Various minutes, "ONWA Membership Report," ONWA Records, box 1; 1986, 1994, 1995 ONWA Membership Rosters, Snure Holdings; Linda Crider, ONWA president, telephone interview by author, 19 May 1998.

13. France, "Toledo Press," p. 11.

14. Foster, "Women in Journalism," p. 1145.

15. "Profile of the Ohio Newspaper Woman," typed copy, presented 25 October 1969, ONWA convention, ONWA Records, box 2; also printed on unnumbered newsletter page, hand dated 12–69, Snure Holdings.

16. Constitution.

17. Bylaws.

18. France, "Toledo Press."

19. Constitution.

20. Ibid.

21. Press release, Lee Steele, the *Toledo Blade*, Toledo, 1971, ONWA Records, box 2.

22. Ohio Newspaper Women's Association convention program, 1977, ONWA Records, box 1.

23. Press release.

24. "Members Debate ONWA Name Change," ONWA newsletter, November 1985. p. 2.

25. "Meet You in Mansfield Oct. 25," ONWA newsletter, September 1986, p. 1; "Animated Meeting Held in Mansfield," ONWA newsletter, December 1986, p. 1.

26. "Board Ponders Future of Our 'Women's Group,'" ONWA newsletter, March 1988, p. 1; "What Lies Ahead for ONWA? Come to Springfield March 26," ONWA newsletter, March 1988, p. 1.

27. Michele Toney, "The Word from the Top: It's Time for Identity Crisis to End," ONWA newsletter, August 1988, p. 2.

28. "Return to Original Purpose, Group Agrees," ONWA newsletter, May 1988, p. 1.

29. Ibid., p. 4.

30. "Several Bylaws Changes Face Members during Annual Meeting," ONWA newsletter, August 1994, p. 4.

31. Press release.

32. Steve Stokes, "The Last Word: And I Didn't Have to Discuss Childbirth . . . ," ONWA newsletter, December 1988, p. 4.

33. Linda Crider, telephone interview by author, 19 May 1998.

34. Foster, "Women in Journalism," p. 1142.

35. "Profile."

36. "Newswomen Criticize Themselves, Cite Some Self-Made Progress Blocks," Ohio Newspaper Women's Association newsletter, unnumbered page, hand dated 9–58.

37. "Profile."

38. "Newswomen Criticize Themselves."

39. "Profile."

40. "Women's News Job Opportunities Bright, Dim Future for Executive Posts, Survey Shows," *Ohio Newspaper Women's Association Bulletin*, December 1958, p. 1.

41. "Newswomen Criticize Themselves."

42. "Women's News Job Opportunities."

43. "Profile."

44. Jo-Ann Albers, "Ad-Libs by Jo-Ann," ONWA newsletter, winter 1972, p. 1.

45. Letter to board signed "Meg" [Marguerite Miller McMullen, ONWA president], n.d. [1966], ONWA Records, box 3. Both activities have since been discontinued.

46. ONWA executive board minutes, 24 October 1975, various correspondence, ONWA Records, box 3.

47. ONWA convention program, 1989, Snure Holdings.

48. ONWA Ballot, annotated, 12 October 1995, President's Holdings, Linda Crider, *Dayton Daily News*, ONWA president.

49. Denger, "ONWA Year Moving Along at Top 'Speed.' " ONWA Newsletter, February 1996, p. 1; Linda Crider, telephone interview by author, 26 May 1998. The minority scholarship is sponsored by a different Ohio newspaper each year.

50. Recent conference attendance has dwindled to the point that those attending the 1996 convention at Cleveland were characterized as a "small group." Lynn Hulsey, "Word from the Top: Common Survey Response: 'No Time,' " ONWA newsletter, August 1994, p. 1; Laurie Denger, "The Prez Sez: Was It Something We Did?" ONWA newsletter, March 1997, p. 1.

51. Hulsey, "Word from the Top: Common Survey Response: 'No Time.' "

52. Laurie Denger, past ONWA president, telephone interview by author, 19 May 1998.

53. Crider, telephone interview by author, 19 May 1998.

INFORMATIONAL SOURCES

Constitution and Bylaws, as amended 1988. Pamphlet Collection, Ohio Historical Society, Columbus, Ohio.

Crider, Linda. Ohio Newspaper Women's Association President's Holdings, Dayton, Ohio.

Neely, Ruth, ed. *Women of Ohio: A Record of Their Achievements in the History of the State*. Cincinnati: S. J. Clark, ca. 1939.

Ohio Newspaper Women's Association (newsletter), 1972–present, passim. Uncatalogued Newsletter Collection, Ohio Historical Society, Columbus, Ohio.

Ohio Newspaper Women's Association Records, Manuscript Collection 773. Ohio Historical Society, Columbus, Ohio.

Snure, Melody. Personal Holdings, Wooster, Ohio.

INSTITUTIONAL PROFILE

Ohio Newspaper Women's Association

Dates: Established as **Women's Centennial Press Association**, Toledo, Ohio, October 1902; name changed to **Ohio Newspaper Women's Association**, Columbus, Ohio, October 1903.

Newsletter: *Ohio Newspaper Women's Association Bulletin*, monthly then quarterly, February (?) 1954–?, Helen Geib Fry, editor, Wadsworth, Ohio. Ohio Newspaper Women's Association (newsletter), 1972–97. Editors from 1972–85 were also the association president.

23

Nan Towle Yamane

Pacific Coast Women's Press Association, 1890–19(41)

After coming west to find a newspaper job in San Francisco in the late 1880s, the young midwestern journalist Florence Finch Kelly decided the city's press was "provincial." The city's dailies were just catching up to the latest of eastern newspaper trends, including the hiring of women writers. In an effort to overcome some of the professional barriers that Kelly and other women journalists found on the West Coast, women journalists organized the Pacific Coast Women's Press Association (PCWPA) in 1890. The PCWPA came of age with the metropolis of San Francisco at a time when recent immigrants to the city and its hinterlands were building an infrastructure to their own regional culture. The PCWPA, which survived until 1941, provided women writers with sorority, power through association, and an organization to wield political power in reforming the press. At the same time, it was limited as a professional organization by its race and class bias, its gendered definition of journalism, and its broad membership with conflicting purposes.[1]

Its original purpose was to provide sorority for writers throughout the Pacific Coast states, as well as support for the advancement of women in journalism. It was perhaps most powerful in the mid-1890s under the leadership of Charlotte Perkins Stetson Gilman, when it was infused with the aggressive vision and reform ideals of its founding members. Although by 1900 it was less ambitious in its public role, the PCWPA remained a significant writers' support group. Over time its focus became less journalistic and more artistic, literary, educational, and nostalgic.

ORIGINS AND DEVELOPMENT

The PCWPA was born in an age of flourishing women's associations and became a leader in the California woman's movement.[2] It was forged by a

complicated mix of forces: San Francisco's professional culture, reform journalism, a woman's movement, and the assertion of middle-class interests in a
city known for its strong labor organization. San Francisco, powerful "queen"
city of the Pacific Coast, was a professional city full of financiers, lawyers,
politicians, and writers. These professions were dominated by men probably to
a greater degree than other areas of the nation, and women struggled to win
entry into medicine, law, and journalism.[3]

Many of the women who gathered to organize the PCWPA were writers with
political interests and, like their male counterparts, were architects building a
foundation for the reform-centered Progressive Era.[4] Like clubwomen elsewhere,
they expanded their access to the public sphere by organizing associations, cir-
culating petitions, lecturing, writing laws and lobbying for their passage, and
demanding more access to the press. "Women's interests" provided not only
professional opportunities for women but a growing financial base for newspaper
expansion as well.[5]

The PCWPA was also influenced by issues of class. Largely middle-class, the
association found itself between growing class factions dividing San Francisco
and its press. The *Chronicle* represented the interests of labor, the *Call* and the
Bulletin reflected middle-class views, and the *Examiner* broadened its readership
to a more inclusive lowest common denominator. Most PCWPA members were
empowered both by their ideas of what women could accomplish as well as by
their socioeconomic caste, a necessarily aggressive middle class envisioning new
possibilities for the perfection of society through association, reform, and
women's participation.[6]

It was in this context that after three years of preparation, freelance writer
Emilie Tracy Y. Parkhurst sent out 150 invitations to newspaper women and
authors "in good standing on this coast" to meet at her home in San Francisco.
Fifty "responded in person," attended the meeting, and drafted a "Constitution
and By-laws" based on that of the New England Woman's Press Association
(NEWPA),* founded in 1885. In Parkhurst's own words, the PCWPA was organized for the "protection, benefit and advantage of the working newspaper
woman and woman author." The association's statement of purpose was taken
nearly verbatim from that of NEWPA: "To elevate the work and the workers;
and to forward by concerted action through the Press, such good objects in
literary, serial, industrial, philanthropic and reformatory lines as may from time
to time present themselves."

Fellowship and solidarity to promote both economic and literary work, as
well as contemporary reform interests, represented the PCWPA's original vision.
These are reflected in the program from its first semiannual convention, held in
1891, at which members presented papers on contemporary reforms, economics,
women, and clubs; on issues involving writers; and on women in journalism.
The convention also honored the genteel form of the era and included poetry,
music, and a valedictory.[7]

Women with literary interests dominated the PCWPA, though it always included a component of journalists who worked for the daily press, notably the

San Francisco Bulletin, San Francisco Call, and *Oakland Tribune*, as well as country weeklies and East Coast publications. In 1890, the organization's 114 members included a number of newspaper and magazine contributors and full-time reporters, editors, and at least one publisher. Founder Emelie Tracy Y. Parkhurst represented the breadth of the work produced by some of the members: She wrote articles for the daily press, published poetry, and was the author of an opera libretto based on the novel *Ramona*.[8] Nellie Blessing Eyster, the association's first president, wrote for magazines, as did many of the founding members. Among the first thirteen officers, only four were employed full time as members of the press; of these, Frances Bagby and Isabel Raymond were both reporters for dailies and Mary Hall-Wood was an editor for the *Santa Paula Independent*.[9]

Many of the members were also reform activists. Sarah B. Cooper of the *San Francisco Bulletin*, for example, was active in kindergarten reform, and Mary Grace Edholm of the *Oakland Tribune* was a temperance worker. In the first year, the residences of members ranged from Vancouver to San Diego to Guatemala. The PCWPA's first categories for membership were active (including journalists, authors, and correspondents), associate, honorary, and life.[10] By 1919, few if any of the members represented the younger generation of full-time newspaperwomen. By the 1930s, PCWPA writers had to compete with other organizations such as San Francisco's branch of Sorosis, established in 1893 for women interested in "literary, scientific, and philanthropic pursuits," and the National League of American Pen Women,* established in 1897.[11]

REFORM AND POLITICS

The PCWPA provided women writers with sorority in their work, linked Pacific Coast women to the regional and national woman's movement, helped to build support for both women's public power and reform of the press, and created more jobs for women journalists. The accomplishments of its members rested on the broad foundation of the growing demands of middle-class women in the region.

The value of the sorority provided by the organization is especially clear when compared with the experiences of the region's earlier women writers who encountered a great deal of prejudice. Some of the first women writers of the area wrote for San Francisco's *Golden Era* in the 1850s and 1860s, yet their work was less than well received, as evidenced by the publication's male editor, who claimed that "the poor *Era* was killed by their school-girl essays." When Janette H. Phelps tried to address woman's rights in the *Golden Era*, she "was treated so discourteously by the men weaklings of the hour that she makes a dignified farewell and is heard no more." When the PCWPA created a forum for these women, Oakland journalist and activist Mary Edholm observed that "Columbus could not have been more happy in discovering America than these women journalists in discovering each other."[12]

The PCWPA also connected Pacific Coast women to the regional and national woman's movement. Meeting in San Francisco, members met reform leaders such as kindergartners Sarah Cooper and Kate Douglas Wiggin; temperance worker Mary Grace Edholm; and woman's rights activists Adeline Knapp and Alice McComas. In turn, these regional activists built links to the national woman's movement through leaders like Caroline Severance and feminist Charlotte Perkins Gilman. Gilman became PCWPA president (1893–94) and served as editor of the association's journal *The Impress* (1893–95). The PCWPA established an official affiliation with the Illinois Economic Association in 1890 and by 1902 became a member of the General Federation of Women's Clubs.[13]

In spite of a professed policy of nonpartisanship, the PCWPA became involved in a variety of issues by the mid-1890s, including public improvements of roads, streets, parks, libraries, kindergartens, and "anything and everything that tends to the building up of the country, regardless of creed, precedent or personal prejudice." The PCWPA also supported "the suppression of criminal details of sensational cases in newspapers" and the "suppression of criminal advertising." The organization's centerpiece effort was an attempt to change the definition of news through the press purity movement.[14]

Charlotte Perkins Gilman and the PCWPA's first journal, *The Impress*, championed these reforms. Gilman claimed *The Impress* to be the only one "on the coast as a non-sectarian, non-reformatory (i.e., not dedicated to any special reform) woman's paper." Gilman felt *The Impress* should be, not politically propelled but, rather, motivated by objectives that "thinking women" decided to be worthy goals. In the search for truth, wrote Gilman, the PCWPA's paper would be "literary and progressive," as well as advocating "a better appreciation of the laws of truth and beauty in all the departments of life," or, as the PCWPA "hopes to [be] as a body," a "strong influence on the right side of things, and moving always upward." In addition to publishing *The Impress*, PCWPA members also planned to publish a series of monographs, publishing one on "country roads and streets." These were mailed to all members, as well as to government officials and to members of the American Economic Association.[15]

In its campaign for press purity, the PCWPA engaged in a number of activities. An entire afternoon session of its 1892 convention was devoted to the issue, resulting in a resolution that deplored the publication of "details of crime reports of divorce courts and other demoralizing matter." In November 1893, the PCWPA, along with almost every other woman's organization in the city, presented the *Examiner*, its special target, with a petition signed by 17,000 women:

We approve of our papers in their energy and enterprise, but we believe the time has come for them to take a higher stand on the question on the exposure of crime. We deplore "personalities," not the public announcement of personal acts. We believe it is a minority of your readers who demand sensational, personal or immoral details, rather than the clean statement of facts and truth. There is too often a minuteness of detail in the press which can gratify only prurient and vulgar curiosity, or awaken such curiosity in innocent and inexperienced minds. We feel that spreading broadcast vicious and debasing news in our homes and among our children, and the consequent knowledge and easy familiarity with crime in all its forms, has a tendency to lower the tone of thought among the best of our people, and to strengthen the worst instincts among the morally lower classes.

The PCWPA included telegrams of support it had received from the New York Press Club and *Century Magazine*. Women, in alliance with women's groups and churches, organized mass meetings of up to three hundred women and circulated petitions.[16]

The PCWPA reached its political peak by 1895 under the leadership of Gilman, Sarah Cooper, and Adeline Knapp. Inspired by the women's sessions at Chicago's World Columbian Exposition in 1893, the PCWPA joined with other women's organizations to plan a Women's Conference in 1894 at the Midwinter International Exposition in San Francisco. This involvement in reform politics and especially the plan for the women's conference, however, created a split in the organization, with the result that a group of writers located in the southern part of the state pulled out of the PCWPA to form the Southern California Women's Press Club (SCWPC)* in March 1895.[17]

CONTRIBUTIONS AND LIMITATIONS

In building a woman's movement and strengthening the power of women as a group, the PCWPA created a press market for more news about women. At the very least, even San Francisco's daily press felt compelled to cover women's events; and at most, editors were forced to acknowledge the growing public interests of its women readers. Further, women writers excelled at feature and women's interest writing, which were the fastest-growing departments of San Francisco's newspapers in the 1880s and 1890s.[18] By 1899, the *Examiner* staff included four women: two activists, a reporter, and assistant Sunday editor Helen Dare. In the same year, the *Chronicle* had four women on its local staff. The *Bulletin* hired at least six women, including two artists, and the *Call* had eight women on staff, including its society editor, known only as "Miss L. Veiller" and a special correspondent in Washington, D.C., C. C. Carleton. The number of women working for these papers was actually greater; for many, who were not counted as staff, worked as occasional contributors and correspondents.[19]

The power of the PCWPA as an organization of journalists, however, eventually dissipated because of issues of race, class, and gender, leaving the association primarily a group of literary women, rather than working journalists. As a professional organization, the PCWPA failed to win a legitimate role among women journalists precisely because of its broader connections to middle-class women reformers exacerbating conflict between newly defined professional goals of journalists and those of authors. The PCWPA became more identified with the woman's club movement than with the profession of journalism.

Race became an issue for the PCWPA in 1891 when Mrs. R. M. Lockett, a black woman, applied for membership and was rejected. The PCWPA board did not state race as the reason for her rejection but said she was too aggressive and that her participation would alienate the rest of the membership. Not all PCWPA members held the same view on excluding potential members on racial grounds, however. Ten years later, when the California Women's Clubs in 1901–2, along with the General Federation of Women's Clubs at their national convention in Los Angeles in 1902, addressed this same question, PCWPA member Mabel Clare Craft (later Deering) argued for the admission of "colored" women. Craft, who wrote for the *Chronicle*, couldn't "reconcile this prejudice with twentieth century logic or our boasted progress in civilization."[20]

Class issues between middle-class and working-class women were especially divisive. Although most of PCWPA's members believed in the importance of equal work opportunities for all women, there was tension between women striving to support themselves by their work and middle-class women working part time for "creative satisfaction." The nature of these class tensions was evident in some of the arguments made during the Press Purity campaign, which attributed sensationalism in the press to publishers' attempts to appeal to the baser appetites of the lower classes. Class tensions also surfaced during the Women's Congress of 1894, when *Examiner* reporter Winifred Black ("Annie Laurie"), exemplifying hostility toward the woman's movement in general and the PCWPA in particular, accused Congress organizers of ignoring women "whose influence is neither moral nor uplifting." Black's criticism, aimed at an underlying current of moral superiority that ran through PCWPA ranks, ignored the work of many PCWPA members like Gilman, who in fact represented the "diverse left-wing perspectives" of socialists and labor activists.[21]

This division also represented a generation gap among PCWPA members that revealed a much deeper division among women writers and journalists created by attitudes regarding gender and work. The majority of PCWPA's members were "literary women" who occupied the traditional women's world of writing that consisted of poetry, fiction, features, or women's interest news for weekend newspaper editions. Although these expanded editions had increased publication and job opportunities for women writers, younger women like Black frequently found themselves rejecting this traditional work in order to adopt male standards. This strategy sometimes succeeded, and Black was one of the few women in her time to occupy the male world of reporting. One male co-worker praised her, writing in 1902 that even though "a woman in a newspaper office is ordinarily a nuisance, [Black] asked no favors on account of her sex, and appeared to desire only that she should be treated like any other reporter."[22] By separating themselves from the PCWPA and the traditional women writers, however, women like Black isolated themselves. Although she and a few others were given honorary membership in the male San Francisco Press Club, they remained distinctly female in a male world.

As Black and other emerging women journalists struggled for acceptance in a man's world, the PCWPA clung to the more traditional literary work of women writers. After 1896, the association was characterized by its focus on poetry, literature, education, and a detectable mood of nostalgia. Authors and poets took over the association's leadership and continued to provide support for women writers, to plan social programs, to encourage young girls to write, and to produce a handful of publications. In 1923, the PCWPA presented to the public a literary pageant entitled "California's Dream of Fair Women," or an "Annual Tribute to California Literature, Music and Art." PCWPA members, "young writers," and "friends" put together the pageant, which began with music, poetry inspired by Ina Coolbrith's "California," readings from *Ramona*, old Spanish songs, and an act from *Narcissa*, an American historical opera in four acts. It was both artistically creative and wistful of California's past.

Similarly, PCWPA journals were full of poetry, literature, and discussions of art and music. Writers might address difficulties with their work, as did journalist Sophie E. Skidmore when she wrote that in spite of progress, women still needed to use their pens for better conditions and pay. However, their literary forms, like their social programs, revealed strong continuities with the traditional female writing of the past that often confined women to certain jobs.[23]

Between 1905 and 1919, the association claimed between 116 and 184 members, averaging 80 to 90 active members in any given year. With the exception of a handful of journalists who had joined in the 1890s, few members represented San Francisco's new wave of women reporters.[24]

CONCLUSION

The PCWPA was created at a time when "literary ladies" working for newspapers were gradually being replaced by full-time reporters. The PCWPA not only found work for women in traditional areas of their writing experience—poetry, fiction, and feature writing—it also led the woman's movement on the Pacific Coast and helped incorporate women's news into Sunday magazine sections. In San Francisco, where conflicts from issues of race, class, and gender created a tough barrier for middle-class women professionals, the work of women journalists became characterized by two distinct worlds—one represented women's particular interests and traditional writing forms, and the other represented the press "fraternity."

A few individuals like Charlotte Perkins Gilman attempted to direct the PCWPA on a path between these two gender-defined worlds, but the PCWPA chose to remain "traditional." For a variety of reasons, it appears that women who defined themselves as "working journalists," especially those writing for urban dailies, kept their distance from the PCWPA by the end of the 1890s. As Elizabeth Burt writes, "professionalism" in journalism had created a clear divide between "career women" working full time, on the one hand, and those perceived as "dabbling literary ladies," on the other.[25] Thus, PCWPA's influence on women journalists, and the journalism profession itself, declined in the twentieth century, and the organization disappeared after 1941.

NOTES

1. The last evidence of the organization to be located was a program for the 1941 PCWPA annual breakfast. Florence Finch Kelly, *Flowing Stream* (New York: E. P. Dutton, 1939), pp. 128–33, 548.

2. Gayle Ann Gullett, "Feminism, Politics, and Voluntary Groups: Organized Womanhood in California, 1886–1896" (Ph.D. diss., University of California at Riverside, 1983), pp. 104–29; and Nan Towle Yamane, "Women, Power, and the Press: The Case of San Francisco" (Ph.D. diss., University of California at Los Angeles, 1995), pp. 227–42.

3. Yamane, "Women, Power, and the Press," pp. 317–19, 38–50; Ella Cummins, *Story of the Files* (San Francisco: World's Fair Commission, 1893); Michael Schudson, *Discovering the News: A Social History of American Newspapers* (New York: Basic Books, 1978); Marion Marzolf, *Civilizing Voices: American Press Criticism, 1880–1950* (White Plains, N.Y.: Longman Publishing Group, 1991).

4. William Deverell and Tom Sitton, eds., *California Progressivism Revisited* (Berkeley: University of California Press, 1994).

5. Karen J. Blair, *The Clubwoman as Feminist: True Womanhood Redefined 1868–1914* (New York: Holmes and Meier, 1980); Anne Firor Scott, *Natural Allies: Women's Associations in American History* (Urbana: University of Illinois Press, 1993).

6. Gullett, "Feminism, Politics, and Voluntary Groups," pp. 104–29; Sheri Katz, "Socialist Women and Progressive Reform," in *California Progressivism Revisited*, ed. Deverell and Sitton, pp. 117–43; Yamane, "Women, Power, and the Press," pp. 317–19.

7. Quote from PCWPA, "Constitution and By-Laws," p. 1; Emilie Tracy Y. Parkhurst, "Pacific Coast Women's Press Association," *Californian*, September 1893, pp. 526–27; PCWPA, "First Semi-Annual Convention of the PCWPA," program, San Francisco, California, 1891.

8. Parkhurst's writing career was cut short by her early death at the age of twenty-nine.

9. Membership lists from PCWPA, "Constitution and By-Laws"; Gullette, "Feminism, Politics, and Voluntary Groups," pp. 109–12; Cummins, *Story of the Files*, pp. 383–98.

10. Ibid.

11. *San Francisco Blue Book, 1931* (San Francisco: Jed Hoag, Publisher, 1931), pp. 533–35.

12. Cummins, *Story of the Files*, pp. 24–28, 377; Edholm quoted in Gullett, "Feminism, Politics, and Voluntary Groups," p. 107.

13. Agnes Snyder, *Dauntless Women in Childhood Education, 1856–1931* (Washington, D.C.: ACEI, 1972), pp. 89–123; Gullett, "Feminism, Politics, and Voluntary Groups," p. 107; Mary Armfield Hill, *Charlotte Perkins Gilman: The Making of a Radical Feminist* (Philadelphia: Temple University Press, 1980), pp. 238–58; Joan M. Jensen, "After Slavery: Caroline Severance in Los Angeles," *Southern California Quarterly* forty-eight (June 1966); 175–86.

14. Parkhurst, "PCWPA," pp. 528–29.

15. Ibid.; *The Impress*, April 1894, p. 2; Hill, *Charlotte Perkins Gilman*, pp. 238–58.

16. PCWPA, "Second Annual Convention of the PCWPA," program, San Francisco, California, 21–23 September 1892, p. 2; *San Francisco Examiner*, 26 November 1893, p. 11; PCWPA, "Constitution and By-Laws," 1893–94, Gullett, "Feminism, Politics, and Voluntary Groups," pp. 117–29; Yamane, "Women, Power, and the Press," pp. 238–40.

17. Gullett, "Feminism, Politics, and Voluntary Groups," pp. 250–64; Rose L. Ellerbe, *History of the Southern California Woman's Press Club* (Los Angeles: Rose Ellerbe 1930), pp. 9–12.

18. Yamane, "Women, Power, and the Press," pp. 238–76; Gullett, "Feminism, Politics, and Voluntary Groups," pp. 109–12; Cummins, *Story of the Files*, pp. 383–98.

19. Cummins, *Story of the Files*, pp. 383–98, 403–25; *San Francisco Blue Books*, 1890–95 and 1899.

20. Gullett, "Feminism, Politics, and Voluntary Groups," pp. 107–8; Rudolph M. Lapp, "A Young Woman of Advanced Ideas: Mabel Craft Deering," *California History* 66, no. 3 (September 1987): 162–69; quote from Judith Rafferty, "Los Angeles Club-women and Progressive Reform in *California Progressivism Revisited*, ed. Deverell and Sitton, pp. 145, 167.

21. Gullett, "Feminism, Politics, and Voluntary Groups," pp. 125, 256–58; Hill, *Charlotte Perkins Gilman*, pp. 243–53.

22. "The Real Annie Laurie," *San Francisco Chronicle* 18 December 1892, p. 13.

23. *San Francisco Blue Books*, 1905–1919; PCWPA, "California's Dream of Fair Women," program, 1923, Ella (Cummins) Sterling Mighels Collection, box 283, folder 4, California State Library, Sacramento; Sophie E. Skidmore, "Power of the Press," chap. in *La Copa de Oro* (San Francisco: PCWPA, 1905).

24. *San Francisco Blue Books*, 1905–1919.

25. Elizabeth V. Burt, "A Bid for Legitimacy: The Woman's Press Club Movement, 1885–1900," *Journalism History* 23, no. 2 (summer 1997): 72–84.

INFORMATIONAL SOURCES

Unpublished Sources

Bio Card and Bio Letter/Information Files. California State Library, Sacramento, California.

Ella Sterling Mighels Collection. California State Library, Sacramento, California.

Gullett, Gayle Ann. "Feminism, Politics, and Voluntary Groups: Organized Womanhood in California." Ph.D. diss., University of California at Riverside, 1983.

Yamane, Nan Towle. "Women, Power, and the Press." Ph.D. diss., University of California at Los Angeles, 1995.

Published Sources

Cummins, Ella Mighels. "Woman's Press Association." In Cummins, *Story of the Files*. San Francisco: World's Fair Commission, 1893.

Daggett, Emerson L., ed. *History of San Francisco Journalism*. San Francisco, California: W.P.A., 1940.

The Impress, 1894–95, passim.

North-Whitcomb, E. M. "Pacific Coast Women's Press Club: Its Origin, Development and Effect." *Everywoman*, July 1915, p. 9.
Parkhurst, Emelie T. Y. "Pacific Coast Women's Press Association." *Californian* (September 1893): 526–34.
Young, John P. *California Journalism*. San Francisco: Chronicle Publishing Company, 1915.

INSTITUTIONAL PROFILE

Pacific Coast Women's Press Association

Dates: Organized 27 September 1890 in San Francisco, California; last meeting recorded in 1941.

Publications: *The Impress*, edited by Charlotte Perkins Gilman and Helen Campbell, 1893–95; *Green Star Magazine*, 1913, Huntington Library; PCWPA Anthologies, 1935, 1937, and 1939.

Archives: A significant amount of material related to PCWPA and its members is contained in the California File, California State Library, Sacramento, California.

24

Nan Towle Yamane

Southern California Women's Press Club, 1893–19(39)

Women journalists in the southern California region first organized in 1893 as an auxiliary to the Pacific Coast Women's Press Association (PCWPA),* which had been organized three years earlier. In 1895, the group split off from the PCWPA to form its own organization because of conflicts over dues, location, writing opportunities, and politics. Although the Southern California Women's Press Club (SCWPC) never became as "large and important" as its mother organization, it was a significant arm of the Los Angeles woman's movement. It took root in an environment supportive of middle-class women reformers, professionals, and journalists, and its membership included some of the most active clubwomen in Southern California. The SCWPC succeeded in building a practical support, educational, activist, and work network for its members, one that operated within the bounds of organized womanhood and survived at least through 1939.[1]

ORIGINS AND DEVELOPMENT

When women journalists first organized in California in 1890, they called their organization the Pacific Coast Women's Press Association and included women from all parts of the state as well as from nearby territories—Oregon, Nevada, and Washington. However, the majority of members were from the San Francisco Bay area; women living in the southern part of the state, particularly in and around Los Angeles, found it useful to establish an auxiliary, which they did in September 1893. The auxiliary became an official branch, the Southern California Chapter of the Pacific Coast Women's Press Association, in 1894.

At first the PCWPC and its auxiliary functioned in tandem, with women of the southern group attending business meetings in the fall and conventions in the spring, and holding their own regular monthly meetings locally. But by 1895, it became clear that there were other, more serious, differences than geography separating the two groups. The decision to break off as a separate organization and the reasons for that decision were reported by the auxiliary's corresponding secretary, Clara Spaulding Brown, in a letter to PCWPA's corresponding secretary, Lillian Plunkett Ferguson, in 1895: "The tidings which I have to convey to you, I fear, will not be welcome, but I trust the cordial feeling of the writers in our Association for the writers in the North will not be questioned."[2]

Brown explained that for a handful of reasons, there had been a unanimous vote for the formation of a separate association. First of all, she explained, the group's name—Southern California Chapter of the Pacific Coast Women's Press Association—was too "unwieldy." Second, members of the group wanted the annual dues reduced to the original $1 per year. Also, because the PCWPA's *Impress* had ceased publication, southern California writers found the PCWPA to be "less advantageous" to them.[3] Finally, but most importantly, the southern California women desired a more practical focus on "press work," and less on the political and social issues to which the PCWPA was devoting much of its energy. They wanted to advance their professional interests, "being very practical and opposed to spending time and thought on women's congresses or any work not coming directly into line of press work." Some writers who were not willing to join the PCWPA were willing to join the SCWPC, wrote Brown.[4]

The goals of the SCWPC were to promote acquaintance among journalists, good fellowship, and cooperation among women writers of the coast and to advance the professional interests of women journalists. Any woman resident of southern California who was a journalist or illustrator for a publication was invited to join. Founders desired high standards of membership, a high initiation fee, and low dues. The organization's first convention, held in March 1895, reflected its interests in journalism and literature, and members presented papers on topics such as "Idealism in Literature," "Personal Reminiscences of Literary People," and the "The Possibilities of a Press Club."[5]

Twenty women signed the original constitution, and another ten joined before the next meeting. Like those who joined the PCWPA, the first members were an assortment of "press women," newspaper and periodical writers and contributors, as well as authors of poetry and fiction. Many members had moved to the Los Angeles area either from the East or from the San Francisco Bay area, and they lived as far away as Redlands, Ventura, and San Diego. According to a reporter from the *Los Angeles Herald*, members were active "on regular staffs of local and suburban newspapers and magazines, and special contributors and correspondents to periodicals all over the United States." Some joined the SCWPC, but also belonged to the PCWPA. Clara Spaulding Brown, an editor of the Women's Department of the *Los Angeles Evening Express*, for example, became president of the SCWPC in 1899. One of the southern group's founders, she retained her membership in the PCWPA. One of the club's first functions in 1896 was a reception for writer Rebecca Spring, an acquaintance of Margaret

Fuller and her husband, Giovanni Angelo Ossoli. At her reception, Spring told stories of famous writers, recited her own work, and was accompanied by the art, poetry, and music of other club members.[6]

Though literature was important to the SCWPC, the organization also managed to keep a journalistic focus on issues of the day. This focus was kept sharp by the many newspaperwomen who made up the membership over the years. One writer commented in 1916:

In the Press Club's active membership are almost all the local newspaper women of the various dailies of the city. Directing the policies of the club in the last year has been Mrs. Lavinia Griffin Graham, of the Examiner staff, as president, and her term of office has been exceptionally brilliant. Mrs. Graham is one of the busiest, most influential and widely known newspaper women of the city. Dorothy Willis, of the Tribune-Express staff, has been a prominent factor in the club's success of the year also with her clever pen and personal endeavor.[7]

Other members representing Los Angeles newspapers at this time included Ruth Sterry and Juana Neal Levy of the *Herald*, Dorothy B. Johnson of the *Times*, Lenore King ("Charlie Angeleno") of the *Examiner*, and Estelle Lawton Lindsey of the *Record*. Others listed as members were editors and publishers such as Clara Shortridge Foltz, publisher of the *New American Woman*, and Harriet Barry, the editor of *Woman's Bulletin*. Among members described as authors and contributors were Anna Dwight Satterlee, Lillian Pelee, Adeline Stanton, Ella Duffield, Lillian Ballagh, and Inez Townsend Tribet. By 1920, the club had 213 members; 181 of these were classified as "active."[8]

ACTIVITIES

The SCWPC served as a venue in which members could discuss professional issues as well as social and political issues of the day. This was accomplished through the club's monthly meetings and annual conventions as well as through the work published by its members. The club was successful in providing sorority for its members, supporting members' work, and educating members for the purposes of press coverage. It retained a practical focus on press work and the advancement of women in the press.

One of the most important functions of the SCWPC was to support members' work. This it did by a variety of activities. It acquired copies of books written and edited by members for its library so that these accomplishments could be shared within the organization at its various meeting places. After more than ten years of planning and discussion, it established a "Marketing Bureau" in 1924 that acted as an agent for procuring assignments for members and placing their work. The bureau, which operated for only about a year, ran at a loss (its expenses were about $200 a month, but the bureau made only an average of $80 a month), though it was prolific, producing forty-seven short stories, one novelette, two books, twenty articles, sixty-four "lecture and program arrangements," and a "very few sets of verse." With the advent of radio, the club sought to establish its presence through this new medium and in 1924 sponsored a monthly radio show on KFI–Los Angeles that featured the work of its members. In the same year, it also held two contests, one for best poetry and the other for best fiction. It also briefly published a newsletter, *The Bulletin*, during 1924 and launched a campaign to raise funds to build a clubhouse. This project, however, was never completed, and the club met in various locations, finally settling at the Friday Morning Club headquarters.[9]

Educating members was an important goal of the SCWPC. Along with building a library for its own use, it planned programs on topics of the day and held debates to enrich members' press work with depth of understanding. It held classes in the arts, encouraged greater cooperation between the press and the public, and sponsored discussions and speakers on such topics as suffrage, world peace, world war, and the latest technology, radio.

The club's educational role often dovetailed with its members' interests in reform and occasionally led to endorsements of particular reforms or direct action. In 1896, for example, the SCWPC passed a resolution to honor the work of California's women in the "press purity" movement, supporting the suppression of lurid and criminal details in newspapers. Many members were involved in temperance and suffrage as well: Mary Todd Ives, for example, wrote for the state Women's Christian Temperance Union publication, the *White Ribbon*, and Alice Moore McComas wrote for the suffrage movement's *Woman's Journal*. In 1911, the SCWPC held debates on woman suffrage, and when Huntington Wright of the *Los Angeles Times* spoke against the reform, the reaction to him was overwhelming: "He had proposed a paper which contained statements so offensive to his feminine audience that some of them were hissed."[10] Wright was so flustered by the reaction that he forgot the rest of his speech. At the conclusion of that event, the 147-member press club voted for suffrage. When the reform passed at the state level in 1913, the SCWPC membership claimed part of the credit:

Los Angeles press women have to their credit the making of history, especially the great campaign for woman's suffrage, when they worked with brains and typewriters to make the dream of California women come true. The victory in that campaign was due as much to women writers as to the justice of men voters.[11]

SCWPC members felt, in fact, that "every great movement started by women's clubs . . . has had the support of press women." In 1914, the membership supported world peace, but once the United States entered World War I, supported the war effort. By 1919, it had formed a Service Committee to aid the war effort, invested in War Bonds, and supported the work of the Red Cross.[12]

The SCWPC also engaged in activities of a more social nature that created and sustained a strong sense of community and harmony among its members. It took pride in "fairness, frankness, loyalty, and good fellowship." According to Rose Ellerbe, who published the group's history in 1930, members "rejoiced" in the "spirit of harmony among members and in the confidence exhibited by the public towards its simple, unpretentious methods to promote unity of action and good fellowship among literary women." The club organized many socials, such as a banquet in 1898, which members claimed to be the "largest if not the only affair of this kind that has ever been given in Southern California, being a gathering of women, some of national reputation." SCWPC members, wrote a *Los Angeles Herald* reporter, were "thoroughly alive to the importance of making their club one of lasting and beneficial enjoyment and influence, not only individually but collectively, and to the section they represent [the press]." But these women did not isolate themselves within their club; they enlarged their social and support network in 1897 by affiliating with the California State Federation of Women's Clubs.[13]

CONCLUSION

The SCWPC was perhaps limited by the homogeneity of the region, the very factor that made it strong as one organization among many in the region. The class conflict so characteristic of San Francisco was minimized in Los Angeles, where the clear majority of the white and middle-class population resulted in closer ideological and personal connections between women and men reformers. Club members embraced organized womanhood and the women's world of reporting, finding positions with the local dailies as writers and editors for women's departments. Less divided by race and class than their sisters to the north, members of the SCWPC shared cultural ideas with each other and with their men. Shared class and cultural identity was the very strength of the SCWPC, and it resulted in a higher percentage of working women journalists in Los Angeles than in San Francisco. In 1910, for example, women accounted for 40 percent of the professionals in Los Angeles and 37 percent of the professionals in San Francisco. Women comprised 17 percent of Los Angeles's "Editors and Reporters" reported in the census, compared to 11 percent in San Francisco.[14]

However, such homogeneity might have resulted in a less aggressive first generation of women journalists, a group less likely to demand new kinds of work for women on the most powerful of dailies. In 1894, the *Los Angeles Herald* reported the reception of Mary S. Lockwood, the president of the International Woman's Press Association, and other national press leaders by the SCWPC. According to the *Herald*, the visitors "were a somewhat free and easy lot, and rather shocked their more demure hostesses of the Southern California Branch of the PCWPA." On balance, the southern California group was more conservative in action than its northern California counterpart. In 1895, for example, SCWPC member Alice McComas addressed the caricature of aggressive and masculine women drawn by anti-suffragists, writing, "[They] may be found in the blue grass country, . . . but they are not a product of the glorious climate of California."[15]

Generally speaking, Los Angeles–based press women were strong in organizing on behalf of women's interests, but less aggressive in demanding work outside their traditional areas of fiction, features, fashion, family, and news directed to women. Those who were more aggressive, it might be noted, were *not* members of the press club. For example, Aggie Underwood—who started out as a switchboard operator for the *Record* in 1902, was a news reporter by 1918, and slowly made her way up the ranks until she became the city editor of the *Los Angeles Herald and Express* in 1947—was not a member of the SCWPC.[16] Underwood's success represented a major victory outside of the women's world of reporting, as well as a reaction to the very movement that contributed to women's first opportunities with the press establishment. More typical of the younger generation of journalists of her time, Underwood was characterized in 1918 as one who "[walks] through fire lines, trails killers, weeps with divorces and rides anything from airplanes to mules to reach the spot that in newspapers is usually marked with an arrow or an X. What a gal!"[17] In her autobiography, Underwood wrote, "I do not regard the fact that I am city editor of a metropolitan newspaper as a triumph in emancipation of womanhood, equality of the sexes—or votes for wimmin [*sic*]." Rather, she felt, being "able to do the work is not a matter of sex."[18] Getting the first opportunities in newspaper work, though, was a matter of sex, and southern California's women writers notably justified their first work as an extension of their feminine roles.

Overall, it must be said that the SCWPC was significant and successful in its support, education, political organization, and advancement of women writers and journalists. It provided a nurturing environment for women writers and journalists, especially those writing in traditional areas of women's journalistic work. Begun as an independent organization in 1895, the club survived at least through 1939.

NOTES

1. Rose L. Ellerbe, *History of the Southern California Women's Press Club* (Los Angeles: Rose L. Ellerbe, 1930), p. 26; *Los Angeles Blue Book*, 1939, p. 245.

2. Ellerbe, *History*, pp. 13–14.

3. *Impress* was published by Charlotte Perkins Gilman from 1890 to 1894.

4. Ellerbe, *History*, pp. 12–16.

5. Ibid., pp. 22–25.

6. Ibid., pp. 25–27; "The Woman's Southern California Press Club," *Los Angeles Herald*, 7 April 1895, p. 16; and Laurie James, *Men, Women, and Margaret Fuller* (New York: (Golden Heritage Press, 1990), pp. 381–99.

7. Ellerbe, *History*, pp. 48–49.

8. Ibid.

9. Ibid., pp. 36–38; 51–54; *Los Angeles Blue Books*, 1921–1939.

10. Ellerbe, *History*, p. 36.

11. Ibid., p. 48.

12. Ibid., pp. 51–53.

13. Ibid., 6–8; "The Woman's Southern California Press Club," *Los Angeles Herald*, 7 April 1895, p. 16.

14. Robert M. Fogelson, *Fragmented Metropolis: Los Angeles, 1850–1930* (Cambridge, Mass.: Harvard University Press, 1967); Judith Rafferty, "Los Angeles Clubwomen and Progressive Reform," in *California Progressivism Revisited*, ed. William Deverlee and Tom Sitton (Berkeley: University of California Press, 1994), pp. 144–74; "Table III.–Total Persons 10 years and over engaged in each specified occupation, classified by sex, for cities of 100,000 inhabitants or more: 1910," in *Fourteenth Census of the United States, 1910*, vol. 4, pp. 176–77, 204–5.

15. Nan Towle Yamane, "Women, Power, and the Press: The Case of San Francisco, 1868–1896" (Ph.D. diss.:, University of California at Los Angeles, 1995), pp. 38–51; "The Woman's Southern California Press Club," *Los Angeles Herald*, 7 April 1895, p. 16; "Alice Moore McComas on Woman Suffrage," *Los Angeles Herald*, 7 April 1895, pp. 13–14.

16. Bruce Henstell, "Newspaperwoman Tells All about It," *Los Angeles Free Weekly Reader*, 31 July 1981, p. 108; Aggie Underwood, *Newspaperwoman* (New York: Harper and Brothers Publishers, 1949), pp. 2–3.

17. *Los Angeles Herald*, 11 November 1918, p. C4.

18. Henstell, "Newspaperwoman Tells All about It"; Underwood, *Newspaperwoman*, pp. 2–3.

INFORMATIONAL SOURCES

Caroline Severance Papers. Huntington Library, San Marino, California.

Ellerbe, Rose L. *History of the Southern California Woman's Press Club, 1894–1929*. Los Angeles: Rose L. Ellerbe, 1930.

Gibson, Mary S., ed. *A Record of Twenty-five Years of the California Federation of Women's Clubs*. Los Angeles: California Federation of Women's Clubs, 1927.

Gullett, Gayle Ann. "Feminism, Politics, and Voluntary Groups: Organized Womanhood in California." Ph.D. diss., University of California at Riverside, 1983.

Jensen, Joan M. "After Slavery: Caroline Severance in Los Angeles." *Southern California Quarterly* 48 (June 1966): 175–86.

Los Angeles Blue Book, 1894–1940.

Rafferty, Judith. "Los Angeles Clubwomen and Progressive Reform." In *California Progressivism Revisited*, ed. William Deverell and Tom Sitton. Berkeley: University of California Press, 1994.

Ruddy, Giles, ed. *The Mother of Clubs: Caroline M. Seymour Severance*. Los Angeles: Baumgardt Publishing Company, 1906.

Williamson, Martha Burton Woodhead. *Ladies Clubs and Societies: Los Angeles in 1892*. Los Angeles: Historical Society of Southern California, 1925.

INSTITUTIONAL PROFILE

Southern California Women's Press Club

Dates: Established in September 1893 as an auxiliary of the Pacific Coast Women's Press Association (PCWPA); became the **Southern California Chapter of the PCWPA**,

10 March 1894; became a separate organization, the **Southern California Women's Press Club**, 12 March 1895. The organization continued until at least 1939, the last year in which it was listed in the *Los Angeles Blue Book*.

Newsletter: *The Bulletin*, published in 1924.

25

Kate Peirce

Texas Professional Communicators, 1893–Present

(Formerly Texas Woman's Press Association and Texas Press Women)

ORGANIZATION

In 1893, Houston newspaperwoman Aurelia Hadley Mohl believed that Texas women writers needed to be in closer touch with each other and decided to take action. Mohl organized a meeting in Dallas to discuss creating a women's press club. More than thirty women accepted her invitation.[1]

Mohl, a reporter for the *Houston Post* who had experience in Washington, D.C., as well, knew that one of the obstacles in the path of advancement for women was a lack of appreciation for organized effort. She would need to persuade the women writers that it was time to organize. Here, she succeeded, and it did not take long for the Texas Woman's Press Association (TWPA) to become what it is today, the second oldest women's organization in Texas. Thirty-four women—newspaperwomen, authors, and poets—representing eighteen towns became charter members.[2]

Mohl was the group's first choice for president, but she chose to be corresponding secretary, and Sidney Smith, a newspaper correspondent from Dallas, was elected president. The rest of the meeting that year was spent creating a constitution and bylaws, one of which defined the organization: "The objects of this Association shall be to advance and encourage Texas women in literary work, to promote fraternal intercourse with kindred associations outside the State and to secure all the benefits arising from organized effort." The group adopted the motto "Lofty Aims and High Ideals."[3]

Charter members of the group came from all over the state and wrote for a variety of publications. Of the thirty-four, fewer than one-third worked for newspapers as regular staff or correspondents. Newspaper staff members included Mrs. Charles Culmore of the *Houston Press*, Lottie Cameron Efnor of the *Hemp-*

stead Press, Virginia Goffe of the *Dallas Times Herald*, Mrs. M. R. Walton of the *Ft. Worth Gazette*, and Allie Wilson of the *Lockhart Register*. Correspondents included Era Hall of Ft. Worth, Sydney Smith of Dallas, and Elizabeth Strong Tracy of Houston. Another thirteen of the charter members were contributors to newspapers and magazines, and seven identified themselves as authors.[4]

Women writers throughout the state greeted news about the organization enthusiastically. "A better time for women writers and for southern literature also, let us hope, dawned with the birth of the Texas Woman's Press Association," wrote Bride Neill Taylor, an author of novelettes, in the *Galveston Daily News*. "It will be encouragement to the timid and a source of inspiration to the disheartened. Every woman writer who wishes to be helped or to help her sisters should become a member."[5]

THE EARLY YEARS

The first convention of the TWPA was held in Fort Worth in July 1893, and it set the tone for future conventions with social functions as important as the business of the organization. Members in the host city made sure sightseeing was part of the program, and many went to great lengths to entertain out-of-towners. Civic leaders were invited to participate in the activities and often opened their homes for receptions and meals for the participants. In the early years, the women also stayed with families who lived in the town where the convention was being held.[6]

The association's third annual convention was held in the state's capital, Austin, where it was characterized by the local press as "the most notable gathering of women ever assembled in the state."[7] Male visitors, used to the noisy behavior of male legislators, were amazed that the women did not all talk at once and that they would yield the floor when the chairwoman instructed them to do so. One visitor presented them with a gavel made of inlaid Texas woods, which the women, who did not need it, promptly lost.[8]

A story in *The Bohemian*, a literary magazine based in Fort Worth, documented every minute of the 1902 convention in Waco and Stamford.[9] One reads of "the purple-velvet sofa of a coach on a Houston and Texas Central Train" that carried the anonymous author to the convention site, the TWPA badge, blue with black lettering, and the convention schedule. Business was transacted during the morning session, songs and instrumental music were interspersed among the more serious matters of the day, and papers and debates filling the afternoon. A grand reception was held on the mayor's lawn with ladies of the reception committee, elegantly attired, greeting each woman of the press. In the middle of the convention, the women changed locations, traveling by train from Waco to Stamford, a town only two years old that became a center for the production of cotton, oil, and flour. There the women continued their business, music, poetry readings, and, of course, sightseeing and socializing.

One paper in particular at that 1902 meeting caught the women's attention: "The Press [Club] Member and What Is Required of Her as a Member." The author wrote that to be a member meant more than meeting friends, but that it "must in the highest and best sense bring interchange of ideas and united effort for the good of our fellow creatures. Does it not widen the doors of heart and brain to thus come in contact with strangers today and friends tomorrow?"[10]

On occasion, members became involved in activities taken up by other women's organizations of the time. During its early years, some members wrote in favor of abolishing child labor laws or passing the suffrage amendment. The organization as a whole occasionally sponsored civic programs. For example, it sponsored a campaign for a building fund of $1 million for a new home for the state library in 1939. In 1915 TWPA petitioned the Texas Board of Regents to establish a school of journalism at the University of Texas. Words one member wrote on the back of a program from the 1915 meeting in Waco illustrate the importance of the journalism school: "An article from half the members of this association in her own style setting forth the value of the school of journalism would result in a higher appreciation of that school and in an increased attendance thereby adding to our prestige and things educational," the note predicted. "Every article we write that helps create public sentiment for the needs of our educational institutions is patriotism for we are doing constructive work."[11] The school was established in 1916, and the Texas Woman's Press Association was the first organization to provide a scholarship for a female journalism student enrolled in the school.[12]

Concern about social issues continued. One of TWPA's ongoing activities has been to monitor issues of concern to women and to journalists. To aid in this, the organization created a legislative committee whose job it was to keep members informed of relevant bills and encourage them to speak up on important issues. The importance of this function was stressed in 1947 by TWPA Legislative Chairman Louise Miller Henely. "As women of the press and platform, we wield a greater power than we know. Others look to us for information about pending legislation," she wrote. "Are you informed? Do you know the impact of the bills in question? The part newspaperwomen take in writing and talking helps greatly in moulding public opinion. 'The pen is mightier than the sword.' The power is in your hands. The world today is looking toward woman to do her part."[13]

In the early days, women involved in literary writing were as welcome in the organization as those working in journalism.[14] But in those days the lines were blurred between fact and fiction in newspapers as well, with poetry appearing alongside—or even as—editorials. Adelaide Tate Barbour, editorial writer for the *Gonzales Inquirer*, frequently wrote "poetorials" for her paper:

> You can live today but once
>   So make it count!
> Yesterday' sun is lost to sight,

Tomorrow's sun's yet hid by night
Today you stand forth in the light;
    So make it count![15]

But as journalistic writing changed from poetic editorials and first-person accounts of accidents and events to "objective" third-person reports, so did the Texas Woman's Press Association change. In 1940, after the organization affiliated with the National Federation of Press Women (NFPW),* authors and poets were no longer eligible for membership; only women actively involved in mass communication news media were invited to join. In 1961, the organization shortened its name to Texas Press Women (TPW).[16]

THE WRITING LIFE

That the primary purpose of the organization was to promote its members as writers and to document their work is clear from the letter sent to members by Decca West, chair of the history committee, in 1918. Telling them it was her duty to collect and preserve their published work, she wrote: "All matter that has appeared in print that the writer feels is representative of her work should be sent even if it is the 'Hack' work that sometimes wearies."[17] The letter generated quick responses. Cora Mellon Cross wrote of sending clippings from her newspaper, *Farm News*, which was published by the *Dallas News*. She had not written much of a literary sort, she said, because "the cry has been so great for potatoes instead of poetry."[18]

Belle Costello of the *Houston Chronicle*, in contrast apparently had plenty of time to do it all. "If I should send clippings of my work I would have a hard job to choose which deserved to go down to the future, as I have always two columns of work each day in the *Chronicle*, and when I have time to write a feature story and illustrate the same as staff artist I have much more," she wrote. "I have found time this past year to contribute several stories and little verses to magazines and done some really creditable work. Since the boys began to leave for the front, I have been working on a regular man's "beat" in addition to my own old work."[19]

Eventually, members were able to submit their best work to the organization's annual writing contest. Members were urged early on to prepare submissions and obtain a note of authenticity from the boss. "It would be well to start drafting those original letters and put them before your boss for his signature before he takes off for the holidays" suggested an article in the organization's newsletter in 1970.[20] And members responded. In 1971, the contest judge wrote that her Q-Q (quantity-quality) rating of contest entries was excellent, especially in the classifications of news, features, special articles, interviews, columns, photography, publicity, and public relations.[21]

Although the organization was made up of writers, it did not have a newsletter until the 1950s.[22] With two exceptions, the publication was called *Texas Press*

Woman until 1995, when its name was changed to *Topics*. In 1959 it was published as *Texas Woman's Press Association News*, and in 1970–71 it was called
the *Distaffer*. No matter the name, the publication has always contained news
about future conventions, reports of past conventions, officers' reports, and information on membership and members' activities. Contest facts and figures as
well as contest results are also included. TWPA also became involved in broader
issues concerning women. In 1974, for example, the organization petitioned the
governor to establish Texas's Third Commission on the Status of Women.[23]

TWPA'S MOST FAMOUS MEMBER

Throughout the organization's existence, much attention was paid to Dona
Coulter Carnes, born in Bryan, Texas, in 1878. Society editor of the *Bryan Daily
Eagle* from 1901 to 1930, she was a life member and served as president in
1938–39. One newspaper article written about her during her presidency provides an amusing picture of how Carnes got started in journalism: "She began
wrangling with a distraught editor of her husband's newspaper that 'she couldn't
write if her life depended on it' and ended about 35 years later president of
WPA of Texas."[24] In 1961, the woman fondly known as "Honey Chile" and
"Miss Dona" was named "Ambassador of Goodwill" by Texas Governor Price
Daniel, and at a "gay nineties" party held on her ninetieth birthday in 1978,
congratulatory letters addressed to "Miss Dona" arrived from President and Mrs.
Lyndon Baines Johnson.[25]

Carnes is credited with increasing membership in Texas Press Women and
encouraging young women journalists to write news instead of society columns.
In 1969 she addressed the organization of which she had been a member for
seventy-five years, and in March 1970 she was, at ninety-one, the oldest member
to attend the convention of the San Jacinto district. "Miss Dona" died July 3,
1980, at age 101.[26]

CHALLENGES

Like many other women's organizations, TPW began to see a decline in
membership after the 1970s, and this became a chief concern during the 1990s.
By 1995, membership had, for the first time, dropped below 200. At 150 members, it was half the size it had been three years earlier. In an effort to reverse
the trend, the group debated changing its name. Board members feared that the
name Texas Press Women represented an aging organization that was no longer
attracting younger members or all those eligible to join: men as well as women
who worked in all areas of mass communication. Believing a new, more inclusive name might attract more members, the board of directors called for ideas.
Texas Professional Communicators (TPC), the name most often suggested, was
adopted in 1995. The newsletter, *Texas Press Women*, also got a new name,
Topics, which was derived from an expansion of the group's new initials.[27]

In another effort to attract members, Kirsten Dietz spent her year as president elect encouraging new chapters and the growth of existing ones. In her year-end report in 1995, she said she believed that with a new name and rededication of members, the organization could have a bright future.[28] This reversal, however, did not come about; a few months into her presidency and worried the organization would fold, Dietz was still asking why membership had fallen, saying hard work and history were in jeopardy.[29]

Both Dietz and her predecessor, Ginger Carnes, were adamant about the importance of preserving the organization. In her 1995 president's report, Carnes listed the organization's activities and characteristics that made it worthwhile, including TPC's scholarships, high school contests, annual contests, diverse membership, and opportunities offered by its connection to the NFPW. "Everyone needs a mentor," she wrote. "To many, TPW is the "only game in town.""[30]

But neither the reorganization nor the continued dedication of members made an impact on the slipping membership, which, by 1998, had dropped to 104. Kathie Magers, president in 1997 and 1998, said she believed it was a sign of the times. People were no longer joiners, and with corporate downsizing, there was a smaller professional population to draw from. She said the group would continue to attempt to recruit new members and pursue its longtime goals: to promote journalism as a career for high school students, to attract qualified people into the profession, and to further journalism as a profession. Both Magers and Dietz were optimistic that the organization would continue, though not with the strength in numbers it once had.[31]

As the world moves toward the twenty-first century, it seems one thing has both changed and not changed with the Texas Professional Communicators: The group still issues a wardrobe advisory, but this has been updated to reflect a sense of common-sense practicality. In 1959 the membership was advised that "the trip to Ft. Hood presents a bit of a 'what shall I wear' problem.' For this occasion, TWPA president Florence Bosl suggests your best suit, plus hat and gloves, since there'll be no returning to your hotel before cocktails and dinner."[32] By 1995, members were being told that "flat shoes are strongly advised for both the Friday afternoon tours and Friday night's fish fry, cruises and COA presentation. . . . Heels are not allowed in the yachts."[33] One can imagine the wardrobe advisory for the 200th anniversary of the Texas Professional Communicators, which Magers and Dietz are determined *will* take place in 2093: "For intergalactic travel, a number-nine spacesuit is a must."

NOTES

    1. Mary R. Walton, "A History of the Texas Woman's Press Association, 1893, 1908, 1908" (unpublished paper presented to the Texas Woman's Press Association, 16 June 1908), p. 2, The Woman's Collection, Rare Book Collection, Texas Woman's University Library, Denton, Texas.
    2. Ibid., p. 3.
    3. Ibid., p. 4.

4. Mrs. F. M. B. Hughes, "The History of the Texas Woman's Press Association," Texas Professional Communicators Archives (hereafter TPC Archives), box 2.325/Q11, Center for American History, University of Texas at Austin, Texas.

5. Bride N. Taylor, "The Woman's Press Association," *Galveston Daily News*, 18 June 1893, TPC Archives, Vertical File.

6. Walton, "A History."

7. Pauline Periwinkle, *Dallas Morning News*, 31 May 1896, p. 15, TPC Archives, Vertical File.

8. Walton, "A History," p. 7.

9. A Bohemian, "Past and Present of Texas," *The Bohemian* 3, no. 4 (1902): 54–77, TPC Archives, Vertical File.

10. Walton, "A History," p. 7.

11. TPC Archives, box 2K341.

12. *Press Woman*, June 1976, pp. 39–40, TPC Archives, box 2.325/B70.

13. Louise Miller Henely, *Press Woman*, June 1947, TPC Archives, box 2.325/V64.

14. *Press Woman*, June 1976, pp. 39–40.

15. TPC Archives, box 2.325/V56. The editorial is included in a scrapbook of clippings from the early 1900s but is without a date. Barbour resigned as editorial writer in 1915 after five years at the paper, according to another editorial.

16. *Press Woman*, June 1976, pp. 39–40.

17. Decca West to Texas Woman's Press Association membership, 20 April 1918, TPC Archives, box 2K341.

18. Cora Mellon Cross to Decca West, 26 April 1918, TPC Archives, box 2K341.

19. Belle Costello to Decca West, 24 April 1918, TPC Archives, box 2K341.

20. Mary Day, *Distaffer*, December 1970, p. 1, TPC Archives, box 2.325/B103.

21. Mary Day, *Distaffer*, February 1971, p. 1, TPC Archives, box 2.325/B103.

22. The organization did, however, publish a column in the *Texas Press Messenger* during the 1940s.

23. Holly Wood to executive committee, 15 April 1974, TPC Archives, box 2.325/B103.

24. Beverley Colomb, "Woman Editor Backs Her Sex against Men on Newspapers," *New Orleans Picayune*, 7 December 1938, TPC Archives, box 2.325/B70.

25. Eliza Bishop, *Texas Press Woman*, September 1978, p. 1, TPC Archives, box 2.325/B70.

26. TPC Archives, box 2.325/B70.

27. Kirsten Dietz, *Topics*, March 1995, p. 2, TPC Archives, box 2.325/A123a.

28. Kirsten Dietz, year-end report, March 1995, TPC Archives, box 2.325/A123a.

29. Kirsten Dietz, *Topics*, August 1995, p. 2, TPC Archives, box 2.325/A123a.

30. Ginger Carnes, President's Report, March 1995, TPC Archives, box 2.325/A1232a.

31. Author interview with Kathie Magers, April 24, 1998, and interview with Kirsten Dietz, 25 June 1998.

32. *TWPA News*, September/October 1959, p. 4.

33. Kirsten Dietz, *Topics*, February 1996, p. 7, TPC Archives, box 2.325/A123a.

INFORMATIONAL SOURCES

A Bohemian. "Past and Present of Texas." *The Bohemian* 3, no. 4 (1902): 54–77.
Distaffer, newsletter of Texas Press Women, 1970–71.

Texas Press Woman, newsletter of the Texas Woman's Press Association and Texas Press
    Women, 1958–94, passim.
Texas Professional Communicators Archives. Center for American History, University
    of Texas at Austin, Texas.
Topics, newsletter for Texas Professional Communicators, 1995.
Walton, Mary R. "A History of the Texas Woman's Press Association 1893–1908." Paper
    presented to the Texas Woman's Press Association, 16 June 1908.

INSTITUTIONAL PROFILE

Texas Professional Communicators

Dates: Organized as **Texas Woman's Press Association** Dallas, Texas, May 1893;
changed name to **Texas Press Women** in 1961; Changed name to **Texas Professional
Communicators** in 1995.

Newsletter: the association had a column in the *Texas Press Messenger* during the 1940s.
From the 1950s until 1995, it published a newsletter, *Texas Press Woman* (although
the name was changed during two periods—in 1959 it was *Texas Woman's Press
Association News*, and in 1970–71 it was called *Distaffer*). When the organization
changed its name to Texas Professional Communicators in 1995, the newsletter was
renamed *Topics*.

Archives: Texas Professional Communicators Archives, Center for American History,
University of Texas at Austin, Austin, Texas; The Woman's Collection; Rare Book
Collection, Texas Woman's University Library, Texas Woman's University, Denton,
Texas.

Contact: Kathie Magers (president, 1998–99), 114 N. Edgefield Ave., Dallas, TX 75208,
tel. (214) 943–7755.

26

Sherry Baker

Utah Woman's Press Club,
1891–1928

ORGANIZATION

The Utah Woman's Press Club (UWPC) was organized in Salt Lake City, October 31, 1891 at the office of the *Woman's Exponent*, an influential Mormon women's newspaper. The announcement of the club's organization appeared in the November 15, 1891, edition of the *Exponent*, and reports of its meetings were published regularly in the *Exponent* thereafter.[1] According to the club's constitution, its objective was "to further the literary development and interests of women, and to foster and strengthen individual efforts by means of organization." Membership eligibility was to "any woman who writes for a creditable journal, newspaper or other publication."[2] Most of the members of the Press Club had a Mormon background, although those who didn't were "readily accepted."[3]

Emmeline B. Wells, editor of the *Woman's Exponent*, was founder and first president of the UWPC. She started the club at the request of Belva A. Lockwood following the formation of the Woman's Press Club of New York City* in 1889.[4] Wells was a leader among Utah women. In addition to editing the *Exponent*, she was president of the Woman's Suffrage Association of Utah, founder of the Reapers Club, a writer, and an activist.

Other prominent local women served as founding officers in the Press Club, including Susa Young Gates, daughter of Brigham Young, and founder and editor of *The Young Woman's Journal*; Lula Greene Richards, founder and first editor of the *Woman's Exponent*; Josephine Spencer, later a writer for the *Los Angeles Examiner* and author of *The Senator from Utah* and *Other Tales of the Wasatch*; and Dr. Ellis R. Shipp, physician, writer, and coeditor of the *Salt Lake Sanitarian*. Club members included women who published their work in local as well as national publications: Nevada Davis of the *New York Herald*; Ada Pattersen, drama critic for the *New York American* and author of a biography of Maude Adams, the Broadway actress from Utah; Ruth May Fox, poet; Joyce Cochran, historian; Lucy A. Clark, editor of the *Farmington Flash Light*; and Ellen Lee Jakeman, a contributor to several newspapers and magazines.[5] By 1897, the club had grown to include forty members, twenty of whom were described as "active workers."[6]

Most club members, however, were not active press women. Romania B. Pratt, president of the UWPC in 1897, explained: "In a strict sense, the name of Press club in our case is a misnomer, so few of us are regular or special correspondents or contributors to newspapers and periodicals, and only three of our number are bona fide editors."[7] This circumstance was not unique to the Utah club. Agnes Hooper Gottlieb has written about the Woman's Press Club of New York City that "in an era when women journalists were still a rarity and exclusion from newsrooms was the norm, the founding members of the New York club deliberately created a broad definition of qualifications for membership."[8] In Utah, a broad definition of qualifications was even more necessary than in New York City, for the number of women journalists in this sparsely settled state was even smaller because of the state's small number of newspapers and urban centers.

The UWPC joined the International Woman's Press Association in March 1892 and incorporated in 1898.[9] Its colors were heliotrope (lavender) and Nile (sage) green. In April 1893 it adopted a pin that depicted a Greek lamp with "UWPC" on the bowl. Club meeting schedules and locations varied. Meetings were usually held once a month, with committee business conducted at additional meetings. In the early years these meetings were held in the parlor of the *Exponent* office or in members' homes; after 1914, they were held in the Salt Lake City Public Library. Membership fees in the early days were $1 per year. Although membership requirements were broad, "applications for membership were presented in writing and approved by a credential committee" and then voted on by the membership. Members could bring guests to meetings, but no guest could attend more than three times a year.[10]

ACTIVITIES

Club activities included the reading of "at least two original compositions" each month, discussion of current topics, and the reading of articles from national magazines that were usually concerned with some aspect of women's clubs, writing, or a current event. The meeting agendas were diverse and often addressed social and political issues, especially woman's suffrage, but their primary purpose was to critique club members' writing. Members were expected to contribute to these agendas regularly, and those who failed to make their assigned presentations at meetings received fines of up to twenty-five cents.[11]

Each October, club members celebrated the October 31 founding of the

UWPC at the annual meeting. In keeping with the Halloween date, members dressed in costumes of their choice depicting significant female literary or historical figures. Assigned members then delivered brief biographical sketches of or a piece of writing by the figure they represented.

Many of the UWPC's activities were closely affiliated to the general woman's club movement of the period as well as to other women's press organizations. In 1891, for example, the UWPC was invited to attend the first meeting of the National Federation of Women's Press Clubs in Boston. Although the newly organized club was not able to send representatives, Wells saluted the enterprise in the *Exponent* and expressed her belief in the value of women, particularly women journalists, organizing.

Letters, telegrams and notes of invitation have been sent to us to be present at the first meeting for the Federation of Women's Press Clubs in Boston on the eleventh of the present month [November 1891]—it has been a source of deep regret that we were unable to attend and help on with the enterprise started last winter in Washington. . . . Such opportunities are rare and ought not to be neglected, they are the milestones that count woman's progress in the path of progression and enlightenment. . . . The women of the press have an immense power for good, to mold the minds of others, to influence the multitudes that may never see them or hear their voices, yet they can wield a potent sway by means of the pen, and so subtle is this impress that it is not perceptible, but grows to giant proportions without scarcely a sound even a whisper. . . . Some of the brightest and brainiest women in the world, will be gathered at the hub in this Federation. . . . To see a large concourse of women who can earn money by the pen is a picture worth gazing upon. . . . The very fact of these women coming together is one of the signs of the times, telling in trumpet tones of the rapid strides being made towards woman's emancipation from ignorance and bondage.[12]

Though the UWPC was not represented at that first national meeting of women's press clubs, it was active in other women's organizations. When the Utah Federation of Women's Clubs (UFWC) was organized April 7, 1893 (the second state federation of women's clubs to organize in the Union), the Utah Woman's Press Club was one of its six charter members. According to Jane Cunningham Croly, who published a history of the woman's club movement in 1898, "There [was] no club in the Utah Federation which [did] more original work than the Utah Woman's Press Club."[13]

One of the primary objects of the organization was to "encourage young writers and cultivate all their literary possibilities," reported Dr. Ellis R. Shipp at the third annual convention of the Utah Federation. "Although many of the results would not perhaps shine with Shakespearean brilliancy yet we have listened to many choice thoughts that would otherwise never had birth," she told those attending. "In reviewing our past year's work one is surprised with the amount of original work done by this club, the greater part of every session being devoted to this line of work."[14]

These women did not enjoy the same possibilities for publication as women writers living in metropolitan areas and the more heavily populated East Coast, but they did find outlets for their writing in Wells's *Exponent* and Gates's *Young Woman's Journal*.[15] And for those who might think the talents and abilities of these women might suffer from geographic or cultural isolation, Wells had the following assurance:

To those unacquainted with the history of Utah, it may seem surprising to tell them that women writers here compare favorably with their sisters in the East, it is however perfectly true; some of them have been born and educated there, and in England and other lands, and have also the broad free spirit of the West . . . Great things in the way of literature are expected from the native born children of the inter-mountain country. Even now we have many young women whose journalistic work is well worth commending, and of whose career we are justly proud.[16]

Despite its isolation, Salt Lake City was the crossroads of the West. Consequently, the UWPC frequently entertained well-known visitors from outside Utah. In May 1891, the club hosted members of the Woman's National Press Association (WNPA) on their return from an excursion to the West Coast. According to the *Exponent*'s account of this event, the visitors included, among others, Mary S. Lockwood, WNPA president and editor of the *American Monthly Magazine*; Mrs. H. W. Balston, correspondent for the *Woman's Tribune*; Emily Hawthorne, poet and correspondent for *Advanced Thought*; Julia A. Anderson, correspondent for the *Philadelphia Daily News*; and Elvira Bliss Sheldon, correspondent for the *Washington Daily Times*.[17]

In its review of activities for the club year ending October 1896, the UWPC reported that members had been addressed by "many renowned speakers both of national reputation and local fame" including Dr. Sarah J. Elliott, "a friend and champion of Clara Barton," and Laura M. Johns, an organizer and speaker of the Woman Suffrage Association. Also in 1896, the UWPC assisted the "gentlemen of the local press" in entertaining the Convention of Western Editors "then enroute for the Pacific Coast."[18] Two years later, the club gave a grand reception at the Bee Hive House (the former residence of Brigham Young) for F. Marion Crawford, "the world renowned author." "Most of the noted women of the Salt Lake Clubs attended," the *Exponent* reported. "It was quite a brilliant and social affair."[19] Other visitors over the years included the Honorable Phoebe Cousins of St. Louis in December 1894; "the Misses Chase of Boston" in November 1895; suffrage speaker Elizabeth Upham Yates in July 1896; and Denver newspaper woman Helen Margaret Ring in August 1900. In March 1897, the guest of honor was Miss A. M. Beecher, who in response to a request from the members, gave an informal talk on economics, the influence of women in politics, and the political status of the Eastern woman.[20]

This last topic was of particular interest to the members of the UWPC, since many of its members were active in the woman's rights movement locally, nationally, and internationally. For years, the *Exponent* served as a voice for the

Utah suffrage movement, and Wells was a strong proponent for the cause and its leaders. Following the death of Elizabeth Cady Stanton, the *Exponent* extolled her as "one of the most extraordinary women the nineteenth century has produced." Wells wrote: "The writer hopes to publish some personal reminiscences of Mrs. Stanton from her own acquaintance and correspondence with this brilliant, attractive, magnificently gifted woman."[21]

Members were involved in other women's organizations as well. In 1893, several members represented the club at the "great congress and fair" held in Chicago in 1893.[22] Susa Young Gates was selected by the National Council of Women to serve as chair of its powerful press committee for three years, to speak at the International Council for Women in London in 1889, and to serve as sole delegate for that council in Denmark in 1902. Four UWPC members—Wells, Gates, Margaret Caine, and Lydia D. Alder—together with other Utah women attended the Quinquennial Congress in London in June 1899. Alder also attended the Quinquennial Congress in Berlin in June 1904.[23] The club was proud of these activities in support of women, and club historian Lydia D. Alder wrote that "perhaps no club in the state or nation has been represented like the U. W. Press [Club] in the congresses of the world."[24]

In addition to women's rights, the UWPC supported local and national civic causes. One of the club's interests was the kindergarten movement. When it was asked in 1902 by a national organization of women's clubs to "take the initiative step in calling together the representatives of Salt Lake clubs to pursue some line of educational work which would benefit the schools of our city," the UWPC called for a community meeting "to consider the subject of improved educational facilities" and the needs of the city schools. The eventual meeting was attended by delegates from most of the city's schools, and discussion expanded to include sanitation and the introduction of temperance literature.[25]

Other civic activities in which the club participated were the George Washington Memorial Association,[26] the traveling library, for which the UWPC provided a library case full of books,[27] and the Red Cross effort during World War I. The UWPC maintained associations with other women's clubs and often held combined meetings with related groups such as the Reapers Club and the Ladies' Literary Club.[28] Press club members also were involved in promoting the social and political interests of the Utah Federation of Women's Clubs.

Members of the UWPC felt its work was important, and they attended meetings regularly to accomplish its purposes. The club encouraged women to write and provided a means by which members could improve their writing. Through Emmeline B. Wells's *Woman's Exponent* and Susa Young Gates's *Young Woman's Journal*, the club provided opportunities for club members to be published and helped members find other markets for publication. The club also financed the second edition of Wells's *Musings and Memories*, and maintained a fund to assist other members in publishing their work.

The members of the UWPC made no distinction between the promotion of women's writing and the promotion of women's rights. To do one was to do the other; each led to and reinforced the other. The club also fulfilled intellectual and social needs. It provided a forum for discussion and study of current and literary topics, and hosted parties and outings for recreation and enjoyment.

EMMELINE B. WELLS AND THE *EXPONENT*

Emmeline B. Wells was the driving force behind the UWPC. She was described as "the main support of the club," and by 1903, a portion of each February meeting was devoted to celebrating "Aunt Em's" birthday.[29] In February 1911, for example, the *Exponent* reported that "February is the natal month of that esteemed and beloved Utah woman, Mrs. Emmeline B. Wells, and during that month her numerous friends vie with each other in showing her their love and appreciation." Among the guests included in the 1911 celebration were prominent members of the Mormon church hierarchy, including President Joseph Fielding Smith, who made a "graceful and tender presentation speech."[30]

In its May 1912 edition, the *Exponent* celebrated its fortieth anniversary by publishing a history of the periodical, of which Wells by this time had been the editor for more than thirty-five years. The article, written by Annie Wells Cannon (Wells's daughter), noted "the untiring efforts of the editor to bring out young writers, uplift the discouraged, help people to discover themselves, develop latent talent and encourage women in different avocations."[31] Of the *Exponent*, which had served as a voice for the Utah Woman's Press Club since 1891, she wrote:

Perhaps after forty years some think its dress old-fashioned, perhaps some think its style not up-to-date; but its struggles and victories have endeared it as it is to patrons as well as publisher; while as to its past, the record and recital of the trials and triumphs, not only of the women of Utah, but of the women of the world, as told in its columns, old-fashioned though its form may be, has been more truthfully and forcefully given than in any other paper in existence.[32]

The sense of the club's grounding in the personage of Wells and in her generation is evident in reports as early as 1906, when Lydia Alder wrote: "Many of [the UWPC's] old members still attend, and give of their best efforts for its up-building. That the Press Club is dear to 'Aunt Em's' heart, goes without saying, and that true and lasting friendships have grown out of the associations formed in its members by delving into the world of thought and events."[33]

But perhaps precisely *because* the character and activities of the UWPC were so much an expression of the interests and passions that drove Emmeline B. Wells, the club and the *Exponent* faltered as she and its early members aged. In 1899, the club lost one of its earliest members, Julia Ivins McDonald; others followed.[34] In 1914, publication of the *Exponent* ceased, and in 1921, Wells died at the age of 93. The club became inactive and "began on the road to its eventual demise."[35] Rather than allowing the organization simply to fade away, remaining members held a final "abandonment party" to bring the UWPC to an official end. Susa Young Gates, the original vice president, who had described the club as "too wonderful to die out," acted as hostess and officiator at the event. The Utah Woman's Press Club was thus formally dissolved on December 6, 1928.[36]

NOTES

1. *Woman's Exponent*, November 1891, p. 77. In addition to the minutes of the UWPC, the *Exponent* often published news from other women's press organizations and women's rights organizations such as the National Federation of Women's Press Clubs, the Pacific Coast Women's Press Association,* the National Council of Women, and the Utah Federation of Woman's Clubs.

2. Ibid.

3. Linda Thatcher and John R. Sillito, "Utah Woman's Press Club: 1891–1928," (unpublished manuscript, Utah State Historical Society, Archives Salt Lake City, Utah), ca. 1983, p. 4.

4. Rose Mary Pedersen Budge, "Literary Women Formed Press Club," *Deseret News*, 10 March 1983, p. C1.

5. Kate B. Carter, *Heart Throbs of the West*, vol. 2 (Salt Lake City: Daughters of the Utah Pioneers, 1950), pp. 213, 231; Thatcher and Sillito, "Utah Woman's Press Club," p. 5; Budge, "Literary Women"; also *Woman's Exponent*, September 1893, pp. 28–29; January 1902, p. 71; and February 1914, pp. 100–102.

6. Jane Cunningham Croly, *The History of the Woman's Club Movement in America* (New York: Henry G. Allen & Company, 1898), p. 1109.

7. Thatcher and Sillito, "Utah Woman's Press Club," p. 4.

8. Agnes Hooper Gottlieb, "Networking in the Nineteenth Century: Founding of the Woman's Press Club of New York City," *Journalism History* 21, no. 4 (winter 1995): 156–63.

9. Carter, *Heart Throbs*, p. 231; *Woman's Exponent*, May 1902, p. 112.

10. *Woman's Exponent*, November 1891, p. 77; Thatcher and Sillito, "Utah Woman's Press Club," p. 3.

11. *Woman's Exponent*, November 1891, p. 77, and December 1901, p. 63; Thatcher and Sillito, "Utah Woman's Press Club," pp. 6, 10; Carter, *Heart Throbs*, p. 231.

12. *Woman's Exponent*, November 1891, pp. 76–77.

13. Croly, *History*, pp. 1108–117. Croly was also the founder of Sorosis, one of the first women's clubs, established in 1868, and the founder and first president of the Woman's Press Club of New York City,* established in 1889. She was one of the first woman newspaper columnists in the country.

14. *Woman's Exponent*, June 1896, p. 2.

15. See Sherry Baker, "Creating a Shared History: Serial Narratives in *The Young Woman's Journal*, 1889–1894" (M.A. thesis, University of Utah, 1988).

16. *Woman's Exponent*, September 1893, p. 28.

17. Ibid., April 1894, p. 115, and May 1894, pp. 132–133.

18. Ibid., December 1896, p. 73, and June 1896, p. 2.

19. Ibid., May 1902, p. 112.

20. Ibid., January 1902, p. 72; February 1902, p. 80; and September 1902, p. 26.

21. Ibid., November 1902, p. 45.

22. Ibid., October 1907, p. 31.

23. Ibid., September 1902, p. 26, October 1907, pp. 31–32; and April 1908, p. 71.

24. Ibid., October 1907, p. 31.

25. Ibid., September 1902, p. 26. According to the *Exponent* article, the invitation came by letter from the "United Federation of Women's Clubs." This was probably the General Federation of Women's Clubs.

26. Ibid., May 1902, p. 112, and April 1908, p. 71. The UWPC subscribed $5 for charter membership in the George Washington Memorial Association in 1902 and apparently collected donations from school children for several years.

27. Ibid., September 1902, p. 26, and December 1913, p. 84. The UWPC supported the traveling library from about 1900 until some time after 1913.

28. Thatcher and Sillito, "Utah Woman's Press Club," p. 42.

29. *Woman's Exponent*, November 1904, p. 35.

30. Ibid., February 1911, p. 53.

31. Ibid., May 1912, p. 66.

32. Ibid., The *Woman's Exponent* was never declared the official organ of the UWPC, although it frequently reported the club's minutes, reports, and activities, as it did for other women's organizations in the state.

33. Ibid., April 1908, p. 71.

34. Ibid., September 1902, p. 26.

35. Thatcher and Sillito, "Utah Woman's Press Club," p. 10.

36. Carter, *Heart Throbs*, p. 231; Budge, "Literary Women," p. C1.

INFORMATIONAL SOURCES

Baker, Sherry. "Creating a Shared History: Serial Narratives in *The Young Woman's Journal*, 1889–1894." M.A. thesis, University of Utah, 1988.

Budge, Rose Mary Pedersen. "Literary Women Formed Press Club," *Deseret News*, 10 March 1983, p. C1.

Carter, Kate B. *Heart Throbs of the West*. Vol. 2. Salt Lake City: Daughters of the Utah Pioneers, 1950.

Pye, Mary F. Kelly. "Utah Women's Press Club: History." Unpublished manuscript, Utah State Historical Society, undated.

Roberts, B. H. *Comprehensive History of the Church*. Vol. 6. Provo, Utah: Sonos Publishing, 1991 (reprint of 1930 text).

Smith, Barbara, and Blythe Darlyn Thatcher, eds. *Heroines of the Restoration*. Salt Lake City: Bookcraft, 1997.

Thatcher, Linda, and John R. Sillito. "Utah Woman's Press Club: 1891–1928." Unpublished manuscript, Utah State Historical Society, Salt Lake City, Utah, ca. 1983.

Woman's Exponent, 1891–1914, passim.

INSTITUTIONAL PROFILE

Utah Woman's Press Club

Dates: Organized 31 October 1891, Salt Lake City, Utah; became inactive 1921; disbanded 6 December 1928.

First president: Emmeline B. Wells; first vice president, Susa Young Gates.

Newsletter: No official newsletter was published, but reports of UWPC activities were published in the *Woman's Exponent*, Salt Lake City, Utah; editor, Emmeline B. Wells. Hard copies of *Woman's Exponent* are available at Historical Department, Church of Jesus Christ of Latterday Saints, 50 E. North Temple, Salt Lake City, Utah. Microfilm copies are also available in various locations, including Special Collections, Harold B. Lee Library, Brigham Young University, Provo, Utah. Some editions are available in hard copy and microform at Special Collections, J. Willard Marriott Library, University of Utah, Salt Lake City, Utah.

27

Karla K. Gower

Woman's Press Association of the South, 1886–18(90)

ORGANIZATION

In fall 1886, Miss Mamie Hatchett, editor of the *Southern Woman*, sent out a letter "calling for an expression of sentiment" regarding the possibility of forming an association of southern female editors.[1] Receiving many favorable responses, Hatchett scheduled a meeting of those interested to be held in Greensboro, North Carolina, on Wednesday, November 3. Female writers, as well as editors, were encouraged to attend. Prior to the meeting, the *Greensboro North State* quoted Hatchett as saying that "the number of women pursuing journalism in the South as a profession is very large and that the attendance at the Press Association will be large enough to make it a success from the first."[2]

Apparently Hatchett was correct because a second meeting was convened at Greensboro on December 18, at which time the Woman's Press Association of the South was officially organized.[3] The stated object of the organization was to "develop, help, and encourage womanly intellect among us in every way possible." Using as its motto "Woman's Work for Woman," the association was meant to provide encouragement and assistance to women who were "timid and distrustful" of their talents so that they could become "all that our Maker meant they should." Mrs. Sallie F. Chapin of Charleston, South Carolina, was unanimously elected president, and Hatchett was named secretary. A vice president was to be selected at a later date for each of the seven southern states represented—North and South Carolina, Florida, Georgia, Louisiana, Texas, and Virginia.[4]

One of those present at the convention was Elizabeth Oakes Smith, who gave a paper on Margaret Fuller, a personal acquaintance. Originally from Maine, Smith was well known before the Civil War as a literary figure in New York and as the first woman to speak on the lyceum platform throughout the country.[5] The presence of Smith, at the time a prominent woman's rights advocate and journalist, suggests how seriously these southern women journalists took the formation of this organization.

WOMEN JOURNALISTS IN THE SOUTH

Journalists in the New South that developed after the Civil War were important and influential in their communities. In the predominantly rural South, local editors helped give their readers the sense of direction and hopefulness necessary to reconstruct their lives. At the end of the Civil War, only 182 weeklies were still publishing in the region. By 1868, there were 499, and twenty years later there were 1,827 weeklies in twelve states.[6] The federal census for 1880 revealed 1,054 periodicals in the seven states represented by the Woman's Press Association of the South.[7] This growth in newspapers offered a venue for women journalists. Writing was one area in which a southern lady could establish a name for herself without fear of damaging the "lady" image, and rural papers, particularly, depended on female correspondents to provide local color and gossip.[8] Southern women especially excelled in fiction writing. Hatchett, for example, had published a novel in 1884 and a series of poems.[9]

Despite the number of southern women who published their writing in newspapers and magazines as "letter writers," correspondents, and contributors, census data for 1880 reveal that only fifteen actually identified themselves as journalists in the seven states represented by the association.[10] By the census of 1890, however, that number had grown to forty-five and another 108 classified themselves as authors or literary persons.[11] Thirty of those women, representing the "best talent of the South," were present to elect Chapin president at the launching of the association.[12]

Chapin was in many ways a natural choice. Born in Charleston, she was the eldest of the four children of a Methodist minister. She attended a girls academy in Abbeville County, South Carolina, and married Leonard Chapin in 1847.[13] A "literary scribbler," with one published novel to her name, Chapin was not a working journalist; she was, however, an organizer.[14] In that respect, Chapin was the product of the Civil War.

Before the Civil War, southern women lacked a tradition of volunteerism and lagged behind their northern sisters when it came to organizing into clubs. Northern women had the benefit of exposure to the abolitionist cause, regular woman's rights conventions beginning in 1848, and the temperance and other reform movements. When they became involved in these activities, they had the opportunity to hone their organizational skills. Women in the South, instead, lacked both a cause and the opportunities for mingling with other women because of the rural nature of the antebellum South.[15] And perhaps most important, women in the South had the image of the "southern lady" working against them. The southern lady had a special role in the South and southern men and women were hostile to any changes, such as women entering the public sphere, that might threaten the image.[16]

But the Civil War had been a catalyst for change in the South on many levels, including women's place in society. During the war, there was an immediate need for women to mobilize and organize. They suddenly became involved with Soldiers' Relief Societies and volunteered at hospitals. After the war, the South was left with, as one scholar described it, "a generation of women without men."[17] There were no more wounded to care for, but the need for action remained and the women responded to the call. The Soldiers' Relief Societies became the Ladies Memorial Associations, and churches, such as the Methodist Church, provided a venue for women to become involved in reform work.[18]

Anne Firor Scott, in her examination of the changes in the role of southern women after the Civil War, noted that although behind those of the North by about ten years, women's clubs developed rapidly in the South during the period 1884 to 1887. She attributed the growth in women's clubs to the war effort, church and temperance societies, and the influence of northern women such as Women's Christian Temperance Union (WCTU) president Frances Willard.[19] Evidence of such influence can be found in the weekly *Greensboro* (North Carolina) *Patriot* that in 1882 sang the praises of northern women who were helping the South: "Woman's influence has always been peculiarly powerful in the South and if now it is further strengthening itself by organization its results will be more beneficial than anything that can come from political effort."[20]

One scholar has suggested that the women who successfully broke out of the southern lady mold were actually those who were able to reinforce the lady image of the Old South while at the same time promoting the economic order of the New South.[21] As southerners struggled to create a New South, they had to reinterpret the meaning of womanhood to fit with changing realities. Organized women, especially in groups such as the WCTU, were leaders in trying to combine the best qualities of the southern lady with the new woman of the South.[22]

BREAKING THE MOLD

Chapin fit well within this group of "conservative progressives," following the pattern of other southern women of her generation. During the war she was president of the Charleston Soldiers' Relief Society, and after the war she continued her involvement by participating in the Ladies Christian Association, for which she served as president for twelve years, and the Ladies Memorial Association.[23] But her real legacy as a clubwoman came after the death of her husband in 1879. The following year Chapin attended a temperance convention at Ocean Grove, New Jersey. Called upon unexpectedly to speak, Chapin apparently discovered she had a talent for public speaking. One newspaper account described her as having "masculine familiarity with politics, and eloquent exhortation," indicating "a masterly mind and a womanly heart."[24] She thereafter became heavily involved in the WCTU, forming the Charleston WCTU, the first in South Carolina, in June 1880. It was Chapin with whom WCTU president Frances Willard stayed on her first trip south in 1881 and who accompanied Willard on the rest of that southern tour. Two years later, Chapin again toured the South, this time as national superintendent of the WCTU's Southern Works, a post she held until 1889, when the organization voted to abolish the position.

Anne Gordon, assistant to Willard, described Chapin in 1881 as "a thorough rebel."[25] And author and temperance worker Caroline Merrick, of New Orleans, in her memoirs said of Chapin, "Both in appearance and speech she was intense, tragic, and pathetic. . . . Mrs. Chapin lived and died an "unreconstructed Rebel."[26] The extent of Chapin's influence can be seen in the *Charleston* (South Carolina) *News and Courier*'s coverage of her death in April 1896:

When, a few years ago, there came a request to The News and Courier to indicate who was worthy to be named among the truly great women of America, the answer included among the foremost the name which forms the caption of this article—a name which, yesterday, ceased to represent one still among the living.[27]

In fall 1886, then, Chapin was in a unique position with her contacts throughout the South and her organizational skills to serve as president of the Woman's Press Association of the South.

Whereas Chapin had the organizational skills, Hatchett had the professional journalism experience. Hatchett was born in Virginia and educated at the Mecklenburg Female College, where, according to her obituary, "she showed a decided aptitude for writing," publishing a novel at age eighteen.[28] She was described in the press of the day as a "talented and well known" writer and as "a capable newspaperwoman."[29] Although she had to suspend publication of *Southern Woman* in September 1886 "because of insufficient patronage,"[30] she immediately thereafter accepted a position as editor of the *Orphan's Friend* published in Oxford, North Carolina.[31] In 1889, she married Col. Al Fairbrother, who was managing the *Lincoln Daily Call* in Lincoln, Nebraska, at the time. Apparently Fairbrother had contacted Hatchett after reading a feature story that she had written for a New York daily and that bore her photograph.[32] Together they spent the rest of their lives establishing and running newspapers and magazines, moving from North Carolina to Virginia to Georgia and back to North Carolina.[33] They were also considered leading advocates of social and civic reforms.

Like Chapin, Hatchett was involved with various women's clubs during her lifetime. She was one of the founders of the Greensboro, North Carolina, Woman's Club and served as its third president. She was also active in the North Carolina Federation of Women's Clubs until 1926 when she and her husband moved to Long Beach, California. Whereas Chapin appears to have followed a rather traditional path in terms of southern club women, however, Hatchett presents the image of the professional clubwoman. She was single when she started *Southern Woman*, and although she belonged to women's clubs, there is no evidence she belonged to either church groups or the WCTU.

Despite the differences in the two women—Chapin was an Old South, middle-class clubwoman, and Hatchett was a New South, professional club-woman—they shared an interest in the role of women and social reform. There are no surviving records to say how long Hatchett's press association existed or even to chronicle its accomplishments, although Marion McBride, in her report to the 1890 Convention of the National Editorial Association, identified the organization as one of the women's press associations then in existence.[34] But given the nature of the two women involved and the association's stated object, the organization's focus undoubtedly extended beyond journalism and women journalists.

What information does exist about the association comes solely from news-paper accounts. It passed bylaws and a constitution and no doubt kept records of its meetings and activities, but those records are not listed in any archive or manuscript collections. One of the difficulties in researching women's history is that the letters and documents of women and their organizations were not always kept safe. They were exposed to the ravages of time and the shortsight-edness of individuals. The concept of history did not, at the time, include in many cases the activities of women, and hence their documents had little or no historical value. The result is that despite the efforts and apparent success of Mamie Hatchett to bring the female editors and writers of the South together to form a network of women journalists across seven states, little evidence remains of the Woman's Press Association of the South.

NOTES

1. *Raleigh* (North Carolina) *News & Observer*, 18 September 1886, p. 4. *Southern Woman* was a newspaper published in Henderson, North Carolina.

2. *Greensboro* (North Carolina) *North State*, 16 September 1886, p. 4.

3. "Woman's Work for Woman," *Charleston* (South Carolina) *News & Courier*, 22 December 1886, p. 5. The railroads gave reduced rates to convention delegates, and the Woman's National Press Association, the New England Woman's Press Association,* and other women's societies sent telegrams of congratulations.

4. The information about the organizational meeting was taken from "Woman's Work." Information about the states represented comes from Marion McBride, "Report to the 1890 Convention of the National Editorial Association," *The Journalist*, 5 July 1890, p. 12.

5. Mary Alice Wyman, ed., *Selections from the Autobiography of Elizabeth Oakes [Prince] Smith* (New York: Arno Press, 1980), p. 9. At the time of the convention in Greensboro, Smith was living in Hollywood, North Carolina. Mary Alice Wyman, *Two American Pioneers: Seba Smith and Elizabeth Oakes Smith* (New York: Columbia University Press, 1927), pp. 228, 231.

6. Thomas D. Clark, *The Southern Country Editor* (Indianapolis: Bobbs-Merrill Company, 1948), p. 20.

7. U.S. Census Office, *Tenth Census of the United States, 1880* (Washington, D.C.: Government Printing Office, 1883).

8. Clark, p. 87.

9. "Mrs. Al Fairbrother Passes in California," *Greensboro* (North Carolina) *Daily News*, 21 June 1936, p. 12.

10. *Tenth Census, 1880.*

11. U.S. Census Office, *Eleventh Census of the United States, 1890* (Washington, D.C.: Government Printing Office, 1895).

12. "Woman's Work."

13. "Chapin, Sarah Flourney Moore," *Notable American Women, 1607–1950: A Biographical Dictionary*, vol. 1 (Cambridge: Belknap Press, 1971), p. 321.

14. Ibid.

15. Anastasia Sims, "Feminism and Femininity in the New South: White Women's Organizations in North Carolina, 1883–1930" (Ph.D. diss., University of North Carolina at Chapel Hill, 1985), p. 28.

16. For a full discussion of the image of the southern lady and her special place in the South, see Anastasia Sims, *The Power of Femininity in the New South: Women's Organizations and Politics in North Carolina, 1880–1930* (Columbia: University of South Carolina Press, 1997).

17. Anne Firor Scott, *The Southern Lady: From Pedestal to Politics, 1830–1930* (Chicago: University of Chicago Press, 1970), p. 106. According to Scott, a quarter of a million men died in the war. In 1870, in four of the seven states represented by the Woman's Press Association of the South, there were more women than men. There were 25,000 more women than men in North Carolina, 36,000 more in Georgia, 15,000 more in Virginia, and 8,000 more in South Carolina.

18. Sims, p. 29.

19. Scott, pp. 152, 155.

20. "Northern Women Helping the South," *Greensboro* (North Carolina) *Patriot*, 1 September 1882, p. 3.

21. Sims, p. 28.

22. Ibid., p. 2.

23. "Mrs. Sallie F. Chapin Dead," *Charleston* (South Carolina) *News & Courier*, April 20, 1896, p. 2.

24. Quoted in *Notable American Women*, p. 322.

25. Letter from Anne Gordon to Mary Hill Willard, 18 March 1881, quoted in Ruth Brodin, *Frances Willard: A Biography*, p. 115.

26. Caroline E. Merrick, *Old Times in Dixie Land: A Southern Matron's Memories* (New York: Grafton Press, 1901), p. 179. Merrick was a longtime president of the Louisiana WCTU and wrote extensively on temperance. She was also a successful orator, addressing the Louisiana state legislature in 1879. Frances E. Willard and Mary A. Livermore, eds., *A Woman of the Century: Fourteen Hundred Seventy Biographical Sketches of Leading American Women* (Buffalo, N.Y.: Charles Wells Moulton, 1893; reprint, Detroit: Gale Research Company, 1967), p. 499 (page references are to reprint edition).

27. "Mrs. Sallie F. Chapin Dead."

28. "Mrs. Al Fairbrother Passes in California," *Greensboro* (North Carolina) *Daily News*, 21 June 1936, p. 12. The obituary does not contain a birthdate. If the book of fiction she published at the age of eighteen is the one published in 1884, then Hatchett

would have been twenty when she organized the Woman's Press Association of the South.

29. Ibid.; *Raleigh News & Observer*, 11 March 1930, p. 11.

30. *Raleigh News & Observer*, 24 September 1886, p. 4, quoting the *Oxford* (North Carolina) *Torchlight*.

31. According to its masthead, the *Orphan's Friend* was an "industrial feature of the Oxford Orphan Asylum, designed to instruct the boys of the institution in the art of printing and if possible to yield a small revenue to the Asylum."

32. *Greensboro Daily News*, 21 June 1936, p. 12.

33. The Fairbrothers took charge of the *Durham* (North Carolina) *Globe* in 1890. Then they moved to Danville, Virginia, and established the *Danville Evening Bee*. They went on to write advertising copy in Boston and later established a magazine called *Everything* in Atlanta. They returned to North Carolina in 1902 and issued *Everything* in Greensboro. In 1916 they purchased the *Greensboro Daily Record* and published it until 1919, when they retired and sold the paper. In the years before Colonel Fairbrother's death in 1930, they resided in California. In his obituary, Fairbrother is credited with founding thirty-five newspapers. *Raleigh News & Observer*, 11 March 1930, p. 11; *Greensboro Daily News*, 10 March 1930, pp. 1, 5.

34. Marion McBride, "Report to the 1890 Convention of the National Editorial Association," *The Journalist*, 5 July 1890, p. 12. *The Journalist* lists the date as the autumn of 1882, but the "2" appears to be a typographical error.

INFORMATIONAL SOURCES

Clark, Thomas D. *The Southern Country Editor*. Indianapolis: Bobbs-Merrill Company, 1948.

Merrick, Caroline E. *Old Times in Dixie Land: A Southern Matron's Memories*. New York: The Grafton Press, 1901.

Scott, Anne Firor. *The Southern Lady: From Pedestal to Politics, 1830–1930*. Chicago: University of Chicago, 1970.

Sims, Anastasia. "Feminism and Femininity in the New South: White Women's Organizations in North Carolina, 1883–1930." Ph.D. diss., University of North Carolina at Chapel Hill, 1985.

———. *The Power of Femininity in the New South: Women's Organizations and Politics in North Carolina, 1880–1930*. Columbia: University of South Carolina Press, 1997.

Wyman, Mary Alice, ed. *Selections from the Autobiography of Elizabeth Oakes [Prince] Smith*. New York: Arno Press, 1980.

———. *Two American Pioneers: Seba Smith and Elizabeth Oakes Smith*. New York: Columbia University Press, 1927.

INSTITUTIONAL PROFILE

Woman's Press Association of the South

Dates: Founded 18 December 1886, Greensboro, North Carolina; continued through 1890; date of cessation unknown.

First officers: Mrs. Sallie F. Chapin, Charleston, South Carolina. (president); Miss Mamie Hatchett, Henderson, North Carolina (secretary).

28

Paulette D. Kilmer

Woman's Press Club of Cincinnati, 1888–1988

Fiction writers and journalists established the Woman's Press Club (WPC) in Cincinnati to help all "lady authors" who published their works succeed in the male-dominated world of print. For almost a century, the press club filled its members' social as well as professional needs. This chapter will focus on the ironic transformation of the organization's motto from a clarion for action at the turn of the twentieth century into a death knell nine decades later. Because the members focused heavily on one another to uphold the pledge of Dumas's three musketeers, "Each for All and All for Each," the press club stopped evolving with the times.[1]

ORGANIZATION

The WPC grew out of a national wave of unrest that countered middle-class women's sense of isolation with the establishment of women's clubs.[2] According to women's historian Karen J. Blair, the women's clubs founded in the nineteenth century provided a haven for "domestic feminists." Here, women were able to meet soul sisters, gain power through unity, and learn how to remain "ladies" while defying social conventions to participate in public arenas, including newsrooms.[3] Women fought to be recognized as legitimate journalists. Women's clubs like the WPC helped them as well as "lady" graduates of high schools, normal schools, and colleges to apply their education to community service and to advance in careers formerly reserved for men.[4] Economic hardships and hostility from those who resisted social change spurred women to seek solidarity in press clubs.[5]

At the WPC's Golden Jubilee celebration in 1938, WPC president Frances Eminger concluded that the club had always served both "the woman who writes to live and the woman who lives to write."[6] In fact, the founder of the organization, Mrs. S. C. Hazlett-Bevis, had invited colleagues she had met while covering events for the *Cincinnati Penny Post* as well as local literary women to discuss launching a woman's press club. Hazlett-Bevis had just returned from attending the International Congress for Women in Washington, D.C., in April 1888. Over cups of tea at the Gibson House, one of Cincinnati's most posh hotels, the women elected Hazlett-Bevis president and decided to limit membership to those who published or gave public lectures. Although they appointed a librarian, most records chronicling the early years of WPC history have vanished.[7]

Eventually, journalists, magazine editors, poets, novelists, and authors of cliffhangers and short stories as well as historians, composers, and later, radio continuity writers joined the WPC. The organization blossomed for decades, peaking between the 1930s and 1970, with as many as fifty members in the early decades. The membership dropped to fewer than twenty in 1970 and declined even further during the 1980s. Economic changes in the mass media would make the WPC as obsolete as rhyming newspaper verses, Wedgewood Blue teas, and white gloves. In 1988, the group would be forced to disband.

PROGRAMS AND ACTIVITIES

The WPC and its members were firmly rooted in the woman's club movement that had begun during the last quarter of the nineteenth century. Most of the club's members participated in philanthropic and service organizations,[8] and the WPC became a charter member of the Ohio Federation of Women's Clubs in 1890 and was among the first to join the National (today General) Federation of Women's Clubs the same year.

During its early years, programs offered at the club's meetings reflected WPC ties to the woman's club movement. Topics were varied and often provocative, frequently touching on political issues such as "Women and the Ballot," "Symposium on Capital and Labor," and "Social Standards." By the turn of the twentieth century, however, the programs lost their political bite and acquired a more literary and, in some cases, entertaining character, with topics such as "Mythology of the Acropolis" and "What about a Sandwich."[9] Club members after the turn of the century eschewed controversies that might cause disastrous partisan splits within the organization. Although the suffrage movement and the rise of women's clubs coincided at many points, many women still opposed the passage of a suffrage amendment.[10] Indeed, Florence Goff Schwarz, a poet who later served as WPC president from 1928 to 1930, ran the Ohio office of the Anti-Suffrage League, waging anti-suffrage campaigns in Wisconsin, Tennessee, Pennsylvania, and other states.[11] Obviously, outspoken, passionate leaders like Schwarz could have commanded a following but might have splintered the WPC. Controversy was avoided, therefore, and the club officially outlawed discussions of both politics and religion.[12]

The WPC, instead, adhered to its central mission: to foster women's professional opportunities through solidarity. They considered themselves part of the

Buckeye creative tradition that began with Harriet Beecher Stowe and the Cary sisters, Alice and Phoebe, who sold poetry to all the Cincinnati papers. At the Diamond Anniversary celebration in 1958, past president Phyllis M. Swisher (1952–1954) said that like their literary predecessors, WPC members had always felt an "urgent need to express themselves in poetry and prose, not just for their own personal enjoyment, but as professionals whose words would be read and remembered."[13] They incorporated these aspirations in the Constitution of 1896 and declared the club's goal was to foster the mutual improvement of women writers and to secure for them all the benefits arising from organized effort.

Article VII of the WPC constitution spelled out membership requirements: Only writers for standard publications were eligible; candidates had to submit proof of publication to the Committee on Credentials; and four negative votes would defeat a nominee.[14] Initially, two categories of membership were offered: regular for those who sold their work and associate for those who received no remuneration. Over the years, the associate level was sometimes dropped, and in later decades, the club introduced corresponding membership for women who no longer lived in Cincinnati. WPC monthly social events gave members the opportunity to bring guests, including prominent society matrons as well as, occasionally, their husbands or other men.

THE HEYDAY OF SOLIDARITY

The WPC's monthly social gatherings introduced writers to the most powerful social leaders in the region as well as to other pen women. Detractors disparaged these essential networking opportunities. In fact, in 1905, former president Grover Cleveland accused women of joining women's clubs to punish their wayward husbands, therein jeopardizing domestic tranquility. In a critical newspaper article, WPC member Virginia G. Ellard denounced Cleveland's glittering generalities. Ellard suggested that working together gave clubwomen a sense of purpose and made them feel respected for the tasks they did in their homes. Moreover, she wrote, through club service, women gained compassion and participated in necessary crusades to rehabilitate homeless girls, to help the poor, and to seek labor reforms, including equal pay and safe working conditions.[15]

Most WPC members joined local women's clubs to implement reforms. From the press club, instead, they sought professional opportunities. Established authors conducted bimonthly workshops on marketing manuscripts as well as writing them. "The club [was] a stepping stone for many aspiring authors, for it [existed] only [to aid] by experience and example those who [were] young in literary life," wrote one city historian.[16] Members also gained a sense of inspiration from some of the club's leaders who served as role models for generations to come. "[Many] of us . . . [stood] in a bit of awe of those earlier members," wrote one member in the 1960s. "They . . . set [for] us standards of achievement and inspired in us a respect for the creative writing profession . . . which added to our stature as an organization and to us as individuals."[17]

These women helped one another convert dreams into a lifestyle. Jealousy seldom erupted because this sisterhood emphasized character first and ability second. "Each is proud of [anyone else's] success in [her] chosen line of work," historian Charles Goss wrote in 1912.[18] Private lives often became interwoven with the official business of the club. Notes about club business in archive records are often jotted down on a slip of paper or on an old envelop containing a family's grocery list for wieners, brown sugar, and white tissues. These intrusions of the real world into the club's regimen suited many, including two poets, Helen D. Berning and Leona F. Westland. When Berning died at the age of seventy-nine in 1971, Westland delivered her eulogy at a WPC meeting. She remembered her friend's coat, the long chats they enjoyed on the bus en route to WPC events, and their service together as club officers.[19]

These friendships strengthened the resolve of members to apply the club motto, "Each for All, and All for Each," to their professional lives. "The loyalty of the [members of the] Woman's Press Club to one another [was] proverbial," wrote Westland in her eulogy to Berning.[20] As editors or founders of poetry journals, some WPC stars created precious space for their pen sisters' verses. For instance, Katherine Hunter Coe (president 1940–41) featured sister poets in two poetry anthologies she published in the early 1930s.[21] George Elliston, who proved she could handle the biggest stories in competition with the best male reporters, published many of her sisters' work in her magazine, *The Gypsy*. She also sponsored Chautauqua programs where WPC colleagues shared their work.

Annette Patton Cornell (president 1941–43) read poems on her show for two radio stations for seventeen years. She and B. Y. Williams (president 1926–28) published club sisters' work in *Talaria*, a poetry magazine they started during the Depression that thrived until World War II.[22] The WPC gave beginners chances to have their work reviewed by masters, like Cornell whom in 1974 the National League of American Pen Women* called the greatest poet of the past fifty years.

THE SLOW FADE

In many ways, the WPC embodied a "fiction factory," a cottage industry for authors.[23] During the late nineteenth and early twentieth centuries, many writers gained regional fame by selling their wares to multiple markets. It was the era of payment by the column inch. The line delineating who was a reporter and who was a magazine contributor remained fuzzy. For example, Amoretta Colby Fitch (president 1923–25), prospered both as a "woman story chaser" and as a poet in Queen City. "The little old lady," as folks called Fitch, rode a bicycle to gather news for the *Cincinnati Commercial Tribune* and also sold items to magazines. By the 1940s, when she was well into her eighties, Fitch set records as the oldest living female reporter in the Midwest.[24] Born in 1857, she helped establish the WPC in 1888 and the Ohio Newspaper Women's Association* in Toledo in 1902 as well as other local clubs. She started out as a reporter at the *Commercial Tribune*, where she became a columnist writing about women's interests and eventually served as editor of its women's department. Besides winning prizes for her writing, she impressed novelist Jack London, who sent her "Morning Prayer" to a British labor union that "adopted [it] as voicing the spirit of the faithful worker":[25]

> I pray thee, Lord, I may not shirk
> If I should die before the night
> I pray thee, Lord, my work's all right.

In 1921, another colorful member of the WPC, journalist Ruth Neely, wrote some amusing articles for a spoof tabloid, *The Scoop*, a "Night Extra." One of these, in which she skillfully lampooned the tenets of objectivity to report an imaginary event, made the front page under the headline "Awful Mishap; Times-Star Is Gloom Stricken":

With a crash that resounded off Price Hill, shook Ft. Thomas and alarmed Cumminsville, Ruth Neely, lost in a mental fog engendered by trying to decipher some of her copy early this morning, collided with her ego and was badly injured. The ego, who is larger than a boulevard light pole, and far brighter, was unimpaired by the impact.... Miss Neely recovered, however, and ... is, as usual, laughing to herself over the cleverness of some copy she is evolving for the Woman's Page.[26]

Poetry, fiction, and imaginative writing such as Neely's were highly prized by the WPC. Perhaps personal ties between WPC members prevented them from elevating factual accounts and discrediting fanciful narratives or vice versa, and unlike other press clubs that agonized over deciding who qualified as a woman journalist,[27] WPC welcomed writers of every kind. So did the press, for many newspapers ran poetry and cliffhangers as well as occasional sermons and essays until after World War II.

This climate, however, slowly began to change with the new century. Journalism historian Elizabeth V. Burt suggests that many women writers felt torn between listening to their inner voice and upholding the clinical professional standards of the newsroom. As intellectual currents swept away sentiment, fact and its retinue of pragmatic, objective, and scientific approaches to knowledge spread.[28] As Progressive Era historian Robert H. Wiebe puts it, "For the lack of anything that made better sense of their world, people everywhere weighed, counted, and measured it."[29] In the early twentieth century, journalism became synonymous with hard, cold facts, and therein intuitive emotional or creative work were devalued.[30] Women struggled to balance their need for professional recognition in a male arena with their equally compelling need to remain sensitive and empathetic.

WPC members in Cincinnati gave each other moral support and practical advice; however, the hallmarks of mentoring, nurturing, and even sacrificing for one another characteristic of the women's press clubs became obsolete as serving self-replaced altruism. By the early twentieth century, people equated efficiency, competition, and productivity with success.

By the 1950s, this became even more pronounced. In terms of economics, the increased emphasis on productivity and competition spelled doom for magazines and newspapers that could not compete with television. Consolidation, liquidation, and editorial upheavals decimated the magazines that had once published poetry. In its glory years, the *Saturday Evening Post* had showcased Norman Rockwell covers that echoed the same homespun themes dear to the Cincinnati women bards: home, children, seasons, nature, Christmas, patriotism, and courtship. But readers now demanded editorials, exposés, political commentaries, and how-to information. When the *Post* switched to quasi-muckraking articles in 1961, the reign of poetry ended.[31] To exasperate matters, television cut into essential advertising revenue, reducing further the amount of space in magazines and even the number of magazines continuing publication.[32]

The WPC (and the careers of many of its members) existed as long as there were outlets for poems, short stories, and personal essays as well as jobs on newspapers and magazines for the women who edited this material. "I thought I was Edna St. Vincent Millay," said one of WPC's last presidents, Kathryn Evans McKay, who began contributing to *Child Life* and *Cosmopolitan* as well as to metropolitan newspapers in 1927, when she was thirteen.[33] But Hunter, Cornell, Williams, and other WPC poets who had regularly published their work in or worked as editors for magazines such as the *Saturday Evening Post, Colliers, Ladies Home Journal*, and *Pictorial Review* as well as newspapers with special columns devoted to poetry, were losing their market by 1960.[34]

By 1960, the newspaper jobs remained, but general-interest magazines for the masses were losing their audiences and going out of business at an alarming rate.[35] By the 1970s, lady poets were an endangered species, and their impending extinction was affecting the vitality of the press club. Although records indicate that through the mid-1970s, from thirty to fifty members and guests attended WPC social gatherings and writers continued to participate in bimonthly workshops, the club was on the wane.

By the early 1970s, WPC membership had dropped to thirty. Pollyanna Sedziol, a poet who had sold one thousand works to eighty magazines, explained that no one joined between 1974 and 1988. Old age, transportation problems, death, and relocation struck down even the most loyal members. Only seven of the fourteen surviving members remained active in the final year. Ironically, the same number, six, attended the last supper in 1988 and the very first planning session in 1888. "My feeling is that poets are out there," said Sedziol, the club's last president, in 1988. "Most women's magazines and many magazines, generally, used to carry a poetry column. Now there are none."[36]

The survivors decided to disband the club after its centennial celebration in 1988. Sedziol and McKay, WPC's last two presidents, were unsure why membership declined. Perhaps the club's solidarity had kept members from making adaptions to appeal to new members. A local historian called the WPC sisterhood one of the oldest and most conservative women's clubs in Ohio.[37] McKay said writers who used four-letter language were not welcome. Sedziol thought the double duty of working and raising their families made it impossible for women to join clubs.[38] Perhaps, also, the WPC was no longer necessary because it had done its job so well. A century ago, women's clubs empowered members to make a difference in their communities at a time when they were shut out of most public forums. By the late 1980s, thanks to organizations like the WPC, women were able to speak in a myriad of public forums.

Officially, the WPC ended in 1988, but as club president Sedziol assured the "Word Worthy Women" in her last official letter, "In 1988 our organization will no longer be a supporting element, but we ourselves will continue viable, and our affection for each other will endure."[39] Thus, the motto, "Each for All and All for Each" outlived its parent organization, proving the words penned by Cornell were right: "Friendship is a golden rose branded upon the heart. . . . No petal drifts."[40]

NOTES

1. Alexander Dumas, *The Three Musketeers* (Boston: Little, Brown, 1893).

2. The Women's Press Club of Cincinnati was apparently sometimes referred to as the Cincinnati Newspaperwomen's Association (CNWA). For example, the subject-index card at the Public Library of Cincinnati and Hamilton County refers patrons looking under "Cincinnati Newspaperwomen's Association (CNWA)" to see "Clubs, Woman's Press Club." The WPC Collections contains only sketchy references to the CNWA.

3. Karen J. Blair, *The Clubwoman as Feminist: True Womanhood Redefined, 1868–1914* (New York: Holmes and Meier, 1980).

4. Eleanor Flexner, *Century of Struggle: The Woman's Rights Movement in the United States*, rev. ed. (Cambridge, Mass.: Belknap Press of Harvard University, 1975), pp. 240–41.

5. Elizabeth V. Burt, "A Bid for Legitimacy: The Woman's Press Club Movement, 1881–1900," *Journalism History* 23, no. 2 (summer 1997): 72–84; Agnes Hooper Gottlieb, "Networking in the Nineteenth Century: Founding of the Woman's Press Club of New York City," *Journalism History* 21, no. 4 (winter 1995): 156–63; Maurine H. Beasley, "The Women's National Press Club: A Case Study of Professional Aspirations," *Journalism History* 15, no. 4 (winter 1988): 112–21.

6. Frances Eminger, *History of the Woman's Press Club, 1888–1938*, written for the Golden Jubilee on 3 December 1938, the Women's Press Club Collection, 1888–1979 (hereafter WPC Collection), box 1, folder 1, Cincinnati Historical Society Library, Union Station Terminal, Cincinnati, Ohio.

7. Ibid. According to Eminger, documents from the early years of the Women's Press Club were lost after the WPC changed the location of its meetings and inadvertently left the club's records behind in the move. Some records were reestablished when Amoretta Fitch donated her yearbooks in 1938.

8. Charles Goss, *Cincinnati—the Queen City* (Cincinnati: Cincinnati Historical Society, 1912), vol. 2, p. 521.

9. Eminger, *History*, p. 4.

10. Burt, "A Bid for Legitimacy"; Blair, *The Club Woman as Feminist.*

11. "Florence Goff Schwarz Dies; Clubwoman Wrote Poetry; Was Active Antisuffragist," 15 August 1946, WPC Collection, box 3, 1946–47 Scrapbook; Goss, *Cincinnati*, vol. 1, p. 303. Although she opposed women's political activity by opposing suffrage, Schwarz was herself quite politically active. During World War I, she worked on the mayor's victory committee.

12. Mary Linn White, "Writers Club Hopes to Reach Century Mark," *Cincinnati Post*, 1986 [no date, month, or page], WPC Collection.

13. Phyllis M. Swisher, "Just Remembering" (paper presented on 4 October 1958) WPC Collection, box 1, folder 1.

14. WPC Constitution (in the yearbooks) WPC Collection, box 2.

15. Virginia G. Ellard, "Practical Results of Women's Clubs" [no newspaper name, page number, or date], WPC Collection, box 1, folder 1.

16. Goss, *Cincinnati*, vol. 2, p. 521.

17. Mary Hoge Bruce, "Cincinnati Woman's Press Club—Decade of the Forties" (essay read at the seventy-fifth anniversary, 5 October 1963), pp. 4–5, WPC Collection, box 3, 1953–62 Scrapbook.

18. Goss, *Cincinnati*, vol. 2, p. 521.

19. Leona F. Westland, untitled eulogy, WPC Collection, box 3, 1967–1971 Scrapbook.

20. Ibid.

21. Katherine Hunter Coe, ed., *Poems of America*, vols. 1–3 (London: Channing Press, 1932–34) and *Poems of All Nations*, vols. 1–3 (London: Channing Press, 1932–34).

22. *Talaria*'s largest circulation areas were in Germany and Japan. Its demise is attributed to distribution problems caused by the war.

23. Paulette D. Kilmer, *Fear of Sinking: The American Success Formula in the Gilded Age* (Knoxville: University of Tennessee Press, 1996), pp. 42–44.

24. Born in 1857, Fitch died in 1949 at the age of 92.

25. "Oldest Newspaperwoman, Poet, Succumbs at 92" [no newspaper name indicated], 5 May 1949. Also, see "Newspaper Woman's Poem Again Spotlighted" [no date or newspaper name indicated], both in WPC Collection, box 3, 1949–1950 Scrapbook. Goss praises Fitch's versatility, noting that she published poems, essays, character sketches, feature stories, and motto cards as well as gave lectures. See Goss, *Cincinnati*, vol. 2, p. 520.

26. Ruth Neely, "Awful Mishap; *Times-Star* Is Gloom Stricken," *The* (Queen City, Ohio) *Scoop, Night Extra*, no. 2 (12 November 1921): 1, WPC Collection, box 3, 1910–37 Scrapbook. Ruth Neely married William Cook France in 1908 but continued to publish under her maiden name. In articles about the WPC, however, she is referred to as Ruth Neely France. See Ruth Neely, ed., *Women of Ohio: A Record of Their Achievements in the History of the State* (Cincinnati: S. J. Clarke, ca. 1939), p. 1223.

27. Burt, "A Bid for Legitimacy," p. 81.

28. Ibid.

29. Robert H. Wiebe, *The Search for Order, 1877–1920* (New York: Hill and Wang, 1986), p. 43.

30. Burt, "A Bid for Legitimacy," p. 81.

31. Theodore Peterson, "The Troubled Giant," chap. in *Magazines in the Twentieth Century* (Urbana: University of Illinois Press, 1964), especially pp. 198–99.

32. Roland E. Wolseley, *The Changing Magazine: Trends in Readership and Management* (New York: Hastings House, 1973), pp. 5, 10.

33. Kathryn Evans McKay quoted in Mary Linn White, "Writers' Club Hopes to Reach Century Mark," *Cincinnati Post*, 1986 [no month, day, or page indicated], WPC Collection.

34. That newspaper verse was a popular and lucrative market is indicated by the *Davis Anthology of Newspaper Verse*, which was first published in 1919. In 1940, Davis selected 225 poems from seventy-two newspapers, including 10 from the *Cincinnati Times-Star*. See Clark D. Firestone, poetry ed., "Cincinnati Verse Gives Queen City High Rank," *Cincinnati Times-Star*, 25 April 1940, WPC Collection, box 3, 1938–40 Scrapbook.

35. A. J. van Zuilen, *The Life Cycle of Magazines: Decline and Fall of the General Interest Mass Audience Magazines in the United States during the Period of 1946–1972* (Uithoorn, The Netherlands: Graduate Press, 1977).

36. Martin Hogan, Jr., "Press Club: That's All She Wrote: Woman's Group Bringing to an End 100-Year-Old Entity," *Cincinnati Enquirer*, 14 August 1988, p. B4 Metro.

37. Goss, *Cincinnati*, p. 520.

38. White, "Writers' Club Hopes to Reach Century Mark."

39. Undated letter signed "Pollyanna" [Sedziol], WPC Collection, box 1962–88, folder 10. Sedziol's letter is on club stationary containing an emblem for WPC with its years "1888–1988." The letter closes with the phrase "until Oct. 16."

40. Annette Patton Cornell, verse card, WPC Collection, box 1, folder 7.

INFORMATIONAL SOURCES

Goss, Charles. *Cincinnati—the Queen City*. Vols. 1 and 2. Cincinnati: Cincinnati Historical Society, 1912.

Kilmer, Paulette D. *Fear of Sinking: The American Success Formula in the Gilded Age*. Knoxville: University of Tennessee Press, 1996.

Peterson, Theodore. "The Troubled Giant." Chap. in *Magazines in the Twentieth Century*. Urbana: University of Illinois Press, 1964.

van Zuilen, A. J. *The Life Cycle of Magazines: Decline and Fall of the General Interest Mass Audience Magazines in the United States during the Period of 1946–1972*. Uithoorn, The Netherlands: Graduate Press, 1977.

Wiebe, Robert H. *The Search for Order, 1877–1920*. New York: Hill and Wang, 1986.

Women's Press Club Collection, 1888–1979. Arranged by Mary Jane Neely. Cincinnati Historical Society Library, Union Station Terminal, Cincinnati, Ohio.

Women's Press Club Collection, 1962–1988. Arranged by Mary Jane Neely. Cincinnati Historical Society Library, Union Station Terminal, Cincinnati, Ohio.

INSTITUTIONAL PROFILE

Woman's Press Club of Cincinnati

Dates: Organized summer 1888; disbanded October 1988. Occasionally referred to as the **Cincinnati Newspaperwomen's Association**.

Archives: Women's Press Club Collection, Cincinnati Historical Society in Union Station
   Terminal, Cincinnati, Ohio. A collection of the poetry and other writings of members
   is held by the Public Library of Cincinnati and Hamilton County.

29

Ann Mauger Colbert

Woman's Press Club of Indiana, 1913–Present

The Woman's Press Club of Indiana (WPCI) was formed on February 18, 1913, in the tearoom of an Indianapolis department store. It is a founding member of the National Federation of Press Women (NFPW),* begun in 1936, and still meets regularly. WPCI was created by twenty-eight working women journalists who met to form an advocacy group for their professional concerns. These women journalists were not the first in the state to be organized for the purpose of association and professional development. In fact, four women had been original members of a mixed-sex press club in Indianapolis thirteen years earlier in 1890, and many (including founders of the WPCI) were associated with the Western Association of Writers, a group formed in Indiana in 1888.[1]

The WPCI originally limited its membership to women who were working members of the press, but it has expanded to include public relations professionals and others involved with related professions such as photography and teaching. In the eighty-six years since its establishment, the organization has undergone other changes, as will be clear from the following discussion. One of the most interesting of these has been the organization's relationship to political activity; it appears to have gone from a behind-the-scenes advocacy group to one interested primarily in professional development. Although it initially had a quiet but broad agenda on women's issues and reform, by the 1990s it had come to deal primarily with political issues as they are concerned with the First Amendment.

BEGINNINGS

Because Indiana's nineteenth-century women journalists were not excluded from the earliest local press clubs and writing groups, their association patterns were different from those of their eastern journalistic sisters. Interestingly, the exclusion of women from male press clubs, as in New York City, in the 1860s was to be extended to Indiana by the early part of the twentieth century. This exclusion became codified in 1934 when the Indianapolis Press Club was incorporated and restricted itself to male newspapermen only.

However, Indiana's women's clubs provided a strong heritage for the twenty-eight women who organized WPCI because the women's clubs in the state were clearly among the oldest in the country. Extremely important to the development of women's clubs in the state was the settling of New Harmony, a community that advanced education for all children and equal opportunity and voting rights for women in the 1820s. Frances Wright, outspoken and forthright, did her earliest journalistic work there with the *New Harmony Gazette* and *Free Enquirer* and helped found the New Harmony Minerva Club, Indiana's first women's club, in 1825.[2]

As historians of the club movement have observed, those women members of the press who formed their own clubs, often because of exclusion from mainstream press clubs, were hoping to find an outlet for their social needs while striving for a sense of professional identification.[3] The same was true in Indiana, particularly in the case of New Harmony, where the "social" aspect of mutual support took precedence.

Clearly the separation between social and professional activities is difficult to define, as seen in the case of Sorosis, founded in New York City in 1868. So many members of that early woman's club were writers that some had debated calling the organization the "Order of the Pen."[4] That group had an important New Harmony connection because Ella Dietz (later Clymer-Glynes), an early president of the Minerva Club, was one of the founders of Sorosis and went on to serve as its president. Dietz was also to serve as the chair of the ratification committee of the General Federation of Women's Clubs (GFWC) in 1889 and created the motto for that group—"Unity in Diversity."[5]

At the same time women were joining the GFWC, an early federation of mixed-sex clubs in Indiana, the Indiana Union of Literary Clubs, was already successfully uniting all writers and journalists throughout the state and working to create an awareness of a national literature rather than one controlled by an eastern group of critics. But gender was to become an issue in these groups. What had been a fairly equitable distribution of membership between men and women changed as women joined the woman's club movement and the number of men in literary groups dwindled. Of the seventy-four clubs attending the fourth annual convention of the Literary Union in Fort Wayne in 1893, only ten were represented by men. Because there were men in the literary clubs and the Literary Union, these groups were reluctant to join the GFWC, since that organization did not allow male members.

Thus, by 1913, Indiana women and men who had long belonged to the same writers' groups were separating into their own gender-based clubs. Evidence of the influence of other women's press organizations can be seen in the WPCI itself, for the founders included two women who already belonged to other women's press groups—Mrs. Wray, a representative from a Pittsburgh press group, and Blanche Foster (later Boruff), a woman who had worked on the Ypsilanti Press in Michigan, where she also belonged to a women's press club.

ORGANIZATION

Several versions of the founding of WPCI exist. According to one account, the club was an outgrowth of a lobbying and press committee appointed by the Indiana State Federation of Women's Clubs at its convention in Fort Wayne in 1912.[6] Another account, written in 1945 by Boruff, suggests the creation of the WPCI was the result of action by an informal group that became a legislative council of Indiana women (later the Woman's Suffrage League) for the state federation. Whatever the details of the club's birth—and they may never be completely clear—the accepted story of the creation of WPCI is that it was founded by Indianapolis newspaper women who were seeking mutual support and by correspondents based in Indianapolis who were sending legislative stories to their hometowns.

There was a clear connection between the GFWC legislative council and the WPCI. One of the founders of the press group, for example, was Louella Frances Smith McWhirter, who had also been one of the original members of the GFWC legislative council. Another was Albion Fellows Bacon, a writer for Evansville papers and the *Indianapolis News*, who is credited with accomplishing the passage of Indiana's first statewide housing code in 1913. Like Bacon, the founders were women from around the state who had come to the capital city to cover events for their local newspapers and sometimes ended up writing for papers in Indianapolis. That many were also involved in promoting measures in which they were vitally interested—suffrage, good housing, and teachers' pensions, for example—suggests that even though they were covering events for hometown papers, the press women had a primary interest in writing stories which would result in support for or against various legislative measures. Almost all the founding members were newspaper writers—a majority, not surprisingly, from Indianapolis dailies. During the early years, membership requirements were that a woman had to have served at least a year as a regularly published writer.

The first president of the club, credited with guiding the group through that first year of organizational issues and criticism from newspaper editors, was Hester Alverson Moffett, the publisher of the *Elwood Daily Record*, which she had edited with her husband since 1897.[7] Another of the founders was Juliet V. Strauss, whose column, "The Country Contributor," appeared weekly in the *Rockville Tribune*, which she owned with her husband. Strauss's column promoted home values and the idea that the commoner things mattered most. On the question of suffrage, Strauss's biographer described her as "indifferent." Strauss marketed her writing to the *Indianapolis News* and later to Edward Bok of the *Ladies Home Journal*. Although she described herself in 1906 to reporter

William Herschell as not much of a clubwoman,[8] she was memorialized by the WPCI in 1922, when a statue was erected in her honor at Turkey Run State Park, near her hometown of Rockville.

Strauss and Moffett were two founders whose views on some of the political questions were probably opposed, but there is no doubt about the views of Grace Julian Clarke, who was actively involved in the woman's movement and whose father had introduced a woman suffrage amendment in Congress as early as 1853. Clarke was the president of the International Federation of Women's Clubs from 1909 to 1911, became press chair of the national GFWC from 1912 to 1916, and is credited with being influential in winning support for the woman suffrage cause among women's clubs. She was a founder of the Woman's Franchise League in Indiana, the organization that promoted woman suffrage from 1912 until its passage seven years later. Clarke also wrote a column of club notes for the *Indianapolis Star* and later edited its women's pages.

Charter members also included other women who are less familiar to readers of Indiana history but who were working reporters and considered achievers for their time. One such is Laurel Conwell Thayer, who first covered social issues and work in Washington, D.C., and later was involved in studies of social issues in Indiana. She was what might be called a muckraker and was a member of the staff of the *Indianapolis Sun* and later wrote for the *Indianapolis Times*. She worked toward housing reform, investigated the incarceration of the insane in county jails, and aroused public interest concerning the importance of psychiatric wards in hospitals.

Other founders, like Clarke, were primarily engaged in writing about women's clubs, even though their politics were sometimes considered radical. Nevertheless, current views are that the founders' goals were primarily social, as evidenced by records that say that the founders did not want their group to be a typical women's club with papers and minutes.

PROGRAMS AND ACTIVITIES

WPCI founding members, then, came together because they had a mutual interest in legislative issues as well as a need for companionship and mutual support. They sought the benefits of organization, a way to network and work to further their own professional and personal interests.

The local journalism community's response to the new organization was not entirely positive. According to Boruff, then a reporter for the *Indianapolis News*, the managing editors of daily newspapers were not happy about the founding of the WPCI, probably because of the clear connection many of the women had to the suffrage movement. But the editors were assured by the women that the whole purpose of the club was to provide a means of communication among women writers, that the members had no "ulterior" motives.[9]

Club meetings were initially held on Tuesdays, seven times a year, with a vacation in the summer. These were held in Indianapolis, where members from newspapers around the state gathered to cover the legislature. With improved transportation and communication, members traveled home more frequently and sometimes didn't spend much time in Indianapolis at all. To accommodate members who lived and worked out of town, meetings were eventually scheduled on Saturdays.

The meetings were primarily based on professional concerns, although they sometimes dealt with issues of broader concerns. The group also promoted itself, apparently to show that "advanced" women were competent in their efforts to approach issues of social concern. In 1916, for example, the WPCI sponsored a "telegraph tea" to publicize its work and prominence among women's groups. The WPCI invited prominent women writers to send their comments by telegraph to be shared during the meeting. The comments dealt with various topics and were often wryly amusing. Louisville writer Alice Hegan Rice, for example, addressed a common dilemma faced by many of the women who were club columnists or wrote women's news. Rice saluted the WPCI's society "editresses, those heroic characters that are denied the crumbs of gossip that fall from the rich man's table." She continued her telegram with a salute to the "untiring brains behind the Woman's page, who affiliate themselves with beauty hints when their mind, perchance, is bent on Ibsen." According to one description, more than five hundred women from all parts of the state came to send and receive the telegraphed messages. A clever talk by Blanche Foster introduced the event: "Man has not necessarily deteriorated, but woman has advanced," she told her appreciative audience.[10]

During World War I, the WPCI became a supporter of the French Relief Fund, and a writer from Indianapolis who lived in Paris helped keep the WPCI women informed. "I used every effort in press work to relieve every war situation that could be relieved without actually shouldering a gun and marching against the Hun," wrote Laura A. Smith of her role in Paris during the war.[11] Over the years, prominent women of national fame were guest speakers at the WPCI meetings, including suffragists Carrie Chapman Catt, Alice Stone Blackwell, and Sylvia Pankhurst. Other speakers included Indiana author Meredith Nicholson and cartoonist Kin Hubbard, Mrs. Lamberton Becker of the *Saturday Evening Post*, and the author and lecturer Frederick Landis.

In 1937, the WPCI was a founding member of the National Federation of Press Women (NFPW),* which increased members' links to other women writers throughout the country. The WPCI hosted the national federation in 1963 and 1979, and several women from Indiana have also been involved with leadership at the national level. During World War II, the gas shortage threatened the ability of many of the members from outlying areas of the state to drive to Indianapolis for meetings, but the WPCI continued to hold its meetings and watched its membership grow as more women found newspaper jobs to replace male journalists going off to war. As the war came to an end, however, many of these women lost their jobs to the very men they had replaced.

During the 1940s, WPCI's membership continued to be composed primarily of newspaper writers, though the categories for membership were broadened to include radio script writers, fiction writers, and college teachers of journalism. At this time, the club included editors and writers for Bobbs-Merrill Company, a major book publisher. This connection was valuable to many members, as the lists of books written by members frequently were published by Bobbs-Merrill.[12]

In the 1950s and 1960s, openly feminist topics were discussed again, but the comments were usually framed so as not to give offense. Sometimes, as when Phyllis Battelle of the International News Service spoke in May 1956, the comments were more pointed. "Chivalry wasn't dead," she asserted; "it had never existed," and to succeed, women had to work doubly hard and be warned against the pitfall of many women reporters—being overly emotional. Also during the 1950s many of the speakers addressed the women about the communist threat. The Cold War and its presence in every woman's life took on a sinister presence.

Other activities focused on the promotion of women in journalism and the writing profession. The WPCI sponsors a high school writing contest, and scholarships for women returning to journalism are named for Louise Eleaner Ross Kleinhenz, a former WPCI president. The group also sponsors a Prison Writing Contest and the Margaret Scott scholarship, which supports attendance at the Indiana University and the Ball State writing conferences. Each year the WPCI presents its highest honor, the Kate Milner Rabb Award, to a member for outstanding achievement and contributions in her profession and to WPCI.

Over the years, the membership has opened to representatives of the electronic media as well as public relations professionals and others involved in related professions such as photography and teaching. Recent membership rolls show an increase of members identified as publicity specialists, with seventy-two in that category. Many of these, however, are women who worked in media prior to going into public relations, so the appearance may belie the reality.

Membership of the organization in the 1970s was more than two hundred, but it has since dropped, according to former president (1982–84) and historian Joan Bey. Bey notes that the decline of membership can be seen in many of the older press organizations throughout the state. Although air travel and easy access to national organizations may play a part in the decline of interest in local professional activities, members of WPCI are still active in professional concerns. WPCI members continue to provide support to women in the field, especially to newcomers. The support goes beyond that which might be measured in terms of encouragement of peers; indeed, financial support from WPCI has aided in those wishing to return to the newspaper profession or attend writing conferences.

NOTES

1. The four early women press club founders were Anna Nicholas, Ida Husted Harper, Nettie Ranford, and Laura A. Smith, also a founder of WPCI in 1913.

2. Caroline Dale Snedeker, *The Town of the Fearless* (New York: Junior Literary Guild, 1932).

3. Maurine H. Beasley, "The Women's National Press Club: A Case Study of Professional Aspirations," *Journalism History* 15, no. 4 (winter 1988): 112–21.

4. Agnes Hooper Gottlieb, "Networking in the Nineteenth Century: Founding of the Woman's Press Club of New York City," *Journalism History* 21, no. 4 (winter 1995): 156–63.

5. Grace Gates Courtney, comp., and Acada Stark Balz, ed., *History of the Indiana Federation of Clubs* (Fort Wayne, Ind.: Fort Wayne Printing, 1939), pp. 20–21.

6. My thanks to Joan Bey, WPCI historian, who has provided information and who let me use the files kept by her as historian of the group.

7. Moffet continued to publish the newspaper for two years after her husband's death in 1917 and then sold the paper. She is credited with founding the Elwood Public Library and garnering support for it through editorials promoting public, rather than private, facilities. In 1989, she was inducted into the Indiana Journalism Hall of Fame Association.

8. Ray E. Boomhower, *The Country Contributor: The Life and Times of Juliet V. Strauss* (Carmel: Guild Press of Indiana, 1988).

9. Scrapbook, Papers of Woman's Press Club of Indiana (hereafter WPCI Papers), W. H. Smith Memorial Library, Indiana Historical Society, Indianapolis, Indiana.

10. Typed note, undated, WPCI Papers, box 9.

11. Blanche Foster Boruff, "The Woman's Press Club of Indiana," *Press Woman*, April 1945, p. 16.

12. This connection was lost when the publisher was acquired by International Telephone and Telegraph in 1966, then by Macmillan Company in 1985.

INFORMATIONAL SOURCES

Boomhower, Ray E. *The Country Contributor: The Life and Times of Juliet V. Strauss.* Carmel: Guild Press of Indiana, 1998.

Boruff, Blanche Foster. "The Woman's Press Club of Indiana." *Press Woman*, April 1945.

Courtney, Grace Gates, compiler, and Acada Stark Balz, ed. *History of the Indiana Federation of Clubs.* Fort Wayne, Ind.: Fort Wayne Printing, 1939.

Woman's Press Club of Indiana Collection. W. H. Smith Memorial Library, Indiana Historical Society, Indianapolis, Indiana.

INSTITUTIONAL PROFILE

Woman's Press Club of Indiana

Dates: Founded 1913; joined National Federation of Press Women in 1937 as a founding member.

Newsletter: *The WPCI Bulletin*, published from the 1930s to present, quarterly.

Papers: Woman's Press Club of Indiana Collection (1913–present), W. H. Smith Memorial Library, Indiana Historical Society, Indianapolis, Indiana.

Contacts: Joan Bey, WPCI Historian, 5872 North Keystone Ave., Indianapolis, IN 46220, tel. (317) 251–6242; Ida Chipman, President (1999–2000), 9010 State Rd. 17, Plymouth, IN 64563, tel. (219) 936–1124.

30

Agnes Hooper Gottlieb

Woman's Press Club of New York City, 1889–1980

LOOKING BACK

On March 8, 1980, members of the Woman's Press Club of New York City (WPCNYC) reluctantly voted to dissolve the ninety-year-old organization. Like its membership, the club was suffering the ailments of old age: Its coffers were low; its monthly bulletin had deteriorated into a single, mimeographed sheet often filled with death notices and health updates on aging members; and it had trouble finding women to fill elected and appointed positions.

Loyal members, so fond of their club and its traditions, tried to avoid dissolution, but it was not to be. As one board member privy to the discussions explained, "Many recommendations and proposals of the board members were discussed at length but failed to meet approval, primarily because they were not practical or in keeping with the prestige and past history of the Woman's Press Club."[1]

The prestige of the club, indeed. In its heyday, all important women journalists working for New York's many newspapers and periodicals sported its insignia pin. The club provided a support system, a professional network, and a social outlet for women who were engaged in newspaper and magazine journalism in the largest city in the world. The women themselves were so proud of their organization and its membership that the club archives, now housed at Columbia University, are filled with press clippings by and about members.

For nine decades the WPCNYC provided a forum for important speakers and aired topics that could affect the women and their writing. It annually honored a New York journalist whose writing ameliorated life in the city and awarded an annual scholarship to a woman student at Columbia University's Graduate School of Journalism. When it was incorporated in 1893, the club's stated purpose was "to gain for women all advantages arising from unity, fellowship and cooperation with those engaged in literary and similar pursuits, including extended aid to members when needed and to further advance the interest of the profession of journalism."[2]

By 1980, that was all gone, along with the days of ladylike journalism. The Women's Caucus of the *New York Times* and a group of women at the Associated Press had filed suits for discrimination against the old boys' networks that reigned; the National Press Club in the nation's capital had succumbed to pressure and had admitted women; and "auxiliary" organizations like the Woman's Press Club of New York City were no longer deemed vital by up-and-coming women reporters who were making headway in important journalistic corners.

The WPCNYC was one more victim that, like general women's clubs, church leagues, and service clubs, lost prestige and importance as women abandoned volunteer positions for paying jobs in professional careers. The generation of women journalists who came of age in the 1960s and 1970s were juggling carpools along with careers and simply had no time for card parties, genteel cocktail hours, and white-glove luncheons.

When it folded in 1980, the WPCNYC listed 101 active members, but board members lamented that as many as forty had failed to pay their dues. Among its membership were few full-time newspaper journalists, although there were representatives of the *New York Times*, the *Washington Post*, and the *Jersey Journal* of Jersey City. The membership list included, however, magazine writers, public relations practitioners, authors, poets, radio announcers, columnists, and a minister.

The composition of the club, in fact, reflected the sentiment of its founders who had voted to accept as members "all women who are writers or of kindred professions."[3] Then, they loosely defined what a "kindred profession" actually was to include anyone who earned part of her living through writing. The earnings requirement was abandoned during the Great Depression, when so few women earned anything at all.[4] During its lifetime, the club also included lawyers, college professors, artists, and teachers.

That the club never limited its membership to full-time working journalists probably led to its ultimate demise among women who had no time for social niceties but would have maintained membership in a strictly professional organization. At the time of its founding in 1889, the charter members were explicit in their desire to be expansive in opening membership to as many women as possible because they wanted to encourage women in the writing professions in a society that allowed women to follow few career paths. They also wanted to provide a network and social outlet that could only be satisfied in a press club.

ORGANIZATION

When the country's first woman's club, Sorosis, was created in 1868, the founders—all writers—toyed with making it a writers club. They ultimately rejected that idea in favor of a more broad and general club, but the notion so appealed to Sorosis founder Jane Cunningham Croly that she resuscitated it twenty-one years later. A prominent New York journalist who wrote under the pen name "Jennie June," Croly had been the motivating force behind organizing Sorosis after she had been refused a ticket to a Charles Dickens lecture being sponsored by the all-male New York Press Club.

By 1889, conditions had changed enough to support a full-fledged women's press club. The number of women working at newspapers had increased, though women still comprised fewer than 4 percent of the nation's journalistic workforce, and a good number of them worked in New York or for New York papers. Croly's situation had also changed, so she was in a better situation to propose such an organization. She was now a widow, her children were older, and her career was well established. Thus, in November 1889, Croly invited fifteen women to her home at 148 East 46th Street to discuss the organization of a women's press club. The women who attended included a half dozen women in newspaper or magazine work: Florence Carpenter Ives of the *New York Press*; Eliza Putnam Heaton of the *New York Recorder*; Helen Watterson of the *New York Sun*; Sarah Clarke Lippincott, who wrote for the *New York Times* as "Grace Greenwood"; Margaret Manton Merrill, founder of the *Colorado Temperance Gazette*, and Mary F. Seymour, editor of the *Business Woman's Journal*.

Those gathered at Croly's home that evening agreed that a women's press club in New York City, the epicenter of American journalism, was long overdue. As Croly told the women, "As other cities throughout the union could boast of flourishing press clubs, surely New York, the very center of American Journalism should not be without one."[5] Croly was elected president, according to the meticulous minutes that were kept throughout the club's life, and the women agreed that annual dues would be $5. They decided who could qualify for membership and accepted the constitution that Croly wrote. The insignia featured "NY" in a circle superimposed over a torch and a feather. The words *Woman's Press Club* were engraved on the circle itself.

The club flourished. Women writers throughout the city flocked to its doors. By 1891, new members included some important women journalists of New York. Among them were Dr. Louise Fiske Bryson of the *New York Medical Journal*; Edith Sessions Tapper, the New York correspondent of the *Chicago Daily Herald*; syndicated writer Isabel A. Mallon; Miriam Leslie, publisher of *Frank Leslie's Ladies' Journal*; Mattie Sheridan of the *New York Daily Graphic* and the *Daily Continent*; Emma Trapper of the *New York Press*; and, Lee C. Harby, a contributor to *Ladies Home Journal*. In December of that year, Croly sponsored Elizabeth Cochrane, "Nellie Bly," the flamboyant stunt reporter of Joseph Pulitzer's *New York World*, for membership.

Croly remained president of the club until her death in 1901, though she attempted to resign several times during the 1890s because she wanted to infuse the club with younger blood. The members, however, routinely refused to accept her resignation. Even though she was absent from the club for long periods in 1898 after breaking her hip, Croly was reelected in absentia by acclamation and remained president of the club until her death in 1901. During her tenure, Croly was the group's driving force and members often deferred to her on matters of importance. Croly had worked at the *New York World*, provided articles for newspapers around the country, and edited a number of magazines, including *Demorest's, The Home Maker, The Woman's Cycle, The New Cycle*, and *Godey's Lady's Book*, during her long career. Since she was one of the most prominent women journalists in New York, it was only logical that her fellow club members, many of them younger and less experienced, deferred to her and begged her opinions on press matters. When she was absent for ill health, Croly wrote letters back to her friends in the club. "I resign my place among you with less reluctance because the Woman's Press Club is now strong and well able to guard its own interests and direct its own affairs," she wrote in one fruitless attempt to resign the presidency. "It will, I am sure, be all the better and stronger from being thrown upon its own resources."[6]

Croly was the guiding light of the WPCNYC for its first twelve years. When she retired to England in 1900, she tried once again unsuccessfully to quit her position as president, but the members once again refused to accept her resignation. Only after her death would the club elect a new president, the Reverend Phoebe Hanaford, who held office until 1906. During the next seventy years, nineteen different women held the presidency.[7]

ACTIVITIES

In many ways the character and activities of the WPCNYC were molded by the interests and activities of its founder. Croly authored several books and wrote columns on women for her many publications and was the most prominent clubwoman in America. In 1890, she organized the General Federation of Women's Clubs (GFWC), which still exists today as an umbrella organization for women's clubs groups.[8] The press club, naturally, was one of the earliest members of the GFWC, which led it to conform to the organizational structure dictated by the federation. Like other clubs affiliated with the GFWC, the press club involved itself in the many social reform projects promoted by the federation. Committees established by the press club often reflected these interests, and by 1897, the WPCNYC had six standing committees: Literature and Journalism, Art, Progress, Current Topics, Entertainment, and Education and Citizenship.

Of these, the Education and Citizenship Committee was the most active. Led by the chair, a woman identified in club records only as Mrs. Clarence Burns, the committee worked on behalf of summer vacations, schools, public playgrounds, and increases in teacher salaries. For example, in December 1898,

Burns brought for discussion "the deplorable state of our public school system" because she wanted the women who were writing for New York newspapers to "excite public interest in behalf of the public educational affairs of our city." Burns described how five thousand children had been turned away because there was no room for them in the schools, how new schools stood empty because they had no furniture, and how teenagers were called upon as monitors because of a shortage of teachers. "Yet, in the meantime, we have a speedway that cost several million dollars," she lamented.[9] The club approved her resolution that members engaged in journalism would lobby on behalf of education in their writing. A month later, Burns announced that four schools had opened and that seventeen new ones were promised. This activism by the WPCNYC on behalf of social problems was exactly what Croly had in mind. She saw the club movement as an alternative to the more radical suffrage movement as a way of giving women a public voice on matters that concerned them.

The club held eight business meetings each year between October and May. Only members were allowed to attend, and attendance at these nuts and bolts gatherings was usually low, with only about two dozen members participating. The meetings, originally held in members' homes, moved in later years to other locations, including hotels and Carnegie Hall. During its last years, the club held most of its meetings at the Hotel Statler Hilton at Seventh Avenue and 33rd Street, although informal meetings and board of directors gatherings were sometimes still held in the women's homes.

The club also sponsored monthly programs or social meetings to which members were allowed to bring guests. These events often attracted quite a crowd. Typical of these social meetings was the gathering on April 24, 1897, which was attended by sixty-six members and ninety-four guests, both men and women, including a representative of the New York City Woman's Suffrage League and the president of the Health Protection Association. Miriam Leslie, the publisher of *Frank Leslie's Illustrated*, spoke about "The Publisher"; Ella Starr discussed "The Woman Reporter"; the Countess de Montague explored fashion writing; and Cynthia Westover-Alden of the *New York Tribune* described her job as editor of the woman's page.[10]

In 1921 the club established a scholarship fund and thereafter held an annual card party to raise money for an endowment. The women also had annual anniversary luncheons in February, which, during the 1930s, were often attended by Croly's daughter, Vida Croly Sidney, as an honored guest. Beginning in 1949, the annual anniversary party also featured the presentation of a special award to the New York journalist whose writing that year had contributed most to the city and its people.

DECLINE

The 1970s proved a difficult period for the club. Many longstanding members were dying and new members were no longer joining to revitalize the club's ranks. The board of directors often had trouble filling positions, which included chairs of the annual card party and luncheon and of the press award and scholarship, editor of the newsletter, *The Bulletin*, and parliamentarian.

By the time the last president, Gladys M. Sherman, took office in 1976, the club was embroiled in an investigation by the Internal Revenue Service because it had failed to file tax returns. Sherman's presidency was marked by frequent meetings with IRS representatives in her ultimately successful battle to have the heavy penalties imposed by the IRS removed. The drawn-out tax fight, though successful, took the starch out of the organization.

In its final meetings to dissolve the club, the board of directors tried to envision other options to keep the club afloat, including fewer meetings, cheaper meeting rooms, or additional fund-raising. But the women's primary concern was to preserve "the high standards of the Woman's Press Club" and to leave enough money in the treasury to perpetuate its scholarship. The only way to ensure that, the board decided, was to dissolve. The club's last official meeting was held on May 10, 1980.

NOTES

1. Elvira DeLiso to Mrs. Louis [Anna] P. DiBella, 24 April 1980, Archives of the Woman's Press Club of New York City (hereafter WPCNYC Archives), Butler Library, Columbia University, New York.

2. Articles of Incorporation, 1893, WPCNYC Archives.

3. WPCNYC minutes, 24 November 1889, WPCNYC Archives.

4. "Annual Report of Historian and Press Award, May 10, 1980," p. 2, WPCNYC Archives.

5. WPCNYC minutes, 24 November 1891, WPCNYC Archives.

6. Croly letter to the club reprinted in the program of the Fifty-first Anniversary Luncheon, 24 February 1940, WPCNYC Archives.

7. Subsequent presidents were Dr. Frances W. Monnell (1906–07), Baroness Katharine Evans Von Klenner (1907–12), Haryot Holt Dey (1912–16), Ida Powell Priest (1916–18), Haryot Holt Dey (1918–22), Amy Wren (1922–26), Haryot Holt Dey (1926–28), Mrs. Louis Reed Welzmiller (1928–30), Mary Ellen Wilson (1930–34), Harriet Bishop Waters Christie (1934–38), Minna Hall Carothers (1938–40), Amelia Berndt Moorfield (1940–42), Carla Whittaker Morrissey (1942–46), Jessie B. Chamberlin (1946–50), Hilda Juanita Couch (1950–54), Katharine M. Clayberger (1954–58), Hilda Juanita Couch (1958–62), Berth E. Wood (1962–66), Grace Harden (1966–68), Jessie B. Chamberlin (1968–72), Violet Van Wagner Lopez (1972–76), and, Gladys M. Sherman (1976–80).

8. GFWC headquarters are located in Washington, D.C.

9. WPCNYC minutes, 10 December 1898, WPCNYC Archives.

10. WPCNYC minutes, 24 April 1897, WPCNYC Archives.

INFORMATIONAL SOURCES

Gottlieb, Agnes Hooper. "Networking in the Nineteenth Century: Founding of the Woman's Press Club of New York City." *Journalism History* 21, no. 4 (winter 1995): 156–63.

Woman's Press Club of New York City Archives, Butler Library, Columbia University, New York City.

INSTITUTIONAL PROFILE

Woman's Press Club of New York City

Dates: Organized in November 1889; incorporated in 1893; became a charter member of the NFPW in 1937; dissolved in May 1980 (although the board of directors met after this to conclude outstanding financial business).

Newsletter: *The Bulletin*, available in club archives (below).

Organizational Records: Woman's Press Club of New York City Archives, Butler Library, Columbia University, New York City.

31

Sheila J. Gibbons

Women, Men and Media, 1987–Present

INTRODUCTION

Women, Men and Media traces its roots to 1987. Not a press club, not a membership organization, it has operated as a floating debate society and force for change in media portrayal of women. Women, Men and Media has monitored the advancement of professional women working in the news, advertising, and entertainment industries and urged speedier integration of women into these businesses at every level.

Women, Men and Media's founders—social critic and author Betty Friedan and longtime news executive Nancy Woodhull—linked journalists, media executives, film makers, screen writers, academics, social activists, and other creative thinkers in a network of discussion and debate about how to improve media treatment of women. With Friedan as executive director, aided in the project's administration by a series of program directors at universities where Friedan was based, symposia were organized several times a year. These were usually held in Los Angeles, New York, and Washington, but they were occasionally offered in other cities, such as Atlanta, Chicago, and Rochester, New York. At some of these gatherings, Women, Men and Media would release the findings of studies it commissioned to track progress—or lack of it—in mass media's connection with and treatment of women. These studies ranged from evaluating women's images in advertising and in women's magazines to analysis of the roles and prominence assigned to women in the columns of daily newspapers and on network television newscasts and morning programs. Women, Men and Media became especially well known for its studies of newspapers, which were conducted annually from 1989 to 1996.

Since its founding, Women, Men and Media has had a board of advisers who lent their names and resources to Friedan and Woodhull's efforts to draw attention to inequity in the media's treatment of the sexes. The advisory board had neither the standing nor the obligations of a board of directors. Rather, its members offered support and ideas to Friedan and Woodhull's debate-discussion-research initiatives. Membership on the board varied as the program moved from the West Coast to the East Coast, and then from New York to Washington, reflecting the types of media executives, academics, and social activists most associated with those locales.

Throughout most of its existence, Women, Men and Media has been an academic project housed in whatever institution of higher education Friedan was affiliated with at the time. These have included the University of Southern California, New York University, and Mount Vernon College in Washington, D.C.

BACKGROUND

The 1970s and 1980s saw the beginning of organized protest against the portrayal of women in and by the meda as well as the limited opportunities for women working in the communication industries. Nearly every major news organization found itself confronting threats of complaints to the Equal Employment Opportunity Commission or lawsuits from women employees receiving lower pay and fewer career-enhancing assignments than their male colleagues.[1] On the outside, activist groups such as the National Organization for Women and the Los Angeles Women's Coalition for Better Broadcasting applied pressure to print and broadcast news organizations, alleging they had failed to address substantive issues of concern to women and had stereotyped women in much of the coverage they had produced. Whereas women working in the industries asked for employment equity and compensation for past discrimination, these groups demanded more quantity and quality in coverage and depiction of women.[2]

Initially, many of the news organizations so confronted renewed their pledges to improve but did little or nothing to redress grievances. In her outstanding chronicle of the New York Times's women's struggle in the 1970s, Nan Robertson described the sluggish response to complaints of gender discrimination at one of the nation's most venerable news organizations. She quotes John Mortimer, the Times's vice president of industrial relations in the early days of the controversy in 1972:

There was a lot of noise at this stage and very little action. I had to make it clear to the decision makers that Punch [Sulzberger, then-publisher of the New York Times] and I wanted to see results and that they would be evaluated. But when you come down to the old cruncherooni and you tell a manager that you're going to judge him on something like unfairness, when all through his career he's been judged on something else—holding down costs, putting out a first-class product—it's hard to reach him. I'd go around every month with a little list and say, 'How're you doing?' and they'd say, 'Fine, fine, yes,

yes, we're going ahead on the women and the minorities.' I couldn't break into the inner depths of these guys. The progess was so glacial we'd all have been 99 years old before we got there.[3]

Betsy Wade, one of the members of the *New York Times* Women's Caucus,* put it more bluntly: "Plenty of sweet talk to our faces and carrying on just the same behind our backs."[4]

The battle between women staffers and management at the *Times* dragged on for six more years and was finally settled just as a trial was imminent. Most discrimination complaints brought against news organizations were not settled until after legal action was threatened and in some cases under way. Generally, to avoid litigation, the employers offered monetary compensation and set hiring and promotion goals. The plaintiffs usually gained very little for themselves after their bruising battle with management, but they did succeed in opening the doors a little wider for the women who followed them.

Even after more women began to be hired and promoted in news organizations, women as a group remained disproportionately undercovered in comparison to men. In an analysis of fifteen studies conducted between 1973 and 1988 on the way in which women were portrayed in newspapers, Marilyn Greenwald found "a consistent pattern of unequal treatment in the news pages":

Interestingly, the treatment of women on the news pages seemed to improve only slightly—or not at all—from the National Organization for Women's 1973 study until recently, despite the entrance of more and more women into the work force since the mid-1970s, and despite the increasing media coverage given to the women's movement and women's rights.[5]

In a comprehensive study of how newspapers covered women's issues, conducted at the George Washington University in 1983, it was determined that ten of the United States's most outstanding newspapers largely ignored or missed opportunities to inform their readers about the impact of changing trends in domestic relations, the Equal Rights Amendment (ERA), national and international women's conferences, pay equity, and lack of enforcement of laws prohibiting discrimination in education.[6] News coverage of women and of matters of interest to women was no better in weekly newsmagazines or on local or national television.

ORGANIZATION

In 1987, Betty Friedan was on the faculty of the University of Southern California (USC), heading a think tank that analyzed the evolving roles of women and men in society. Her groundbreaking work on modern women, *The Feminine Mystique*, had been published nearly a quarter century earlier.[7] It was no less than revolutionary, revealing the myth of the happy homemaker to be just that—a myth—and making the case for the importance of women's being able to choose the directions their lives would go in, rather than being automatically assigned a role.

Friedan had assumed a key, highly visible role in the modern women's movement. She was a founder of the National Organization for Women and its first president and believed in the power of collective action for change. In 1985, she wrote: "Neither I nor any woman could break that vicious circle alone. We found our strength by confronting the condition that made us what we were as women, and by acting together to change them."[8] Friedan knew firsthand the sting of employment discrimination, having been denied maternity leave and fired from her job with a labor newspaper when she became pregnant with her second child. She felt strongly that the media helped to further the myth of women's satisfaction with a narrow set of life choices. Friedan believed, she said, that her work as a contributor to women's magazines had helped foster that very myth.[9]

By 1987, from her USC post in Los Angeles, Friedan felt the time had come to build a new awareness of the imbalance and distortion in the coverage and representation of women and men in a variety of media, and also to monitor the media workplace for evidence of gender discrimination. Friedan saw media images of women as "a Rorschach test, *reflecting* what's happening in the larger society, and also *shaping* what's happening in the larger society."[10] Friedan and her think tank's "kitchen cabinet" began to plan a conference to be held early in 1988. The conference would gather what was known at that point about women's status in the media, carefully considering whether promises to hire and promote women had been kept, and whether film, television, and print media had changed with women's increased participation in the media workforce.

Among those Friedan invited to the conference was Allen H. Neuharth, then chairman and CEO of the Gannett Company, the newspaper and broadcasting conglomerate. Neuharth had established a reputation as a firm believer in the importance of having women move up the ranks at Gannett's newspapers and radio and television stations. In a speech to women journalists in 1970, he had said:

The press is overmanned, especially at the top. Far too many publishers, editors, managing editors, city editors, magazine editors, broadcast station managers, are men. As a result, most of our news and editorial products are still designed primarily by men, even though they are aimed primarily at women, that's bad. Bad for you. Bad for our society.[11]

Neuharth began to hold his managers accountable for developing gender, ethnic, and racial diversity among Gannett employees and ensuring representation of diverse viewpoints in news coverage. He tied the managers' compensation to their success in this regard and began obtaining the kind of results that put Gannett at the front of the news industry in its employment of women and minority executives. Though Neuharth felt strongly that this approach was simply good business, few of his peers in the media business shared his passion about this.

Neuharth could not attend Friedan's Los Angeles conference, but he sent Gannett news executive Nancy Woodhull in his place. Friedan was disappointed that Neuharth could not attend, but she and Woodhull established a quick rapport. Woodhull had begun her newspaper career in 1964 at the *News Tribune* in Woodbridge, New Jersey. Later she became a reporter for the *Detroit Free Press* and then managing editor of Gannett's Rochester newspapers. She was one of the founding editors of *USA TODAY*, and at the time she appeared at Friedan's conference, Woodhull was president of Gannett News Media and Gannett News Service.

At that landmark conference, "Breakthroughs and Backlash," held in late winter 1988, Friedan and Woodhull discussed the idea of creating an entity that would pay close attention to the issues of media gender diversity that both of them cared so much about. They agreed to work together and established Media Watch: Women and Men. Within a year, the name was changed to Women, Men and Media. The name was deliberately inclusive of men, reflecting Woodhull and Friedan's thinking that change could not occur without taking into account the views and participation of males.

"One of the ideas that Betty and I had was to create an organization that would do studies and create roundtables and seminars around the country that would discuss the issues, to get opinions about what needed to be done, and to make the press more aware of how to do this job of covering women," Woodhull was to recall eight years later. "Hopefully, in having those conversations, we would be able to promote change."[12]

The two served as co-chairs, with Friedan also acting as executive director. The Gannett Foundation provided the first grant to make it possible for Women, Men and Media to conduct studies and arrange conferences and symposia. It continued this support after it changed its title to the Freedom Forum, and over the years other organizations also provided funding, including the Times Mirror Foundation, Capital Cities/ABC, Inc., the Skaggs Foundation, and the Eugene and Agnes E. Meyer Foundation.[13]

ACCOMPLISHMENTS

Although Women, Men and Media was based in Los Angeles, it collaborated with another organization, Women in Film (WIF), and stepped up pressure on Hollywood's film and television industry to provide more opportunities and better roles for women. According to playwright and screenwriter Gloria Goldsmith, a former president of WIF and a member of Friedan's California "kitchen cabinet" who also organized many of the Los Angeles events, "What Betty did [in Los Angeles] was to let the industry know that there are qualified women at all levels of the entertainment business, as well as make the public and the industry conscious of the depiction of women in film and TV."[14]

To get that message out, Women, Men and Media began giving "Break-through Awards" recognizing individuals and companies who were responsible for changing stereotypes and for crossing boundaries in entertainment. Among the early recipients were Callie Khouri for her film *Thelma and Louise*, David Kelly for his strong women characters in the television series *Picket Fences*, and Barbra Streisand for directing films showing women's strength and complexity.

Friedan and Woodhull shared the moderating duties at the various Women, Men and Media symposia. They typically posed questions to symposia participants, asking them to react to what Women, Men and Media research showed and asking for their views. Occasionally, they would use a panel discussion format, but they preferred the roundtable as a model for discussion and debate. With this method, they were able to elicit input from a broad range of individuals and bring forward a wealth of anecdotal detail and suggestions for solutions to problems.

The Women, Men and Media Breakthrough Awards came to include others who had elevated women's views to higher levels. Recipients included Blanche Wiesen Cook for her biography of Eleanor Roosevelt; the American Women in Radio and Television* foundation, and Capital Cities/ABC for their public service campaign to combat sexual harassment; Barbara Reynolds, then a columnist for *USA TODAY*, for her strong voice in questioning the status quo; Jones Intercable for its support of research on diversity in the cable television industry; and CNN for its high level of employment of women in key positions throughout the organization.

In 1992, Friedan left Los Angeles for New York, where she had been offered a faculty appointment at New York University. Here she teamed up with long-time friend and veteran broadcast journalist Marlene Sanders to teach a seminar on women and media. Thus, the Women, Men and Media programs were expanded to New York, with Sanders as program director, though some programs were still occasionally held in Los Angeles. Women, Men and Media sponsored discussions on topics including how women figured in the coverage of politics, abortion and family issues, the impact of male-dominated talk radio, and the image of women in women's magazines. Programs were open to the public, usually for free or at a modest cost, and featured knowledgeable participants who were recognized experts in their fields.

Women, Men and Media also collaborated with Women in Communications, Inc.,* in 1991 to examine the influence of advertising images on society. In 1993, it collaborated with Women in Cable to discuss whether it is possible to restructure work to include the values women espouse, and still serve the bottom line. Joint ventures with organizations such as these helped to export Women, Men and Media's discussion and debate content into allied communication industries.

By 1992, Woodhull had her own consulting business in Rochester, New York, and was a trustee of the Freedom Forum, headquartered in Arlington, Virginia.

In 1995, Friedan relocated to Washington, D.C., to become a Woodrow Wilson Center fellow and to teach at Mount Vernon College. Thus, by the mid-1990s, the Washington, D.C., area came to be an important location for the two women and the Freedom Forum world headquarters became a regular site of Women, Men and Media symposia.

In addition to facilitating freewheeling debate, which was often covered by the press and the trade media, Women, Men and Media commissioned research that illuminated the status of women in media and challenged media executives to do better. Foremost among these reports were the annual analyses of newspapers, conducted by M. Junior Bridge of Unabridged Communications, Inc., in Alexandria, Virginia. During the 1980s, Bridge had been a media relations director for the National Organization for Women and, in that capacity, heard from many women about unbalanced coverage of issues of interest to women and stories of persistent stereotyping in news reporting. She had also heard complaints from journalists about the lack of female influence on news values. Bridge was considering mounting a study of newspaper coverage when she met Woodhull, who encouraged her to proceed with the project. Woodhull introduced Bridge's results at a Women, Men and Media conference in Washington in 1989, along with the work of others who had been studying women and media, such as Kathy Bonk of the Communications Consortium in Washington, D.C., and Jean Gaddy Wilson of New Directions for News at the University of Missouri in Columbia.

Bridge's first study analyzed a month's worth of ten U.S. dailies. Later the sample was doubled to twenty, and Bridge conducted the study for Women, Men and Media every year through 1996. Throughout the eight years of the study, the numbers changed somewhat, but only incrementally. The 1996 results of front-page references capped two years of declining mentions of women. In that year, Bridge found, front-page newspaper references to females amounted to only 15 percent of total front-page references to women. When females were covered on key pages as the main figures of stories, more than half were victims or perpetrators of crimes or alleged misconduct. Stories about women as persons of accomplishment and achievement were few. Fewer than 1 percent of the references in front-page political stories were to females. Women in power in both the public and private sectors received minimal coverage, either as newsmakers or sources of important information.[15]

The annual studies pushed newspaper organizations to examine themselves. A number of them began using the Women, Men and Media analysis model to assess their own progress toward reaching internal goals.[16] Other groups began conducting their own assessments of their local newspapers to determine if they were continuing to shortchange women.[17] In most cases, the numbers paralleled the Women, Men and Media results and indicated that new strategies and new thinking were required if women and girls were to see their lives reflected accurately and more frequently in news content.

In 1997, the productive collaboration of Friedan and Woodhull came to a tragic, premature end with Woodhull's death from lung cancer at the age of fifty-two. Now under Friedan's sole leadership, though with the assistance of a program director and program adviser, Women, Men and Media continues with its mission to raise awareness about media's role in the lives of women and men and continues to organize symposia and commission research. In 1997, the Freedom Forum Media Studies Center in New York City began to sponsor the annual analyses of media Women, Men and Media had long commissioned.

NOTES

1. Among these were the Associated Press, which settled with the Wire Service Guild in 1983 following a ten-year fight by female reporters and African American reporters for equal consideration of pay and assignments with their white male colleagues; the *Detroit News*, which paid more than $300,000 in 1983 to ninety female members of a class-action suit; and the *New York Times*, which in 1978 settled a sex discrimination suit brought by its women employees. That case originated with ninety charges against the *Times* in a complaint to the Equal Employment Opportunity Commission in 1972 and 1973.

2. In 1972, the National Organization for Women's New York chapter filed a petition with the Federal Communications Commission to deny renewal of the broadcast license of WABC-TV in New York on the grounds that the station failed to meet the needs of its female viewers in news and programming and that it discriminated against women in employment. The Los Angeles Women's Coalition for Better Broadcasting reached agreements with local stations to improve their service to women viewers and their record on female employment after indicating they would petition to deny renewal of broadcast licenses. For more on these cases, see Maurine H. Beasley and Sheila J. Gibbons, "Challenges to Mass Media," in *Taking Their Place: A Documentary History of Women and Journalism* (Washington, D.C.: American University Press, 1993), pp. 235–65.

3. Nan Robertson, *The Girls in the Balcony: Women, Men, and the New York Times* (New York: Random House, 1992), p. 157.

4. Ibid.

5. Marilyn S. Greenwald, "The Portrayal of Women in Newspapers: A Meta-Analysis" (paper presented at the annual convention of the Association for Education in Journalism and Mass Communication, Washington, D.C., August 1989), p. 6.

6. "New Directions for News: A Newspaper Study," sponsored by the Women Studies Program and policy Center of the George Washington University, Washington, D.C., September 1983. The newspapers that participated in the study were the *Arizona Daily Star, Atlanta Journal and Constitution, Cincinnati Enquirer, Dallas Times Herald, Denver Post, Detroit Free Press, Los Angeles Times, Miami Herald, New York Times*, and *St. Louis Post-Dispatch*. The independent think tank New Directions for News (NDN), at the University of Missouri is the outgrowth of this landmark research.

7. Betty Friedan, *The Feminine Mystique* (New York: W. W. Norton & Co., 1963).

8. Betty Friedan, *It Changed My Life: Writings on the Women's Movement* (New York: W. W. Norton & Co., 1985), p. 388.

9. Friedan, *The Feminine Mystique*, p. 66.

10. Transcript, Women, Men and Media roundtable, "Marginalizing Women: Front-

Page News Coverage of Females Declines in 1996" (Freedom Forum, Arlington, Va., 16 April 1996), p. 4.

11. Sheila Gibbons, ed., and Pam Janis, writer, *Allen H. Neuharth: The Gannett Years*, (Arlington, Va.: Gannett Co., 1989), p. 21. This was a retrospective book produced at the time of Neuharth's retirement as chairman of Gannett Co., Inc.

12. M. Junior Bridge, *Marginalizing Women: Front-Page News Coverage of Females Declines in 1996* (Washington, D.C.: Women, Men and Media, 1996), p. 1.

13. Women, Men and Media fact sheet.

14. Gloria Goldsmith, interview by author, 6 June 1998.

15. Bridge, "Marginalizing Women," p. 1.

16. Among these were organizations as far-flung as the Capital Women's Journalists Association of China, which released results of its monitoring studies of Chinese newspapers at the NGO Forum held in conjunction with the UN Fourth World Conference on Women held in September 1995 in Beijing. Other news organizations that used the study model were the *Hartford Courant*, the editorial page of *USA TODAY*, and Knight-Ridder newspapers.

17. Among the better known of these efforts is the "Names in the News" study conducted annually by the Minnesota Women's Press. This women's newspaper has been monitoring the state's two largest papers, the *Minneapolis Star Tribune* and the *St. Paul Pioneer Press*, annually since 1992.

INFORMATIONAL SOURCES

Beasley, Maurine H., and Sheila J. Gibbons. *Taking Their Place: A Documentary History of Women and Journalism*. Washington, D.C.: American University Press, 1993.

Empowering Women in the Media. Washington, D.C.: International Women's Media Foundation, July 1996.

The Media and Women without Apology. Theme issue of *Media Studies Journal* 7, no. 1–2 (winter-spring 1993).

Media Report to Women, 1972–present, passim.

Mills, Kay. *A Place in the News: From the Women's Pages to the Front Page*. New York: Columbia University Press, 1990.

Robertson, Nan. *The Girls in the Balcony: Women, Men and the New York Times*. New York: Random House, 1992.

"Study Finds Sex Discrimination at U.S. Newspapers." Reuters wire report, 13 July 1995.

INSTITUTIONAL PROFILE

Women, Men and Media

Dates and places: Founded in Los Angeles as **Media Watch: Women and Men**, 1987–88; name changed to **Women, Men and Media**, 1988. Based in New York City 1992–95; Washington, D.C., 1995–97; Silver Spring, Maryland, 1998–present.

Officers 1999: Betty Friedan, executive director; Sheila Gibbons, program director; Marlene Sanders, program adviser.

Address: c/o Communication Research Associates, P.O. Box 180, Colton's Point, MD 20626, tel. (301) 769–3899.

32

Carolyn M. Byerly

Women's Feature Service, 1978–Present

Women's Feature Service (WFS) is a woman-managed global news agency that specializes in news feature stories about women and development, primarily in nations of the southern hemisphere. Based in New Delhi, India, WFS syndicates 250–300 feature stories each year to both mainstream and alternative media as diverse as India's *Hindustan Times*, the Hong Kong–based *Far Eastern Economic Review*, the Philippines' *The Men's Zone*, Uruguay's *La República*, and the American *Chicago Tribune*. About two-thirds of the agency's stories are written in English, the remainder in Spanish. Stories are circulated to media and other clients electronically as well as through regular mail. The agency also produces documentary video and radio features for broadcast, dossiers on a range of issues, various reports, and occasional books on women's role in national and regional development. WFS also sponsors international seminars to train working journalists employed by other news outlets to expand their coverage of women and development.

This chapter traces the operations and evolution of WFS since its beginnings in 1978, considering in the process how WFS has helped to change news definitions in order to incorporate women's experience in the news and to encourage women's fuller social participation.

BACKGROUND

Women's marginalization by media had already come sharply into focus when the United Nations' Decade for Women began in 1975. Early academic studies and feminist analyses showed that the news and entertainment media systematically excluded, stereotyped, and trivialized women in most of their news and programming.[1] At the end of the 1970s, most media also barely acknowledged the global women's movement that was challenging female secondary status in all nations of the world.

These were serious problems for women. As scholars have shown, all major social movements of the twentieth century have needed the mainstream news media to disseminate their ideas and to mobilize followers, both in the initial and in later stages.[2] Moreover, in today's world, the media have become more generally understood as vehicles through which citizens deliberate matters of common concern and participate in political processes. The extent to which women and other diverse groups succeed in gaining access to those media has become one measure of democracy.[3]

Delegates who attended the official UN meeting in Mexico City in 1975, recognized that women's political and social advancement would require greater access to both mainstream and alternative media. This led them to adopt a "World Plan of Action," which, among other things, noted that "the mass communications media . . . could exercise a significant influence in helping to remove prejudices and stereotypes, accelerating the acceptance of women's new and expanding roles in society and promoting their integration into the development process as equal partners."[4] This document laid the cornerstone for what has become a veritable library filled with UN-sponsored studies and reports on women and communication, as well as for what were to become interventionist programs, like the Women's Feature Service Project and its progeny, the New Delhi–based WFS.

Immediately after the 1975 UN Decade for Women meetings in Mexico City,[5] a small group of activists and journalists met to propose an umbrella project that would represent the modern woman who sought to be a more powerful and political actor and help circulate new ideas about women's problems, achievements, and social analyses to general audiences. After three years of planning, the "Women's Feature Service Project" was launched in 1978 under the administration of UNESCO's Yvette Abrahamson, with short-term funding from the UN Educational, Scientific and Cultural Organization (UNESCO) and the UN Fund for Population Agency (UNFPA).[6]

ORGANIZATION AND STRUCTURE

The organization and structure of WFS have been marked by several distinct stages. The first stage can be characterized as a start-up phase that lasted from 1978 to 1983, under Inter Press Service (IPS) sponsorship. Then headquartered in Rome, IPS allowed two branches of the service—Oficina Informativa de la Mujer, in San José, Costa Rica, and African Women's Feature Service, in Nairobi, Kenya—to operate autonomously. Each branch produced a few dozen stories a year that were circulated in English and Spanish over the IPS news wires and through regular mail.

A second stage, which lasted from 1983 till 1987, is best described as a period of decline. UN start-up funds had ended in 1983, and IPS (itself chronically underfunded) kept only a semblance of women's news alive as it wrestled with how to continue. By 1987, IPS director Roberto Savio had pulled together enough funds to hire international development specialist Anita Anand to consolidate the scattered remains of the women's news project. Between 1987 and 1989, Anand's farsighted leadership guided a reinvigorated WFS through what can be considered the agency's third stage, a period marked by the establishment of regional bureaus, the securing of grants for training female journalists, the expansion of story production from a few dozen to several hundred a year, and the drafting of plans for the agency's move toward independence.[7]

The fourth and present stage, which began in 1990, really marks the emergence of WFS as an autonomous, mature organization with a clear sense of its mission in world news. By relocating its headquarters to India, WFS reaffirmed its commitment to speak primarily for women in developing nations of the Southern Hemisphere, where women have faced the greatest struggles against poverty and lack of access to health, education, and other basic services. WFS correspondents also began to descend *en masse* on major UN (and other) meetings, thereby covering international debates and the policy making that grew out of them. Because women—female professionals and grassroots leaders working through nongovernmental organizations—were by now deeply involved in those debates, WFS stories of those meetings reflected women's involvement in shaping major policies on population, human rights, the environment, and other issues.

By 1998, Women's Feature Service was centrally managed from its headquarters in New Delhi, with regional news bureaus in San José, Costa Rica, and New York City, a national bureau in the Philippines, and contributing centers in the Philippines and the Netherlands. The New Delhi headquarters acted as the central distribution point of English-language stories and overall agency operations and also oversaw general operations of the agency. The offices in Costa Rica and the Philippines were headed by veteran journalists who hired and supervised part-time correspondents, edited stories, and coordinated marketing. The U.S. office covered and produced stories about relevant UN activities, served as liaison to U.S. funding sources, and handled WFS finances.[8]

In that same year, WFS had about forty part-time correspondents, all female. These correspondents, about one-third of whom had more than a decade of experience working with the agency, were typically experienced full-time or freelance journalists who also wrote for a variety of magazine, newspaper, and broadcast media. These contributors usually came to the agency through informal networks of women's press associations and agencies for development in the nations served by WFS. They usually came to the agency with academic training and journalistic specialties in subjects that include politics, economics, international affairs, health, medicine, theater and cinema, psychology, and education. These women were also involved in local, national, or international women's movements.[9]

Like many small news enterprises, WFS has operated with limited resources through the years. However, in the mid-1990s, the agency began to encounter more serious fiscal problems than usual, brought on by escalating costs (particularly in the Latin American region) and changes in funding arrangements with some governmental sponsors. Budget constraints inevitably meant fewer funds for writers' salaries and travel expenses, as well as fewer regional meetings for training and coordination. The agency responded by increasing its story marketing in the South Asian region, particularly its home state of India; expanding its services to include research and technical writing; and shifting added fundraising and marketing responsibilities to its regional directors. These efforts met with some success, particularly in terms of regional marketing and grant writing.[10] The agency's budget in 1997 was just under $400,000, with the majority of revenues coming from contracts and grants from governmental and nongovernmental organizations and private foundations. The balance of revenues were generated by the sale of stories to media.[11]

WFS also embarked on new directions to influence the coverage of women and development in world news. In 1998, the agency received private funding to convene journalists, academics, and leaders of nongovernmental religious organizations in order to explore ways of increasing accuracy and depth in stories about women in religious traditions. The agency also hoped to establish an international training center in India with a certificate program to prepare both female and male journalists to cover gender and development issues from a "progressive women's perspective."[12]

MISSION AND ACTIVITIES

WFS has played both a symbolic and a practical role for women in global news. The agency's mission has been to give women more visibility and voice in order to strengthen them politically, particularly in the developing nations. In addition to filling a significant gap in mainstream news, WFS has also sought to redefine news by placing women's lives and ideas central to stories and by raising critical questions about women's secondary citizenship. These were dramatic departures from how most news agencies across the world were treating women's concerns and activities at the time WFS was founded. The agency has also sought to create an informational bridge among women of all nations who share so many of the same problems, hopes, and success stories, even though their cultural and political contexts might differ. In order to achieve this, WFS has targeted primarily an educated audience with the goal of influencing public opinion and policy with regard to women's status.

Most of WFS's basic journalistic guidelines exhort WFS correspondents to meet the familiar standards of good reporting—focus the story in the lead, seek a range of credible sources and perspectives, include facts, attribute all information, avoid jargon, give examples, tell stories, don't editorialize, and use action verbs. These practices align the agency with other news services, both mainstream and specialized. WFS distinguishes itself from other services, however, by its criteria that reporters use a particular context and gender to frame stories. Thus, writers "look for connections—to the past, the future; to economics, political trends, international agreements, structural adjustment," and other elements necessary for a bigger context.[13] They also provide what the agency has always called a "progressive women's perspective." The WFS style book defines this perspective as "any critique of the existing world view" that includes women's knowledge, wisdom, intuition, and perceptions of their environment. The agency believes that this perspective must be forward looking, not just pointing out failures and problems of the past, but also considering what women, groups, or governments are doing to overcome them.[14] In these ways, WFS journalism both adapts and redefines the concept of development news to include a gender dimension that has often been lacking.[15]

Over the years, WFS has consistently delivered stories that show women as knowledgeable, capable, and effective social actors.[16] Most of the sources in WFS stories are women, in leadership as well as nonelite positions lower in the socioeconomic scale. Not surprisingly, most stories focus on politics, laws, and economics as these affect women. But stories also factor in culture and tradition, showing how these enter into the ways women experience and challenge oppressive practices.

One story published in 1996, for example, asks, "Are buildings gender neutral?" The story reports on women architects in India's west coast city of Mumbai who led a movement to erect women-friendly hostels for working women. The story's central concern is gender-bias in city planning, a problem that has historically resulted in neighborhoods that are unsafe for women to travel and ill designed for them to work together in their dwellings (e.g., in kitchens). Studies on gender and living spaces helped the architects to influence changes in new neighborhood designs. One leader quoted in the story also advocates the incorporation of these gender studies into college architectural curricula.[17]

Another story published in 1996 and datelined Kiev, Ukraine, spotlights women's efforts to address the high rate of birth defects and infant mortality brought on by pregnant women's exposure to toxic chemicals at their work sites. Social and economic crises in the Ukraine made it essential for women to work through their pregnancies, so quitting for the sake of their babies was not an option. In early 1996, a group of thirteen women's organizations formed an umbrella organization, the National Women's Council of Ukraine, to campaign for legislation to improve the health and status of women, including implementation of a major government program for women that had been shelved since 1990 for lack of funds.[18]

Another "typical" WFS story, also published in 1996, recounts efforts by local women to enact laws against sexual harassment in Trinidad and Tobago, where most women need to work outside the home to provide for their families. A national court decision upholding the firing of an employee at Republic Bank for sexually harassing a female colleague helped motivate the campaign. The story mentions that Caribbean women's determination to end sexual harassment had been sparked by their outrage a few years earlier during the Anita Hill-Clarence Thomas Senate hearings in the United States.[19]

WFS CONTRIBUTIONS

Women's Feature Service has played a long-term leadership role in promoting the role of progressive female journalists in world newsmaking, particularly in the developing nations. WFS stories reveal how women take active roles in the serious business of economics, health, politics, laws, war and peace, and cultural traditions—the public realms traditionally dominated by men. Even women primarily associated with the traditional private sphere of home are revealed in WFS stories to be capable of taking on public lives and of having views about matters that concern them and their families.

The agency also demonstrates that female journalists and editors can establish their own international news agencies, and fund and manage them decade after decade in a world news market that is still overwhelmingly dominated by powerful male-owned transnational corporations. WFS has never lost sight of its mission to place journalism in the service of women, even in the face of financial and other challenges.[20]

Though still a small player on a big field, WFS has the potential to remain a significant channel through which women of diverse origins, philosophies, and daily lives can contribute their ideas and analyses to the public sphere, thereby enlarging their roles in society and democratic process. For this reason, women everywhere benefit from—and have a stake in—the survival of alternative world media like Women's Feature Service.

NOTES

1. Major references from this early period show that women were generally marginalized in these ways in all nations of the world, except the northern European nations, where women had achieved greater access to jobs and decision making within the media. See Mieke Ceulemans and Guido Fauconnier, *Mass Media: The Image, Role, and Social Conditions of Women* (Paris: UNESCO, 1979), and Gay Tuchman et al., *Hearth and Home: Images of Women in the Mass Media* (New York: Oxford University Press, 1978).

2. See Richard Kielbowicz and Clifford Scherer, "The Role of the Press in the Dynamics of Social Movements," *Research in Social Movements, Conflicts and Change* 9 (1986): 71–96.

3. Edward Herman and Robert W. McChesney, *The Global Media: The New Missionaries of Global Capitalism* (London: Cassell, 1997).

4. *World Plan of Action, 1975*, paragraphs 161–62, cited in UNFPA Project Request, 1 July 1976.

5. There were three meeting sites in all during the decade: Mexico City (1975), Copenhagen (1980), and Nairobi (1985). The ten-year follow-up meeting was held in Beijing, in 1995. Each "meeting" was actually two events: the official UN meeting, attended by representatives picked by the heads of states belonging to the UN, whose job it was to adopt recommendations to governments for advancing women's status; and

a second independent forum, sponsored by nongovernmental organizations and open to any women who wished to attend.

6. Abrahamson was a program specialist in UNESCO's Population Division.

7. Carolyn M. Byerly, "News, Consciousness and Social Participation: The Role of Women's Feature Service in World News," in *Feminism, Multiculturalism and the Media*, ed. A. N. Valdivia (Thousand Oaks, Calif.: Sage, 1995).

8. Carolyn M. Byerly, "Countdown for Women's Feature Service: Gender, News and Development in an Era of Globalization" (unpublished paper presented at the annual convention of the International Communication Association, Jerusalem, July 1998).

9. Byerly, "News, Consciousness and Social Participation" and "Countdown for Women's Feature Service."

10. Gretchen Sidhu, executive director, WFS-USA, personal communication to author, spring 1998; Byerly, "Countdown for Women's Feature Service."

11. Byerly, "Countdown for Women's Feature Service."

12. Gretchen Sidhu, personal communication to author, fall 1998.

13. Gretchen Sidhu, "Eleven Things to Remember When Writing a WFS Story," 1998.

14. *WFS Style Manual*; Gretchen Sidhu, personal communication with author, 1998.

15. The "development news" style emerged as a format used widely by news agencies serving the developing nations in the 1970s. Its intent was to overcome the shortcomings of the long-dominant "Western news" format, which tends to be oriented toward crises or other unusual events, relies on official (mostly powerful male) sources, and often contains little historical or other background. Moreover, development news assumed the role of shining a spotlight on the issues and processes in the lesser-developed nations, so often neglected by the giants of international news—Associated Press, Reuters, Agence France Press, and, at the time, United Press International. In terms of gender, however, Western and development news agencies—both of which were controlled and staffed mainly by male journalists—did little either to hire women or to cover women's concerns in the 1970s and 1980s. See C. Anthony Giffard, Carolyn M. Byerly, and Catherine Van Horn's unpublished report, "The World of Inter Press Service" (The Hague, Netherlands: International Association for Mass Communications Research, 1991); Margaret Gallagher, *Unequal Opportunities: The Case of Women and the Media* (Paris: UNESCO, 1981).

16. Byerly, "News, Consciousness and Social Participation" and "Countdown for Women's Feature Service."

17. Sharmila Joshi, "Only Men Live Here," WFS wire story (Mumbai, India), 21 May 1996.

18. Svitlana Bozhko, "Cash Strapped Workers Opt for Hazardous Jobs," WFS wire story (Kiev, Ukraine), 10 September 1996.

19. Joseph Avian, "Landmark Case Condemns Whistles at Work," WFS wire story (St. Joseph, Trinidad and Tobago), 30 April 1996.

20. Margaret Gallagher, *An Unfinished Story: Gender Patterns in Media Employment* (Paris: UNESCO, 1995); International Women's Media Foundation, *Women Reporting on International News*, June 1997.

INFORMATIONAL SOURCES

Byerly, Carolyn M. "Countdown for Women's Feature Service: Gender, News and Development in an Era of Globalization." Unpublished paper presented to the International Communication Association, Jerusalem, Israel, July 1998.

————. "News, Consciousness and Social Participation: The Role of Women's Feature Service in World News." In *Feminism, Multiculturalism and the Media: Global Diversities*, ed. A. N. Valdivia. Thousand Oaks, Calif.: Sage, 1995.

Ceulemans, Mieke, and Guido Fauconnier. *Mass Media: The Image, Role and Social Conditions of Women*. Paris: UNESCO, 1979.

Gallagher, Margaret. *Unequal Opportunities: The Case of Women and the Media*. Paris: UNESCO, 1981.

————. *An Unfinished Story: Gender Patterns in Media Employment*. Reports and Papers on Mass Communication, No. 110. Paris: UNESCO, 1995.

Giffard, C. Anthony, Carolyn M. Byerly, and Catherine Van Horn. "The World of Inter Press Service." The Hague, Netherlands: International Association for Mass Communication Research, 1991.

International Women's Media Foundation. *Women Reporting on International News*. Washington, D.C.: International Women's Media Foundation and Women's Foreign Policy Group, June 1997.

WFS Style Manual. New Delhi, India: Women's Feature Service, undated.

Women's Feature Service. *The Power to Change: Women in the Third World Redefine Their Environment*. New Delhi, India: Kali Press for Women, 1992.

INSTITUTIONAL PROFILE

Women's Feature Service

Dates: Founded and headquartered in Rome under sponsorship of Inter-Press Service in 1978; relocated headquarters to New Delhi, India, in 1990.

Purpose: To produce and disseminate stories about women, especially in developing nations.

Contacts: Anita Anand, Executive Director (1999), 1 Nizamudin East, New Delhi 110013, India; Gretchen Sidhu, North American Regional Coodinator (1999), 269 Varick St., no. 2-G, Jersey City, NJ 07302. To arrange for a weekly log of stories, contact Sidhu at <gsidhidhu@igc.org>

33

Donna Allen

Women's Institute for Freedom of the Press, 1972–Present

The Women's Institute for Freedom of the Press (WIFP) was founded in early 1972 by women activists in the peace, civil rights, civil liberties, and women's movements who had also worked in movement media or mass media. They recognized the need for media equality to enable everyone's information to be heard by the public, and they wished to focus on building a new, more democratic communications structure. According to their papers of incorporation in the District of Columbia as a nonprofit organization, their purpose was

to engage in research on all aspects of communication as they relate to implementing the purpose of the First Amendment of the United States Constitution in its provision for freedom of the press; to study ways in which freedom of the press may be extended to more Americans and expanded to cover more facets of American life; to inform women who have a special interest in the media of new developments in mass media ideas, actions, facts and philosophy as they relate to the freedom of the press; and to conduct seminars among such women that will examine the First Amendment principles underlying these developments and to work on an internship basis with individual women who wish to learn more about the application of the First Amendment to mass media communication, with particular attention to its structure, its technology, and the community and individual interest in a free press.[1]

The four women who signed the letters of incorporation were typical of the women involved in the creation of WIFP.[2] These four had some previous involvement with the media and had been active in social movements for some time. Margot Burman was an artist and photographer who made posters for peace movement organizations. Karen Lunquist was a writer for environmental and other movement publications and subsequently founded *The Girls and*

Women's Tai Kwan Do Newsletter, which she published for more than a decade. Donna Allen was active in the women's movement and had been a contributor to the early women's movement publication *No More Fun and Games*. Sara Altherr Reitz was a reporter at the *Washington Post*.

WIFP has never been a membership organization. Rather, its officers have directed and facilitated a number of projects and activities aimed at fulfilling the purpose stated in its papers of incorporation. Individuals can volunteer to participate in these activities and can subscribe to its various publications and reports. There are no membership fees; however, donations are accepted, and subscription fees were eventually charged for specific publications. Over the years WIFP has conducted studies, supervised internships, and issued a number of publications, notably *Media Report to Women* and *Directory of Women's Media*.

ACTIVITIES

It was no coincidence that WIFP arose when it did. By the early 1970s, new segments of the public were clamoring to be heard and were demanding a "media democracy." The World War II invention of the offset press had made publishing affordable to anyone. This relatively inexpensive technology made possible the rise of the underground press and the various presses of the many reform movements of the time, including the environmental, peace, civil rights, civil liberties, and women's movements. Through these publications society began to hear from people whose information had rarely been taken into account in the nation's decision making. The result was significant change in societal values.

A major goal of the women who established the WIFP was to build media networks as a first step to more democratic communications. Despite the possibilities offered by the offset press, they believed information from women was not reaching the public fast enough to change the stereotypes that supported inequalities facing not only media women, but all women. During the early 1970s, women working for print and broadcast media had begun to sue their employers for sex discrimination and to challenge the license renewals of broadcasters who discriminated against women in their hiring, compensation, and promotion policies. WIFP hastened the process by helping to get the word around about these actions through its publication *Media Report to Women*. WIFP also assisted women in becoming aware of and networking with other women's media outlets through its *Directory of Women's Media*.

MEDIA REPORT TO WOMEN

The first action taken by WIFP was to create a network through which women could raise and discuss their media issues. On June 15, 1972, it published the first issue of *Media Report to Women*, which carried the subtitle "Facts—Actions—Ideas—Philosophy." Although the group had no outside funding, Karen Lunquist and many other interested women scraped together enough to buy an Army surplus mimeograph machine for $125. At first WIFP had no regular publication schedule for *Media Report*. Whenever the women working on the publication were able to collect enough information about women's efforts to change the media to fill nine pages (which could be mailed at the cost of two first-class stamps), they would print and mail out a new edition.

The circulation list was decided in an equally uncomplicated manner; they sent *Media Report* free to all the women they knew who were working in the media or who were concerned about the media. This list expanded as other women saw the publication and asked to be added to the mailing list. Costs were minimal—less than $10 for envelopes, less than $50 for postage—and were covered by voluntary contributors who were interested in seeing this information get out. During this period, as in later years, WIFP acted in "movement style," that is, without formal structure. In 1974, *Media Report* began to list Donna Allen as its editor, since she was taking the primary responsibility in getting it out, but everyone available participated in its publication.

After WIFP had published three issues of *Media Report* in 1972 and three more in 1973, five hundred women were asking to receive the publication. This convinced the WIPF that it could publish the report on a regular basis and create a structure for subscriptions. WIPF decided to publish it monthly and charge a nominal subscription price to cover the cost of printing and postage—$10 per year for women and $15 for men ("until the ERA is ratified") and to those subscribing with institutional checks. The staff involved in putting together the publication was to remain voluntary.

The publication's circulation and content grew rapidly. Media women in the United States and other countries sent in information to spread the word about their own communication actions, which were not otherwise being reported in mass media. For example, in 1972, the members of the New York chapter of the National Organization for Women (NOW) sent in the text of their 1972 petition to the Federal Communications Commission to deny the license renewal of WABC-TV.[3] After their petition was published in *Media Report*, subsequent issues published stories about other license renewal challenges across the country, many of which were probably encouraged by knowledge of the NOW petition.

Media Report to Women illustrated the viability of the WIFP principle that people should speak for themselves, that their messages should be published in their own words. No one reported other people's information; there was no third person reporting. Each group or individual told their own stories; the stories about them that appeared in *Media Report* were made up of quotes from the source. This principle was reaffirmed in the following words, which *Media Report to Women* frequently included on page one: "The Women's Institute for

Freedom of the Press believes that the world's communications systems must be restructured—both by our daily media decisions and in our plans for the future—on the fundamental principle that people should speak for themselves."

The publication's impact was broadened as its circulation list expanded to include libraries and institutions. By the early 1980s, more than two hundred of its subscribers were journalism schools, women's studies programs, and general libraries with repository subscriptions that included all back issues as well as the annotated cumulative index that WIFP began publishing in 1974. In 1987, in anticipation of sizeable increases in typesetting costs that were greater than it could handle, WIFP sold *Media Report to Women* (for a nominal fee) to Communication Research Associates in Silver Spring, Maryland, an organization that had the resources necessary to continue its regular publication. There, under the direction of Sheila Gibbons and Ray Hiebert, it is published quarterly and continues to report on issues of concern to women.[4]

OTHER PUBLICATIONS AND RESOURCES

WIFP also expanded its impact through its close cooperative relationship with the Association for Education in Journalism and Mass Communication (AEJMC), of which Donna Allen was a member, and through the publication in 1977 of two other important resources. These were the *Syllabus Sourcebook on Women and Media*, edited by WIFP vice president Dana Densmore, and *Women in Media: A Documentary Sourcebook*, edited by Maurine Beasley and Sheila Gibbons of the University of Maryland. This text was used widely in journalism courses and courses in women and the media. Beasley and Gibbons created it to meet the lack of information about women in journalism they encountered when teaching a course on women and media.[5]

In 1977, a group of women who were making the kind of progress for women that was regularly reported in *Media Report to Women* formed a "WIFP Associates" network. Their goal was to work together and as individuals for the WIFP goals they shared. The Associates network grew to more than eight hundred women who worked for the media or were interested in how the media covered women and their concerns. Each of the associates signed a slip indicating her agreement with the "WIFP Associates Statement," which is printed on the back of all WIFP stationery and in the 1978, 1979, and 1983 editions of the *Directory of Women's Media*. It reads, in part:

Women are increasingly becoming dissatisfied with the inadequacies of the present structures. We seek improvements both through expanding women-owned media and through our equal presence in other media at all levels—in employment, in news coverage, and in the accurate reflection of our abilities and our political, economic, and social options. We are working together to register our unity, to aid each other's media efforts, and to increase the resources allocated to constructive changes that move us toward equality between men and women in our ability to reach the whole public. . . . For women to continue to make progress, it is essential that we expand the outreach of women's information.[6]

A women's media structure was rapidly building itself. Compared to the 1950s, when there were virtually no women-owned media except occasional membership newsletters published by women's organizations, the number of women's media had grown to the hundreds by the 1980s. *Media Report to Women* offered exchanges with these publications and checked their contents for items about women in the media and women's media it could use in its own pages. It reported topics as varied as the creation of a new women's health periodical, the progress of a group analyzing mass media coverage of women's news, studies made of the role of women in film, and new women's recording companies. These items used the exact words used by the women's paper in which they had appeared and always provided the name and address of the source.

Because the number of women's publications was growing so rapidly, WIFP decided to create a directory listing these many women's groups and publications. The job was taken on by Martha Leslie Allen, who since 1969 had been working in the South in the civil rights movement and had founded a women's media organization in Memphis that successfully increased the number of women and minorities in broadcast hiring in that city. Convinced that a women's media network was key to achieving media democracy and thus key to all other issues of importance to people, Allen moved to Washington to become a major contributor to WIFP and to create its *Directory of Women's Media*.

In keeping with WIFP's belief that people should speak for themselves, Allen did not "list" individuals and organizations to be included in the *Directory*. Rather, if they wanted to be in it, they had to request a listing and supply the information each year. Over the years, the number of groups and individuals requesting a listing grew dramatically. The first issue of the *Directory*, published January 1, 1975, recorded the existence of 154 women's periodicals (130 of which were published in the United States); by 1989, it listed 702, with more than 300 published in countries outside the United States.

Similar growth was reflected in other forms of the media. For example, the 1975 *Directory* listed only twenty-four women's presses and publishers (three of which were in other countries); the 1989 edition listed 111, with 30 in other countries. The three women's news services that were listed in 1975 grew to eleven in 1989; twenty-four women's music groups listed in 1975 grew to fifty-five by 1989; twenty-six women's art, graphics or theater groups in 1975 increased to sixty by 1989, and the forty-five women's bookstores listed in 1975 numbered ninety in the 1989 *Directory*. In 1989, more than five hundred individuals listed themselves in the "Media Women and Media-Concerned Women" section. A dozen other media categories, such as radio, TV, film, and speakers bureaus, also showed similar growth figures from 1975 to 1989. In 1990, WIFP passed the job of publishing the

Directory to the National Council for Research on Women in New York City, which published further editions, in 1992 and 1994.[7]

Women's publications also began exchanges among each other, enabling, for example, the *Maine Freewoman's Herald* to report women's news found in *The Feminist Bulletin*, a San Diego women's paper—or in papers published outside the United States. Newly established women's news services, such as Her Say and the Associated Women's Press, also helped cross-circulate women's news.

It can be said that the women's movement created itself through the communications structure it built. This women's media movement grew without mass media's recognition or, more realistically, perhaps, because mass media ignored the issues women's own media were reporting, speaking for themselves. It was women raising issues in their own media, however, that eventually forced society—and mass media—to address these issues. For example, violence against women was ignored almost entirely by the mass media until women had succeeded through their various media and activities, such as conferences and lobbying, in making it a subject of legislation. Thus, once it became a "legitimate" topic for coverage, it began to appear in news stories. Similarly, women's media spread the word about sexual harassment; when the number of sexual harassment lawsuits had increased significantly, this also became a news story in mass media.

PROJECTS

By the late 1980s, WIFP began to refocus its energies toward projects that dealt more directly with its goal of restructuring the communications media. The results of one of these appeared in the last WIFP edition of the *Directory*, published in 1989—a thirty-page section by Martha Allen entitled "Women Working toward a Radical Restructuring of the Communications System." This was Allen's analysis of the material published in *Media Report to Women* for the last fifteen years that led her to believe that women's media had certain unique characteristics that were different from men's media. Allen found eight such different qualities and provided nine pages of examples of each characteristic taken directly from women's papers.[8]

In 1990, WIFP began to publish a booklet series, *Looking toward a Radical Restructuring of the Communications Media*. The goal of the series was to stimulate thinking about women's media in relation to mass media and how their own media based on people speaking for themselves was beginning to change the world's communications systems to a more democratic structure. By 1998, five booklets had been published: *Media without Democracy and What to Do about It; What's Wrong with Mass Media for the Women Half of the Population—Re-building the System; The Media Technology Road to Democracy and Equality; The Source of Power for Women: A Strategy to Equalize Media Outreach*; and one on a solution to the campaign spending problem, *A National Citizens' Network of Radio and Television*.

WIFP also organized seminars in Washington, D.C. These covered a long list of topics such as the philosophy of the First Amendment, cable and public access television, license challenges and other community actions, satellite communication, public broadcasting, proposed legislation, problems of the print media, discrimination in media employment, the creation of stereotypes, and the structure of the communications industry. In addition, WIFP has run an internship program since 1972 and has had a steady stream of interns from this country as well as from a dozen other countries. Each intern has undertaken a publishable research project on women and media, documenting the causal relationship between women having a means of communication and the progress they make politically, legislatively, economically, or socially toward a more democratic communications media structure. Two examples of such studies published by WIFP are Kimberlie A. Kranich's "Celebrating Diversity / Women of Color Periodicals: 1968–1988" (published in the 1989 *Directory of Women's Media*) and Hearly Mayr's *Muslim Women and the Cyberspace Revolution*, published as a WIFP booklet in 1997.[9]

In 1978, WIFP conducted the first of seven annual conferences entitled "An Annual Conference on Planning a National and International Communications System for Women." The first six of these were held at and with the assistance of the National Press Club in Washington, D.C., which at the time had just admitted women to membership and was eager to show it no longer discriminated against women. Attendance at these conferences steadily grew in size with, for example, the April 1982 conference attended by 124 women from thirty-two countries. Out of these conferences grew several projects from women who had communications technology foremost in their minds. This was an interest that was shared by WIFP, which knew how key new technologies were to making women's voices be heard. In 1973, for example, WIFP worked with women in several cities, first to establish a cable TV channel for women, and then to form a Women's Cable Television Clearinghouse. In 1977, WIFP worked with the 109 women's organizations of the National Women's Agenda on a proposal to seek a NASA-sponsored experimental satellite.

In 1980, WIPF acted on one of the most ambitious new technology conference ideas. It conducted four hours of international interactive teleconferencing by satellite between women gathered in six U.S. cities and women who were official delegates from Third World countries to the Second U.N. World Conference on Women in Copenhagen, Denmark. Five years later, the technology was no longer new, but at the next UN World Conference on Women held in Nairobi, WIFP organized four more hours of teleconference time between Third World official delegates and women gathered in U.S. cities and several other countries.[10] By 1998, new technology work by WIFP focused on women's use of the electronic media and the World Wide Web.

NETWORKING WITH OTHER ORGANIZATIONS

Especially important to WIFP has been its work with other organizations seeking media change, such as the Minority Media and Telecommunications

Council and the Cultural Environment Movement, as well as other women's organizations. Some of the women's organizations it has worked with include women's media organizations such as Women in Communications, Inc. (WICI),* Journalism and Women Symposium (JAWS),* the International Women and Media Foundation, American Women in Radio and Television (AWRT),* and the National Federation of Press Women (NFPW).*

In working with general women's organizations, WIFP has focused on the media aspects of their work. This included, for example, work during 1997–99 with dozens of women's organizations to create a U.S. organization of women's nongovernmental organizations that would serve as a national communications system for all women. Initially named U.S. Women Connect, this organization was still in the planning stage in 1999.

WIFP has contributed its philosophy of media equality and democracy in working with other organizations on shared concerns such as freedom from violence, pay equity and affirmative action, equal political representation, and elimination of racism. Thus, over the years, WIFP has shared resources with women's organizations such as the National Council of Women's Organizations, the National Woman's Party, the Feminist Majority, the National Organization for Women, the Young Women's Christian Association, National Women's Political Caucus, National Council of Negro Women, Business and Professional Women's Clubs, National Women's Conference, and the Women's Vote Project. This cooperation has at times included sharing the expertise of WIFP interns. In one such case, in 1997, an intern helped a sister organization, the National Women's Conference, build a World Wide Web page.

Most recently, WIFP has worked with Women Leaders Online and its media network, news and discussion groups, and electronic Women's Voting Guide, a project that has been of particular concern in light of WIFP's belief that the new technology has the potential of making possible significant advances toward media democracy.

Future areas of WIFP concentration will focus on expanding women's use of new technology in all forms of media as the most promising way to carry out the goals for which WIFP was founded: to enable everyone to be heard speaking directly to the public rather than having to go through others. The new technology offers exciting opportunities that are increasingly being utilized in ways that result in a more viable and democratic society for everyone.

NOTES

1. District of Columbia Articles of Incorporation, 17 May 1973. The board of directors throughout the 1980s and 1990s has consisted of Donna Allen, president; Dana Densmore, Indra Dean Allen, and Paula Kassell, vice presidents; Martha Leslie Allen, secretary and WIFP director; and Karen Lunquist, treasurer.

2. That these four were the women to sign the papers of incorporation was purely circumstantial. They were closest to the Washington, D.C., courthouse, where the papers were filed, and all were available at the same time.

3. *Media Report to Women*, 15 June 1972, pp. 5–8.

4. Editor's note: In spring 1999, Communication Research Associates relocated to Colton's Point, Maryland.

5. In 1989, the American Journalism Historians Association recognized WIFP work with an award to its president Donna Allen "For Her Efforts to Preserve Documents Important to the History of American Journalism."

6. See, for example, "Associates Statement," in Martha Leslie Allen, ed., *1983 Index Directory of Women's Media* (Washington, D.C.: Women's Institute for Freedom of the Press, 1983), p. 44.

7. WIFP had published the *Directory* on an IBM typesetting machine that was phased out by IBM in the late 1980s. Without the typesetter, and lacking the funds to purchase new typesetting machinery, WIFP found it impractical to continue to publish the *Directory*.

8. These points are discussed at length in Allen's dissertation. See Martha Allen, "The Development of Communication Networks among Women, 1963–1983" (Ph.D. diss., Howard University, 1988).

9. Kranich was a graduate student in journalism at Northwestern University who spent a five-week internship with WIFP in summer 1988. Mayr was a graduate student in journalism at Columbia Union College in Takoma Park, Maryland.

10. The satellite time for these conferences was contributed by Comsat in 1980 and by Intelsat in 1985.

INFORMATIONAL SOURCES

Beasley, Maurine H. and Sheila J. Gibbons, ed. *Women in Media: A Documentary Source Book*. Washington, D.C.: Women's Institute for Freedom of the Press, 1977.

Directory of Women's Media. Annual editions 1975–89. Editions through 1987 titled *Index/Directory of Women's Media*. Washington, D.C.: Women's Institute for Freedom of the Press.

The First Annual Conference on Planning a National and International Communications System for Women: A Report. Report on conference held 7–8 April 1979 at the National Press Club, Washington, D.C.

Five Year Index to Media Report of Women, Annotated Index of Media Activities and Research, 1972–76; 1977–81; 1982–87; 1987. Washington, D.C.: Women's Institute for Freedom of the Press.

Media Report to Women, What Women Are Doing and Thinking about the Communications Media, 1972 to present, passim.

INSTITUTIONAL PROFILE

Women's Institute for Freedom of the Press

Dates: Founded February 1972, Washington, D.C.

Officers: Dr. Donna Allen, founder and president (1972–1999). Dr. Martha Leslie Allen, director (1975–present).

Primary Publication: *Media Report to Women*, 1972–87. Publication of *Media Report to Women*, was assumed by Communication Research Associates, Silver Spring, Maryland, in 1987 and continues to be published quarterly.

Archives: WIFP Papers, National Women and Media Collection, Western Historical Manuscripts Collection, Ellis Library, University of Missouri, Columbia, Missouri.

Address: 3306 Ross Place, N.W., Washington, D.C. 20008–3332, tel. and fax (202) 966–7783; e-mail: <wifponline@igc.apc.org>, Web site: <http://www.igc.org/wifp/>.

34

Maurine H. Beasley

Women's National Press Club, 1919–1970

During the middle decades of the twentieth century, the Women's National Press Club (WNPC), located in Washington, D.C., brought together an elite corps of women journalists who strived for recognition in a male-dominated occupation. With Eleanor Roosevelt its most prominent member, before and during World War II the club played an influential role in the nation's capital, both publicizing the achievements of its members and recognizing the accomplishments of women of distinction. Founded in 1919 as an outgrowth of the suffrage movement, the club provided a social and professional outlet for women journalists who were excluded from the National Press Club (NPC), where male journalists, along with publicists and lobbyists, gathered news by meeting with national and world leaders. The WNPC club offered visibility to Washington women journalists and allowed them to band together to seek the same access to news sources as men journalists had. Although some of its members—notably Eileen Shanahan of the *New York Times* and Peggy Simpson of the Associated Press—covered the women's movement of the 1960s, the club itself did not embrace broad feminist concerns but attempted to uphold the ideal of journalists as neutral observers.

With the advent of equal opportunity legislation that brought greater participation of women in the journalistic workforce, the WNPC ceased operation as a woman-only organization. In December 1970 it voted to admit men and changed its name to the Washington Press Club (WPC). A month later the men-only NPC voted, 227 to 56, after a bitter struggle, to accept applications from women and admitted an initial twenty-four. Both press clubs operated until 1985, when the WPC, which then had five hundred members, merged with the NPC. An outcome of the merger was the creation of the Washington Press Club Foundation to promote equality and excellence in journalism. One of its projects has been the collection of oral histories of some sixty pioneer women journalists.

The preservation of this historical material has been a fitting tribute to the WNPC, an organization that gave women journalists, many of whom were limited to writing either women's feature stories for general news sections or material specifically for women's and society pages, a sense of professional identity at a time when their male colleagues refused to accept them as equals. The WNPC provided psychological support to enhance members' feelings of self-worth as they fought discrimination and created their own forum for meeting with newsmakers, socializing, and advancing their careers. Although the WNPC and its successor group never had more than a fraction of the members of the NPC (which numbered 4,673 for its golden anniversary in 1958), the WNPC offered an alternative to the isolation of individual women fighting personal battles to be taken seriously. Not all members were journalists, however; some were publicists, the term given those involved in public relations work in the early decades of the twentieth century. To maintain the news orientation of the club, women in public relations were not allowed to become president and were accepted only on the basis of one to every two journalists admitted.

ORGANIZATION

Six women—three who wrote for newspapers, and three who were publicists for the National Woman's Party, the militant arm of the suffrage movement—founded the WNPC in 1919. The most distinguished of the newspaperwomen, Cora Rigby, highly-regarded bureau chief for the *Christian Science Monitor*, was known for her dignified manner and professional accomplishment. Joining with her were Carolyn Vance Bell, who wrote features for the Newspaper Enterprise Association, and Elizabeth King (later Stokes), a reporter for the *New York Evening Post*.

The publicists were Florence Brewer Boeckel, Eleanor Taylor Marsh Nelson, and Alice Gram Robinson, who were seeking new clients after Congress passed the Nineteenth Amendment in June 1919, and it appeared certain that women would get the right to vote. The three had formed a partnership to handle news for the Visiting Nurses Association and other women's groups and wanted to stay in close touch with the women journalists whom they had gotten to know during the suffrage campaign. The organizational meeting for the WNPC was held at their Washington office on September 27, but in later years it was Bell who took credit for originating the idea of the club to facilitate useful contact between women in the news field.[1]

All the founders except Robinson signed a letter of invitation sent to women who worked for newspapers, news bureaus, and government publicity operations. Nothing was said about bringing together journalists and publicists. Instead, the letter noted that proposed club meetings could provide "an opportunity to hear more intimately than we otherwise could, prominent men and women who come to Washington."[2] The wording represented an indirect protest against the policy of the NPC that barred women from covering its speakers. When the women chose their club name, it was obvious they intended to set up their own parallel group.

Some forty women attended the organizational meeting. Bell, who was pregnant, did not attend, since it was considered shameful at the time for expectant mothers to show themselves in public. Only twenty-eight out of the forty joined the group at first, apparently because some journalists feared their professional independence might be compromised if they were in the same organization with publicity writers.

Over the years the WNPC grew slowly with about 150 members on its rolls in the 1930s. It continued to accept women whose work in public relations brought them in regular contact with the press, but these individuals played secondary roles within the organization. Membership requirements were rigorous, designed to exclude part-time workers and those considered dabblers at the journalistic craft. The club, which excluded men, offered active membership to "reputable publishers, editors, writers, correspondents and reporters, actively engaged in Washington on well-established newspapers, press associations or periodicals including government publications, and deriving therefrom all or the greater part of their income."[3] Members who stopped newspaper or publicity work could remain in the club only on a nonvoting status pending reinstatement if they renewed their press connections.

The club's structure was put in place at its first luncheon-business meeting held at a restaurant on November 6, 1919. Cora Rigby was made honorary president, and Lily Lykes Rowe (later Shepard), a correspondent for the *New York Times*, active president. A year later Rigby took over as active president, a position she held until 1926. Among the most outspoken early members was Winifred Mallon, the first woman political writer hired by the Washington bureau of the *New York Times*, who believed the club was needed to fight against male attempts to diminish the importance of women on newspapers. She became president in 1935.[4]

Patterning itself after the NPC, the women's group held luncheon gatherings featuring speakers of note. The first guest, Margaret Bondfield, a British labor leader, appeared on November 13, 1919. At a subsequent luncheon, Lowell Thomas, the world-famous traveler, told of his experiences with Lawrence of Arabia. Unlike the NPC, which owned an impressive building near the White House, the WNPC was never able to afford its own clubhouse. Sessions were held at restaurants, hotels, and the headquarters of women's groups like the American Association of University Women. In later years it used office space in the NPC building even though members were barred from the actual men's club itself.

When Warren G. Harding, owner of the *Marion* (Ohio) *Star*, was elected U.S. President in 1920, the fledgling NWPC enjoyed special privileges. Harding's wife, Florence, who had managed the newspaper and was comfortable with journalists, invited the group for a cruise on the presidential yacht and entertained them at a White House tea. Camaraderie developed among WNPC members, as expressed in these verses written by Frances Parkinson Keyes, Washington correspondent for *Good Housekeeping* and later a best-selling novelist, at a luncheon in her honor before she left on a trip around the world in May 1925:

> Remember too I shall return
> From Athens, Naples, and Lucerne;
> From castles I have found in Spain—
> And then I'll see you all again,
> Whenever I can get the chance.
> For Persia, Palestine, and France
> Can give me nothing much, I guess,
> That I'll love better than the Press
> Club, so for Monday lunch
> I'll soon be back here with the bunch;
> And don't let anybody cry
> Because I now must say goodbye.[5]

A SPLIT IN THE RANKS

Although important to the group as a whole, social events were taken more seriously by some of the members than others. Those employed on society pages found them of greater interest, both professionally and personally, than women who wanted to focus on luncheons with serious speakers. This led to the alienation of a group of society reporters who withdrew from the WNPC in 1932. Margaret Hart and Katharine M. Brooks, both society reporters for the *Washington Evening Star*, co-founded the rival Newspaper Women's Club. Fourteen women, all employed on Washington's four major newspapers, were listed as organizing members.

In contrast to the WNPC, which prided itself on restricting membership to full-time journalists and publicists, the new group established a special associate member category for prominent women who were prime sources of women's and society news. In addition, an honorary membership category was established for women known either in their own right or as the wives of important men. The organization eventually bought a clubhouse near Washington's famous Embassy Row and remains in existence today as the American News Women's Club with a membership that includes women in public relations. In spite of some hostility, the clubs eventually had considerable overlapping membership.

The WNPC remained the domain of the women who covered general news, were associated with major newspapers, and competed directly with men. Its rolls read like a "Who's Who" of Washington women journalists, with many of its members establishing notable records of journalistic accomplishment in spite of the prevailing prejudice against women. Among its presidents, for example, were Genevieve Forbes Herrick (1933), a correspondent for the *Chicago Tribune*; Doris Fleeson (1937), a political columnist for the *New York Daily News*; and Esther Van Wagoner Tufty (1941), who ran her own news bureau.

INFLUENCE OF ELEANOR ROOSEVELT

As first lady from 1933 to 1945, Eleanor Roosevelt formed close ties with club members. Many of them attended her press conferences that were limited to women only so news organizations would be compelled to hire newspaperwomen to cover them.[6] Unlike Grace Coolidge and Lou Henry Hoover, her immediate predecessors in the White House, Roosevelt accepted invitations to the club's annual "stunt parties," elaborate theatrical affairs that started during the Coolidge administration. These events, which satirized Washington politics, were similar to the male-only Gridiron Club dinners traditionally attended by the president.[7]

The subject of much "stunt party" humor, Eleanor Roosevelt joked with club members and gave off-the-record reactions to their satire, which influenced her actions on at least one occasion. After she was lampooned in a 1933 skit called "Babies, Just Babies," she gave up editorship of a magazine for new mothers with that name. The skit made fun of the inexperience of the new Roosevelt administration, beginning, "We are new to the business of running the show. We're babies, just babies, just babies."[8]

Special invitations to the "stunt parties" went to women members of Congress and famous women like Amelia Earhart and Margaret Sanger. The events displayed the members' creativity and presence on the capital scene. With the exception of the war years, they continued until 1963, when they were dropped because club members were too busy with their careers and other activities to devote time to them. Apparently because its members were so involved with their jobs, the club did not have a journal or formal newsletter, although it issued press releases and sent announcements to its members.

In 1938 club members voted to accept Roosevelt herself as an active member on the basis that she was a professional journalist because for two years she had written a daily syndicated, diarylike column, "My Day." Fleeson proposed her for membership and was seconded by Ruby Black, who owed her job as the first woman hired by the United Press to Roosevelt's refusal to admit men to her press conferences. Also seconding the motion was Bess Furman, an Associated Press reporter who worked for the *New York Times* and became WNPC president in 1945. Nine votes were cast against Roosevelt's admission, presumably because she did not conform to the club requirement that membership was limited to those who earned most of their living by writing. When Roosevelt's name came up for membership, Black, who was WNPC president in 1939, had to deny erroneous rumors that she was the first lady's "ghost writer." A strong admirer of the first lady, Black wrote Roosevelt's first biography (1940).

Roosevelt's involvement helped increase the organization's visibility in Washington. In 1941, on the eve of World War II, President Franklin D. Roosevelt spoke to the group on the part women could play in the national defense effort. This occasion marked the first luncheon President Roosevelt had attended since he arrived in Washington eight years earlier. In 1943 Elmer Davis, director of the Office of War Information, chose to appear before the WNPC apparently to make amends to the press after he had criticized Washington journalists for paying too much attention to bureaucratic bickering.

Following World War II, which led to an expansion of opportunities for women journalists in Washington, WNPC membership rose, reaching more than four hundred by 1960, including broadcasters, who first were admitted in 1944. Presidents Truman, Eisenhower, Kennedy, Johnson, and Nixon, along with foreign dignitaries and candidates for high office, attended WNPC functions as well as those of the far larger NPC. In 1946 the women's group decided to allow men to cover its annual dinner, but a quarter century more elapsed before gender restrictions in press club memberships finally disappeared.

THE FIGHT TO END DISCRIMINATION

The issue of eliminating discrimination in membership first arose in connection with efforts to desegregate both clubs. A petition to admit women to the NPC was circulated in 1955 by a NPC member opposed to the admission of the club's first African American member, Louis Lautier of the National Negro Press Association. Lautier, nevertheless, was elected by a majority vote with supporters contending the club was a professional, not a social, organization. About the same time the WNPC accepted its first African American member, Alice A. Dunnigan of the Associated Negro Press.

Responding to the NPC petition, the NWPC president, Elizabeth Carpenter, a *Houston Post* correspondent who later became press secretary to Lady Bird Johnson, maintained that women had no strong desire to become NPC members. She took this position because club members did not want to be associated with the move to keep African American journalists out of the NPC. The clubs then tried to work out a compromise agreement that would allow women to cover NPC luncheon speakers.

This led to an infamous arrangement that confined women journalists to the balcony overlooking the club dining area, where they could watch, but not join, their male colleagues as they lunched prior to hearing speeches by leading figures. Women journalists were allowed to eat alongside the men only once—in 1959 after Soviet Premier Nikita S. Khrushchev stated he would not speak at the NPC unless women journalists were given the same privileges as men. After Khrushchev's appearance, however, the women had no option but to return to the crowded balcony, where they could not hear well and had no chance to ask questions.

In 1962 women journalists received support from President John F. Kennedy when they protested against being relegated to the balcony during a speech by

Jawaharlal Nehru, prime minister of India. Kennedy said at a press conference that he personally believed all reporters should be permitted into the NPC on a basis of equality to cover a state visitor. In reply, the WNPC president, Bonnie Angelo, a *Time Magazine* correspondent, criticized the U.S. State Department for arranging for heads of state to speak at the NPC because of its discriminatory policy toward women.

The following year the NWPC president, Elsie Carper, a *Washington Post* reporter, expressed outrage when another woman reporter for the *Post* was taken off a civil rights story because she was not allowed to cover a press conference at the NPC. Subsequently, Carper and Frances Lewine, an Associated Press reporter and former WNPC president, brought pressure on Harold Wilson, head of the British Labour Party, not to speak at the NPC on a forthcoming trip to the United States. Carper and Lewine sent cables to women in Parliament who were members of the British Labour Party asking that they urge Wilson to boycott the NPC. In response, the prime minister announced that he would speak at the British embassy instead. Although some members of the WNPC objected to what they viewed as Carper's unladylike tactics, the protests were ultimately were successful.

Prompted by Elizabeth Carpenter, President Lyndon B. Johnson, following his election in 1964, directed the U.S. State Department to inform the NPC that either it allow women journalists to cover speakers on the same basis as men or visiting dignitaries would no longer would be scheduled there. At that point the club agreed to permit women reporters to attend its luncheons, although it wanted them to use a back door. The women refused to do so, however, and entered the club through the front door. Their steps forward marked a symbolic end to the need for a separate women's organization. The passing of the WNPC from the capital scene in 1970 testified to its success in leading the way for women to be fully accepted as Washington journalists.

NOTES

1. Carolyn Vance Bell, "Founding," typescript, 1968, pp. 4, 7, Women's National Press Club Files (hereafter referred to as WNPC Files), Cora Rigby Archives, National Press Club, Washington, D.C.

2. Typed copy of open letter, 23 September 1919, WNPC Files.

3. WNPC membership qualifications as listed in 1924 directory, WNPC Files, box 32.

4. Winfred Mallon, "The Whole Truth, As Far As It Goes about Us," typescript, July 1937, p. 1, WNPC Files, box 23.

5. Frances Parkinson Keyes Papers, box 1, Special Collections, Tulane University Library, New Orleans.

6. Eleanor Roosevelt, *This I Remember* (New York: Harper & Brothers, 1947), p. 102.

7. The exclusive Gridiron Club, made up of a select number of leading Washington journalists, did not accept women until 1974.

8. Joseph P. Lash, *Eleanor and Franklin* (New York: Signet, 1971), p. 494.

INFORMATIONAL SOURCES

Beasley, Maurine H. "The Women's National Press Club: A Case Study of Professional Aspirations." *Journalism History* 15, no. 4 (winter 1988): 112–21.
Black, Ruby. *Eleanor Roosevelt: A Biography.* New York: Duell, Sloan and Pearce, 1940.
Furman, Bess. *Washington By-Line.* New York: Alfred A. Knopf, 1949.
Women's National Press Club Papers, Archives of the National Press Club, 529 14th St., N.W., Washington, DC. 20045.

INSTITUTIONAL PROFILE

Women's National Press Club

Dates: Founded September 1919, Washington, D.C.; ceased operation as a woman-only group in 1970 when it became the **Washington Press Club**; merged with the National Press Club in 1985. At the time of merger the Washington Press Club Foundation was created to promote equality and excellence in journalism.

35

Kathleen L. Endres

Women's Press Organizations in Cleveland, 1886–1970s

INTRODUCTION

Founded in 1886, the Cleveland Woman's Press Club was the first women's press organization to be established in Ohio. In its more than eighty-year existence, this writers organization changed its name, character, and constituency several times, conforming to the needs of its members as well as the changing climate of the times.

In 1889, for example, it merged with the Cincinnati Women's Press Club* to form the Ohio Woman's Press Association (OWPA),* though it kept its own leadership and continued to hold its own activities as the Cleveland Branch of the OWPA. This union was dissolved in 1912 when the group changed its name to the Cleveland Women's Press Club. During the next decade, the group apparently split into two organizations, the Cleveland Women's Press Club and the Cleveland Writers' Club, a distinction that apparently separated journalists from authors of fiction and poetry, though several members over the years "crossed the lines."

Both these organizations thrived through the 1920s and early 1930s, but the Cleveland Women's Press Club disappears from the historical record after 1937. The Cleveland Writers' Club, instead, which came to include men as members, remained active until the mid-1970s. This chapter traces how the Cleveland Woman's Press Club and the organizations it spawned contributed to the professional climate for women writers in Ohio.

THE CLEVELAND WOMAN'S PRESS CLUB

The 1880s were a time of enormous energy and creativity in the city of Cleveland. This energy and creativity were especially evident in two areas—the literary and publishing arena and the women's social and benevolent community. Those two venues coalesced in 1886 to create the first women's press club in both the city and the state, the Cleveland Woman's Press Club. Three groups of women—newspaperwomen, "occasional contributors" to newspapers and magazines, and book authors—joined together to create this organization.

By the 1880s, the three largest dailies in the city—the *Leader*, the *Plain Dealer*, and the *Press*—had hired a small but growing cadre of women journalists who covered society and benevolent news for their "women's sections." Gertrude Van Rensselaer Wickham, probably the first woman to hold an editorial position on a Cleveland newspaper, had been a popular columnist at the *Leader*. Sarah Holden Bierce, sister of L. E. Holden, editor and publisher of the *Plain Dealer*, worked for that paper, as did Estella Bone, editor of the popular newspaper column "Family Council."

But that cadre of women newspaper journalists was not large enough to start a professional organization. They needed the additional backing of women who carried the title of "occasional contributor," women who were essayists for religious papers and out-of-town newspapers and magazines. Typical of this group of writers were women like Harriet Arey, a contributor to the *Boston Transcript* and *Boston Traveler*, and Mrs. M. C. Hickman, a contributor to the *New York Advocate* and *Pittsburgh Advocate*, who submitted stories and essays periodically to newspapers and magazines while continuing in their principal occupations as wives/mothers or teachers.

Another group of women who joined the press club also maintained a twofold designation, that of book author and wife/mother or teacher. Mrs. J. R. Bell, author of the *W.C.T.U. Mother Goose*, was typical of this group.

Until 1886, Wickham, Bierce, Bone, Arey, Hickman, Bell, and the other women who became charter members of the Cleveland Woman's Press Club worked independently in this city of about 190,000. Aside from their immediate circle of friends and relatives, they received little guidance, advice, or moral support in their professional pursuits. But then an out-of-towner brought these women focus and unity. She was Marion McBride of the *Boston Post*, who had helped organize the National Woman's Press Association in 1885.[1] It is unclear why McBride was in the city or how great a role she played in organizing the group, that is, whether she merely suggested the idea or took a more active role.[2] Nonetheless, after her visit to Cleveland in 1886, ten women joined together to create the Cleveland Woman's Press Club. From this early start of ten women committed to improving themselves, the club grew and evolved.

For two years the Cleveland Woman's Press Club was the only woman-based press association in the state. Women across northern Ohio—from Toledo and Ashtabula to Bellfontaine and Berea—joined the Cleveland organization. The first president, Harriet Arey, was an occasional contributor to Boston and Cleveland newspapers, the author of two books—*Household Songs: And Other Poems*, published in 1855, and *Home and School Training*, published in 1884—

and a teacher, mother, and widow.[3] Arey remained president six years, through the club's first shift in direction—and its first change of name.

OHIO WOMAN'S PRESS ASSOCIATION, CLEVELAND BRANCH

The latter half of the 1880s saw the establishment of women's press organizations in many states, with sometimes more than one in a single state or city. Ohio was no exception, and in 1888, the Cincinnati Women's Press Club* was organized. The next year the Cincinnati and Cleveland clubs merged to form OWPA—the Ohio Woman's Press Association. The first meeting of this group was held in Cleveland following the Ohio Woman Suffrage Association, indicating perhaps that at least some of OWPA's founders were active in the suffrage movement. About twenty-five to thirty women attended that first OWPA meeting and were wined and dined by L. E. Holden, the millionaire proprietor of the *Plain Dealer* and the brother of Sarah Bierce, a charter member of the original Woman's Press Club of Cleveland. The membership of the new organization cut across generations. As one reporter explained, some members were "mere girls" with youthful enthusiasm, whereas other members were older, "more somber ones who have fought life's battle to its meridian, and even beyond."[4]

Although the Cincinnati and Cleveland branches shared a single name, they retained their own leadership and programming and, in effect, were distinct organizations. The Cleveland Branch worked to achieve a practical end to help the press club's membership with their work, "giving help to the Novelist, the Essayist, the Poet, the Reviewer, etc."[5] Those aims illustrated that the Cleveland Branch always had a strong literary base. Notwithstanding the name of the OWPA, newspaper and/or other forms of nonfiction writing often took a secondary position within the new organization. Both the membership and the programming seemed to suggest this. Of the fifty members in 1890, for example, only thirteen were on editorial staffs or were regular contributors to periodicals, and the book authors (ten) and the "occasional contributors" dominated the group. The programming for the year also reflected that strong literary bent—as well as an interest in current affairs.

The Cleveland Branch met every month at some member's home and discussed everything from the "Moral Responsibility of the Novelist" to "Elements of Success in Fiction," from the "Dismemberment of Poland" to "Catharine of Russia" and the "Siberian Exile System." Not that nonfiction was ignored. Wickham of the *Cleveland Leader*, for example, provided an overview of "The Newspaper Press," and another member offered perspectives on "The Work of the Reviewer." Each presentation was a paper prepared by the member, who did the research on the topic. Sometimes the papers were so good that the members submitted them for publication in newspapers or magazines.

That literary emphasis continued when Linda Thayer Guilford, a popular teacher, city activist, author of *The Story of a Cleveland School from 1848–1881*, and "occasional contributor" to newspapers and magazines, took over as president of the Cleveland Branch of the OWPA when Arey left the city.[6] Guilford was the retired principal of the prestigious Cleveland Academy and had developed a network of friends through her various civic activities, especially those of the Women's Christian Temperance Union (WCTU). Although not one of the organization's charter members, Guilford certainly had the energy and imagination to lead the group and its programming. The Cleveland Branch's activism during her presidency reflected that energy and imagination.

Programs continued to emphasize literary topics and current affairs. Members continued to provide the greatest number of presentations—with topics such as "Harriet Beecher Stowe and Women in American Fiction," "Fiction and Fiction Making," and "The Literary Style and How to Attain It"—but outside speakers and experts offered their perspectives as well. In 1892, for example, *Cleveland Herald* editor John C. Covert talked about "General Newspaper Work" and historian Dr. Elroy M. Avery lectured on "How to Use a Library." Sometimes this guidance came by way of a letter. Harper Brothers offered "What the Public Wants in Fiction," and Mrs. M. E. Songster, an editor at *Harper's*, provided her perspectives on "What the Editor Wants in Fiction." Other members dealt with current issues and events, with topics such as "The Chinese Question" and "The Modern Blue Stocking." Under Guilford's leadership, the organization also reached out to make its presence felt across the nation. In 1890, OWPA helped organize the mixed-sex International League of Press Clubs.

The Cleveland Branch had a reputation for "exclusiveness," according to one newspaper story.[7] Although general guidelines for membership do not suggest this, the procedure for membership does. Membership was open to "any reputable writer, author or journalist," but each woman had to be nominated by three members and had to receive approval from two-thirds of the association's active members. Those restrictions apparently did not limit the organization's growth during this period, and by 1891, the Cleveland Branch had fifty-seven regular members. By 1896, it had seventy-four, only thirty-four of whom lived in Cleveland. As had been the case from its earliest days, the Cleveland Branch of the Ohio Woman's Press Association continued to draw its membership from across northern Ohio as well as from outside the state. Members could be found in Toledo, Ashtabula, Berea, Ravenna, Norwalk, and Oberlin in Ohio—and in Kokomo, Indiana, Wichita, Kansas, and New York City. The large number of members across northern Ohio prompted a change to the constitution that encouraged this dispersed membership; at least one-half of the vice presidents had to be women *not* living in Cleveland.

In spite of the growing size of the Cleveland Branch, its personal character had not been sacrificed. Indeed, the Cleveland Branch of the OWPA seemed to balance professional objectives with friendship goals. Perhaps Mary Richardson, an early member of the organization, explained it best:

I felt greatly honored that I—almost a stranger in Cleveland at that time—had been selected as an associate of writers and authors, and was thus recognized as having a creative mind, and their cordial greeting and courteous attention made me feel that I was not only privileged to enjoy such association, but that I had "fallen among" friends. The fraternal feeling in this club was very pronounced—a *camaraderie* that has ever been one of the beautiful features of the Cleveland Branch of the Ohio Women's Press Club.[8]

The new century brought a push for greater professional standards among the new members. A candidate now had to "submit samples of work for which she received pay and names of publishers." Nonetheless, the restrictions did not reduce the number of members, and by 1901, the Cleveland branch had eighty-one members. Shortly after, however, membership began dropping; and by 1904, it was down to sixty-nine women. Precisely what happened is unclear. Dues remained the same—a $1 initiation fee and annual dues of $1. Programming remained at the same high caliber with members preparing papers on a wide range of literary and journalistic topics and current events. The meetings were still held in downtown Cleveland, within easy access of the largest number of members. The only thing that was different was the location. The monthly meetings were no longer held at the meeting rooms of the WCTU but were, instead, held in a variety of locations.

REORGANIZATION—CLEVELAND WOMEN'S PRESS CLUB

Whatever the reason, the Cleveland Branch was unable to stop the drop in its membership, and by 1912 had only fifty-nine members. That same year, it redefined itself—and returned to its roots.[9] Under the leadership of Mrs. John F. Fisher, the Cleveland group reverted to its original name (with a change in spelling of "Woman's"), the Cleveland Women's Press Club. That action caused some consternation and debate within the organization. Longtime member Gertrude Wickham did not support the name change. The Ohio Woman's Press Association was a designation recognized by the business world and differentiated the organization from "literary societies composed of amateurs," she wrote.[10]

Wickham, however, was apparently in the minority. Under its new name, the Cleveland Women's Press Club grew once again—albeit slowly and never to the size it had been at the end of the nineteenth century and start of the twentieth. Programs continued to include a balance of practical information (e.g., "Materials and Methods of Fiction," "The Freelancers") and the inspirational (e.g., "Noble Lives and Noble Deeds," "As Nature Whispers").

The press club came to see itself as part of the greater woman's club movement in the city and the state. In 1916, it formally affiliated with the city's Federation of Women's Clubs and in 1919 joined the Ohio Federation of Women's Clubs. Although each of these moves suggests that the press club was prepared to play a broader role within the city, it first had to deal with a crisis within its own organization.

In 1922, some of the press clubs' members of a more literary bent broke away to form their own organization, the Cleveland Writers' Club (see below).[11] This left the Cleveland Women's Press Club clearly journalistically based, and membership was limited entirely to "women actively engaged in either newspaper or editorial publicity work."[12] During the 1920s the press club held an annual dance, "The Second Edition Ball," and in 1936 hosted a tea for the correspondents covering the GOP convention held in Cleveland. Luminaries attending included Mrs. Robert Taft, whose husband was seeking the GOP presidential nomination, Florida gubernatorial candidate E. E. Callaway, and the esteemed columnist Walter Lippman. After 1937, when the organization was described as lampooning "British royalty" at its ball, references to the Cleveland Women's Press Club disappeared from the local press and the organization seems to have ceased to exist.[13]

CLEVELAND WRITERS' CLUB

Much better known—and much more fully covered—was the Cleveland Writers' Club, which claimed 1886 as its founding date and the Ohio Woman's Press Association and the Cleveland Women's Press Club as its ancestors. But the Cleveland Writers' Club was quite different from those organizations. First, it opened its doors to men who were "accredited professional writers in greater Cleveland" and had sold at least two manuscripts for publication.[14] A number of men did join; in fact, two of them—Dr. Samuel W. Kelley, a Cleveland physician and author of a book on surgical diseases of children, and a W. G. Vorpe—even held office.[15] However, the largest number of members were women. Second, though the club remained a means to improve—one Writers' Club president characterized it as a "clinic, a working group for those learning to write"—it also became a way to showcase the talents of members.[16] "Hitherto we have kept the attitude of students," one program asserted,[17] but now the group would reward the best writing in the city. The group began by offering three prizes of $25 each for the best short story, poem, and one-act play. Prizes for best article, radio script, and juvenile fiction were added in later years.[18]

Ironically, an editor from the *Cleveland Press*, May C. Whitaker, was elected the club's first president. It apparently struck a responsive call in Cleveland literary circles, for by 1927, the club had eighty-two active members, which made it as large as the OWPA had been in its best years. In addition, two male journalists, Wilson G. Smith of the *Cleveland Press* and James H. Rogers of the *Cleveland Plain Dealer*, were named "honorary members."

Like many other professional organizations, the club had its problems during the Depression. The number of members dropped, and individuals who retained their memberships were slow to pay their dues. In the 1933–34 yearbook, members were reminded: "Please pay dues before December first. Our treasury is low and funds are needed to finance programs and postage." The character of the membership of the club itself was changing as well, reverting to its original profile. By the late 1930s, few men were listed as active members. Indeed, by 1938, only one man—Franklin Bishop, DDS—was listed among the active members. To counteract this drop in membership and the resulting impact on its treasury, the club added a new membership category—associate member. These members were required to pay twice the annual dues as regular active members. Associate members came from two groups, "those producing prose and poetry of good quality but not marketed" and "persons who are paid for lectures or radio broadcasts of 'satisfactory quality.' "[19]

Besides continuing its established programs and competitions, the group also sponsored some interesting activities. On one occasion, three members were given the same story plot but told to develop it in their own way. Each sold her story to a national publication: Mrs. W. B. Neff sold hers to *Century*, Mary Agnes Griffin to *Harper's*, and Marian Hill to *McClure's*.[20]

During World War II, the Cleveland Writers' Club continued offering a variety of programs dealing with members interests. In 1941–42, it offered several programs on writing nonfiction. Ralph Turner, general manager of the Newspaper Enterprise Association, explained "How a Newspaper Syndicate Works," and publisher Agust Fehranback gave a "writing clinic" on "Trade Journals." Not that fiction was ignored, for other writing clinics dealt with short stories and poetry. Nor was radio ignored, either. Waldo Pooler, head of the dramatic and script department of WTAM, outlined "Ideas for the Airwaves." That heavy emphasis on nonfiction disappeared in 1944–45, when the largest number of topics on the club's programs dealt with short stories, plays, and poetry. That type of programming was in keeping with the writing awards the organization was giving each year, and the high point of the club's season was the announcement of the awards.

The progress of the Cleveland Writers' Club is difficult to chart after World War II. Isolated references in newspapers indicate it continued to give writing awards until at least 1950,[21] and a recent history of the city indicates that the club remained active into the 1970s and issued a monthly newsletter, *Write Face*.[22]

CONCLUSION

Though it changed its name, its constituency, and its mission over the years, what started out as the Cleveland Woman's Press Club outlived most of the women's press clubs founded in the nineteenth century. Its lifespan of more than eight decades, in and of itself, was quite an achievement. Few women's press associations have been as long lived. What made the Cleveland press club so different?

The Cleveland club arose from the same impulses that triggered the organization of other women's press clubs across the country: a desire for camaraderie and self-improvement. But unlike many other press associations that disbanded after a few years or decades, the Cleveland club survived because of the diversity of its membership base, its innovative programs, and its ability to change along with changing conditions.

The Cleveland association was never strictly a "press club." From its beginning, the members were never solely journalists or editors. Their repertoire was broader than that. They were poets, book authors, essayists, and short story writers. They all shared the desire to improve their writing and a wish for the companionship of other writers. They achieved both at the club's monthly meetings. A member or two would prepare and present papers that not only would inform the membership but could lead to publication in newspapers and magazines. The meetings were not solely for business and information; time was also set aside for socializing and for camaraderie.

The club also survived because it evolved from a press club that carried one city's name (although members were from across northern Ohio) to a city branch of a state organization, back to a Cleveland press club, and finally, to a writers' club. Its final name, the Cleveland Writers' Club, was probably truest to its membership base and its original purpose.

NOTES

1. Elizabeth V. Burt, "A Bid for Legitimacy: The Woman's Press Club Movement, 1881–1900," *Journalism History* 23, no. 2 (summer 1997): 74–75.

2. Undated, unidentified newspaper clipping in yearbook, "Ohio Woman's Press Association—1891–1892, Cleveland Branch," Ohio Woman's Press Association Collection (hereafter OWPA Collection), Western Reserve Historical Society, Cleveland, Ohio.

3. Mrs. H.E.G. Arey, *Home and School Training* (Philadelphia: J. B. Lippincott & Co., 1884) and *Household Songs: And Other Poems* (New York: J. C. Derby, 1855).

4. "Ohio Woman's Press Association," *Cleveland Commercial*, 29 May 1889, Gertrude Van Rensselaer Wickham Collection (hereafter Wickham Collection), Western Reserve Historical Society, Cleveland.

5. "Ohio Woman's Press Club, Cleveland, Ohio," yearbook, 1890–91, unnumbered page, OWPA Collection.

6. Linda Thayer Guilford, *The Story of a Cleveland School from 1848–1881* (Cambridge, Mass.: J. Wilson & Son, 1890).

7. "In Journalism," undated, unidentified clipping in "Ohio Woman's Press Association—1891/92, Cleveland Branch," yearbook, OWPA Collection.

8. Mary E. M. Richardson to Gertrude Wickham, East Cleveland, 5 June 1911, Wickham Collection.

9. No explanation for the Cleveland Branch's withdrawal from OWPA was provided in any of the newspaper stories or the organization documents.

10. Undated typescript, Wickham Collection.

11. Clintie Winfrey, "Club Members Write Histories, Cook Books, Detective Stories, Essays, Magazine Articles," *Cleveland Press*, 25 August 1939, *Cleveland Press* Collection, Cleveland State University, Cleveland, Ohio. Another account has the entire press

club changing its name to the Cleveland Writers' Club. See Marian J. Morton, *Women in Cleveland: An Illustrated History* (Bloomington: Indiana University Press, 1995), p. 159, and "Year Book of the Cleveland Writers' Club, 1927–28," Cleveland Writers' Club Collection, Western Reserve Historical Society. Subsequent stories about the Cleveland Women's Press Club and its activities in the city's newspapers, however, lend credence to the former account.

12. "Mrs. Maude Truesdale Press Club President," *Cleveland Press*, 22 October 1927, *Cleveland Press* Collection.

13. Alice Kuehn, "Women Scribes Plan for Ball," *Cleveland Press*, 23 November 1928; "Women's Press Club Plans Novel Entertainment for Second Annual Celebration," *Cleveland Press*, 13 December 1928; Eleanor Clarage, "City Good Host, Verdict at Tea," *Cleveland Plain Dealer*, 12 June 1936; " 'British Royalty' Honored at Ball," *Cleveland Plain Dealer*, 2 May 1937; all in *Cleveland Press* Collection.

14. "Year Book of the Cleveland Writers' Club, 1927–28," Cleveland Writers' Club Collection; Winfrey, "Club Members Write Histories."

15. Dr. Samuel W. Kelley, *The Surgical Diseases of Children: A Modern Treatise on Pediatric Surgery* (New York: E. B. Treat, 1909).

16. Winfrey, "Club Members Write Histories."

17. "Year Book of the Cleveland Writers' Club, 1927–28," unnumbered page, Cleveland Writers' Club Collection.

18. "Six Prizes Given by Writers Club," *Cleveland Press*, 23 April 1950, *Cleveland Press* Collection.

19. "Year Book of the Cleveland Writers' Club, 1938–39," Cleveland Writers' Club Collection.

20. Winfrey, "Club Members Write Histories."

21. See, for example, "Six Prizes Given by Writers Club," *Cleveland Press*, 23 April 1950, *Cleveland Press* Collection.

22. David V. Van Tassel and John J. Grabowski, *The Encyclopedia of Cleveland History* (Bloomington: Indiana University Press, 1987), p. 283.

INFORMATIONAL SOURCES

Cleveland Press Collection. Cleveland State University, Cleveland, Ohio.

Cleveland Writers' Club Collection. Western Reserve Historical Society, Cleveland, Ohio.

Gertrude Van Rensselaer Wickham Collection. Western Reserve Historical Society, Cleveland, Ohio.

Ingham, Mrs. W. A. *Women of Cleveland and Their Work, Philanthropic, Educational, Literary, Medical and Artistic: A History.* Cleveland: W. A. Ingham, 1893.

Morton, Marian J. *Women in Cleveland: An Illustrated History.* Bloomington: Indiana University Press, 1995.

Ohio Woman's Press Association Collection. Western Reserve Historical Society, Cleveland, Ohio.

Van Tassel, David V., and John J. Grabowski. *The Encyclopedia of Cleveland History.* Bloomington: Indiana University Press, 1987.

INSTITUTIONAL PROFILES

Cleveland Women's Press Club

Dates: Founded in 1886 as the **Cleveland Woman's Press Club**; merged with the Cincinnati Women's Press Club in 1889 to become the **Ohio Woman's Press Association, Cleveland Branch**. In 1912, changed name back to the **Cleveland Women's Press Club**; continued activities until 1937, date of cessation unknown.

Archives: Ohio Woman's Press Association Collection, Western Reserve Historical Society, Cleveland, Ohio.

Cleveland Writers' Club

Dates: Descended from **Cleveland Woman's Press Club**, the **Ohio Woman's Press Association**, and the **Cleveland Women's Press Club**; broke away from the latter in 1922; continued activities until the mid-1970s.

Newsletter: *Write Face*, exact years of publication unknown, no holdings located.

Archives: Cleveland Writers' Club Collection and Ohio Woman's Press Association Collection, Western Reserve Historical Society, Cleveland, Ohio.

36

Susan Weill

Women's Press Organizations in Mississippi, 1894–Present

MISSISSIPPI WOMEN'S PRESS CLUB, 1894

In 1892, Kate Markham Power defied the hackneyed image of repressed southern womanhood and joined a group of six hundred newspaper editors, mostly men, on a railroad trip from St. Louis to Seattle. She was only twenty-seven at the time, and the journal she kept during that adventure, *A Bunch of Letters from the Great Northwest*, was published as a book by the *Jackson Clarion-Ledger*, the Mississippi newspaper where she was employed as city editor.[1]

Kate Power (1865–1946) was born in Jackson, Mississippi, at the close of the Civil War. She was formally educated at Mary Baldwin Seminary in Stanton, Virginia, and began her news career in the early 1880s as society editor for the *Clarion-Ledger*. Over several decades, Power served in nearly every staff position at the newspaper, from city editor to editor-in-chief.[2] Referred to affectionately as "Miss Kate" by other staffers,[3] she was respected for her "sleuth-like mind"[4] and "great initiative."[5] Power's lifelong interest in the news media led her to observe in 1936 that the social issues reported in newspapers in the 1930s sounded "ominously like the newspapers of one hundred years ago."[6]

Kate Power was interested in the advancing rights of women, as evidenced by her coverage in *Kate Power's Review* of the "triumphal entry" into the practice of medicine by Mary Morrison in California.[7] Power often discussed and promoted woman suffrage in her role as a journalist and wrote, "After asking men why they object to allowing women to vote, I have yet to hear one single, sound logical reason."[8] *Kate Power's Review*, a tabloid published every Saturday from September 1894 through October 1895, featured poetry, sermons, book reviews, "Town Talk," short fiction, recipes, a "Children's Corner," and extensive advertising. The front-page banner headline in the inaugural issue was

"Well! Well! Well!" and the ensuing introductory article written by publisher J. B. Lusk noted that "women are coming to the front as they should."[9] Power reported the establishment of the Mississippi Women's Press Club (MWPC) in *Kate Power's Review*:

This club, organized last summer [1894] at Greenwood is, of course, in its very early infancy, but it is a vigorous infant that has never entered the troublesome stage of Existence. Organized with a membership of eleven, it has grown up and spread out until it now embraces about forty of the leading literary women of the State. The club membership is not confined entirely to writers, but illustrators and even women of pronounced literary tastes and accomplishment. Indeed, the roll now shows a collection of women, each of whom is a celebrity in her own way and is an ornament to her State.[10]

The purpose of the first official MWPC meeting in 1895 was to prepare for the summer gathering on the Mississippi Gulf Coast. "Programs are being arranged now, and the group will be treated to the best within the power of their members," Power wrote. The "best" included "musicians, poets, elocutionists and essayists of note" and the hope that "perhaps Mrs. French Sheldon will tell of her African explorations."[11]

MISSISSIPPI PRESS WOMEN

After this promising beginning, however, the MWPC, like many of the other women's press organizations of the late nineteenth century, dissipated, leaving behind few traces,[12] and it was not for another fifty years that Mississippi press women would organize again. In 1947, the Mississippi Press Women (MPW) was launched by Mary Cain, the socially conservative editor of the *Summit Sun* and a member-at-large of the National Federation of Press Women (NFPW).* Perhaps ironically, Kate Power's younger sibling, Anabel, who never mentioned her sister's earlier attempt, was a charter member of MPW.[13] Kate Power died in 1946, the year before the second group was founded.

In a brief history of the MPW published in 1972, charter member Flora Langley observed that the group was "born in labor and nurtured in fortitude."[14] According to Langley, a lack of archival material kept her historical documentation of the group minimal. "Those pioneers who mothered [MPW] shared one lack, they didn't have time for all that paper work. Records are sketchy. [I am] limited by faulty memories and stymied by ex-officials who stand firmly on 'executive privilege' to remain silent," Langley wrote.[15]

Cain was elected the first president of MPW, and Hazel Brannon Smith of Durant, the first woman to be awarded a Pulitzer Prize for editorial writing, was elected vice president. Cain and Brannon Smith, as newspaper publishers and editors, were also members of the predominantly male Mississippi Press Association (MPA), an organization founded in 1866 exclusively for newspaper publishers and editors. MPW's other charter members were primarily the wives of members of the MPA, since women publishers, editors, and reporters were relatively scarce in the Mississippi press before the 1940s.

At the organizational meeting of MPW on June 6, 1947, nineteen women joined the group. Similar to the women who established other press women's associations elsewhere, they came together for advice and support.[16] By the time the list of members was submitted for the 1947–48 NFPW *Directory*, there were nearly forty members, including Mississippi writer Eudora Welty, whose brief membership raised a bit of controversy. According to Maurine Twiss, who joined MPW in 1951, "Miss Welty was not really a newspaper journalist, and some members thought she should not be allowed." Another debate regarding membership once raged. "In the early years, some of the members objected to there being public relations or electronic media people, and Hazel Brannon Smith wanted print people only," Twiss recalled. Both of these debates were settled by the MPW bylaws, however, which state that membership is open to "professional writers," not just print journalists.[17]

ACTIVITIES AND PROGRAMS

The MPW gathered for two meetings each year. In the fall, meetings were devoted to the election of officers and workshops. In the spring, the MPW met with the MPA on the Mississippi Gulf Coast.[18] From the beginning, MPW decided to offer workshops for members because most of the press women in Mississippi at the time had never received "formal schooling in newspapering."[19] These workshops were a major factor in the recruitment of members, and topics such as photography, interviewing, reporting, layout, editing, marketing, and media law were offered by MPW members and outside media practitioners. Speakers included Kathryn Wyndham, journalist turned novelist; Helen Thomas, from the White House Press Corps; and Ed Arnold, a New York journalism professor who held a seminar on newspaper layout. Juanita Hight, who joined MPW in 1949, said the workshops were vital to her work as an award-winning journalist: "It was at a workshop meeting of MPW that I learned what little I know about newspaper writing."[20] Twiss agreed: "In those early years, the workshops were perhaps the only source of professional enhancement for women. College classes were minimal. Most of the women who were in the press had come in through a side door. We were not trained."[21]

The activities of MPW also advanced the status of women journalists in Mississippi and helped obtain public acceptance of women in the business.[22] The workshops and awards were regularly reported as news in the state's press. "MPW played a great part in advancing respect for women journalists," Hight recalled,[23] and a significant benefit of the enhanced status of Mississippi women journalists was their sudden inclusion into the Mississippi media network. By the early 1960s, women journalists were being invited to press conferences that in prior years only men had been invited to attend.[24]

One much-publicized activity sponsored by MPW was the college scholarship and loan program in which grants and other financial support were made available for women journalism students. "The bequests were small, only about a hundred dollars, but they were important for their times, and every loan was paid back," said Twiss.[25] Funds for the project came from donations and workshop fees as well as profits from the 1958 NFPW conference held in Jackson. During that convention, Mississippi governor and Mrs. J. P. Coleman hosted a reception in the governor's mansion and a postconvention tour on chartered buses attracted 125 participants for a statewide tour through twenty towns and communities. National conferences of the NFPW were also held in Mississippi in 1977 and 1995.

DIVERSE AND TALENTED LEADERSHIP

The presidents of the MPW were an interesting group and reflected the diversity of the membership. The first president, Mary Cain (1947–49), studied journalism at Louisiana State University and began publication of the weekly *Summit Sun* in 1936, "with $250 cash, much faith and much ignorance."[26] She was the first woman to seek the office of Mississippi governor, although defeated in both her 1951 and 1955 campaigns. Cain's political philosophy supported states' rights, and her opposition to "increasing federal encroachment" landed her in the national spotlight in 1952 when she refused to pay Social Security taxes for herself or her employees. When the Internal Revenue Service padlocked the door of the *Sun* to force her to do so, Cain simply sawed the lock off and went back to work. That act of defiance earned her the nickname "Hacksaw Mary."[27]

Many of the early presidents of MPW married into newspaper families but made names for themselves in the business. Lyda Emmerich (1949–50) trained as a court reporter and began her career at the *McComb Enterprise-Journal* when she became the wife of the publisher, J. O. Emmerich. She wrote a popular column and worked in all areas at the newspaper, including editorial, circulation, and advertising. Velma Johnson Taylor (1950–51) studied journalism at Louisiana State University and married the publisher of the *Mississippi Sun*, which was published in Charleston. Besides being an award-winning writer, Taylor became the associate editor of the *Mississippi Sun* and associate editor and publisher of the *South Reporter*, which was published in Holly Springs. Lois Anderson (1952–53) was a school teacher who began working at the *Ripley Southern Sentinel* in 1938 after she married the publisher. The first southern woman elected to an office of the NFPW, Anderson won more than 150 journalism awards during her long career. Lillian Thornton (1952–53) became a newspaper woman after her husband purchased the *Neshoba County Democrat*, published in Philadephia, Mississippi, in 1944; and Juanita Hight (1953–54) found herself employed by the *Winston County Journal* in Louisville soon after she married the son of the editor. Hight, who served as NFPW secretary in 1954, became an award-winning writer of news and features.

Others had a wide range of professional experience before assuming the MPW presidency. Louise Morehead, president from 1954 to 1956, wrote for daily newspapers in Little Rock, Arkansas, and Washington, D.C., before moving to Mississippi. The next MPW president, Hazel Brannon Smith (1956–58), majored in journalism at the University of Alabama and then moved to Mississippi in 1943 to purchase the *Durant News* and *Lexington Advertiser*. Brannon Smith received many awards for her writing, including the Pulitzer Prize in 1964. She challenged southern tradition with her editorials and aroused the ire of many white Mississippians by advocating equal justice for all people, including African Americans. She believed it was her duty to take a stand on controversial issues and once wrote: "There are already too many jellyfish in the world. We don't need anymore in the form of editors."[28]

Margaret Phillips, who served two terms as president (1960–62 and 1964–66), was editor and publisher of the *Tunica Times-Democrat*. Mary Alice Bookhart (1962–64), who began her journalism career in 1932, was women's editor at the *Jackson Clarion-Ledger* for more than three decades and received eighteen awards from the NFPW. Mildred Dearman (1966–68), associate editor of *The Carthaginian*, which was published in Carthage, was one of the first women to be elected president of a local Chamber of Commerce. Of Dearman, the *Clarion-Ledger* once wrote, "Run a blood analysis on Mildred Dearman and you would likely find more printer's ink than plasma."[29]

Jessie McKay (1968–70) was society editor at the *Pass Christian Tarpon-Beacon*, and Mary Lou Webb (1970–72) started co-publishing the *Meadville Advocate* with her husband David in 1962. Webb, who also served as president of NFPW from 1987 to 1989, initiated the MPW's Woman of Achievement awards in 1971. The first recipient of the award was Hazel Brannon Smith. The prestigious annual award is made to a woman who is nominated by her peers, and letters of support are garnered from politicians, university presidents, and media industry leaders.

ISSUES AND CHANGES

By the 1970s, the professional affiliation of the MPW had begun to shift away from pure journalism toward related fields and several members had left their jobs with the print media for the more financially lucrative field of public relations. Maurine Twiss became head of public information at the University of Mississippi Medical Center in 1955, a position later held (in 1998) by Barbara Austin (MPW president, 1972–74). NancyKay Sullivan Wessman (1980–82), a former journalist, became deputy director of information services at the Mississippi Department of Health. To reflect this shift in the membership, the MPW constitution was altered in 1977 to include "all professional communicators," a transformation that was "fashionable at the time," according to Twiss.[30] Also in 1977, the MPW constitution eliminated any reference to gender and Steve Wilkerson, of WLOX-TV in Biloxi, became the first male member.[31] In 1993, MPW removed the word *women* from its name and adopted a new, more inclusive title—Mississippi Media Professionals (MMP)—"to change our image to fit modern journalism."[32]

While many press women's organizations "expanded their purview to include social and economic reform,"[33] this was not the case with MPW, although individuals might take a stand on a particular issue. According to former president Twiss, "There were many sensitive times and most of the members individually, or their papers, disagreed with the more liberal views, but we did not take issue with these non-traditional views at MPW meetings. We were polite. The most comfortable way to deal with it was to avoid it."[34]

Thus, in 1948, when the Mississippi Democrats stormed out of the national Democratic convention in protest of President Harry Truman's civil rights platform, the Dixiecrat walkout was not discussed at MPW meetings. MPW charter member Harriett Gibbons, the only woman editor of a daily Mississippi newspaper at the time, took the unpopular stance of denouncing the walkout in the *Laurel Leader-Call.* "We don't believe Mississippi gained anything in particular by walking out of the convention," she wrote in an editorial.[35] Interestingly, when Eleanor Roosevelt was asked by President Truman to run as his vice president that year, Gibbons was the only editor of a daily Mississippi newspaper who failed to cover the story.[36]

In 1954, when the Supreme Court ruled in *Brown v. Board of Education* that public schools must be racially integrated, the MPW once again remained silent. And once again Gibbons took a position, writing: "That Mississippi is in for a period of most difficult and trying times is conceded by us all. Such an era must be met with an even temper, with self-control, with a determination to work out what faces us in the spirit of Americanism."[37]

Freedom Summer in 1964 was another story that affected all journalists working in the state. Jean Perry (MPW president, 1974–76) had moved to Mississippi in 1963 and joined the *Meridian Star* as a reporter. She remembered the long hot summer of 1964 as "quite an introduction to Mississippi for a Yankee from Ohio."[38] MPW member Hazel Brannon Smith risked her life by advocating change in Mississippi's racially biased system of justice and that summer was hailed as "a courageous woman," by the *St. Louis Post-Dispatch* for her dedication to gaining "equality before the law" for all people.[39] The *Arkansas Gazette* praised Brannon Smith as "a segregationist who took the position that her county sheriff ought not to have shot a Negro in the thigh for what seems to have been the hell of it."[40] When the Civil Rights Act of 1964 was approved by the U.S. Congress, Brannon Smith encouraged her readers to give the legislation a chance, and when the civil rights workers arrived in the state to assist blacks in voter registration, she was the only Mississippi editor who openly praised them. "The truth is, these young people wouldn't be here if we had not ignored our responsibilities to our Negro citizens," she wrote.[41]

Among her editorial colleagues in MPW, Brannon Smith was alone in her nontraditional beliefs. More typical in her views was Margaret Phillips of the *Tunica Times-Democrat*. Phillips interpreted the Civil Rights Act of 1964 as a political ploy to "court" the black vote and condemned federal intervention in states' rights.[42] Mary Cain at the *Summit Sun* concurred with Phillips and complained in her editorial column, "I believe the races are far happier—and better behaved—when they are separated."[43] Cain, who reflected some of the fears and beliefs of Mississippians, referred to the civil rights workers as "buttinskis who have absolutely no business here and they'd better get on home where they belong."[44] Also president of Women for Constitutional Government, Cain declared in her column the same day that Communism was behind the civil rights summer project.[45] Cain also blamed the bombings of local black churches that summer on the congregations themselves. "I wouldn't put it beyond some of the hare-brained Negroes to set off these blasts in an effort to get federal goons into Mississippi," she wrote.[46]

Interestingly, when the first African American woman applied to MPW in the early 1960s, Mary Lou Webb remembers that she was easily accepted. Either the Mississippi group was more open-minded than the Georgia Women's Press Club, remembered for "[withdrawing] from the General Federation of Women's Clubs because the Federation had admitted to membership three Negro women's press clubs" in 1895,[47] or the half century that had intervened had seen the evolution of dramatic changes in southern social acceptance.

Although most political party and civil rights issues were carefully skirted at MPW meetings, one issue that caused an uproar was the Equal Rights Amendment (ERA). According to NancyKay Sullivan Wessman, a discussion about whether the group should endorse the ERA was denounced by Mary Cain, whose diatribe against the amendment caused Sullivan Wessman and several other women to walk out of the meeting.[48] In 1974, Cain described her opposition to the ERA in an interview with one sentence, "Just imagine putting men and women who don't even know each other in the same barracks!"[49] A year later, however, the MPW voted at its fall business meeting to support passage of the amendment in Mississippi[50] and in 1978 drafted a resolution requesting that the Mississippi legislature allow a floor debate of the ERA. This public endorsement of political action was unprecedented in this otherwise apolitical group, and it caught the attention of the media. MPW's resolution was announced in the *Jackson Daily News* under the headline "State Presswomen Urge ERA Debate."[51]

PRESENT AND FUTURE

Although MPW changed its name to Mississippi Media Professionals in 1993 to reflect a broader membership base including men and women and those from a range of communication professions, membership that had peaked in 1980 at nearly two hundred fell to only twenty by 1996. Maurine Twiss, a member of the group since 1951, observed: "I'm still a member, but not involved. The organization kind of fell apart, numbers fell. It seems to me that it just dwindled away."[52]

Finances were one reason for the group's decline. The organization's inability to compete with the stronger Mississippi Press Association (MPA), which began accepting women members by the 1980s, may also be a reason. Once the MPA opened its workshops to all journalists, not just to editors, newspapers stopped paying membership dues and workshop fees for their employees who were MPW members. It seemed the same services were made available to those same women through the MPA, to which the newspapers already paid fees. According to Webb, women who might have had their MPW dues paid by their newspaper would now have to pay those dues themselves. "When you're a working woman, if you have to choose between paying your electric bill or your club dues, you pay the bill," she said.[53]

The MPA not only attracted the dues once paid for MPW membership and some of the programs the MPW had previously offered, it also began to co-opt MPW's leadership. Carolyn Wilson, for example, who joined the MPW during the 1980s, became executive director of the MPA in 1985 and held that position through 1998. According to Wilson, "The programs and concerns of the MPW have been pretty much absorbed by the MPA since I came on board as director in 1985."[54]

From the founding of the Mississippi Women's Press Club in 1895 to the fight for survival of the Mississippi Media Professionals in 1998, Mississippi women media practitioners have attempted to raise the status of women in the field and to meet their needs with limited resources. Although many believe the organization is "phased out" or "falling apart," some hold onto the hope that the future is not so dim. In 1996, MMP president Peggy Keyes Gray sent a survey to the remaining twenty members asking whether the group should continue, and only four positive responses were returned.[55] By 1998, however, the membership numbers had doubled and Faye Moreland, a recent arrival in the state, was elected MMP president. Longtime member and former NFPW president Mary Lou Webb saw Moreland's election as a good sign: "Maybe these new members can reinvigorate the organization so that there will be a resurgence. I certainly hope so."[56]

NOTES

1. J. L. Power Family Papers, Mississippi Department of Archives and History (hereafter MDAH), Jackson, Mississippi.

2. Kate M. Power Papers, 1936 file, MDAH.

3. Purser Hewitt, managing editor of the *Jackson Clarion Ledger*, to Kate Power, 23 November 1937, Kate M. Power Scrapbook, box 3, MDAH.

4. Susie Powell, Works Progress Administration of Mississippi, to Kate Power, July 1937, Kate Power Scrapbook.

5. L. A. Fuller to Alabama Red Cross, March 1919, Kate Power Scrapbook.

6. Kate M. Power Papers, 1936 file, MDAH.

7. "Dr. Mary Morrison," *Kate Power's Review*, 22 December 1894, p. 3.

8. Kate Power, "The Suffrage Question," *Kate Power's Review*, 11 November 1894, p. 5.

9. J. B. Lusk, "Well! Well! Well!" *Kate Power's Review*, 1 September 1894, p. 1.

10. "The Women's Press Club," *Kate Power's Review*, 22 December 1894, p. 4.

11. Ibid.

12. Elizabeth V. Burt, "A Bid for Legitimacy: The Women's Press Club Movement, 1881–1900." *Journalism History* 23, no. 2 (summer 1997): 72.

13. Juanita Hight, telephone interview by author, 20 June 1998; Maurine Twiss, telephone interview by author, 18 June 1998.

14. Flora Langley, "MPW Mini-History," Louisville, Mississippi, 1972.

15. Ibid.

16. Agnes Hooper Gottlieb, "Networking in the Nineteenth Century: Founding of the Women's Press Club of New York," *Journalism History* 21, no. 4 (winter 1995): 158; Burt, "A Bid for Legitimacy," p. 74.

17. Twiss interview.

18. Ibid.

19. Langley, "MPW Mini-History."

20. Hight interview.

21. Twiss interview.

22. Ibid.

23. Hight interview.

24. Mary Lou Webb, telephone interview by author, 3 July 1998. Webb became a member in 1961.

25. Twiss interview.

26. "Biographies of Presidents of Mississippi Press Women," compiled by Pat Sellers (1974), p. 4, in the possession of NancyKay Sullivan Wessman, Jackson, Mississippi.

27. Ibid., pp. 6–7.

28. Ibid., p. 47.

29. Ibid., p. 58.

30. Twiss interview.

31. Anne Washburn McWilliams, "MPW-MMP Highlights, 1975–1997," in "Mississippi Media Professionals 50th Anniversary, 1947–1997," Jackson, Mississippi, p. 13, Mississippi Media Professionals Files, Fant Library, Mississippi University for Women, Columbus, Mississippi.

32. Ibid., p. 8.

33. Burt, "A Bid for Legitimacy," p. 76.

34. Twiss interview.

35. Harriet Gibbons, "It's Over," *Laurel Leader-Call*, 15 July 1948, p. 4.

36. Susan Weill, " 'In a Madhouse's Din': Civil Rights Coverage by Mississippi's Daily Press, 1948–1968" (Ph.D. dissertation, University of Southern Mississippi, 1998), p. 40.

37. Harriet Gibbons, "Take It Easy," *Laurel Leader-Call*, 18 May 1954, p. 4.

38. "Biographies of Presidents of Mississippi Press Women," p. 69.

39. "To a Courageous Woman," *Lexington* (Mississippi) *Advertiser*, 4 June 1964, p. 2.

40. "Honoring Courage," *Lexington* (Mississippi) *Advertiser*, 11 June 1964, p. 2.

41. Hazel Brannon Smith, "Through Hazel's Eyes," 2 July 1964, p. 1.

42. Margaret Phillips, "The Democrat's Albatross," *Tunica Times Democrat*, 4 June 1964, p. 4.

43. Mary Cain, "Mary Cain's Column," *Summit* (Mississippi) *Sun*, 30 July 1964, p. 1.

44. Mary Cain, Ibid., 11 June 1964, p. 1.

45. Ibid.

46. Mary Cain, "Mary Cain's Column," *Summit Sun*, 25 June 1964, p. 1.

47. Burt, "A Bid for Legitimacy," p. 77.

48. NancyKay Sullivan Wessman, telephone interview by author, 8 July 1998.

49. Mary Cain, interview by author, 1 October 1974.

50. McWilliams, "MPW-MMP Highlights," p. 13.

51. "State Presswomen Urge ERA Debate," *Jackson Daily News*, 9 September 1978, p. 2.

52. Twiss interview.

53. Webb interview.

54. Carolyn Wilson, telephone interview by author, 20 June 1998.

55. McWilliams, "MPW-MMP Highlights," p. 17.

56. Mary Lou Webb, telephone interview by author, 28 September 1998.

INFORMATIONAL SOURCES

"Biographies of Presidents of Mississippi Press Women." Compiled by Pat Sellers (Mississippi Press Women president, 1976–78), 1974. Private collection of NancyKay Sullivan Wessman, Jackson, Mississippi.

J. L. Power Family Papers. Mississippi Department of Archives and History, Jackson, Mississippi.

Kate M. Power Papers. Mississippi Department of Archives and History, Jackson, Mississippi.

Kate Power's Review. September 1884–October 1895, passim.

Mississippi Media Professionals Files. Fant Library, Mississippi University for Women, Columbus, Mississippi.

Power, Kate M. *A Bunch of Letters from the Great Northwest, for the "Daily Clarion," Jackson, Mississippi*. Jackson, Miss.: *Jackson Clarion Ledger*, 1892.

INSTITUTIONAL PROFILE

Mississippi Women's Press Club

Dates: Founded summer 1894 by Kate Markham Power; years of activity unknown.

Newsletter: Material concerning the club was published in *Kate Power's Review*. September 1884–October 1895.

Archives and papers: J. L. Power Family Papers (Kate M. Power), Mississippi Department of Archives and History, Jackson, Mississippi.

Mississippi Media Professionals

Dates: Founded 6 June 1947 in Jackson, Mississippi, as **Mississippi Press Women**; name changed in 1993 to **Mississippi Media Professionals**.

Newsletter: Written and published occasionally at the discretion of each MPW/MMP president.

Archives and papers: Mississippi Media Professional Files, Fant Library, Mississippi University for Women, Columbus, Mississippi; MPW File, Mississippi Department of Archives and History, Jackson, Mississippi; and personal holdings of various past presidents.

Contact: Faye Moreland (president, 1998–2000), 1822 West Jackson St., Tupelo, Mississippi 38801–3127, tel. (601) 842–4567.

37

Betty Houchin Winfield

Women's Press Organizations in Missouri, 1896–Present

Freaks, perhaps, these earliest women journalists.

Sara L. Lockwood, 1924[1]

EARLY DAYS

From the late nineteenth century, with such few numbers and their unexpected female roles, Missouri women journalists were indeed "freaks." Men edited the earliest Missouri newspapers for and with other men, even when little-recognized Missourian Eliza Patten assisted her husband in typesetting the *Missouri Intelligencer* and *Boons Lick Advertiser* in 1819.[2] Though their numbers were unrecorded in the 1870 census,[3] Missouri women did become reporters, editors, and publishers, and grew enough in numbers to be taken seriously, as independent and self-conscious professionals. And, for more than 125 years they participated in organizations to support their efforts.

Missouri's earliest state journalism organization, the Missouri Editors and Publishers' Association, founded in 1866, initially listed only men in attendance at conventions, although wives and other women were noted at meetings by 1870.[4] Starting with regional meetings,[5] nearly one hundred editors and publishers sought uniformity for "bargaining" rates between advertisers and individual papers. By 1867, Missouri editors and publishers had formed a second organization, the Missouri Press Association (MPA).

Eight years later, when 108 editors presented their credentials for membership, Dora Sankey of the *Holden Enterprise* became the MPA's first female member.[6] During the next few years, five other women joined Sankey: Miss. A. V. Casebolt of the Cape Girardeau *Marble City News* (1877); Kate M. Jones of the

Clinton Advocate (1878); Mrs. O. F. Reagan of the *Jefferson City People's Tribune* (1878); Julie M. Bennett of the *Hannibal Courier* (1879); and Etta L. Hume of the *Kirkwood Star-Republican* (1879).[7]

By 1879, women not only were members but began taking a more public, active part in the MPA's annual convention. Julie Bennett recounted the reality of being an editor, reading her poem "The Editor's Dream." Ironically, she defined the editor as being male by using the masculine pronoun, even though she was an editor herself:

> Clipping, and jotting down neighborhood news,
> Rewriting some nonsense, he dare not refuse,
> Hearing the gossip spun out by some bore
> Who needed no asking to enter the door,
> Sending out bills which came back unpaid,
> Some with requests that he pay in trade.[8]

Women like Sankey and Bennett were definitely members of a very small group, for few Missouri women were officially recognized as journalists at that time; just 1.5 percent of the journalistic workforce registered in the 1880 census were women, with only 9 women listed among the 585 individuals who designated themselves as journalists.[9] Many a Missouri press woman attended MPA meetings because she had married the editor "and found herself to be a newspaper woman."[10] Many of these women continued as "newspaper women" after the death of their husband and often inherited their husband's politics along with his newspaper. Of the twenty-five newspapers edited by women who were listed in official manuals of Missouri during the last decade of the century, three were Democratic, five Republican, two Populist, and eleven independent.[11] The women editors of political journals included Mrs. Sue J. Rittenhouse of the *Jonesburg Journal* (Democratic), Mrs. M. A. Smith of the *Warsaw Times* (Republican), Mrs. Gertrude Ebbs of the *Windsor Republican*, and Mrs. W. J. Powell of the *Rolla New Era* (Republican).[12]

By the late 1800s, however, these women began to see journalism as a place where women could intentionally seek a career. In 1881, Susie McK. Fisher, wife of the editor of the *Farmington Times*, read her treatise "Women in Journalism" at the MPA convention. She argued that it was time for women to enter journalism despite their scarcity and the limited acceptance of those few who were recognized journalists. Fisher acknowledged that "women sometimes have entered journalism from a very love of the power it gives," but that for the newspaper as a whole, there would be a gender advantage. "The tone of a newspaper with a woman on the staff is purer and more deserving of a place in every household," she argued.[13]

This connection to the MPA provided the only formal venue in which Missouri women journalists could meet, although many were active in and wrote about a number of social reform movements, including the kindergarten movement, greater public morality, and temperance.[14] An early attempt to organize women journalists occurred in 1884, when Mrs. Louis M. Pavy of the *St. Louis Republican* joined a handful of women at the North, South and Central Exposition in New Orleans to establish the National Woman's Press Association. The charter members were to return home to establish city, state, and regional chapters, and by 1890, more than a dozen had formed throughout the country.[15] Missouri was slow to follow; but as the number of women journalists in the state grew, organization became possible.[16]

MISSOURI WOMAN'S PRESS ASSOCIATION

Thus, in 1896, *The Journalist* reported the formation of the Missouri Woman's Press Association (MWPA) with Mrs. Holden E. Day of St. Louis serving as president. The association membership requirements were broad, open to any Missouri woman "who has published original matter in any form, or who has been, or is now connected with any reputable publication as editor, reporter, contributor, reviewer, correspondent, compiler, or illustrator."[17] By 1898 MWPA's membership had increased to sixty-one state members, with fifteen residing in the St. Louis area. Executive board member Victoria C. Whitney of the St. Louis Bar Association was empowered to file articles of incorporation with the secretary of state.[18] Other officers included Alice Speece Lybarger of Butler as first vice president; H. Jeanne Tracy of Springfield as second vice president; Anna E. Bigelow of Nevada (Missouri) as third vice president; Frankie Van Slyke of St. Louis as treasurer; Adah B. McDaniel of St. Louis as recording secretary; and Anna N. Miller, also of St. Louis, as corresponding secretary. Mrs. Alice J. Jones, Virginia C. Whitney, and Susan C. Hulsart constituted the executive board. The association reached out beyond the state borders and sent a delegation to the Nashville Exposition in October for the Women's Press Day.[19]

In addition to pursuing its professional interests, the group began raising money for worthwhile causes. In 1898, the MWPA gave a euchre party at the Southern Hotel in St. Louis to provide a library and reading room for the soldiers stationed at the Jefferson Barracks during the Spanish-American War. According to the *Fourth Estate*, which reported the event, "A handsome sum was realized."[20]

During the first decades of the new century, the MWPA became less active, despite the fact that Missouri, similar to other state organizations, had fluid membership standards and was open to all women writers. In fact, the MWPA seemed to fade from the scene, even though during World War I and after the advent of suffrage, women journalists as full-time professionals appeared as a serious presence.[21] By the 1920 census, almost a quarter of all Missouri journalists listed were women, 267 out of 1,076.[22] At the same time as MWPA was passing out of existence, Missouri women found a new venue in which they could elevate their professional education. The newly founded School of Journalism at the University of Missouri began a program in 1908 for "leadership in journalism with high ideals and special training." The educational emphasis was for "well-equipped men"; nevertheless, the first undergraduate journalism class had thirteen women among the ninety-seven students. Of the six students who formed the first graduating class in 1910, one was a woman, Mary Gentry Paxton. During World War I, the number of women in the program greatly increased, and by the 1920s, females comprised just under one-third of the graduates. For example, by 1923, 151 women along with 281 men had graduated with a B.J. in the first fifteen years of the Missouri School of Journalism.[23]

The women students soon organized. They established a "Women's Journalism Club" and were eligible for membership in Theta Sigma Phi (TSP; later renamed Association for Women in Communications*), the national women's journalism honor society established at the University of Washington in 1909.[24] Shortly after, the University of Missouri became the third university to establish a local TSP chapter. Women remained active in the organization even after they graduated college, and in 1918, Kansas City established TSP's first alumnae chapter.

MISSOURI WOMAN'S PRESS CLUB

Missouri women journalists did not organize on the state level again until November 1936, when they gathered in St. Louis in response to a call from the Illinois Woman's Press Association (IWPA)* to create a national organization of press women. The women gathered to consider IWPA's suggestion that Missouri organize a group that could then become a charter member of what was to become the National Federation of Press Women (NFPW).* The seventeen women who attended liked the idea and decided to hold the organizational meeting during the annual Journalism Week at the University of Missouri.[25] The founders included Jewell Ross Davis Mehus, who taught and did public relations for Central Missouri State Teachers College in Warrensburg, and Bertha Iseman Bless of the *Weston Chronicle*, who was to become NFPW's first president.[26]

Thus, on May 19, 1937, the Missouri Woman's Press Club (MWPC) was organized.[27] The club's original goal was to "secure the benefits of organized effort; to foster mutual improvement through association; and to promote the highest ideals of American journalism."[28] Though many women remained members of the male-dominated MPA, they now had their own organization. Membership was limited to women engaged in journalism as a profession for at least one year immediately prior to their written application. An applicant had to submit three samples of recently published work and win the approval of the membership through a secret vote. Honorary members were admitted by a majority vote of the active members in recognition of achievements in the world of letters and came to include national radio host Mary Margaret McBride (1941)[29] and Vi Edom, co-founder of the University of Missouri photojournalism sequence and the Missouri Photo Workshop (1961).

Among the thirty-five charter members were practicing journalists and journalism educators, including Jewell Ross Davis of Central Missouri State Teachers College and Miss Frances Grinstead of the School of Journalism at the University of Missouri, Columbia. Elected president was Bertha Iseman Bless of the *Weston Chronicle*. The vice presidents were Mrs. Dorys Farley of the *West Plains Journal*, Miss Ella Pearl Smith of the *Clinton Eye*, Mrs. Osa McGraw of the *Lead Belt News* in Flat River, Miss Ardis Hamilton of the *Grundy County Gazette* of Spickard, and Miss Dorothy Porter of the *Milan Standard*.[30]

The MWPC became a founding member of the NFPW in 1938 and remained active in the national organization for the next five decades. Bless became NFPW president in 1940 the year the MWPC hosted the federation's annual convention in St. Louis, giving Bless the opportunity to say, "Women from across the land learned what Missouri women were doing and what they could do."[31] MWPC once again hosted the NFPW in 1949, when the national convention was held in Kansas City in honor of its new president, Catherine Dines Prosser, a Fayette, Missouri, native who was then the women's editor at the *Denver Post*.

Initially, the organization leaned heavily on the male-dominated MPA. Yet by 1939, the group met at least once a year on its own. Thus, it met three times yearly with two specified dates: once in conjunction with the fall meeting of the MPA, and once in Columbia with the School of Journalism during Journalism Week. Speakers were invited to these events, usually from the state press or government agencies, but national figures occasionally appeared as keynote speakers, including President Harry Truman in 1957 and former first lady Eleanor Roosevelt in 1959. In 1958, the club shortened its name to Missouri Press Women (MPW).[32]

As the MPW grew, it established several regional chapters to become accessible to women throughout the state. The largest were in St. Louis and Kansas City.

ACTIVITIES

Throughout the years, MPW has tried to encourage journalism as a worthwhile career in numerous ways. One of its major efforts has been to raise funds to benefit a woman student at the School of Journalism at the University of Missouri. That fund was named the Sara Lockwood Williams Scholarship and Loan Fund in 1961, in honor of the University of Missouri's first woman professor of journalism. The scholarship, which is awarded to a woman in her junior year, continues today.[33] In 1974 the organization began publishing pamphlets on careers in journalism in both print and broadcasting. It also offered other scholarships to students through the St. Louis and Kansas City chapters and since 1971 has sponsored yearly high school newspaper competitions.[34] The St. Louis chapter sponsored numerous charity benefits within the city and gave an annual Quest Award for life excellence within the community.[35]

During the 1970s, MPW faced the issue of women's rights. Perhaps to avoid divisiveness, the debate over the Equal Rights Amendment became a verboten topic after strong opposition from the St. Louis regional chapter. Despite discussion, the state organization did not formally take a stand on job discrimination. Despite the fact that MPW members were also automatically members of the MPA, only two women have been president of that organization in its 133-year history: Mrs. Avis G. Tucker of the *Warrensburg Daily Star-Journal* in 1982 and Betty Simpson Spaar of the *Odessa Odessan* in 1988.

MPW remained a NFPW affiliate and continued to meet twice a year, with the fall meeting devoted to workshops and the spring meeting held in the state capital in Jefferson. But the years and changing times took their toll. Whereas MPW once had nearly four hundred members, its membership dropped to seventy in 1997–98.[36] At the same time, the St. Louis chapter, with approximately ninety members, was acting as an independent organization without state or national sanction.[37]

To consolidate its strength and efforts, MPW took several steps. In 1998, members voted to change its name to National Federation of Press Women, Missouri Affiliate (NFPW/MO) "to establish a stronger, more visible alignment with the national organization." In April 1999, the state organization and the St. Louis chapter merged to combine their efforts. The state organization moved its headquarters from the home of its president (which changed each time a new president assumed office) to St. Louis. The reorganized NFPW/MO now has two co-presidents, each of whom is elected for two years, with elections held on odd-numbered years.[38]

Missouri women journalists in the late nineteenth century may have been an aberration because of their small numbers; yet by the end of the twentieth, they represented a substantial portion of the journalistic field. Women made up 66 percent of the 1998 University of Missouri School of Journalism graduating class of 645. Missouri women journalists are no longer called "freaks," as they once were, and now have numerous professional organizations, including NFPW/MO, available to them.

NOTES

1. Sara L. Lockwood, "Women and the Newspaper," Journalism Series No. 30, 10 September 1924 (Columbia: University of Missouri, 1924).

2. Alma F. Vaughan, "Pioneer Women of the Missouri Press," *Missouri Historical Review* 64, no. 3 (April 1970): 289.

3. Under journalists, and cross-listed by gender, no women were listed in Missouri in 1870, although 262 were tabulated. "Selected Occupations, with Age and Sex, and Nativity," *The Statistics of the Population of the United States, Ninth Census*, vol. 1 (Washington, D.C.: Government Printing Office, 1872), p. 743.

4. Vaughan, "Pioneer Women," p. 290.

5. William H. Taft, *Missouri Newspapers and the Missouri Press Association: 125 Years of Service, 1867–1992* (Marceline, Mo.: Heritage House Publishing, 1992), p. 6.

6. Vaughan, "Pioneer Women," p. 290.

7. Ibid. For the most part, married women used "Mrs." followed by their initials, their husband's name, or their husband's initials; those who simply used their first and last names were usually unmarried. Here, the author will use the names as they appeared in documents of the period.

8. Ibid. Julie Bennett, formerly a special writer for the *St. Louis Republic*, was the editor of the *Hannibal Courier*.

9. "Occupations, Table XXXIV," *Statistics of the Population of the United States at the Tenth Census (June 1, 1880)*, vol. 1 (Washington, D.C.: Government Printing Office, 1883), p. 832.

10. Jewell Ross Mehus and Maude Freeland, eds., "Foreword," *Missouri Press Women: History and Directory, 1965*, Missouri Press Women Papers, folder 15, Western Historical Manuscript Collection (hereafter WHM Collection), Ellis Library, University of Missouri, Columbia, Missouri.

11. Of the remaining four, two were described as society, and two as nonpolitical newspapers.

12. Vaughan, "Pioneer Women," pp. 296–97.

13. Mrs. Susie McK. Fisher, "Women in Journalism," *The Fifteenth Annual Session of the Missouri Press Association: Proceedings of the Missouri Press Association, 1867–1876* (Sedalia, Mo.: J. West Goodwin, 1882), pp. 21–24.

14. See, for example, Mrs. S. B. Ellis, "Importance of the Growth and Ideas in the Kindergarten," *St. Louis Republican*, 13 May 1877; Mrs. T. D. Bogie, lecture at the Missouri Press Association, Seventeenth Annual Session, 1883 (Sedalia), pp. 39–43, Missouri Press Association Records, WHM Collection. Mrs. Maggie A. Bowman, who owned the *King City Democrat*, became editor and publisher of the state Women's Christian Temperance Union newspaper, *The Counsellor*. See Vaughan, "Pioneer Women," p. 293.

15. See Elizabeth V. Burt, "A Bid for Legitimacy: The Woman's Press Club Movement, 1881–1900," *Journalism History* 23, no. 2 (summer 1997): 72–84.

16. By 1890, Missouri women made up almost 3 percent of the state's listed journalists, or 26 out of 893 listed in the census; by 1900, they made up 7 percent, or 87 of the 1,225 journalists listed. See "Statistics of Population, Table 79, Occupations," *Report on Population of the United States at the Eleventh Census: 1890*, part 1 (Washington, D.C.: Government Printing Office, 1897), p. 319; and "Statistics of Occupations, Table 33," *Special Reports: Occupations at the Twelfth Census, 1900* (Washington, D.C.: Government Printing Office, 1904), p. 134.

17. *Missouri Editor*, February 1897, p. 9; Vaughan, "Pioneer Women," p. 304.

18. "Items of Interest to Many Clubs," *Chicago Evening Post*, 16 December 1897; *The Journalist*, October 1897, p. 198.

19. "Special to the Journalist," *The Journalist*, October 1897, p. 198.

20. "Press Club News," *Fourth Estate*, 15 December 1898, p. 3.

21. Maurine H. Beasley, "The Women's National Press Club: A Case Study of Professional Aspirations," *Journalism History* 15, 4 no.4 (winter 1988): 112.

22. "Population," Table 15, *Fourteenth Census of the United States, Taken in the Year, 1920* (Washington, D.C.: Government Printing Office, 1923), p. 89.

23. "Graduates Number 435: Missouri Alumni in Journalism, 1908–1923," Journalism Series No. 27 (Columbia, Mo.: University of Missouri, 1924), p. 7.

24. Women were excluded from membership in Sigma Delta Chi, the male society

founded in 1909 at DePauw University, until the 1970s. The society was later renamed the Society of Professional Journalists.

25. "Missouri Women's Press Club History," *Missouri Women's Press Club, 1949*, Sara Lockwood Williams Papers, folder 793, WHM Collection.

26. Bless also launched the NFPW newsletter, *The Press Woman*, and set up national writing contests to give recognition to women writers in North America. Alma Edmonds, "Bertha Iseman Bless," in *Show Me Missouri Women: Selected Biographies*, ed. Mary K. Dains (Kirksville, Mo.: Thomas Jefferson University Press, 1989), pp. 139–40; Missouri Women's Press Club Charter members, *Missouri Women's Press Club Treasurer's Book, 1937–1964*, vol. 1, 1937, WHM Collection.

27. Mehus and Freeland, *Missouri Press Women*, p. 3.

28. "Missouri Women's Press Club," Sara Lockwood Williams Papers.

29. Ibid.

30. Ibid.

31. Mehus and Freeland, *Missouri Press Women*, p. 8.

32. Ibid., p. 5.

33. Ibid.

34. Betty Rothman Cook, a member since 1958, interview by author, 23 May 1999.

35. Guinn Tuckett Stemmler, president of the St. Louis regional chapter, telephone interview by author, 23 May 1999.

36. It had 359 members in 1965. Mehus and Freeland, *Missouri Press Women*; "Missouri," *National Federation of Press Women Directory, 1997–98* (1998), pp. 44–46.

37. Allison Stein Best, e-mail, 4 June 1999. Best was MPW president in 1998–99 and became co-president of the reorganized NFPW/MO in 1999–2000.

38. Ibid.

INFORMATIONAL SOURCES

Primary Sources

Missouri Press Association Records. Western Historical Manuscript Collection, Ellis Library, University of Missouri, Columbia, Missouri.

Missouri Press Women, Papers, 1961–85. Western Historical Manuscript Collection, Ellis Library, University of Missouri, Columbia, Missouri.

Missouri Women's Press Club, Treasurer's Book, 1937–64. Western Historical Manuscript Collection, Ellis Library, University of Missouri, Columbia, Missouri.

Sara Lockwood Williams Papers, 1885–1961. Western Historical Manuscript Collection, Ellis Library, University of Missouri, Columbia, Missouri.

Published Material

Dains, Mary K., ed. *Show Me Missouri Women: Selected Biographies*. Kirksville, Mo.: Thomas Jefferson University Press, 1989.

Lockwood, Sara L. "Women and the Newspaper." Journalism Series No. 30. Columbia, Mo.: University of Missouri, 1924.

Mehus, Jewell Ross, and Maude Freeland, eds. *Missouri Press Women: History and Directory, 1965*.

Taft, William H. *Missouri Newspapers and the Missouri Press Association: 125 Years of Service, 1867–1992.* Marceline, Mo.: Heritage House Publishing, 1992.

Vaughan, Alma F. "Pioneer Women of the Missouri Press." *Missouri Historical Review* 64, no. 3 (April 1970): 289–305.

INSTITUTIONAL PROFILES

Missouri Woman's Press Association

Dates: Founded 1896; incorporated 1898; ceased ca. 1910.

National Federation of Press Women, Missouri Affiliate

Dates: Founded as **Missouri Woman's Press Club** on 7 May 1937; became an affiliate of the NFPW in 1938; changed name to **Missouri Press Women** in 1959; incorporated on 11 August 1971; changed name to **National Federation of Press Women, Missouri Affiliate** in 1998.

Newsletter: *Life Lines.*

Archives: Missouri Press Women, Papers, 1961–85, and Missouri Women's Press Club, Treasurer's Book, 1937–64, both in Western Historical Manuscript Collection, Ellis Library, University of Missouri, Columbia, Missouri.

Contacts: Co-presidents 1999–2000: Allison Stein Best, 6714 Kenwood Ave., Kansas City, MO 64131, e-mail: <astein@noblefusion.com>; Janice Denham, 528 Pamela Lane, Kirkwood, MO 63122, tel. (314) 965–1079, e-mail: <denham@primary.net>.

Appendix: Chronology

This chronology includes only those women's press organizations profiled in this volume. The organization names are those used in the title of the profile. In those cases where the name was changed, *the most recent name* is listed here. Name changes are indicated in the description with the appropriate dates.

1885: Illinois Woman's Press Association, Chicago.

1885: New England Woman's Press Association, Boston; ceased activity in 1982.

1886: Cleveland Women's Press Club. This was founded as the Cleveland Woman's Press Club. It merged with the Cincinnati Women's Press Club in 1889 to become the Ohio Woman's Press Association, Cleveland Branch. In 1912, it changed its name to the Cleveland Women's Press Club and continued activities until at least 1937; its date of cessation is unknown.

1886: Woman's Press Association of the South, Greensboro, North Carolina.; continued through 1890; date of cessation unknown.

1888: Woman's Press Club of Cincinnati, disbanded in 1988. It was occasionally referred to as the Cincinnati Newspaper Woman's Association.

1889: Woman's Press Club of New York City, dissolved in 1980.

1890: Michigan Woman's Press Association, founded in Traverse City, became inactive ca. 1918. It reorganized in 1937–38; ceased ca. 1940.

1890: Pacific Coast Women's Press Association, established in San Francisco, ceased activities by 1941, date of cessation unknown.

1891: Utah Woman's Press Club, established in Salt Lake City, became inactive in 1921, disbanded in 1928.

1892: Michigan Woman's Press Club, organized in Grand Rapids, became inactive by 1914, date of cessation unknown.

1893: Southern California Women's Press Club, organized in Los Angeles, became inactive ca. 1939, date of cessation unknown.

1893: Texas Professional Communicators. This was organized as Texas Woman's Press Association in Dallas in 1893. It changed its name to Texas Press Women in 1961 and again to Texas Professional Communicators in 1995.

1894: Mississippi Women's Press Club, founded in Jackson, continued until at least 1896, date of cessation unknown.

1896: Missouri Woman's Press Association, founded in St. Louis, ceased ca. 1910, date of cessation unknown.

1897: National League of American Pen Women. This was organized in Washington, D.C., as the League of American Pen Women. It changed its name unofficially in 1921 and legally in 1926 to the National League of American Pen Women.

1898: Denver Woman's Press Club.

1900: Detroit Women Writers. This women's press club was founded in 1900 as the Detroit Press Club. It changed its name to Detroit Women's Press Club in 1908 and Detroit Women Writers Club in 1914. It changed its name once again in 1966 to Detroit Women Writers.

1902: Ohio Newspaper Women's Association.

1909: Association for Women in Communications. Founded at University of Washington in 1909 as Theta Sigma Phi. It changed its name to Women in Communications, Inc., in 1972 and allowed men to become members. Dissolved in 1996 and replaced by the Association for Women in Communications.

1913: Woman's Press Club of Indiana.

1919: Women's National Press Club. Established in Washington, D.C., in 1919. Ceased operation as a women-only group in 1970 when it became the Washington Press Club. It merged with the National Press Club in 1985.

1922: Newswomen's Club of New York. Established as the New York Newspaper Women's Club in 1922, name changed to the Newswomen's Club of New York in 1972.

1922: Cleveland Writers' Club. This club descended from Cleveland Woman's Press Club (founded in 1886, renamed the Ohio Woman's Press Association in 1889, and renamed the Cleveland Women's Press Club in 1912). It broke away from the Cleveland Women's Press Club in 1922 and continued activities as the Cleveland Writers' Club until the mid-1970s. The date of its cessation is unknown.

1937: National Federation of Press Women.

1937: National Federation of Press Women/Missouri Affiliate. This was founded as the Missouri Woman's Press Club in 1937. It changed its name to Missouri Press Women in 1959 and to National Federation of Press Women/Missouri Affiliate in 1998.

1940: Minnesota Press Women, dissolved in 1982.

1941: Kansas Press Women.

1941: Colorado Press Women.

1942: Association of Women Broadcasters. Established by the National Association of Broadcasters as the Association of Women Directors in 1942. Its name was changed to the Association of Women Broadcasters in 1946. It was dissolved in spring 1950 when its parent organization withdrew support and members voted to reorganize as American Women in Radio and Television.

1944: Idaho Press Women.

1947: Mississippi Media Professionals. Group originally founded in Jackson, Mississippi, as Mississippi Press Women; its name was changed in 1993 to Mississippi Media Professionals.

1951: American Women in Radio and Television.

1965: Michigan Press Women. Organized 1965 in St. Joseph, Michigan, as Michigan Women's Press Club, it changed its name in 1984 to Michigan Press Women.

1972: The *New York Times* Women's Caucus.

1972: Women's Institute for Freedom of the Press, organized in Washington, D.C.

1977: Delaware Press Association. Founded 1977 in Wilmington as Delaware Press Women. It changed its name to Delaware Press Association in 1997.

1978: Women's Feature Service, headquartered in New Delhi, India, with a regional coordinator in Jersey City, New Jersey.

1985: JAWS: Journalism and Women Symposium.

1987: Association for Women in Sports Media.

1987: Women, Men and Media.

Bibliography

MANUSCRIPT COLLECTIONS AND ARCHIVES:

Altrusa Club of Boise. "Biographies of Idaho Women." Unpublished manuscript, 1979. Day Northwest Collection, Special Collections, University of Idaho, Moscow, Idaho.

American Women in Radio and Television Collection. Broadcast Pioneers Library of American Broadcasting, The University of Maryland, College Park, Maryland.

American Women in Radio and Television Web page, <http://www.awrt.org>.

Association for Women in Communications, Madison (Wisconsin) Chapter Records. State Historical Society of Wisconsin, Madison, Wisconsin.

American Women in Radio and Television Papers. American Women in Radio and Television, McLean, Virginia.

Bio Card and Bio Letter/Information Files. California State Library, Sacramento, California.

"Biographies of Presidents of Mississippi Press Women." Compiled by Pat Sellers, 1974. Private collection of Nancy Kay Sullivan Wessman, Jackson, Mississippi.

Caroline A. Huling Collection. University of Illinois at Chicago Library, University of Illinois at Chicago, Chicago, Illinois.

Caroline Severance Papers. Huntington Library, San Marino, California.

Chicago Press League Collection. Chicago Historical Society Research Center, Chicago, Illinois.

Cleveland Press Collection. Cleveland State University, Cleveland, Ohio.

Cleveland Writers' Club Collection. Western Reserve Historical Society, Cleveland, Ohio.

Delaware Press Association Collection. Katherine Smigie, Delaware Press Association Historian, 1012 Kent Road, Wilmington, Delaware.

Denver Woman's Press Club Papers. Denver Woman's Press Club Clubhouse, Denver, Colorado.

Denver Woman's Press Club Papers. History Department, Denver Public Library, Denver, Colorado.

Detroit Women Writers Archives. Burton Historical Collection, Detroit Public Library, Detroit, Michigan.

Ella Sterling Mighels Collection. California State Library, Sacramento, California.

Frances Parkinson Keyes Papers. Special Collections, Tulane University Library, New Orleans, Louisiana.

Georgina MacDougall Davis Papers. Manuscripts and University Archives, University of Washington, Seattle, Washington.

Gertrude Van Rensselaer Wickham Collection. Western Reserve Historical Society, Cleveland, Ohio.

Illinois Woman's Press Association Collection. Chicago Historical Society Research Center, Chicago, Illinois.

JAWS: Journalism and Women Symposium Archives. National Women and Media Collection, Western Historical Manuscript Collection, State Historical Society of Missouri. University of Missouri at Columbia, Columbia, Missouri.

J. L Power Family Papers. Mississippi Department of Archives and History, Jackson, Mississippi.

Jones, Elizabeth McLeod. "Ink on Her Fingers." Unpublished autobiography in the collections of the Minnesota Historical Society.

Kansas Press Women Papers, Manuscript Collection 223. Manuscripts Department, Kansas State Historical Society, Topeka, Kansas.

Kate M. Power Papers. Mississippi Department of Archives and History, Jackson, Mississippi.

MaryAnn Yodelis Smith Papers. State Historical Society of Wisconsin, Madison, Wisconsin.

Michigan Press Women Papers. State Archives of Michigan, Michigan Historical Center, Lansing, Michigan.

Mississippi Media Professionals Files. Fant Library, Mississippi University for Women, Columbus, Mississippi.

Missouri Press Association Records. Western Historical Manuscript Collection, Ellis Library, University of Missouri, Columbia, Missouri.

Missouri Press Women, Papers, 1961–85. Western Historical Manuscript Collection, Ellis Library, University of Missouri, Columbia, Missouri.

Missouri Women's Press Club, Treasurer's Book, 1937–1964. Western Historical Manuscript Collection, Ellis Library, University of Missouri, Columbia, Missouri.

New England Woman's Press Association Papers. Massachusetts Historical Society, Boston, Massachusetts.

Newswomen's Club of New York Papers. Newswomen's Club of New York, National Arts Building, 15 Gramercy Park, New York.

Ohio Newspaper Women's Association President's Holdings. Linda Crider, Dayton, Ohio.

Ohio Newspaper Women's Association Records, Manuscript Collection 773. Ohio Historical Society, Columbus, Ohio.

Ohio Woman's Press Association Collection. Western Reserve Historical Society, Cleveland, Ohio.

Press Club of Chicago Collection. Chicago Historical Society Research Center, Chicago, Illinois.

Sallie Joy White Papers. Schlesinger Library, Radcliffe College, Cambridge, Massachusetts.

Sara Lockwood Williams Papers, 1885–1961. Western Historical Manuscript Collection, Ellis Library, University of Missouri, Columbia, Missouri.

Schaefer, Ruth Crane, and Pat Griffith Mower. "Historical Record of the Association of Women Broadcasters." Transcript of tape recording, 3 January 1976. Broadcast Pioneers Library, College Park, Maryland.

Swank, Gladys Rae. "Ladies of the House (and Senate): A History of Idaho Women in the Legislature since Statehood." Unpublished manuscript, 1978. Special Collections, University of Idaho, Moscow, Idaho.

Tad Bartimus Papers. Women in Journalism Oral History Project, Records. 1987–94. Washington Press Club Foundation. Washington Press Club, Washington, D.C.

Texas Professional Communicators Archives. Center for American History, University of Texas at Austin, Texas.

Woman's Press Club of Indiana Collection. W. H. Smith Memorial Library, Indiana Historical Society, Indianapolis, Indiana.

Woman's Press Club of New York City Archives. Butler Library, Columbia University, New York City.

Women's National Press Club Papers. Archives of the National Press Club, 529 14th St., N.W., Washington, DC 20045.

Women's Press Club Collection (Cincinnati), 1888–1979. Cincinnati Historical Society Library, Union Station Terminal, Cincinnati, Ohio.

Women's Press Club Collection (Cincinnati), 1962–88. Cincinnati Historical Society Library, Union Station Terminal, Cincinnati, Ohio.

TRADE JOURNALS, NEWSLETTERS, AND WEB SITES

Agenda (newsletter of the National Federation of Press Women), 1987–98, passim.

Association for Women in Sports Media. Web page, <http://users.southeast.net/~awsm>.

AWSM Newsletter (newsletter of Association of Women in Sports Media), 1998–99, passim.

Banner Lines (newsletter of the Michigan Women's Press Club/ Michigan Press Women), 1965–98, passim.

The Beam (newsletter of American Women Broadcasters), 1947–51, passim.

DelAware Press Woman, 1990–present, passim.

Distaffer (newsletter of Texas Press Women), 1970–71, passim.

Gopher Tidings (newsletter of Minnesota Press Women), 1943–69, passim.

The Impress (publication of Pacific Coast Woman's Press Club), 1894–95, passim.

JAWS: Journalism and Women Symposium Web page, <http://www.jaws.org>.

The Journalist, 1885–1904, passim.

Kate Power's Review. September 1884–October 1895, passim.

The Literary Century, 1893, passim.

The Matrix (publication of Theta Sigma Phi/Women in Communications, Inc./Association for Women in Communications), July 1918–present, passim.

Media Report to Women: What Women Are Doing and Thinking about the Communications Media, 1972 to present, passim.

National Federation of Press Women Web page, <http://www.nfpw.org>.

New York Newspaper Women's Club Bulletin, 1924–present, passim.

Ohio Newspaper Women's Association (newsletter), 1972–present, passim.

The Pen Woman (newsletter of the League of American Pen Women), 1920–23, passim.

Press Woman (newsletter of the National Federation of Press Women), 1969–99, passim.

Radio Daily, 1943–51, passim.

Texas Press Woman (newsletter of the Texas Woman's Press Association and Texas Press Women), 1958–94, passim.

Topics (newsletter of Texas Professional Communicators), 1995–present, passim.

Woman's Exponent, 1891–1914, passim.

PUBLISHED MATERIALS

Allen, Martha. "The Development of Communication Networks among Women, 1963–1983." Ph.D. diss., Howard University, 1988.

Arey, Mrs. H. E. G. *Home and School Training*. Philadelphia: J. B. Lippincott & Co., 1884.

———. *Household Songs: And Other Poems*. New York, J. C. Derby, 1855.

"AWC History." AWC Web page, <http://www.womcom.org>.

Baker, Sherry. "Creating a Shared History: Serial Narratives in *The Young Woman's Journal*, 1889–1894." M.A. thesis, University of Utah, 1988.

Beakes, S. W. *Past and Present of Washtenaw County, Michigan*. Chicago: S. J. Clarke Publishing Co., 1906.

Beasley, Maurine H. "The Women's National Press Club: A Case Study of Professional Aspirations." *Journalism History*, 15, no. 4 (winter 1988): 112–21.

———. *The New Majority: A Look at What the Preponderance of Women in Journalism Education Means to the Schools and to the Professions*. College Park: University of Maryland, October 1985.

Beasley, Maurine H., and Sheila J. Gibbons, eds. *Taking Their Place: A Documentary History of Women and Journalism*. Washington, D.C.: American University Press, 1993.

———. *Women in Media: A Documentary Source Book*. Washington, D.C.: Women's Institute for Freedom of the Press, 1977.

Black, Ruby. *Eleanor Roosevelt: A Biography*. New York: Duell, Sloan and Pearce, 1940.

Blair, Karen J. *The Clubwoman as Feminist: True Womanhood Redefined, 1868–1914*. New York: Holmes and Meier, 1980.

Bliss, Edward, Jr. *Now the News: The Story of Broadcast Journalism*. New York: Columbia University Press, 1991.

Boomhower, Ray E. *The Country Contributor: The Life and Times of Juliet V. Strauss*. Carmel: Guild Press of Indiana, 1998.

Boruff, Blanche Foster. "The Woman's Press Club of Indiana." *Press Woman*, April 1945.

Boyd, Mrs. Frank W. *Rode a Heifer Calf through College*. Brooklyn: Pageant-Poseidon, 1972.

Bradshaw, James. "Mrs. Rayne's School of Journalism." *Journalism Quarterly* 60, no. 3 (autumn 1983): 513–17.

Bridge, M. Junior. *Marginalizing Women: Front-Page News Coverage of Females Declines in 1966*. Washington, D.C.: Women, Men and Media, 1996.

Budge, Rose Mary Pedersen. "Literary Women Formed Press Club." *Deseret News*, 10 March 1983, p. C1.

Burt, Elizabeth V. "A Bid for Legitimacy: The Woman's Press Club Movement, 1881–1900." *Journalism History* 23, no. 2 (summer 1997): 72–84.

Byerly, Carolyn M. "Countdown for Women's Feature Service: Gender, News and Development in an Era of Globalization." Paper presented to the International Communication Association, Jerusalem, Israel, July 1998.

———. "News, Consciousness and Social Participation: The Role of Women's Feature Service in World News." In *Feminism, Multiculturalism and the Media: Global Diversities*, ed. A. N. Valdivia. Thousand Oaks, Calif.: Sage, 1995.

Carter, Kate B. *Heart Throbs of the West*. Vol. 2. Salt Lake City, Utah: Daughters of the Utah Pioneers, 1950.

Cepac, Claudia. "A Historical View: The Editorial Perspective of a 19th Century Woman Newspaper Editor." Unpublished research paper, University of Michigan School of Journalism, 1972.

Cervi, Clé, and Nancy Peterson. *The Women Who Made Headlines: The First 100 Years*. Lakewood, Colo.: Western Guideways, 1998.

Ceulemans, Mieke, and Guido Fauconnier. *Mass Media: The Image, Role, and Social Conditions of Women*. Paris: UNESCO, 1979.

Chapman Brothers, eds. *Portrait and Biographical Album of Lenawee County, Michigan*. Chicago: Chapman Brothers, 1888.

Clark, Thomas D. *The Southern Country Editor*. Indianapolis: Bobbs-Merrill Company, 1948.

Cobb, Margaret. "Gifted Gals." *American Mercury*, June 1928, pp. 199–207.

Coe, Katherine Hunter, ed. *Poems of America*. Vols. 1–3. London: Channing Press, 1932–34.

———. *Poems of All Nations*. Vols. 1–3. London: Channing Press, 1932–34.

Cook, Joan, and Betsy Wade. "One Shot at History." Tape of talk at the Schlesinger Library, Radcliffe College, Cambridge, Massachusetts, 1 May 1986.

Courtney, Grace Gates, compiler, and Acada Stark Balz, ed. *History of the Indiana Federation of Clubs*. Fort Wayne, Ind.: Fort Wayne Printing, 1939.

Cramer, Judith A. "Radio: A Woman's Place is on the Air." In *Women in Mass Communication*, 2d ed., ed. Pamela J. Creedon, pp. 154–66. Newbury Park, Calif.: Sage, 1993.

Crathers, Alice Tarbell. *In Detroit . . . Courage Was the Fashion*. Detroit: Wayne State University Press, 1953.

Creedon, Pamela J., ed. *Women in Mass Communication*. 2d ed. Newbury Park: Sage, 1993.

———. *Women, Media, and Sport: Challenging Gender Values*. Thousand Oaks, Calif.: Sage, 1994.

Croly, Jane Cunningham. *The History of the Woman's Club Movement in America*. New York: Henry G. Allen & Company, 1898.

Cummins, Ella Mighels. "Woman's Press Association." In Cummins, *Story of the Files*. San Francisco: World's Fair Commission, 1893.

Daggett, Emerson L., ed. *History of San Francisco Journalism*. San Francisco: W.P.A., 1940.

Dains, Mary K., ed. *Show Me Missouri Women: Selected Biographies*. Kirksville, Mo.: Thomas Jefferson University Press, 1989.

De La Torriente, Donna Duesel. *So We All Can Be Heard: An History of the Illinois Woman's Press Association, 1885–1987*. Streamwood: Illinois Woman's Press Association 1987.

Deverell, William, and Tom Sitton, eds. *California Progressivism Revisited*. Berkeley: University of California Press, 1994.

Doll, Louis W. *A History of the Newspapers of Ann Arbor, 1829–1920*. Detroit: Wayne State University Press, 1959.

Dooley, Patricia L. "Minnesota Journalists as Elected Officials, 1923–1938: An Historical Study of an Ethical/Conflict of Interest Question." M.A. thesis, University of Minnesota, 1985.

———. "Minnesota Women Journalists during World War II." *Roots*, 17, no. 2 (winter 1989): 22–26.

Eberhard, Wallace B., and Margaret Lee Myers. "Beyond the Locker Room: Women in Sports on Major Daily Newspapers." *Journalism Quarterly* 65 (fall 1988): 595–99.

Ellerbe, Rose L. *History of the Southern California Women's Press Club, 1894–1929*. Los Angeles: Rose Ellerbe, 1930.

Empowering Women in the Media. Washington, D.C.: International Women's Media Foundation, July 1996.

Flexner, Eleanor. *Century of Struggle: The Woman's Rights Movement in the United States*. Rev. ed. Cambridge, Mass.: Belknap Press of Harvard University, 1975.

Fogelson, Robert. M. *Fragmented Metropolis: Los Angeles, 1850–1930*. Cambridge, Mass.: Harvard University Press, 1967.

Friedan, Betty. *The Feminine Mystique*. New York: W. W. Norton & Co., 1963.

———. *It Changed My Life: Writings on the Women's Movement*. New York: W. W. Norton & Co., 1985.

Furman, Bess. *Washington By-Line*. New York: Alfred A. Knopf, 1949.

Gallagher, Margaret. *Unequal Opportunities: The Case of Women and the Media*. Paris: UNESCO, 1981.

———. *An Unfinished Story: Gender Patterns in Media Employment*. Reports and Papers on Mass Communication, No. 110. Paris: UNESCO, 1995.

Gibbons, Sheila, ed., and Pam Janis, writer. *Allen H. Neuharth: The Gannett Years*. Arlington, Va.: Gannett Co., 1989.

Gibson, Mary S., ed. *A Record of Twenty-five Years of the California Federation of Women's Clubs*. Los Angeles: California Federation of Women's Clubs, 1927.

Giffard, C. Anthony, Carolyn M. Byerly, and Catherine Van Horn. "The World of Inter Press Service." The Hague, Netherlands: International Association for Mass Communications Research, 1991.

Goss, Charles. *Cincinnati—the Queen City*. Vols. 1 and 2. Cincinnati: Cincinnati Historical Society, 1912.

Gottlieb, Agnes Hooper. "Networking in the Nineteenth Century: Founding of the Woman's Press Club of New York City." *Journalism History* 21, no. 4 (winter 1995): 156–63.

Graham, Sandy. "A Brief History." In *Colorado Press Women Inc.: 55 Years of Service to Communications*. Denver: Colorado Press Women, 1996.

Green, Norma. *Leading Change for 75 Years: WICI-Chicago, 1919–1994*. Chicago: Women in Communications, Inc., Chicago Professional Chapter, 1994.

Greenwald, Marilyn S. "The Portrayal of Women in Newspapers: A Meta-Analysis." Paper presented at the annual convention of the Association for Education in Journalism and Mass Communication, Washington, D.C., August 1989.

Guilford, Linda Thayer. *The Story of a Cleveland School from 1848–1881*. Cambridge, Mass.: J. Wilson & Son, 1890.

Guimary, Donald L. *Citizens Groups and Broadcasting*. New York: Praeger, 1975.

Gullett, Gayle Ann. "Feminism, Politics, and Voluntary Groups: Organized Womanhood in California." Ph.D. diss., University of California at Riverside, 1983.

Haarsager, Sandra. *Organized Womanhood: Cultural Politics in the Pacific Northwest, 1840–1920*. Norman: University of Oklahoma Press, 1997.

Hage, George S. *Minnesota Newspaper Association*. Minneapolis: Minnesota Newspaper Association, 1992.

Harris, Fran. *Focus: Michigan Women, 1701–1977*. Michigan Coordinating Committee of the National Commission on the Observance of Women's Year, 1977.

Hastings, Lucille. "Colorado." *Press Woman*, June 1976, pp. 30–31.

"Helen Malloch's Vision." *Press Woman*, June 1976.

Herman, Edward, and Robert W. McChesney. *The Global Media: The New Missionaries of Global Capitalism*. London: Cassell, 1997.

Hill, Mary Armfield. *Charlotte Perkins Gilman: The Making of a Radical Feminist*. Philadelphia: Temple University Press, 1980.

"History of Women in Communications, Inc." *1993 Directory*. Arlington, Va: Women in Communications, Inc., 1993.

Hogsett, Vernetta Murchison. *The Golden Years: A History of the Idaho Federation of Women's Clubs, 1905–1955*. Caldwell: Idaho Federation of Women's Clubs, Caxton Printers, 1955.

Hosley, David H., and Gayle K. Yamada. *Hard News: Women in Broadcast Journalism*. Westport, Conn.: Greenwood Press, 1987.

Houston, Jane. "Writers in Residence: The Home of the Denver Woman's Press Club." *Colorado Homes and Lifestyles*, January/February 1990, pp. 77–78.

Huling, Caroline. *Prominent Women of Illinois*. Chicago: Illinois Woman's Press Association, 1932.

Huyler, Jean Wiley. "Past Is Prologue." *Press Woman*, June 1976, p. 1.

Illinois Newspaper Directory: History of Illinois Press Association. Champaign, Urbana: Illinois Press Association, 1934.

Ingham, Mrs. W. A. *Women of Cleveland and Their Work, Philanthropic, Educational, Literary, Medical and Artistic: A History*. Cleveland: W. A. Ingham, 1893.

International Women's Media Foundation. *Women Reporting on International News*. Washington, D.C.: International Women's Media Foundation and Women's Foreign Policy Group, June 1997.

James, Edward T., ed. *Notable American Women, 1607–1950: A Biographical Dictionary*. Vol. 1. Cambridge, Mass.: Belknap Press, 1971.

Jensen, Joan M. "After Slavery: Caroline Severance in Los Angeles." *Southern California Quarterly* 48 (June 1966): 175–86.

Junkin, Susie B. "A Report of the Meeting of the Kansas Woman's Press Association," *The Newspaper West* 4, no. 5 (1896): 155.

Kelly, Florence Finch. *Flowing Stream*. New York: E. P. Dutton, 1939.

Kielbowicz, Richard, and Clifford Sherer. "The Role of the Press in the Dynamics of Social Movements." *Research in Social Movements, Conflicts and Change* 9 (1986): 71–96.

Kilmer, Paulette D. *Fear of Sinking: The American Success Formula in the Gilded Age*. Knoxville: University of Tennessee Press, 1996.

Knapp, John I., and R. I. Bonner. *Illustrated History and Biographical Record of Lenawee County, Michigan*. Adrian, Mich.: Times Printing Company, 1903.

Kulczycky, Larissa C. *The First 85 Years: The History of Women in Communications, Inc.* Arlington, Va.: Women in Communications, Inc., 1994.

Lash, Joseph P. *Eleanor and Franklin*. New York: Signet, 1971.

Lauterer, Jock. *Community Journalism: The Personal Approach*. Ames: Iowa State University Press, 1995.

Lockwood, Sara L. "Women and the Newspaper." Journalism Series No. 30. Columbia: University of Missouri, 1924.

Lord, Myra B. *History of the New England Woman's Press Association*. Newton, Mass.: Graphic Press, 1932.

Los Angeles Blue Books, 1894–1940.

Marshall, Jane P. "Jaws of Hope: Action, Yes, and Replenishment." *The Quill*, February 1990, pp. 43–44.

Marzolf, Marion. *Civilizing Voices: American Press Criticism, 1880–1950*. White Plains, N.Y.: Longman Publishing Group, 1991.

———. *Up from the Footnote*. New York: Hastings House, 1977.

Mayr, Hearly. *Muslim Women and the Cyberspace Revolution*. Washington, D.C.: Women's Institute for Freedom of the Press, 1997.

McBride, Marion. "Report to the 1890 Convention of the National Editorial Association." *The Journalist*, 5 July 1890, p. 12.

McCarthy, Abigail. "Jane Grey Swisshelm: Marriage and Slavery." In *Women of Minnesota: Selected Biographical Essays*, ed. Barbara Stuhler and Gretchen Kreuter. St. Paul: Minnesota Historical Society Press, 1977.

McKay, Anne. "Speaking Up: Voice Amplification and Women's Struggle for Public Expression." In *Technology and Women's Voices: Keeping in Touch*, ed. Cheris Kramarae, pp. 187–206. New York: Routledge & Keagan Paul, 1988,

The Media and Women without Apology. Theme issue of *Media Studies Journal* 7, no. 1–2, (winter-spring 1993).

Mehus, Jewell Ross, and Maude Freeland, eds. *Missouri Press Women: History and Directory, 1965*. Missouri Press Women Papers, folder 15. Western Historical Manuscript Collection. Ellis Library, University of Missouri. Columbia, Mo.

Merrick, Caroline E. *Old Times in Dixie Land: A Southern Matron's Memories*. New York: Grafton Press, 1901.

Michigan Woman's Press Association. *Proceedings of the Second Annual Session*. Battle Creek, Mich.: Wm C. Gage and Sons, 1892.

"Michigan Woman's Press Association." *Michigan History Magazine* 24 (summer 1940): 309–12.

Michigan Woman's Press Club. *Leaves from Our Lives*. Grand Rapids, Mich.: Dean Printing and Publishing Company, 1894.

Miller, Phyllis, and Randy Miller. "The Invisible Woman: Female Sports Journalists in the Workplace." *Journalism and Mass Communication Quarterly* 72 (winter 1995): 883–89.

Mills, Kay. *A Place in the News: From the Women's Pages to the Front Page.* New York: Dodd Mead, 1988; New York: Columbia University Press, 1990.

Morton, Marian J. *Women in Cleveland: An Illustrated History.* Bloomington: Indiana University Press, 1995.

National Federation of Press Women Membership Directory and Information Guides, 1983–1995, and 1998.

Neely, Ruth, ed. *Women of Ohio: A Record of Their Achievements in the History of the State.* Cincinnati: S. J. Clark, ca. 1939.

"New Directions for News: A Newspaper Study." Women's Studies Program of the George Washington University, Washington, D.C., August 1989.

North-Whitcomb, E. M. "Pacific Coast Women's Press Club: Its Origin, Development and Effect." *Everywoman,* July 1915, p. 9.

Parkhurst, Emilie Tracy Y. "Pacific Coast Women's Press Association." *Californian,* September 1893, pp. 526–34.

"Past and Present of Texas." *The Bohemian* 3, no. 4 (1902): 54–77.

Pecora, Norma. "Ruth Franklin Crane (1902–1989)." In *Women in Communication: A Biographical Sourcebook,* ed. Nancy Signorielli, pp. 79–91. Westport, Conn.: Greenwood Press, 1996.

Penson-Ward, Betty. *Idaho Women in History: Big and Little Biographies and Other Gender Stories.* Boise: Legendary Publishing Co., 1991.

Peterson, Theodore. *Magazines in the Twentieth Century.* Urbana: University of Illinois Press, 1964.

Plested, Dolores. "Amazing Minnie: A 19th Century Woman of Today." *Colorado Heritage* 1 (1984): 18–27.

Porter, Philip W. and Norval N. Luxon. *The Reporter and the News.* New York: D. Appleton-Century, 1935.

Power, Kate M. *A Bunch of Letters from the Great Northwest, for the "Daily Clarion," Jackson, Mississippi.* Jackson, Miss.: *Jackson Clarion Ledger,* 1892.

Pye, Mary F. Kelly. "Utah Women's Press Club: History." Unpublished manuscript, Utah State Historical Society, undated.

Rafferty, Judith. "Los Angeles Clubwomen and Progressive Reform." In *California Progressivism Revisited,* ed. William Deverell and Tom Sitton. Berkeley: University of California Press, 1994.

Roberts, B. H. *Comprehensive History of the Church.* Vol. 6. Provo, Utah: Sonos Publishing, 1991 (reprint of 1930 text).

Robertson, Nan. *The Girls in the Balcony: Women, Men, and the New York Times.* New York: Random House, 1992.

Roosevelt, Eleanor. *This I Remember.* New York: Harper & Brothers, 1947.

Ross, Ishbel. *Ladies of the Press.* New York: Harper & Brothers, 1936.

Rouse, Morleen G. "Daytime Radio Programming for the Homemaker, 1926–1956." *Journal of Popular Culture* 12 (fall 1978): pp. 315–19.

Ruddy, Giles, ed. *The Mother of Clubs: Caroline M. Seymour Severance.* Los Angeles: Baumgardt Publishing Company, 1906.

Schudson, Michael. *Discovering the News: A Social History of American Newspapers.* New York: Basic Books, 1978.

Scott, Anne Firor. *Natural Allies: Women's Associations in American History*. Urbana: University of Illinois Press, 1993.

————. *The Southern Lady: From Pedestal to Politics, 1830–1930*. Chicago: University of Chicago Press, 1970.

Sheire, Catherine M. *History of Minnesota Press Women, 1940–1946*. Minnesota Press Women, ca. 1946.

Sims, Anastasia. "Feminism and Femininity in the New South: White Women's Organizations in North Carolina, 1883–1930." Ph.D. diss., University of North Carolina at Chapel Hill, 1985.

————. *The Power of Femininity in the New South: Women's Organizations and Politics in North Carolina, 1880–1930*. Columbia: University of South Carolina Press, 1997.

Sioussat, Helen. *Mikes Don't Bite*. New York: L. B. Fischer, 1943.

Skidmore, Sophie E. "Power of the Press." In *La Copa de Oro*. San Francisco: PC WPA, 1905.

Smith, Barbara, and Blythe Darlyn Thatcher, eds. *Heroines of the Restoration*. Salt Lake City: Bookcraft, 1997.

Snyder, Agnes. *Dauntless Women in Childhood Education, 1856–1931*. Washington, D.C.: ACEI, 1972.

Stone, Vernon. "MU Researcher Tracks Women's Gains as TV News Directors." University of Missouri Web page, http://www/missouri.edu/jourvs.

"Study Finds Sex Discrimination at U.S. Newspapers." Reuters wire report, 13 July 1995.

Stuhler, Barbara, and Gretchen Kreuter, eds. *Women of Minnesota: Selected Biographical Essays*. St. Paul: Minnesota Historical Society Press, 1977.

Sulloway, Frank J. *Born to Rebel*. New York: Pantheon Books, 1996.

Taft, William H. *Missouri Newspapers and the Missouri Press Association, 125 Years of Service, 1867–1992*. Marceline, Mo.: Heritage House Publishing, 1992.

Thatcher, Linda, and John R. Sillito. "Utah Woman's Press Club: 1891–1928." Unpublished manuscript, Utah State Historical Society Archives, Salt Lake City, Utah, ca. 1983.

Underwood, Aggie. *Newspaperwoman*. New York: Harper and Brothers Publishers, 1949.

Valdivia, A. N., ed. *Feminism, Multiculturalism and the Media: Global Diversities*. Thousand Oaks, Calif.: Sage, 1995.

Van Tassel, David V., and John J. Grabowski. *The Encyclopedia of Cleveland History*. Bloomington: Indiana University Press, 1987.

van Zuilen, A. J. *The Life Cycle of Magazines: Decline and Fall of the General Interest Mass Audience Magazines in the United States during the Period of 1946–1972*. Uithoorn, The Netherlands: Graduate Press, 1977.

Vaughan, Alma F. "Pioneer Women of the Missouri Press." *Missouri Historical Review* 64, no. 3 (April 1970): 289–305.

Wade, Betsy. "Surviving Being a Survivor, Or, Whatever Became of What's Her Name?" *Media Studies Journal* 9 (1995): 32–43.

Waller, Judith C. *Radio: The Fifth Estate*. Boston: Houghton Mifflin, 1946.

Walton, Mary R. "A History of the Texas Woman's Press Association, 1893–1908." Paper presented to the Texas Woman's Press Association, 16 June 1908.

Weddon, Willah. *Michigan Press Women, Today and Yesterday*. Stockbridge, Mich.: Weddon Press, 1996.

Weltman, Janie Gordon. *Our First 50 Years, 1885–1935*. Malden, Mass.: Maplewood Press, 1936.

Wheeler, Cora. "Mrs. M. L. Rayne." *The Journalist*. 24 February 1891, p. 1.

Wiebe, Robert H. *The Search for Order, 1877–1920*. New York: Hill and Wang, 1986.

Willard, Frances E., and Mary A. Livermore, eds. *A Woman of the Century: Fourteen Hundred Seventy Biographical Sketches of Leading American Women*. Reprint, Detroit: Gale Research Company, 1967.

Williamson, Martha Burton Woodhead. *Ladies Clubs and Societies: Los Angeles in 1892*. Los Angeles: Historical Society of Southern California, 1925.

Wilson, Jean Gaddy. "At Sea in a Sea Change: Few News Organizations Have Faced up to the New Reality." *The Quill*, February 1990, pp. 29–32.

Women's Feature Service. *The Power to Change: Women in the Third World Redefine Their Environment*. New Delhi, India: Kali Press for Women, 1992.

Women's Feature Service Style Manual. New Delhi, India: Women's Feature Service, undated.

Women's Institute for Freedom of the Press. *Directory of Women's Media*. Annual editions, 1975–1989. Washington, D.C.: Women's Institute for Freedom of the Press.

———. *The First Annual Conference on Planning a National and International Communications System for Women: A Report*. Report on conference held 7–8 April 1979 at the National Press Club, Washington, D.C.

———. *Five Year Index to Media Report of Women: Annotated Index of Media Activities and Research*, 1972–76; 1977–81; 1982–87; 1987. Washington, D.C.: Women's Institute for Freedom of the Press.

Wyman, Mary Alice, ed. *Selections from the Autobiography of Elizabeth Oakes [Prince] Smith*. New York: Arno Press, 1980.

———. *Two American Pioneers: Seba Smith and Elizabeth Oakes Smith*. New York: Columbia University Press, 1927.

Yamane, Nan Towle. "Women, Power, and the Press: The Case of San Francisco." Ph.D. diss., University of California at Los Angeles, 1995.

Young, John P. *California Journalism*. San Francisco: Chronicle Publishing Company, 1915.

Index

Page numbers in **bold** refer to main entries.

About the Contributors

Donna Allen was president of the Women's Institute for Freedom of the Press. She was coeditor of *Communications at the Crossroads: The Gender Gap Connection* (1989) and coeditor of *Women Transforming Communication: Global Intersections* (1996). She died in 1999 as this book was going into production.

Sherry Baker is assistant professor in the Department of Communication, Brigham Young University, Provo, Utah. She recently published "Applying Kidder's Ethical Decision-Making Checklist to Mass Media Ethics," *Journal of Mass Media Ethics* 12, no. 4 (1998).

Maurine H. Beasley is professor of journalism at the University of Maryland, College Park. She is the coauthor and editor of *Taking Their Place: A Documentary History of Women in Journalism* (1993) and has published widely on women journalists. She is a former journalist.

Elizabeth V. Burt is associate professor in the School of Communication at the University of Hartford. She has published articles on women journalists and women's publications in *Journalism and Mass Communication Quarterly, Journalism History, American Journalism*, and in two Greenwood titles, *Women in Communication* (1996) and *Women's Periodicals in the United States: Social and Political Issues* (1996). She is a former journalist.

Carolyn M. Byerly is assistant professor in the Department of Television and Radio, Roy H. Park School of Communication, Ithaca College. She is the author of "News, Feminism and the Dialectics of Gender Relations," in M. Meyers, ed., *Mediated Women: Representations in Popular Culture* (1999). She is a former journalist.

Ann Mauger Colbert is Journalism Program coordinator at Indiana University/ Purdue University (IPFW), Fort Wayne, Indiana. She is the author of "Philanthropy in the Newsroom: Women's Editions of Newspapers, 1894–1896," *Journalism History* 22, no. 3 (autumn 1996). She is a former journalist.

Janet Cramer is assistant professor in the Department of Communication and Journalism at University of New Mexico, Albuquerque.

Patricia L. Dooley is assistant professor in the Elliot School of Communication at Wichita State University. She is the author of *Taking Their Political Place: Journalists and the Making of an Occupation* (1997).

Sonya Forte Duhé is assistant professor in the College of Journalism and Mass Communications at the University of South Carolina.

Kathleen L. Endres is professor in the School of Communication at University of Akron, Ohio. She is coeditor of two Greenwood publications, *Women's Periodicals of the United States: Consumer Magazines* (1995) and *Women's Periodicals of the United States: Social and Political Issues* (1996).

Sheila J. Gibbons is vice president of Communication Research Associates, Inc. She is editor of *Media Report to Women* and coauthor of *Taking Their Place: A Documentary History of Women and Journalism* (1993) and *Exploring Mass Media: Past, Present and Future* (1999).

Victoria Goff is associate professor in the Department of Communication and Arts at the University of Wisconsin at Green Bay. She has published her work in *Women's Periodicals in the United States: Consumer Magazines* (Greenwood, 1995), *American Journalism*, and *Media History*.

Agnes Hooper Gottlieb is associate professor of communication and women's studies at Seton Hall University and is director of the Elizabeth Ann Seton Center for Women's Studies. She is coauthor of *1000 Years, 1000 People: Ranking the Men and Women Who Shaped the Millennium* (1998). She is a former journalist.

Karla K. Gower is assistant professor at the University of Alabama. She has published articles in *American Journalism* and *Journalism and Mass Communication Quarterly*.

Norma Fay Green is director of graduate journalism at Columbia College, Chicago. She is author of "Chicago's StreetWise: Case Study of a Newspaper to Empower the Homeless in the 1990s," in *Print Culture in a Diverse America* (1998), and "Martha Gellhorn: Eager Eyewitness to War, Restless Dreamer of Peace," in *Eye of the Reporter: Literature's Heritage in the Press* (1996). She is a freelance journalist.

Sandra L. Haarsager is associate professor in the School of Communication at University of Idaho. She is the author of *Organized Womanhood: Cultural Politics in the Pacific Northwest, 1840–1920* (1997) and *Bertha Knight Landes of Seattle, Big City Mayor* (1994). She is a former journalist and columnist.

Tina V. Hall is a communications specialist for MidSouth–a Center for Leadership and Training, which is located at the University of Arkansas at Little Rock.

Janice R. Hume is assistant professor at the A. Q. Miller School of Journalism and Mass Communications at Kansas State University at Manhattan. She is the author of "Defining the Historic American Heroine: Heroic Women of Godey's *Lady's Book*," *Journal of Popular Culture* 31, no. 1 (summer 1997), and is a former journalist.

Paulette D. Kilmer is assistant professor in the Communication Department at the University of Toledo. She is the author of *The Fear of Sinking: The American Success Formula in the Gilded Age* (1996). She is a former journalist.

Tina Lesher is associate professor of journalism and chair of the Department of Communication at William Paterson University. She is president of New Jersey Press Women and was the 1992 New Jersey Press Women Communicator of Achievement. She is a former journalist.

Therese L. Lueck is associate professor in the School of Communication at the University of Akron. She has recently published the electronic chapter "Media" in the McGraw-Hill database, Primis. She is coeditor of two Greenwood volumes, *Women's Periodicals in the United States: Consumer Issues* (1995) and *Women's Periodicals in the United States: Social and Political Issues* (1996). She is a former journalist.

Marion Marzolf is professor emerita, University of Michigan. She is the author of *Up from the Footnote* (1977). She is a former journalist.

Michael P. McCauley is assistant professor in the Department of Communication and Journalism at the University of Maine. He is a former broadcast journalist.

Beverly G. Merrick is assistant professor in the Department of Journalism and Mass Communication at New Mexico State University. She has published her work in *American Journalism* and *Journalism History*. She is a former journalist.

Kate Peirce is professor in the Department of Mass Communication at Southwest Texas State University. She is the author of "Women's Magazine Fiction: The Making of a New Woman or an Old Lady?" in *Sex Roles*, October 1997. She is a former journalist.

Linda Steiner is associate professor in the Department of Journalism and Mass Media at Rutgers University. She has published her work in *American Journalism* and *American History*. She is a former journalist.

Katherine Ward is historian of the Delaware Press Association (DPA). She is a past president of the DPA and past editor of *DelAware Press Woman*. She is the author of *A Legacy from Delaware Women* (1987) and *Delaware Women Remembered* (1977).

Willah Weddon is past president of Michigan Press Women. She is the author of *Michigan Press Women, Today and Yesterday* (1996). She received the first annual Martha Rayne Award for Media History Research in April 1999, during the Michigan Journalism Hall of Fame ceremony at Michigan State.

Susan Weill is assistant professor at the University of Alabama. She is author of "Mark Singer," in *Dictionary of Literary Biography: American Literary Journalists, 1945–1995* (1997). She is a former journalist.

Jan Whitt is associate professor in the School of Journalism and Mass Communication at University of Colorado. She is the author of *Allegory and the Modern Southern Novel* (1993) and has published articles on literary journalism, American literature, popular culture, newspaper history, and women's issues. She is a former journalist.

Betty Houchin Winfield is professor in the School of Journalism at the University of Missouri at Columbia. She is the author of *FDR and the News Media* (1994, 1990) and recently published several pieces on Hillary Rodham Clinton in *Political Communication* (1997), *Women, Media and Politics* (1997), and *First Ladies* (1999). She is a former broadcast and print journalist.

Nan Towle Yamane is a lecturer at California State University at Northridge.

ISBN 0-313-30661-3

90000>

EAN

9 780313 306617

HARDCOVER BAR CODE